BILL GILES AND BASEBALL

BILL GILES
and Baseball

John B. Lord

TEMPLE UNIVERSITY PRESS PHILADELPHIA

To my ultra-patient and supportive wife, Joan; to one of the truly great men of baseball, Bill Giles; to my parents, John and Marian, who introduced me to the game . . . and made me a Cubs fan; to our children, Megan, Sean, and Ryan, "kids-in-law," Adam and Lindsay, and the gifts God has given to Joan and me, our grandsons, John Braxton and James Ryan Lord

TEMPLE UNIVERSITY PRESS
Philadelphia, Pennsylvania 19122
www.temple.edu/tempress

Published 2014

Library of Congress Cataloging-in-Publication Data

Lord, John B. (John Brian), 1949–
Bill Giles and baseball / John B. Lord.
pages cm
Includes bibliographical references and index.
ISBN 978-1-4399-0786-3 (cloth : alk. paper) —
ISBN 978-1-4399-0788-7 (e-book)
1. Giles, Bill, 1934– 2. Baseball team owners—United States—Biography. 3. Philadelphia Phillies (Baseball team). I. Title.
GV865.G56L67 2014
796.357092—dc23
[B] 2013043279

♾ The paper used in this publication meets the requirements of the American National Standard for Information Sciences—Permanence of Paper for Printed Library Materials, ANSI Z39.48-1992

Printed in the United States of America

2 4 6 8 9 7 5 3 1

Contents

Acknowledgments

My biggest debt of gratitude goes to William Y. Giles, a great man, who patiently and tirelessly sat for interviews and provided much information about the inner workings of baseball that is unavailable outside the tight circle of owners. Mr. Giles also provided access to other owners and former owners, many of whom consented to be interviewed. I am indebted to these individuals, including Jerry Reinsdorf, Larry Lucchino, John Harrington, Bill Bartholomay, and David Montgomery, and also to Eddie Einhorn and John Ellis, whom I conversed with over the phone. I am similarly grateful to Peter O'Malley, who offered useful commentary via email.

Bob Dupuy, former MLB number two man and a friend of Mr. Giles, offered a wide range of perspectives and valuable information during two interviews. I am also thankful for the opportunity to interview former MLBPA Executive Director Don Fehr and noted baseball economist and author Dr. Andrew Zimbalist, both of whom supplied key insights into baseball's unique economic circumstances and labor relations issues. Dr. Zimbalist also provided a useful early review of my manuscript, and his numerous books and articles on the business of baseball were invaluable in my research.

Thanks also to Agnes Kryst, administrative assistant in the Department of Marketing at Saint Joseph's University, for her work in preparing manuscripts of the interviews; Zoya Pavlovskaya, my graduate assistant, who helped with research; and Monica DeBarberie, Kristen Farrell, Courtney Marzano, and Ally Arthur, undergraduate students at Saint Joseph's, who helped compile and footnotes and the reference list. I owe a debt of gratitude to my friend and fellow Cubs fan Dr. Bill Schwartz and to my brother Kevin, another long-suffering Cubs fan, both of whom read and critiqued early versions of some of the chapters.

I am grateful to the team at Temple University Press, especially Micah Kleit, my editor, and Gary Kramer, publicity manager. Peggy and Doug Gordon of P. M. Gordon Associates put forth a yeoman effort in handling the copy editing and typesetting. Without the help and support of these people, and others who are part of the Temple University Press team, this project would not have been possible.

Introduction

Bill Giles is fond of saying, "Someone pointed out to me recently that I had spent my whole life in baseball. But I told him, 'Not yet, I haven't.'" Bill Giles is a baseball lifer, born in Rochester, New York, where his father, Warren Giles, ran the Rochester club in the International League, and raised in Cincinnati, Ohio, where his dad ran the Reds as president and general manager. As a young man, Bill worked for the Reds, then learned the business from the ground up at one of the team's minor league affiliates, and eventually headed to Houston in 1960 to help launch the expansion Colt .45s, who started National League play in 1962. In the fall of 1969, Bill came to Philadelphia to help publicize and promote the Phillies as the team prepared to move to Veteran's Stadium from aging Connie Mack Stadium. He has been involved with the Phillies ever since, serving as president and general partner from 1981 through 1997 and as chairman since stepping down as president.

No single period in the 138-year history of major league baseball saw more change and turmoil than the sixteen years that Bill Giles served as president and managing partner of the Philadelphia Phillies. Giles purchased the Phillies after the 1981 season, during which baseball experienced its first serious labor stoppage, a fifty-day strike, a disruption in the season caused by a failure of the owners and players to agree on compensation for lost free agents. Free agency in baseball had existed since 1976, and the owners had difficulty adjusting to such a brave new world. From the late 1970s through the mid-1980s, salaries skyrocketed, fueled by a combination of salary arbitration and free agency, both won by the late Marvin Miller, the patron saint of all professional athletes. The owners responded by colluding to rig the free agent market, leading to a temporary halt in the upward spiral of salaries in the late 1980s. But the mistrust and bitterness this episode created among the players toward the owners contributed to more labor problems in 1990 and beyond.

Baseball expanded from sixteen to twenty-six teams between 1961 and 1977, but other cities, typically represented by powerful members of Congress, wanted teams of their own. After threats from Congress about possible loss of baseball's antitrust exemption, the owners agreed to expand again, adding two franchises to the NL in 1993. With expansion came two issues: how to split the franchise fees, which had grown from a few million dollars to almost $100 million per team in fifteen years, and how to align teams within their respective divisions in the NL. Commissioner Fay Vincent's decisions on expansion fees and league alignment proved to be very unpopular with certain owners. As a result of these decisions—and others, as we will see—and of the owners' perception that Vincent was soft on labor issues, baseball's eighth commissioner was forced from office in September 1992. This move created a vacancy in the commissioner's office that was filled by Milwaukee Brewers' owner Bud Selig, who, when he was appointed chair of the owners' Executive Council, became *de facto* acting commissioner. However, for nearly six years, baseball operated without a permanent commissioner.

Not long after Vincent's departure, the owners, unable to agree among themselves on how to share industry revenues that had grown dramatically but left small market teams at a significant economic disadvantage, and unable to agree with the union on how the revenues should be split between the owners and the players, took a hard line on a new labor deal. The players refused to accept the owners' demands for a salary cap and other economic concessions and walked off the job in August 1994. A month later, with the owners and players at loggerheads and no chance for a settlement, Selig canceled the postseason and America was deprived of a World Series for the first time since 1904.

Meanwhile, the owners decided to align the leagues into three divisions each and to introduce an expanded postseason, including a wild card team in each league. The change in the postseason format was delayed by a year because of the strike. Despite continuing labor strife and facing both renewed political pressure and a $280 million assessment for collusion damages, baseball expanded again. After extensive discussion of numerous alternative models, the 1998 expansion into Phoenix and Tampa–St. Petersburg brought with it another round of realignment and a revised schedule format. As part of the labor deal that finally passed in late 1996, interleague play began in 1997.

As these other changes were occurring, the business of baseball continued to grow, particularly in the areas of sponsorships, licensing, and media deals. As commissioner from 1984–1989, Peter Ueberroth had radically changed baseball's approach to marketing, licensing, and sponsorships. Since then, it had become clear to the owners that baseball could no longer do its business with each league functioning separately. Gradually, the owners diluted the power of the individual leagues as baseball centralized its business operations. The owners adopted what amounted to a CEO model in the office of commissioner, and eventually the office of league president was eliminated. At the same time, the owners negotiated with each other over competitive balance and revenue sharing and with the players over the economic structure of baseball. As part of the 1996 collective bargaining agreement (CBA), the owners and players agreed on a revenue-sharing plan, introducing a very significant modification to the economics of baseball.

In July 1998, after six years of saying that he had no interest in being permanent commissioner, Bud Selig—with a big push from many of the owners—finally accepted the job. With the 1996 labor agreement about to expire at the end of August 2002, once again, the drumbeats of labor war sounded loudly. But this time the players and owners reached an eleventh-hour settlement, averting a strike, and marking the first time since 1970 that a CBA had been reached without a labor stoppage. Although baseball again had severe economic problems around 2002, the labor agreement and the period of peace that the new CBA ushered in set the stage for dramatic industry growth over the next ten years.

Although he stepped down as president of the Phillies during the 1997 season, Bill Giles was a key part of the business of baseball during the twenty-one years from his purchase of the team from the Carpenter family after the 1981 season up to the 2002 labor agreement. This book reviews and recounts much that happened off the field in major league baseball during that era. I discuss key issues and decisions—with a focus on those that directly involved Mr. Giles—that have helped shape what we know today as Major League Baseball, a $7 billion-plus business with individual franchises worth as much as $2 billion. I also review some of the key decisions involving the Phillies during the Giles era: his purchase of the club, innovative TV deals, and the new ballpark—decisions that have played a significant role in dramatically changing the fortunes of the only professional sports team in history to lose 10,000 games, although the team is now considered one of the bedrock franchises in all of sports. I focus on Bill Giles—not only what he did but also what he said. Bill Giles is a baseball lifer, a true baseball romantic, and one of the architects of the game. He is also an extrovert and a public figure whom sports writers could always count on for timely and insightful quotes that keep the public tuned in to the inner workings of the national pastime.

BILL GILES AND BASEBALL

1

A Rapid-Fire Exposition of the Business of Baseball from the Beginning to 1981

The 1800s

The business of baseball started shortly after the first recorded game was played on the Elysian Fields in Hoboken, New Jersey, in 1846. Enterprising businessmen understood the attraction of baseball as it quickly became "our national game" and would rope off areas and charge spectators for the privilege of witnessing a contest. By the post–Civil War era, the popularity of baseball was soaring and some of the better "amateur" players were compensated for playing baseball on behalf of companies or enterprising business people as a means of attracting spectators, who were being charged as much as 25 cents to attend the games. Finally, in 1869, the Cincinnati Red Stockings, led by Harry Wright, who was to become manager of the Phillies in the 1880s, became baseball's first openly professional team. The Red Stockings played throughout the northeastern part of the country as an independent club, playing and winning games, and finished its first season with fifty-six wins, no losses, and one tie.

The competitive and commercial success of the Red Stockings motivated other people with means to organize professional "base ball" clubs. This led in 1871 to the formation of the National Association of Professional Base Ball Players, the first professional baseball league. This league was an operation run by players and was rife with organizational and financial problems, not to mention the rowdiness of both players and spectators. This state of affairs led a successful Chicago coal magnate named William Hulbert to found the National League as an operation run on sound business organizational principles and with the goal of creating a "fan-friendly environment." The National League of Professional Baseball Clubs began play with eight franchises in 1876 and today is still known as "the senior circuit."

As baseball's popularity grew and more business people saw an opportunity to turn a profit, other leagues, including the American Association, the Union League, and the Players League, came and went between 1884 and 1890. As competition among teams increased, so did competition for the best players, and many players jumped from team to team to accept better deals. This practice became known as "revolving," and to stop "revolvers," the owners agreed to "reserve" a certain number of players on the teams' rosters. They also agreed not to make offers to the reserved players on opponents' rosters. Thus, the reserve clause was born, and eventually this clause was extended to the entire roster and became part of the standard player's contract, putting the owners firmly in control of the business of baseball.

In the late 1890s, Ban Johnson, a former Cincinnati newspaper writer, took over leadership of a struggling minor league called the Western League. By virtue of his vision and leadership, Johnson added franchises in major cities such as Philadelphia and Chicago and eventually declared the Western League to be a second major league, which he renamed the American League in 1901. To strengthen the league and increase its popularity, Johnson and the club owners recruited several dozen active players from National League rosters, including stars such as Napoleon Lajoie and Ed Delahanty from the Phillies. The bidding war for players by the two leagues led to a rapid increase in salaries, something the owners in both leagues disliked.

The 1900s

The owners in both the National League and the American League ("the junior circuit") agreed to end their bidding wars and negotiated the National Agreement of 1903. This agreement established the modern structure of major league baseball—two eight-team leagues with a World Series between the respective league champions. In addition, a three-man National Commission was formed to govern baseball. The American and National Leagues that existed at the time of the National Agreement, with sixteen teams located in eleven Northeastern cities, remained in place for fifty years, despite two World Wars, the short-term incursion of the Federal League in 1914–1915, and the effects of the Great Depression.

As more successful business people saw the profit potential of America's game, a number of them formed a new league. The Federal League was founded as a minor league in 1913 and declared itself a major league in 1914, thereby challenging the existing leagues. The Federal League played for two years until the owners realized that they simply did not have access to enough good ballplayers, mainly because of the reserve system, which bound major league players to their clubs once under contract, and because National League and American League owners threatened to "blacklist" any player who jumped leagues. The owners of the Federal League sued the owners of the two major leagues on antitrust grounds, but the suit died in the courtroom of Federal Judge Kenesaw Mountain Landis, who happened to be a big Chicago Cubs fan. When the league disbanded, the owners of the American League and National League agreed to compensate the Federal League owners, several of whom were provided cash payments. Some others, including Charles Weeghman, owner of the Chicago Whales, who had built his team a ballpark at Clark and Addison Streets on the north side of Chicago, were given opportunities to own teams in the National League or American League. The owners of the Baltimore Terrapins did not consider their settlement offer adequate and filed a second antitrust suit against the existing major leagues. This lawsuit made its way through the courts, eventually reaching the Supreme Court in 1922, when Chief Justice Oliver Wendell Holmes rendered his notorious decision that declared that major league baseball was not involved in interstate commerce and therefore was exempt from federal antitrust statutes, an exemption that remains, at least partially, to this day.

Meanwhile, the greatest scandal in the history of the national pastime occurred when players on the 1919 Chicago White Sox allegedly conspired with gamblers to "throw" the World Series. This plot was discovered late in the 1920 season, when a grand jury in Cook County, Illinois, was named to investigate another gambling allegation, in a regular season game between the Cubs and the Phillies. The gambling and game-throwing revelations motivated baseball's owners to scrap the ineffectual National Commission, a body rife with conflicts of interest and inequitable decision-making, as the governing body of baseball. The owners realized that they needed a strong central authority to replace the National Commission, and the office of commissioner was created in 1921. Judge Landis, who had come to the attention of the owners because of the stalled Federal League suit, was named baseball's first commissioner with the idea of "cleaning up the game" and restoring public confidence in its integrity. Of course, all baseball fans know that the first major move that

Landis made was to ban the eight suspected members of the 1919 White Sox, the "eight men out," for life.

At the time that Landis suspended the eight White Sox players and three others, the public believed that the Black Sox Scandal, as it came to be known, was a kind of "original sin" for baseball, an isolated incident that tarnished the game and the individuals involved. But years of research and revelations showed that gambling was endemic to baseball and throwing games was a cottage industry for certain players, including the infamous Hal Chase. Sean Deveney has written a fascinating book called *The Original Curse* that alleges that the Cubs threw the 1918 World Series to the Babe Ruth–led Boston Red Sox and that some of the White Sox used this as an example for their decision to "throw in" with gamblers a year later.

The 1920s and 1930s

The 1920s, following the 1919 sale of Babe Ruth by the Red Sox to the New York Yankees, ushered in a period of excitement and, mirroring the U.S. economic boom of the 1920s, a period of great economic growth for baseball. "The Bambino" helped create the modern game and directly led to the building of "the house that Ruth built," the original Yankee Stadium in the Bronx, in 1923. The Yankees, with its "murderers' row" lineup of Ruth, Gehrig, Dickey, and others, dominated the American League and the headlines. During this decade, the first games were broadcast on radio, starting with a game between the Phillies and the Pirates that was broadcast on KDKA in Pittsburgh in 1924.

However, after the stock market crash and the onset of the Great Depression, the 1930s proved to be era of economic struggle for the nation and for major and minor league baseball. Game attendance plummeted as many Americans simply could not afford the price of admission. Connie Mack's Philadelphia Athletics, led by greats such as Lefty Grove, Jimmy Foxx, and Al Simmons, won three American League pennants and two world championships from 1929 to 1931. Although overshadowed by Ruth and Gehrig's Yankees, some baseball observers consider the A's of this era the greatest team ever. However, because the team was his only source of income, Mack was struggling financially, especially as the effects of the Depression set it. He was forced to sell many of his star players, and the A's never recovered. By the middle of the decade, the Yankees re-exerted its dominance and, fueled by a young Joe DiMaggio, won four consecutive world championships, from 1936 to 1939. In the National League, the St. Louis Cardinals, buoyed by a farm system created by the visionary Branch Rickey, emerged as the best team, with competition from the New York Giants and Chicago Cubs, who won three pennants during the decade, its last sustained period of excellence. During this decade, night baseball debuted, thanks to the vision of Larry MacPhail, general manager of the Cincinnati Reds.

The 1940s and 1950s

The country was still largely in the throes of the Depression when World War II came to the United States in December 1941 after the Japanese attack on Pearl Harbor. Shortly thereafter, President Roosevelt sent his "green light letter" to Commissioner Landis, indicating his preference for baseball to continue during the war to help with the morale of the country. World War II had a significant effect on major league baseball because many of the better players joined the war effort, whether in actual combat positions like Bob Feller, Hank Bauer, and Warren Spahn, or largely playing baseball, helping with morale and supporting efforts to sell war bonds to finance the war effort, like Joe DiMaggio. Night baseball became much more prevalent, a necessity because many people worked in the factories making munitions and war materials. The quality of the game deteriorated significantly after 1942, but baseball, including the World Series, was played right through the war. In 1944, the woeful St. Louis Browns won its only pennant, and in 1945, the Cubs won its last pennant, only to be beaten by the Tigers, energized by the return of the great Hank Greenberg after his war experiences, in the World Series.

After World War II, the United States experienced an economic boom and attendance for both the major and minor leagues increased significantly from 1946 to 1949. However, because the owners had 100 percent of the economic control of the game due to the Reserve Clause and the Antitrust Exemption, they successfully held salary increases in check. During the war, labor problems in private industry had been controlled, but once the war ended, there was a great deal of labor unrest and many industries experienced employee strikes. In baseball, some of the players began to push for a pension plan and other benefits common to organized labor. Robert Murphy, an attorney, decided that baseball players could benefit from a union and attempted to organize the Pittsburgh Pirates in 1946—an effort that failed, but showed that players were not satisfied with their economic circumstances. The owners decided at that time to mollify the players and started the first pension plan.

The most noteworthy change that took place in baseball during the postwar years was, of course, Jackie Robinson's signing by Branch Rickey, who had come to Brooklyn from St. Louis to replace Larry MacPhail, who had left the Dodgers to join the war effort. Robinson inked his initial contract in the fall of 1945 and spent the 1946 season leading the Dodgers' Triple-A Montreal Club to the International League Championship and a "little World Series" win over the American Association's Louisville club. Robinson debuted with Brooklyn on April 15, 1947, a date that Major League Baseball now celebrates each year. Many more African Americans and Latinos followed Robinson throughout the 1950s, and in the National League in particular, black players changed not only the face of the game but also the way it was played. One can argue that it was not coincidence that between 1947 and 1956 the Dodgers—the "boys of summer" immortalized by Roger Kahn—buoyed by Robinson, Roy Campanella, Don Newcombe, and other black players, won six National League pennants. The Giants, featuring Willie Mays, Monte Irvin, and Hank Thompson (baseball's first all-black outfield), among others, won pennants in 1951 and 1954; not coincidentally, Mays missed the 1952 and 1953 seasons due to active military duty. Then the Braves, with a roster that included Henry Aaron, Billy Bruton, Wes Covington, and Juan Pizarro (a black Latino), won National League pennants in 1957 and 1958. During this period, despite the overall dominance of the New York Yankees, the National League was clearly the stronger league.

Another significant change to baseball's landscape in the 1950s was the founding of the Major League Baseball Players Association in 1953. The Players Association initially functioned as a "house union" and made very few demands on the owners—certainly not a call for the end of the Reserve Clause—but the foundation had been put in place for seismic changes to baseball's labor relations in succeeding decades.

Despite the postwar economic boom, owners of "second teams" in Boston, St. Louis, and Philadelphia began to realize that their cities could not adequately support two major league teams. As a result, they decided to seek greener pastures for their teams and baseball witnessed its first franchise relocations since the National Agreement of 1903. One ball club moved after each of the 1953, 1954, and 1955 seasons. First, owner Lou Perini moved his Boston Braves to Milwaukee; the following year, Bill Veeck sold the St. Louis Browns to new owners, who moved the club to Baltimore, where it took on the name of a long-standing minor league team, the Orioles; and the next year, the Mack family sold the Philadelphia Athletics to Arnold Johnson, a business colleague of the owners of the New York Yankees, and Johnson moved the club to Kansas City. The Braves, in particular, enjoyed tremendous success as attendance in Milwaukee, historically a strong minor league city, exceeded 2 million for several of the years after its relocation, an unheard of number at that time. Walter O'Malley, who had earlier maneuvered to become sole owner of the Brooklyn Dodgers, took notice of the financial success of the Braves in Milwaukee.

During the late 1940s and early 1950s, television began to have a major impact on the business of baseball. Similar to the situation in the early days of radio, many baseball executives, including National League President Warren Giles, were concerned that televising games would hurt the live gate; as a result, a majority of teams were reluctant to put their games on TV locally. Baseball's jewels, the All-Star Game and the World Series, were televised nationally, and the first national television contracts were negotiated between baseball and the networks. However, baseball continued to earn the lion's share of its revenue through the live gate.

After the 1957 season, O'Malley, keenly aware of the fiscal success of the Braves in its new home and frustrated by New York Public Works czar Robert Moses in O'Malley's quest for a new ballpark in Brooklyn, succumbed to offers by the city fathers of Los Angeles to relocate the team to Southern California; O'Malley decided to move his Dodgers to Los Angeles in 1958. New York Giants owner Horace Stoneham, who made the famous statement, "I feel bad for the kids but I haven't seen too many of their fathers lately," after drawing only 629,000 to the Polo Grounds in 1956, decided to move his New York Giants to San Francisco at the same time. In 1960, Calvin Griffith, decrying his team's circumstances in a demographically changing Washington, D.C., moved the Senators to the Twin Cities. With these franchise shifts, major league baseball had dramatically expanded its geographic footprint, and for the first time, the "national game" was truly national.

Once New York City had lost its two National League teams, pressure mounted to bring another team to New York. Mayor Robert Wagner gave Bill Shea, a prominent attorney, the job of finding a National League team that was willing to relocate to New York. None of the teams he asked, including the Phillies, was interested. As an alternative, Shea came up with the idea of a "third major league" with eight teams in seven large cities that didn't have a major league team, plus New York, which still had the Yankees, but no National League team. This third league—the Continental League—was announced in 1958. The intention of Shea and the potential owners he recruited was to be part of major league baseball, unlike the Federal League, which had attempted to challenge the American League and National League, and league play would start in 1961.

The initiative became much more credible when Branch Rickey, noted for his creation of the modern farm system as well as the integration of baseball in 1947, was named president. Rickey, who was the mentor of Warren Giles and the godfather of Bill Giles, moved the formation of the league forward. At one point, Rickey appeared on the popular 1950s TV show *What's My Line,* and when asked about the prospects of the league actually beginning play, he said that it was "as inevitable as tomorrow morning."[1] While the National League and American League owners welcomed the new league publicly, in private they made every effort to scuttle it before it launched. The league never did start play; the idea was abandoned once the owners, succumbing to pressure from Congress to make major league baseball available in more cities, especially New York, agreed to expand. The American League pulled the trigger on expansion first. In 1961, the expansion Angels joined the Dodgers in Los Angeles and the Junior Circuit welcomed Washington, D.C., back into the league with the expansion Senators. New York and Houston were granted franchises in the National League, and the new National League franchises began play in 1962.

The 1960s

The 1960s was a decade of dramatic social change. The civil rights movement had begun in the 1950s, with Rosa Parks and *Brown v. Board of Education,* but many people believe that Jackie Robinson's debut on April 15, 1947, was just as important, if not more so. Former Negro League player Stanley Glenn said, "Jackie Robinson did more for civil rights than the Supreme Court."[2] The era of social activism really took off in response to the expansion of the war in Southeast Asia, which led to years of protests and upheaval across the Unites States. Baseball mirrored the larger society in which it functioned. The 1960s also ushered in a new executive director for the Players Association in 1966, a former economist for the Steelworkers Union named Marvin Miller. Few realized it at the time, but Miller's hiring and the negotiation of the first CBA between the owners and players in 1968 would lead to a sea change in baseball. Later, the negotiation of the first labor deal between the owners and the players was described by longtime baseball man Paul Richards as "the end of baseball as we knew it."

Just as they had expanded at the beginning of the decade, both leagues expanded again at the end of the decade. In 1969, the National League added teams in Montreal and San Diego, while the American League placed new teams in Kansas City and Seattle, bringing the total number of teams to twenty-four. Expansion led to the creation of six-team divisions and league championship playoffs to determine pennant winners in each league. In 1977, the American League expanded again, adding teams in Kansas City to replace the A's after the team moved to Oakland, and in Seattle, which had lost the Pilots to Milwaukee after its initial 1969 season. In both cases, prominent politicians created pressure on baseball to expand and replace the franchises that the cities had lost.

The decision in 1960 to expand the National League created an opportunity for Bill Giles to obtain his first real job in major league baseball. Gabe Paul, who served under Warren Giles with the Cincinnati Reds and then succeeded him as general manager when the elder Giles became National League president in 1951, left the Reds after the 1960 season to become the first general manager of the expansion Houston franchise. Gabe reached back to Cincinnati and hired Bill Giles as publicity director and traveling secretary for the Colt .45s—later to become the Astros—and Bill's career in major league baseball had officially begun.

The Business of Baseball "Back in the Day"

The business of baseball today is far different from the business of baseball at the time Bill Giles joined the expansion Houston club. At the time, baseball was a much smaller and less sophisticated operation than the $7 billion-plus enterprise it is today. In 1960, total major league revenue was less than $100 million and total attendance had not yet reached 20 million. Marketing consisted of a little bit of radio and TV advertising and promotions such as ladies day and bat day. The executives who ran the baseball business and the various clubs counted on the daily newspapers and the newspaper beat reporters who covered the team to help drum up interest. Only a few years earlier, some baseball executives thought that broadcasting and especially televising games in the home team's market hurt attendance. In fact, national television revenue for the 1960 season, including the World Series between the Yankees and Pittsburgh Pirates, was only about $3.3 million.

Of course, this was before the introduction of the Internet, cable television, and regional sports networks. At the time, there was little in the way of licensing and sales of team merchandise, there were no suites or club seats, and there were no ballpark naming rights—you cannot count Wrigley Field or Busch Stadium, which both were named for owners, not for companies. Revenues consisted primarily of ticket sales; some income from concessions, which, according to Giles, consisted of "a hot dog, a Coke, peanuts, and a scorecard"; a small national TV deal; local radio and TV deals for much smaller numbers than we are used to today; some local sponsors and ballpark signage; and a couple of national sponsorships, including a long-standing deal with Gillette, the company that helped men "look sharp, feel sharp." The scale of baseball was simply much smaller. The only significant changes to the business of baseball in the first fifty years after 1903 were the move toward night baseball, which started in 1935, and the move to offer broadcasts and telecasts of games. Marvin Miller had not yet come on the scene.

The Reserve Clause and the Economics of Baseball

The economics of baseball were governed largely by the reserve system, which permitted an owner to completely control a ballplayer once that player had signed a contract. The "infamous" (at least from the players' point of view) reserve clause in the standard player's contract bound a player to a team virtually in perpetuity. The reserve clause granted the owner an arbitrary right to renew a player's contract, on terms of the owner's choice, for one year. The clause was interpreted to mean that the team could renew year after year and was held in place by baseball's antitrust exemption. In the years immediately after World War II, two different legal cases—involving players Danny Gardella[3] and George Toolson[4]—failed to dislodge the antitrust exemption.

The owners deemed the reserve system necessary to provide stability to a team's roster from year to year, but also to limit bidding on players and therefore control salaries. This was demonstrated by the fact that player salaries had risen during the wars between leagues when there was competition among teams for players, first in 1901–1902, when the American League began to compete with its older rival, the National League, and again in 1914–1915, when the Federal League claimed major league status and tried to sign National League and American League players. Of course, both "wars" ended quickly and the owners moved to re-establish economic control over the game. For most of the history of major league baseball, there was little upward pressure on salaries. Consequently, there was never a great deal of pressure to create new and larger revenue streams. In fact, when the owners were struggling economically during the Great Depression, Bill Veeck's father, president of the Chicago Cubs, proposed integrating baseball as a way of opening up the game to African Americans and a potential new revenue stream—African American fans—but the idea proved too unpopular with the baseball establishment to implement at the time.

After the initial imposition of the reserve clause back in the 1880s, players' attempts to countervail against the power and control of the owners occurred periodically. The first significant move was an attempt by John Montgomery Ward, who was both an excellent player and an attorney, to organize the players into a "brotherhood" in 1885. Ward also led the formation of the Players' League in 1890, a league that gave the players control over their own destiny—specifically, there was no reserve clause in the player's contract—but the new league could not survive economically and lasted only one year. As already mentioned, Robert Murphy unsuccessfully attempted to organize the "Baseball Guild" in Pittsburgh in 1946. He was able to gain some benefits for the players, including compensation for spring training—forever after known as "Murphy Money"—but his organizing effort was largely thwarted.

The major economic issue driving players in the postwar era was a pension plan. To that end, the players formed the Major League Baseball Players Association (MLBPA) in 1953, being careful not to call their association a "union." The legal counsel to the MLBPA was Judge Robert Cannon, whose father had gained notoriety by serving as the attorney representing Joe Jackson and some other members of the infamous Black Sox in their lawsuit against Charles Comiskey, heard in Milwaukee in 1924. Thus, the younger Judge Cannon had some experience with baseball. However, as a labor leader, Judge Cannon was not exactly a rabble-rouser and the MLBPA operated largely as a partner with the owners. Judge Cannon's position was that the players enjoyed terrific salaries and benefits and should be grateful to and cooperative with the owners. It wasn't until Judge Cannon refused to accept the terms of the job of executive director in the mid-1960s that Marvin Miller came to the Players Association in 1966 as executive director. Once Miller—an experienced, hard-line labor representative—took charge, the Players Association began to operate as a real union. As a result, the economics and business of baseball eventually were completely transformed.

The average annual salary for major league baseball players before Miller's arrival was less than $16,000. Historically, the share of revenues paid to players was in the 30 percent range and below, sinking as low as 17.6 percent in 1950 and rising a bit during the decade. Pete Rose came to major league baseball with the Cincinnati Reds in 1963, when the players were still under the economic thumb of the owners. Rose, racing to first base on walks and diving into bases, became known as "Charlie Hustle" and was banging out the hits that would eventually make him "the hit king." Rose frequently claimed that he wanted to be "the first $100,000 singles hitter." Fast forward to 2013 and compare Rose's goal with the megamillions that the Angels are paying Albert Pujols and Josh Hamilton for perspective on baseball salaries then and now.

As executive director of the Players Association, Marvin Miller demonstrated a real knack for both understanding players' concerns and educating players about their rights and the ways in which certain factors, such as independent arbitration of grievances—instead of the commissioner serving as final arbiter—could affect their circumstances. Ultimately, of course, Miller knew that the Holy Grail for the players was free agency, but early on, for the most part, even the players supported the reserve clause, believing the owners who claimed that the reserve clause provided necessary economic and competitive stability to baseball.

During the late 1960s, Curt Flood changed all of that. Most baseball fans are at least somewhat familiar with the story of how Flood, a twelve-year veteran and All-Star centerfielder for the successful Cardinals of the 1960s, was traded against his wishes to the Phillies following the 1969 season. Flood did not want to leave St. Louis, where he had established business interests, or come to Philadelphia, which at the time had a reputation for not treating black players well. Coincidentally, Flood's initial actions to have the trade voided and be declared a free agent took place at exactly the time when Bill Giles was leaving Houston and coming to Philadelphia to join the Phillies as vice president of business operations. The Phillies delayed the announcement of Bill's appointment by a week because of the Flood controversy.

With the somewhat grudging support of the Players Association, Flood filed suit against Commissioner Bowie Kuhn, who had cited the reserve clause in denying Flood's request to be declared a free agent, and major league baseball. With Miller and former Supreme Court Justice Arthur Goldberg at his side, Flood took the case to the courts, where he lost, and he eventually lost in the U.S. Supreme Court in a 5–3 (with one recusal) split verdict, which was announced in 1972. While Flood's grievance and lawsuit did not lead to free agency, the entire process raised consciousness about the issue and put the owners on notice that the institution was under attack.

The case of Catfish Hunter created further incentive for the players to remove their economic shackles. A's owner Charles Finley, an insurance executive, had convinced Hunter to take part of his compensation in the form of a paid annuity, but Finley had missed the contractually obligated annuity payment during the 1974 season. Hunter filed a grievance to have his contract declared null and void and thereby to become a free agent. Because Miller had adroitly included a grievance system in the CBA, the case came to baseball's independent arbitrator, Peter Seitz. Seitz decided that Finley had violated the terms of Hunter's contract and therefore declared the contract null and void. As a result, Hunter, the best pitcher on the three-time defending world champion team and the 1974 Cy Young Award winner, became a free agent. A frenzy of activity followed, with most major league teams—including the Phillies—attempting to sign Hunter. George Steinbrenner, whose group had purchased the Yankees from CBS just a year earlier, signed Hunter to the unheard-of sum of $3.75 million for five years, thereby establishing a pattern of signing expensive free agents for the Yankees that lasted through the signings of Mark Texeira and CC Sabathia some thirty-six years later. Suddenly, the size of Hunter's new deal provided clear and compelling evidence that free agency was a potential golden goose for the players and demonstrated to players the potential value of an open market.

So it was virtually predestined that the reserve clause would be tested. And it was shortly thereafter by Andy Messersmith of the Dodgers and Dave McNally of the Expos. Both men played the 1975 season without signing a contract, thereby "playing out their options." Both Messersmith and McNally then filed grievances against major league baseball, based on the fact that having played without a contract during their option year they had satisfied the condition of renewal for "one year" as stipulated by clause 10A of the standard player's contract and were now legally free agents. The owners disagreed, because for ninety years, the baseball industry had interpreted the reserve clause to mean that owners could renew the players' contracts year after year. The case went to baseball's arbitrator, Seitz. After hearing the case, Seitz strongly urged the owners to negotiate a settlement—but to no avail. Seitz then ruled in favor of the players on the owners' "day of infamy," December 23, 1975. The owners sought redress through the courts and filed suit to have Seitz's decision overturned in federal court in Kansas City, the home of Ewing Kaufmann's Royals. The owners specifically wanted to avoid the "liberal bias" of the East, so they did not file their lawsuit in New York. The Players Association retained a young labor lawyer who had clerked for presiding Judge John Oliver to work on their legal team. The young lawyer's name was Donald Fehr.

Once free agency became a reality, confirmed by the courts after Judge Oliver dismissed the owners' suit, the key issues were implementation of the new system and compensation for teams that lost players due to free agency. Ultimately, the owners and players agreed that, after six years of service in the big leagues, players could gain free agency. What was not decided was compensation. The players believed that direct compensation in the form of a player or players from the signing team, which the owners demanded, would create a significant disincentive for clubs to sign free agents, thereby reducing both demand and upward pressure on salaries. They were correct. The owners refused to back down from their demands for compensation, and this disagreement led directly to baseball's first major strike during the 1981 season. The strike lasted for fifty days and created havoc for owners, players, and fans.

The 1980s

The strike was settled in August 1981 just before the owners' strike insurance ran out. The players went back to work and the owners agreed to a somewhat complex and indirect form of compensation for players lost to free agency. Meanwhile, salaries exploded and owners made crazy offers to free agents. Phillies owner and chief executive officer (CEO) Ruly Carpenter was not at all happy about the changing economics of the game. The average player salary had gone from approximately $19,000 in 1967 to about $52,000 in 1976 to about $144,000 in 1980, a very rapid escalation that frightened the baseball establishment.

The final straw was when Ted Turner, owner of the Braves, offered a mediocre outfielder named Claudell Washington an outrageous contract: a five-year, $3.5 million free agent deal, with a $250,000 interest-free loan and incentives worth $265,000 a year thrown in for good measure. During the spring training after the Phillies first-ever world championship in 1980, Ruly Carpenter decided that his family would exit baseball. So, while Gabe Paul's move to Houston provided Bill Giles the opportunity to get his first real job in baseball, twenty-one years later, Ruly Carpenter's decision to sell the Phillies gave him the opportunity to achieve his lifelong dream of running a major league club.

The strike of 1981 had taken a real toll on the game. In its aftermath, the owners focused a good deal of their anger on Commissioner Kuhn, primarily because Kuhn felt that he was commissioner for all of baseball—owners, players, and fans—while the owners wanted their commissioner to help them make money. The owners who felt that Kuhn was too soft on labor and ineffective on other business matters pushed to have him removed from office and refused to renew his contract beyond the end of his term in 1984. The strike had caused both sides to lose real money. Estimates put the owners' loss at approximately $72 million, net of strike insurance.[5] The players lost about the same amount in salaries. But the real damage was to how the fans felt about both the owners and the players. The common attitude was "a pox on both their houses."

In the fall of 1981, the business of baseball was clearly in the throes of an economic tsunami. Salary arbitration, which the players had won via collective bargaining in 1973, combined with free agency, caused salaries to escalate rapidly. George Steinbrenner had demonstrated the potential value of free agency by turning his Yankees into World Series champions in both 1977 and 1978 after signing Hunter, Reggie Jackson, and others. Owners who wanted to improve their clubs saw free agency as a solution, but at the expense of what they considered runaway salary inflation.

Baseball was just emerging from the era of replacing old neighborhood ballparks, such as Connie Mack Stadium (formerly known as Shibe Park) with multipurpose stadiums with artificial playing surfaces designed for both baseball and football but ultimately good for neither. Roy Hofheinz, owner of the expansion Houston Colt .45s and builder of the Astrodome, created the concept of luxury suites, but they were not yet significant revenue producers for major league baseball. Along with the changes on baseball's labor front and the incursion of publically funded, multipurpose stadiums with artificial turf fields, cable TV was just starting to come of age. ESPN was a fledgling operation in Bristol, Connecticut. Ted Turner had purchased the Braves in 1976 and, using satellite distribution of his signal, had turned WTBS into a "superstation." This was the beginning of a completely new relationship between television and baseball, not to mention higher and higher rights fees (the fees paid by the networks to the property for the right to televise games), especially local rights fees for "big-market" teams.

Attendance was rising. By 1980 total major league attendance had reached 43 million—from less than 20 million in 1960. Some of the attendance gain was attributable to expansion and more teams, but there was also more interest in the game. While the owners abhorred free agency because of its effect on salaries, the fans liked free agency because it allowed teams to improve themselves more easily and quickly than in the past, when they had to rely on player development and trades. In addition, free agency actually helped create more competitive balance, contrary to the fears of the owners, who thought that all of the good players would play for the highest-revenue clubs. With more competitive balance and with the excitement created by significant free agent signings, fans could feel some "hope" that their team could compete for a championship. With hope came interest, and with interest came rising attendance and television ratings—and rising revenues. Revenues per team had reached more than $12 million by 1980. The total revenue from national television contracts for all of major league baseball had reached $47 million per year, and 1980 marked the first time that national TV revenue had surpassed the total of local TV revenue for all twenty-six teams.

It was into this world of major league baseball that Bill Giles became managing partner and president of the Phillies in October 1981, twelve years after his move from Houston to Philadelphia.

2

Bill Giles and Major League Baseball's Network TV Deals, 1983–1995

Television debuted in 1939 at the New York World's Fair, but it did not become commercially viable until after World War II. During the late 1940s and early 1950s the amount of television programming and the number of televisions in American households grew significantly. Baseball was there almost from the beginning. NBC first provided television coverage of the World Series in 1947; Gillette sponsored the game and paid a rights fee of $65,000 for television and $175,000 for radio. National broadcasts of regular season games began in 1953, when ABC became the first network to televise a "game of the week." This arrangement lasted for two years at ABC, after which it was picked up by CBS.[1] As the household penetration of television grew, the sights as well as the sounds of baseball became available in American living rooms. While early on some teams, such as the Brooklyn Dodgers and the Chicago Cubs, embraced television, other baseball executives thought that watching games in the comfort of one's home might discourage attendance. National League President Warren Giles said specifically that he did not want baseball to become a "studio game."

By the end of the 1950s most baseball insiders understood that television was both remunerative—NBC and Gillette paid $3 million a year for the World Series plus $250,000 for the All-Star Game—and could be a highly effective tool for creating interest in the game. Television and sports, in fact, are made for each other. The growth of spectator sports has been fueled by television, and the growth of television, in turn, has been helped by sports as a major programming vehicle. Sports programming is live and original and delivers a desirable demographic to many advertisers. August Busch, chairman of Anheuser Busch in the early 1950s, understood that principle early on when he bought the St. Louis Cardinals. People at the ballpark drink beer; more importantly, the heaviest consumers of beer watch baseball on television.

One cannot overstate the importance of television to major league baseball and other sports, especially football. In late December 1958, in cold and gray Yankee Stadium, Johnny Unitas guided the Baltimore Colts to a thrilling overtime victory over the New York Giants in the National Football League (NFL) Championship game. NBC telecast the game nationally, and this "greatest game ever played" is now considered the seminal event that made the NFL what it has become. More generally, it is fair to say that television has cemented sports into the American psyche and into American culture. In 2001 *Baseball Weekly* listed television as second only to Jackie Robinson's signing in its list of the "top 100 things that impacted baseball in the 20th century." Overall, television has given baseball a large audience; provided significant revenue for owners, which in turn has dramatically increased franchise values; and fundamentally changed the way in which fans follow the game.[2]

One generation after Warren Giles, Bill Giles did not share his father's pessimism about the effect of television on baseball. The younger Giles had a knack for publicity and promotion, and he understood the effectiveness of television as a promotional vehicle for baseball, encouraging fans to go to the ballpark in person, noting, "You could show the excitement of your fans screaming, of families having fun at the ballpark. It was the best promotion you could have."[3]

A Key Player in the TV Game

When Bill Giles and his partners purchased the Phillies, major league baseball was working with a national TV contract that, for the first time, generated total revenue that exceeded the sum of local TV rights. The 1980–1983 deal doubled the old contract, yielding $190 million, or $1.8 million per team per year.[4] By late 1982, Commissioner Bowie Kuhn had failed to gain reelection for another term and was a lame duck. For this and other reasons, the executive council of owners felt that Kuhn should not negotiate a new national TV contract on his own and needed some experienced and knowledgeable owners to work with him. Two owners in particular had experience in negotiating television deals. Giles had put together local radio, over-the-air, and pay television packages in Philadelphia during the 1970s that were models in the industry, according to Kuhn. Giles had worked with Ed Snider of the Philadelphia Flyers to create one of the nation's first multisport regional sports channels in September 1976, and he was eager to serve on the committee as the representative of the National League.

The other owner with television experience was Eddie Einhorn, co-owner of the Chicago White Sox. Einhorn was the founder and chairman of TVS Television Network, a leader in sports programming in the 1970s. The TVS telecast of college basketball's "game of the century" between Houston and UCLA from the Astrodome in 1968 is credited for the growth in popularity of college basketball on television. It also provided an opportunity for Giles, who worked for the Astros at the time, to meet and get to know Einhorn.

The committee, which called itself "KEG"—for Kuhn, Einhorn, and Giles—held preliminary discussions with ABC and NBC in December 1982 and then moved into high-gear negotiations in January 1983. Arthur Watson, president of NBC Sports, and his vice president, Ken Schanzer, represented NBC, while Jim Spence, senior vice president of ABC Sports, handled the responsibilities for ABC.[5] According to the agreement then in place, ABC and NBC had paid $300 million each to split the baseball "jewels," the All-Star Game, the League Championship Series, and the World Series. KEG's goal was to obtain a total of $1 billion for the rights to telecast these events for six years—$500 million each from ABC and NBC.[6] Kuhn commented, "From the outset, we made it clear that we were looking for a substantial deal that we felt we could justify on the basis of recent network arrangements for college and professional football and on the advertising dollars we projected could be generated by the baseball package."[7]

Einhorn and Giles wanted to continue with at least two networks on the next contract, three, if possible. Working with multiple networks spread the financial risks, ensured greater promotion for baseball, and reduced the possibility that blockbuster programming would run opposite baseball. Baseball's leverage lay in a clause in the existing 1980–1983 contract that stated that if either ABC or NBC made an offer on a new deal, the other network could get half the package by matching the offer.[8] Einhorn felt that "the only way we are going to make more money is to play one network against the other."

> The strategy was to get one of them to go for the whole thing, to make the market. Our job was to convince one of them that we were willing to give them the whole thing. It was a matter of meeting with the networks and breaking them down. We needed a stalking horse. I had done a lot of business with NBC, including some Olympic stuff, so we decided to make the initial offer to them. It took a while to get NBC to be willing to be "the stalking horse."[9]

Einhorn approached NBC and told Watson, "Art, the whole package is NBC's for $1 billion. If you don't take it, we're going to ABC and offer them half for $500 million. If they balk at that, it's yours for $900 million. So you can either take half, roll the dice you get it all for $900 million, or take ABC out of the picture right now for $1 billion."[10] Einhorn was well versed in TV through his syndication background and other ventures, so he took the lead in shaping the contract's many intricacies. Unfortunately, he tended to outrun the comprehension of the others. During one long and complex dissertation that Einhorn delivered to both the other members of the committee and the TV executives on a new formula he had devised to split the package, he finished to the sound of absolute silence. Schanzer asked to caucus with Watson and in private asked whether Watson had any idea what Einhorn was talking about. Watson said that he didn't understand a word of what Einhorn had said, so Schanzer and Watson decided to admit to the committee that they didn't understand the presentation. When pressed, Kuhn admitted that he didn't understand it either, and they all laughed, except Einhorn, who just shook his head in bemused frustration.[11]

During the first few months of 1983, Schanzer and Watson for NBC and KEG for baseball negotiated the intricate details of the contract. NBC bid a total of $475 million for half of the package for five years, along with a guarantee to pick up the other half for $425 million if ABC didn't take it. As Ken Schanzer said, "Either we succeeded in getting the whole package or we so crippled our competitor, we made his life hard." KEG took the offer to ABC, and Roone Arledge, head of ABC Sports, passed on it, indicating that ABC's top offer was $300 million. The proposed deal favored NBC, particularly since it gave NBC an extra World Series, three for NBC versus two for ABC over the five-year deal.[12]

The committee and the networks continued to negotiate and ultimately restructured the deal by extending the contract to six years and giving ABC a third World Series. The committee also offered some other concessions, including exclusivity for *The Game of the Week*, which could make a significant difference in the ratings. Finally, ABC consented. The final deal, approved in April 1983, was for ABC to pay $575 million while NBC paid $550 million. Baseball would collect $1.125 billion over the six-year life of the contract, from 1984 through 1989. The revenue for each individual club quadrupled, from $1.8 million per year to $7.2 million per year.

During the negotiations, CBS had maintained a strong interest but was discouraged by the high price, which they felt did not make business sense for them. ABC was not happy with the size of NBC's offer—but, as an incumbent rights holder, did not want to give up baseball, despite the cost.

Einhorn maintained that the size of the deal was predicated on extending the two League Championship Series from a best-of-five to a best-of-seven, which eventually happened in 1985. This part proved to be difficult to get because the most powerful owner in the group, Walter O'Malley, felt that nothing should be as big as the World Series. Consequently, National League President Chub Feeney was not initially in favor either. Giles was immediately in favor of this plan and went with Einhorn to convince the commissioner, which they did. The change was worth a lot of money. Einhorn says, "Our strategy had to be, we make the deal first, then we go back [to the owners] and say 'we made this deal, but we have to do this to get it,' so nobody could kill the deal ahead of time. The contracts gave every club an enormous increase in annual revenue. The twenty-six clubs approved the deal unanimously, after the fact."[13]

Giles recollected that "the committee and the networks eventually consummated the deal while having dinner at a table set up in the kitchen of the '21' Club in New York City. The KEG group was praised for its efforts, and each of us received a grandfather clock with a plaque, thanking us for our good work on behalf of the owners."[14]

An "Almost" That Became a "Never Was"

The work on the contract that the KEG group negotiated with ABC and NBC in 1983 took place at a time when the U.S. media landscape was changing significantly. Cable TV was making significant strides, both generally and in the sports business, due to the vision of people such as Bill Giles, Ted Turner, and also Bill Rasmussen, who put together a little deal called ESPN. As Giles recalls:

> ESPN was just starting, and there were not too many people who could get it because many areas had not been wired for cable. They weren't getting very good ratings at all, and they came to Major League Baseball, to Einhorn and Commissioner Kuhn and me, and offered baseball 50 percent of ESPN for $30 million. I recommended that we look at it and take it before the owners. Kuhn said, "Baseball owners won't go for that. They just don't have the cash flow to spend $30 million on half of ESPN." So that's how Major League Baseball missed out on owning half of ESPN, which as it turns out, would have been one heck of a deal because ESPN is worth $10 billion or something right now.[15] [*Note:* According to Forbes, ESPN is now worth $40 billion as the world's Most Valuable Sports Property.[16]]

At the time, Eddie Einhorn said, "People who control their own product and channel will be the ones who make money."[17] Today, Einhorn reflects back: "ESPN did not want to pay baseball for rights; they came to us and offered a half interest in the network and the owners said 'no'; the leagues couldn't get together on it. Baseball wasn't as financially well set in those days."[18] Einhorn and Giles were ahead of the curve as well as most of the other owners.

Giles explains how the owners' perspective on television was changing thirty years ago:

> The ESPN deal that we didn't make marked the beginning of baseball people thinking about and understanding cable and its potential revenue impact on the industry. Ted Turner was doing his superstation thing at WTBS, and the Braves were just beginning to draw national attention and generate revenue with their TV package. I had a good understanding of cable TV, even at the early stages. In the 1970s, Ed Snider and I created PRISM, which now is Comcast Sports Net, for local telecasts. From 1982 on, I was a big booster of cable television at the national level. To me, for a homeowner, having cable TV is like paying your phone bill each month. Once you get a particular cable channel, you are going to probably keep it for the rest of your life and you will be paying this monthly fee. Plus the programming has advertising. From the beginning, I felt strongly that the combination of subscription fees and advertising was going to be better in the long run than regular over-the-air TV, which is just ads, and that once we have maximized our return from the networks, the next plateau of TV money is cable.[19]

Commissioner Kuhn was not optimistic about buying in to ESPN, but he and some of the owners decided late in 1983 to explore the concept of creating or acquiring baseball's own cable network or superstation that could generate revenue for all of baseball. The KEG group attended a cable convention in Las Vegas and met with industry leaders. The consensus was that baseball had a great product but that the marketplace was already saturated with baseball because of the hundreds of games telecast on the superstations. As a result, the television magnates at that time dissuaded the commissioner and the other committee members from creating a baseball network. Given the lost opportunity and its revenue potential, Kuhn estimated that the superstations were costing baseball in excess of $100 million per year.

Despite what had happened previously, Kuhn's successor, Peter Ueberroth, was one of the few who did believe in a baseball cable channel.

Ueberroth commissioned Giles and two colleagues to explore the concept. The group created income and expense projections and spent a lot of time analyzing the pluses and minuses of an exclusive cable channel for baseball. Giles recollected, "The bottom line was that in five years the channel would have turned a profit, but the owners would have to give up a minimum of $42 million annually in rights fees that were being paid by ESPN. The Executive Council voted against this proposal." Thirty years later, in 2006, "major league owners did vote to approve a baseball channel on a digital sports tier, which would allow MLB to continue their lucrative cable deals with ESPN and WTBS while still having their own channel."[20]

A couple of years after Ueberroth asked Giles to project some financials for a baseball channel, "George Steinbrenner made his big deal for cable [$488 million for twelve years with the Madison Square Garden Network] in New York, and that was the stepping stone to almost every club eventually making some sort of a cable deal. Then, of course, Comcast came around and Fox Sports has cable deals with several teams. That was a big revenue jump for baseball, particularly those clubs in large media markets."[21]

The Ueberroth CBS Mega-Deal and a Move to Cable

Some observers considered the KEG-negotiated $1.125 billion ABC-NBC deal a mistake because it was too one-sided in favor of baseball. Dennis Swanson inherited the contract when he succeeded Roone Arledge as president of ABC Sports in January 1986. When questioned about his goals as successor to Arledge, Swanson responded, "to get out of baseball." By early 1987, ABC projected that it would lose at least $150 million over the six seasons of its baseball deal.[22] Arthur Watson, president of NBC Sports, had negotiated NBC's part of the deal and was less vocal than Swanson, but the terms of the deal made the NBC bosses unhappy as well. This weakened baseball's position for future negotiations.

The ABC-NBC contract lasted through the 1989 season, so it was up to Commissioner Ueberroth to negotiate a new deal. Ueberroth had experience in television negotiations with the Olympics, and the networks considered Ueberroth a plus in negotiating deals. According to WTBS sports boss Bob Wussler, "He knows our business."[23] Moreover, according to both Bill Giles and Eddie Einhorn, his decision-making style differed dramatically from that of Bowie Kuhn; he was much less dependent on committees and he "kept his own counsel" on many key decisions.

Bill Giles reflected on the CBS deal:

> Ueberroth was a big television guy. He did pretty much a lot of things just by himself. He made a deal for all the jewels—the All-Star Game, the playoffs, and the World Series, with one network—CBS. Eddie Einhorn and I always believed it is better to have two networks sharing the postseason because our theory was that if you place your games on only one network, the other networks are going to schedule sporting events and other popular programs against you, which can hurt your ratings. And then the other networks are not going to be sitting at the door wanting baseball again because they have gotten into NASCAR, football, basketball, or whatever. You might get more money, of course, by selling all the rights to one network. When we did the deal with CBS, both ABC and NBC felt betrayed in a way and lost interest in baseball.[24]

Einhorn pleaded with Ueberroth not to make the deal with only one network. According to Einhorn, "the key is not the money; the key is to have two or even three partners. If you get rid of a partner, that partner will hate you and may never come back, because they are going to find something else to put their resources behind."[25]

Ueberroth gave the networks their choice of any or all of four different options: the entire package; one that would alternate between two networks; the entire package minus the League Championship Series, which would then go to cable; or an *à la carte* approach, in which a network could choose an individual season or a targeted piece of the whole package. CBS chose the first option and put in a bid of $1.06 billion. The four-year deal would almost double baseball's existing TV package, and the total was more than $300 million higher than NBC or ABC. CBS got the contract.[26]

Ueberroth signed a deal with CBS, giving the network exclusive rights to twelve weekend games (later increased to sixteen games) during the regular season, plus the All-Star Game, the American League and National League Championship Series, and the World Series, for an average of $265 million per year, from 1990 through 1993.[27] CBS's bid was 37 percent more than ABC and NBC had paid under their combined previous contracts.[28] The twenty-six teams in the big leagues stood to collect a total of more than one-quarter billion annually under the new contract with CBS. Under the previous contract with NBC and ABC, annual revenue amounted to $200 million a year. Before the first ticket was sold, every major league team generated almost $10 million in revenue.[29]

Despite their dissatisfaction with the economics of their current contract with baseball, both NBC and ABC publicly expressed disappointment at the news that both networks were not in baseball's immediate TV future. In a statement, Watson of NBC said that his network had "aggressively" bid to continue its forty-one-year involvement with baseball and was "deeply saddened." Dennis Swanson, president of ABC Sports, noted in a statement that baseball had been a "blue-chip franchise" for the network since 1975 and ABC was "disappointed" to lose baseball.[30]

In January 1989, the other shoe figuratively dropped. Commissioner Ueberroth awarded baseball's first cable contract to ESPN, a subsidiary of ABC, for $100 million annually, starting in 1990. ESPN planned to televise 175 games per year. At the time, ESPN had a subscriber base of 50.1 million of the nation's 90.4 million TV households. Baseball chose ESPN as its first cable partner because its subscription base was higher than those of other bidding networks, including Ted Turner's TNT. Ueberroth wanted to make sure that the maximum possible number of homes could see the product. To protect the local television outlets, Ueberroth and ESPN agreed that blackouts of ESPN telecommunications would occur in the markets of the teams involved if the games were being televised locally.

Starting in 1984, baseball's annual national television revenue had quadrupled from $1.8 million to $7.2 million per team. Just seven years later, starting in 1991, each club stood to receive approximately $14 million annually from the national television contracts. Seemingly, baseball was in clover, but both Jerry Reinsdorf and Eddie Einhorn, owners of the White Sox, expressed the same concern, that is, that the owners spent the extra TV money before the ink was dry on the contract.

The two deals underscored baseball's drift away from over-the-air broadcasts during the regular season; the previous ABC-NBC deal included forty regular season games in 1989, the last year of the contract. Congress responded by threatening to take away baseball's antitrust exemption if baseball continued to reduce the number of games available on over-the-air network and local broadcasts in favor of lucrative cable deals. No one was particularly surprised at this response; since the early 1950s, every time Congress has been unhappy with major league baseball, one or more of its members has threatened baseball's antitrust exemption. Legislators had criticized the contract with ESPN as well as George Steinbrenner's $488 million, twelve-year cable deal with Madison Square Garden. Senator Howard Metzenbaum said that the deal displayed "an arrogance bordering on contempt." By this time, Fay Vincent had taken over as commissioner after Bart Giamatti's tragically short five-month tenure. Vincent defended baseball's television strategy, noting that, despite the increase in cable network programming, the total number of local, free telecasts of baseball games had increased to 1,653 games in 1989 from 1,485 games in 1984.[31]

Trouble in Television City

The CBS deal took effect in 1990, a case of unfortunate timing as a result of baseball's ongoing labor problems. The owners believed that the Players Association had gotten the best of them both in 1981 and again in 1985, and then they were found guilty of collusion in their attempt to tighten the free agent market after the 1985, 1986, and 1987 seasons. Thus, when the 1985 labor agreement expired on December 31, 1989, many owners prepared for war. The owners locked the players out of camp in 1990 in an attempt to gain significant concessions from them in terms of revenue sharing and salary arbitration. Even though Commissioner Vincent brokered a new CBA on March 19 of that year, the opening of the season was delayed and the normal feeling of hope that fans have during spring training was replaced with frustration and disgust that the owners and players couldn't find an equitable way to share their millions.

Labor unrest had created a negative image for baseball that reduced advertising rates and discouraged sponsors. After only one year, CBS sought a partial refund on its rights fee from Major League Baseball, citing losses resulting from the lockout and the late season opener. CBS claimed that it has lost $100 million in 1990 on rights fees totaling $265 million. The negative labor situation was one factor that hurt CBS. A difficult economy hurt all of the networks. More importantly, only fourteen of twenty-one possible postseason games took place in 1990, and the World Series between Cincinnati and Oakland, two small-market teams with limited national appeal, was a four-game sweep by the Reds. Early in year two of the deal, CBS Chairman Laurence Tisch called the contract a "mistake" that he would not make again.[32]

Both CBS and ESPN lost significant sums. Overall, ESPN's estimated losses on its baseball contract in 1990 were at least $36 million. CBS claimed after-tax losses of $55 million for 1990 and estimated a total after-tax loss of $170 million for the life of the four-year deal. CBS was hurt financially not only by overbidding for the contract but also by negotiating for exclusive rights to all postseason games. In previous years, the networks split the contract and thereby split the risks. Einhorn lamented, "We end up with one network [CBS] which lost a lot of money on the deal and we've angered the other networks, our former partners, in the process. ABC and NBC have now gotten along without baseball, and we've lost our leverage in the new negotiations."[33]

Trouble started as early as December 1991. Mark Potts wrote in the *Washington Post,* "There are signs that the profligate spending [on players] may come to a halt—chiefly because of the widely held expectation that the next national television contact signed by Major League Baseball, to go into effect with the 1994 season, will be considerable smaller than the current $1.4 billion four-year pact with CBS and cable network ESPN."[34]

Surrounded by a very difficult set of circumstances—increasingly threatening signs of labor unrest, a shaky economy, and unhappy television networks, not to mention the hundreds of millions of dollars in guaranteed contracts with players signed once the free agent market opened in 1989—baseball had to negotiate new national television contracts.

A New Contract and a New Concept

With the CBS deal due to expire after the 1993 season, baseball once again needed to negotiate a contract for a national television contract, but this time, the power rested with the networks. Both CBS and ESPN had lost a lot of money. Einhorn and Giles both understood that it was going to be hard to justify the amounts of money the networks had been paying. Every knowledgeable source in both Major League Baseball and the media predicted that the networks would drastically reduce their financial commitments to the game. Baseball had been devalued as a broadcast commodity because of declining national interest in the sport and a consequent decline in television ratings.

Baseball's problems resulted from several issues, including fans' unhappiness with continuing labor unrest, the growth in popularity of the NBA, and the oversaturation of baseball on television, brought on by both the ESPN contract, which included 175 games per year on cable, and the impact of the superstations. In addition, baseball's viewership was aging. In the three years between the last year of the ABC-NBC deal and 1992, baseball viewership among boys 12–17 years of age fell 24 percent, while in the same age cohort, viewership was up 31 percent for the NBA and 16 percent for the NFL. Between the recession of the early 1990s and the aging demographic watching major league baseball, advertisers had concerns about the value of baseball, except during the World Series. John Mandel, a senior vice president with Grey Advertising, said at the time, "The advertiser is saying, 'I can put money in the NFL or the Skins Game or in the hot-rodders.'"[35]

Need for a New Approach

Baseball's television committee for the new round of negotiations consisted of Einhorn, Giles, and Tom Werner of the San Diego Padres, a veteran television producer whose credits included *The Cosby Show.* Einhorn understood that baseball's only leverage was that "we have the national pastime. Maybe it doesn't have the same value as before, but we're not going begging." All three members of the committee knew that the new deal would provide significantly less revenue than previous deals; advertising sales had amounted to only 50 percent of what the networks had paid for baseball. The *Chicago Sun-Times* reported that "it is no coincidence that Einhorn's White Sox, Werner's Padres and Giles' Phillies have been three of the most frugal spenders this [1992–1993] winter."[36]

Giles and Einhorn had previously indicated that two networks are better than one, but that fell on deaf ears when Ueberroth negotiated the CBS deal. One network proved to be a mistake. Going into the new negotiations, the owners clearly preferred more than one network for broadcast television. As Eddie Einhorn said, "I would have preferred two networks last time. That would mean two networks that cared about baseball. Now NBC and ABC don't care like they did when they had it. It was there to be done last time."[37]

Another unique dimension of a proposed television package emerged during the early discussions: the idea of revenue sharing in place of rights fees. Giles, in particular, understood that type of arrangement because the Phillies were in the first year of a revenue sharing arrangement he had negotiated with WPHL-TV in Philadelphia. This was a complex deal with a sliding revenue-based percentage split between the team and the network, with a floor below which the team's revenue could not go. The sales staffs of the Phillies and WPHL shared responsibility for selling advertising.[38]

Thus emerged a somewhat radical new approach whereby baseball entered into a joint venture with two networks, which turned out to be ABC and NBC—both returning despite dissatisfaction with their previous deal—which created a separate company to sell advertising on the broadcasts. For the first time, television did not give baseball an upfront rights fee. The deal provided for sharing risk as well as revenue. The networks and baseball provided working capital for the joint venture equally, and advertising had to be sold for any of the partners to reap financial gains. Neal Pilson from CBS pointed out one possible complication, that the unit formed by the three partners—Major League Baseball, ABC, and NBC—also would be in competition with the ABC and NBC sales operations in selling the advertising inventory for other events.

Bud Selig, in the role of head of baseball's ruling executive council and *de facto* commissioner, said about the new venture, "This is the wave of the future. We believe we have control over our destiny in this partnership. Baseball's been criticized for being slow to react and this shows us to be proactive." The Major League Baseball Players Association, on the other hand, was less sanguine. Don Fehr claimed that he had not been apprised of the plan beforehand and was quite miffed at the turn of events. "You'd think they [the owners] would let their partners know what they're doing, but apparently they want to be partners with the networks and not the players. I hope they do well together."[39]

Enhancing the Value of the Deal

Giles, Einhorn, and Werner, plus other baseball executives, discussed several ideas and proposals designed to enhance the value of the partnership. These included allowing interleague play, reducing the length of the regular season, realigning the two divisions in each league into three divisions, and adding a round of playoffs in the form of wild card series in each league. Because the postseason draws by far the highest national TV ratings, this additional advertising inventory would presumably replace some of the revenues that would be sacrificed with the new deal. In addition, adding a new round of playoffs might allow baseball to move these telecasts from broadcast TV to cable without raising the concerns among members of Congress that would inevitably accompany such a plan.

In addition to requiring the approval of the Players Association for any material changes to the structure of the season, an additional playoff series represented additional advertising time to sell. This did not deter Giles, a strong proponent of the extra round in the postseason playoffs, who saw the expanded playoffs as more than just more advertising dollars. He believed that adding a third division winner plus a wild card team to the postseason would create more interest in more cities, especially when the pennant races in the four divisions lacked drama.

Other experts agreed with Giles' assessment. Bryan Burns, a sports television consultant and former MLB executive who worked with Peter Ueberroth on the CBS and ESPN deals, commented, "The question of more inventory is a legitimate issue. But if you're trying to generate more interest in the game generally after Labor Day, expanding the playoffs may be the right direction. If, instead of four teams in contention there are seven or eight, then maybe 12 or 14 teams have some [chance of making it to the playoffs], creating broader interest in the game."[40]

On the other hand, the idea of shortening the season never saw the light of day. Fewer games meant reduced gate and local TV revenues, which would have had to be offset by more national TV income. The members of the TV committee knew well that baseball fans are parochial in terms of their interest in their local team and that local baseball telecasts attracted more fan interest and provided a more stable stream of cash.

Having experienced a big decline in ratings for national telecasts of regular season games and given the realization that baseball has largely local appeal, baseball decided to make a significant change in the pattern of broadcasts with the new TV deal. Using an idea borrowed from professional and college football, baseball moved to regionalize their broadcasts in an attempt to heighten fan interest and therefore the size of the TV audience. Ken Schanzer, a network executive representing NBC in the negotiations, said:

> Our vision started with one thesis: whatever problems baseball has, Job One is to revive the health of baseball and its relationship with television. Once that is on solid footing, at that point you approach the future from a new vantage point. If the patient is sick, he has to walk before he runs. We have to get this patient well. The ratings have been on such a precipitous decline[;] unless we can improve them, it would be very difficult to hold on to a lot of stuff to which we have all been accustomed to [*sic*] over the years.[41]

Eddie Einhorn, expressing similar sentiments, said, "We've got to build it up again. We've got to regenerate interest [in baseball]."[42] Both baseball and the networks were intent on reversing the seven-year decline in regular season TV ratings.

The Baseball Network

The three partners in the joint venture created a new company called The Baseball Network (TBN), which had responsibility for producing televised baseball and for the marketing and selling of major league baseball. ABC Sports president Dennis Swanson called TBN "a true joint venture," with each partner "sharing the cost from day one." Einhorn described the venture as "one-stop shopping for sponsors; in the future sports on TV will be sponsor-driven."[43] TBN had three partners, ABC, NBC, and MLB, and each contributed $10 million in start-up capital. Ken Schanzer assumed the position of president and chief operating officer. The original deal was for six years, covering the 1994 thorough 1999 seasons. The contract specified that if the venture generated a minimum of $330 million in sales during its first two years, the arrangement would automatically renew for two more years.[44]

The long-standing tradition of a national game of the week on Saturday gave way to multiple weekly regional telecasts on selected nights during the week, slots for which TBN had exclusivity—no other national or local telecasts were permitted for competing games. The networks used their own announcers, including Bob Costas and Al Michaels, for two of the regional games; the other games used local production teams and local station announcers.

The terms of the new deal were as follows: Major League Baseball was slated to receive 85 percent of the first $140 million of advertising sold, 50 percent of the next $30 million, and 80 percent of all sales beyond $170 million annually. The "jewels" were split so that one network had the All-Star Game and League Championship Series and the other had the new round of wild card playoffs plus the World Series. The packages rotated from year to year between ABC and NBC. The wild card playoffs, best-of-five series later to be designated the American League Division Series and the National League Division Series, were played simultaneously and aired regionally. The League Championship Series in both leagues were shown regionally and aired simultaneously, except for games 6 and 7, which had staggered starts. The World Series was set up to start on a Saturday so that games 1, 2, 6, and 7 would be played on weekend nights, with the games starting at 7:20 Eastern Time, which was more than an hour earlier than in previous seasons.[45]

Giles estimated that national broadcast revenue would drop from $401 million in 1993, the last year of the CBS deal, to about $200 million in 1994, a decrease from $15.4 million to $7.1 million per team. Giles admitted that "it wasn't going to be pretty," but he also predicted, "We plan to grow this into something." Eddie Einhorn noted that CBS had netted $152 million in advertising during the 1993 season; if an equivalent amount of advertising was sold in 1994, given the revenue split planned for TBN, baseball would get about $134 million. But Einhorn predicted, "We'll do much better than that."[46] Tom Werner said that "in the short run, we're going to take a dramatic hit in central-fund distribution. This unconventional approach would be no worse in the short run when compared to the traditional deal, but in the long run we'll be able to build an asset."[47] ABC's Dennis Swanson said, "It's a different way to do business. Sponsors are looking for value-added now, and they will be able to get it from baseball in this arrangement. It is going to be advertiser-friendly.[48]

Cable TV and Pay-per-View

Regionalizing the postseason represented a significant change for baseball. Regionalization became a trade-off to keep the games on free over-the-air networks. However, another concern voiced by the industry, fans, and Congress was that such regionalization could open the door for pay-per-view distribution of games that the networks did not show in a specific region. Bud Selig countered that expressed fear. During a press conference discussing TBN, Selig said, "All baseball's premiere events will remain a fixture on over-the-air TV. Pay-per-view is expressly excluded from all parts of the contract."[49] Giles admitted that the pay-per-view idea had been discussed as a means to feed markets not shown games on a network. "It was one of 18 million ideas we had floating around. We decided [pay-per-view] was not a good idea," he said, adding that neither NBC nor ABC liked it.[50]

The Demise of the Baseball Network

Despite baseball's best-laid plans, the Baseball Network was doomed almost from its inception. The deal took effect with the 1994 season, a time of increasingly contentious relationships between owners and players, much to the consternation of fans, who just wanted baseball. With the two sides unable to reach a new labor agreement, the players walked out on August 12. The second major player strike in fourteen years eventually forced cancellation of the remainder of the regular season plus the postseason. The strike lasted until the spring of 1995, when a federal judge, Sonia Sotomayor—now Justice Sotomayor of the U.S. Supreme Court—ruled on a grievance brought by the Players Association. In her decision, Judge Sotomayor reinstituted the terms of the labor agreement that had expired on December 31, 1993, and with that, the players went back to work. However, spring training brought with it the possibility of opening the 1995 season with replacement players, and the acrimony and public sniping between the owners and players created an atmosphere that discouraged sponsors from investing in major league baseball. In addition, the season started late. Given such circumstances, it came as no surprise that, by the summer of 1995, the partners in the Baseball Network clearly saw that the $330 million threshold in ad sales was simply not going to be reached by the end of the season.

In May 1995, after the season had finally commenced with regular players, Bill Giles reported that TBN's advertising spots were selling for twice as much as CBS received in the final year of its contract in 1993.

But the financial damage had been done. Moreover, the television landscape had changed from that of 1993, when TBN was created, and baseball suddenly had more options as the emerging Fox network, which had already outbid CBS for NFL games, became a significant player in televised sports. As a result, the television committee, on behalf of the owners, decided against extending TBN and began to look at viable alternatives. Giles said, "There will be a decision [by MLB] in August on the future of The Baseball Network. All of us on the board want to continue the venture. But there are rumors on the street about interest from Fox and CBS, although we haven't heard from them."[51]

When the owners did not step up to extend TBN as the networks had requested, ABC and NBC announced, angrily, that they were walking away. Although it was a mere formality by then, the owners later voted to discontinue the venture. That put an end to TBN. The venture had been the subject of much criticism by fans and the media. Nevertheless, the end of TBN upset Einhorn, who viewed the format as a growing process. "Our ratings were improving; we were holding the line on sales prices," he said. "These things would have helped us to succeed next season. And we would have rebuilt baseball as a TV product while controlling our own destiny."[52]

In retrospect, the members of the television committee acknowledged that the conditions surrounding the 1993 network negotiations had left them few options. According to Giles, "We had no option; we were at the mercy of NBC and ABC. We wanted wild-card games and were limited in our options if we wanted to keep the games on network television. No one wanted these games. Our only other option was cable, and we felt we wanted to keep the games on network television. But the public doesn't like it. So next year, we'll try to sell it to the networks and probably cable as well."[53]

Ironically, one of the major negative effects of TBN was the limited television access to playoff games, which took place only in 1995, after MLB had decided to go in a different direction in the succeeding years. Responding to criticism leveled at baseball, Giles said, "We did the best we could do." Ken Schanzer commented, "Whether one likes regionalization or not, the reality is it's performed exactly what it was projected to do: improve the ratings. In terms of a sport trying to sell itself to a mass audience, these numbers don't lie." As it turned out, while overall 1995 playoff ratings declined from 1993, the ratings in the eight cities with teams in the playoffs were huge. The Mariners averaged a 39 rating in Seattle for the first two games, the Rockies averaged a 33 rating in Denver, Cleveland averaged a 29 rating, and Atlanta averaged a 27 rating. The Yankees, in the No. 1 TV market in the country, had a 17 rating, what one network man described as "a monster rating for New York." The numbers exceeded expectations, according to Schanzer.[54]

After the saga of the TBN had ended, Giles said that the network's creators, Giles, Einhorn, and Werner, had predicted that there would be unhappy people, but wanted to try the concept and see where it could go. In retrospect, Giles admitted that the TBN concept "was always flawed, but it was the best deal we could have gotten two years ago. That has changed now."[55] Looking ahead to the next round of negotiations, Giles said, "There's no question that we want to get more of the postseason games available [on television]. We would like to have all the LCS games available. We would like to do the division series in a different way than The Baseball Network. A lot of us would like to get back a Saturday game of the week."[56]

Baseball Welcomes Fox

Just as the CBS deal suffered from bad timing because of the labor problems in 1990, TBN debuted in 1994, a year that will always live in baseball infamy because, for the first time since 1904, one year after the National Agreement established the major leagues as we know them, baseball did not have a postseason. No postseason telecasts doomed TBN for year one. No postseason, no advertising sales, no revenues. The fact that baseball avoided for one year the "realization of regionalization" proved to be small consolation. But in 1995, criticism of the regionalization of the Division and League Championship Series came from many sources.

The entry of Rupert Murdoch's Fox network changed the media landscape dramatically. In 1993, Fox outbid CBS for the rights to the games of the National Conference of the NFL, which CBS had owned for decades. This one move helped establish Fox as a fourth major network, along with ABC, CBS, and NBC. Fox's success in creating audiences for its shows and attracting local affiliates with the NFL led it to consider becoming a player in the baseball television network stakes. All of a sudden, the rights fees that baseball could not sell after the failed CBS contract, which forced baseball to create a revenue sharing deal, were potentially back on the table.

TBN's contract allowed any of the parties to cancel the deal if revenues during the first year, 1994, did not reach the designated threshold for advertising sales of $330 million, a figure that became impossible to attain with no postseason. While ABC and NBC presumably wanted to give TBN another year or two to determine its economic validity, the baseball owners saw the potential of a lucrative new rights deal with Fox plus additional networks. An unnamed owner said at the time, "Fox changes everything. Now we can make a much better deal just doing things the traditional way [with a rights fee]. It might not end up where the old [CBS] deal was, but it's going to be better than what we have now."[57]

Acknowledging the significant loss from TBN, Bill Giles said that a better TV deal is one way to recoup those losses, and he was sanguine on the future of television in baseball, saying, "In the long run, there's definite growth in television. I'm not so sure about the short-term—this year [1994] and next year. But by the year 1999 or 2000, I think we'll be in good shape there."[58] His words proved to be prescient.

To facilitate the process and enhance prospects for a better deal, Selig appointed Barry Frank of IMG, an experienced television consultant (who is still active today), to serve as negotiator and consultant for the new round of negotiations. IMG is a major sports and media agency, and Frank had served previously as consultant to numerous Olympics organizing committees, the NBA, the NFL, U.S. Open tennis, the America's Cup, and the Orange Bowl, among other groups. Giles said that Frank "is recognized as the premier sports properties negotiator" and also stated that Frank was told to get a deal that included national telecasts of all postseason games. Acting Commissioner Selig restated that playoff games would not be on cable.[59]

In mid-August 1994, MLB owners met in Chicago and officially notified both ABC and NBC that they did not plan to continue TBN, a move that allowed other TV bidders to negotiate as early as October 9. The announcement was a mere formality for the owners because both ABC and NBC had announced in June, after baseball deferred on renewing TBN, that they didn't plan to continue past 1995.

When the negotiations between the television committee and the potential network bidders commenced, Giles outlined a significantly different postseason schedule than was the case with TBN. The plan called for national prime time coverage of the divisional series Tuesday–Monday, with no Thursday off and staggered starts; thirteen other games in the afternoon or late night on cable or the networks; and Wednesday, Saturday, and Sunday starts at 1:00, 4:00, 7:00, and 9:00 or 10:00 P.M. The League Championship Series in each league would also have full coverage. The question of how much cable would be involved was unanswered at that point. Giles made the significant statement that "we're willing to take less to market the game. Exposing more quality players is of equal importance to money."[60]

As negotiations heated up, Giles reported that he and Frank "have been working around the clock looking at all of our options."[61] Ultimately, their efforts bore fruit. Despite continued labor uncertainty and dwindling attendance, baseball negotiated a five-year, $1.7 billion package with multiple networks, including NBC, Fox, ESPN, and Prime Liberty, plus international rights. Fox and NBC shared broadcast rights, with ESPN and Liberty/Fox sharing the cable package.

The package, the most lucrative in the game's history to that point, eliminated TBN's regionalized postseason format in which only one playoff game could be seen per night in a given city. For the succeeding five years, the start times of playoff games were to be staggered so that each game could be shown in its entirety. Selig commented, "There's no question we were extremely sensitive to fans' concerns as we did this television contract. We believe we've alleviated all those problems."[62] Giles reported that, of the twenty potential divisional series games, eight would be on broadcast TV and twelve on cable. Divisional playoffs were scheduled to be telecast on ESPN at 1:00, 4:00, and 11:00 P.M. Eastern Time. Fox and NBC were scheduled to alternate a prime time game each night, with each televising one League Championship Series, rotating the American League and National League series from year to year. Fox Sports President David Hill announced that the network would have a pregame show before its Saturday afternoon telecasts. The telecasts were scheduled to start on Memorial Day weekend.[63]

Broadcasting & Cable magazine reported details of the contract as follows. Fox ($575 million) obtained the rights to the World Series in 1996, 1998, and 2000; the All-Star Game in 1997 and 1999; and up to twenty Saturday afternoon games. Fox planned to produce an hourlong pregame show before their Saturday regional games, of which half were to be devoted to young fans. Fox also received one League Championship Series each season; Fox split division playoff games with NBC and ESPN. NBC ($400 million) got the rights to the 1997 and 1999 World Series and the All-Star Games of 1996, 1998, and 2000. NBC also received one League Championship Series each season and divided division playoff games with Fox and NBC. ESPN ($440 million) retained its exclusive rights to regular season Wednesday and Sunday night games and won the rights to between six and ten division playoff games each postseason, with the proviso that if two games were played simultaneously, one would be carried on ESPN2. Prime Liberty ($172 million), later known as Fox Sports Cable, got a four-year deal to show two games weekly on its choice of Monday, Tuesday, Thursday, or Friday nights. Local baseball telecasts were not to be blacked out in favor of Fox Cable's telecasts.[64] Selig called the new contracts "another significant step in the recovery of our sport."[65]

The reactions in the media at the time included a quote from John Helyar, author of *The Lords of the Realm*, a landmark book about the business of baseball. Helyar said, "Baseball, ailing for the last two seasons, negotiated a surprisingly strong [deal] by playing on the sports appetites of several networks."[66] Another writer commented that the networks are "obviously still willing to shell out big bucks for baseball, despite the sport's tarnished reputation."[67] A third said, "MLB is supposed to be in bad shape; the deal is surprising considering there is still no CBA.[68] A fourth writer called the package "semi-miraculous."[69]

Giles said that, as a result of baseball's new television deal, he was less worried about Congress. Pointing out that NBA playoff games had already migrated to cable from broadcast television without any strong reaction, he said, "We hope Congress will understand. When you see what the NBA does, putting playoff games on cable, I don't see how they can complain.[70]

A Bonus for Baseball's New Network Partners: Interleague Play

Another interesting element of the new television package was the dawn of regular season interleague play. Fox, ESPN, and Liberty/Fox wound up with "first dibs" on interleague games, scheduled to begin in 1997. With the unanimous approval of interleague play between National League and American League teams, baseball's newest partners found themselves in the enviable position of owning rights to televise 15–16 interleague games per team per season. Ironically, baseball's longest running partner, NBC, was left out of interleague regular season play because its deal did not include regular season games. Giles, one of the architects and strongest advocates of interleague play, announced the initial schedule of national interleague telecasts, which consisted of games in two-week blocks around Memorial Day and Labor Day, with Fox televising Saturday afternoon games on the Memorial and Labor Day weekends as part of the *Game of the Week* and ESPN telecasting six interleague games, including two Wednesday double-headers and two Sunday night games. Finally, Fox/Liberty had four interleague games, two on Tuesday night and two on Friday night—on Fox's fX cable channel.[71]

Did this new deal solve all of baseball's problems? Hardly. At the time the contract was announced, the owners and the Players Association still had not agreed to a new labor deal. Free agent contracts had helped send salaries soaring again. And baseball had not yet concluded an acceptable set of revenue sharing deals between owners and players and, just as importantly, between large-market and small-market owners. Giles projected total national broadcast revenue (including radio and superstation) to be $2 billion during the life of the deal. But he also said that an extra $4–$5 million "is not going to help those teams" losing $20 million.[72] Red Sox CEO John Harrington stressed that the increase from the national contract "will be more than offset by the decline from local TV." The Red Sox lost about twelve local games to TBN in 1995, which "eroded the value" of their rights.[73]

Baseball Allows Fox to Be a Little Daring

As part of the new TV deal, baseball agreed to make some changes in its highly traditional telecasts by allowing Fox to make technological enhancements. These included placing microphones inside bases, bullpens, and outfield walls, and on managers—those who agreed to be miked—and placing cameras under the stands so that fans could watch designated hitters taking warm-up swings. Over the years, other enhancements were made, including the camera on a catcher's mask. Not all worked, but the effort was worthwhile and baseball's newly cooperative approach was noticeable. "They've not only gone the extra mile[;] they've gone an extra 15 miles," said John Filipelli, Fox's senior coordinating producer for baseball, who had witnessed several eras of lousy feeling at NBC and TBN.[74]

When asked to whom a network goes for technical go-aheads or simple cooperation, Giles responded that "in the past it was the leagues, in the future it will be the new marketing guru who will be hired soon," a sign that at the end of the 20th century, baseball decided it needed someone to coordinate marketing efforts.[75] "Bud Selig has appointed me to look into it," Giles said. "But we've agreed to let Fox do what's in the contract."[76]

Why did tradition-bound (some would say "stodgy") baseball agree to these changes? Very simply, "it is a matter of baseball recognizing it needs to market itself better and it needs to be a stronger television product," Filipelli said. "We've talked about a lot of these things for years but I think the last couple of years have not been particularly kind to the game and I think the game realizes it needs to be more TV friendly than it has been in the past. And they really have bent over backwards to try and be accommodating. They've been terrific. They've really gone out of their way to give us what we've asked for and to be a true partner."[77]

Bill Giles on Television and Baseball

The distance between the bases has always been ninety feet and will never change. But what has changed over the last sixty years is television and the revenues TV generates. The changes have been dramatic: television has changed the way baseball operates the business of the game. Television revenue created such a disparity in team revenue that it forced baseball to share revenue—unheard of before 1990. When I started my baseball career in 1948, baseball's revenue from television was *zero.* By 2002 television was 30 percent of baseball's total revenue—and that percentage will only get higher.[78]

3

Collusion

The New Economic Reality of Baseball

For literally 100 years, from the founding of the National League in 1876 to Peter Seitz's decision that ushered in free agency in December 1975, owners held virtually all of the economic power in major league baseball. Player salaries as a percentage of team revenues were around 35 percent in the 1930s, but except for a brief period after World War II, from 1946 to 1949, they kept falling to as low to 17.6 percent in 1950. By the 1970s, Marvin Miller had eroded some of the owners' control over salaries and player movement by winning the right to salary arbitration, introduced in the 1972 CBA, and by the "ten and five rule," which was negotiated into the 1973 CBA after the U.S. Supreme Court denied Curt Flood's appeal in his case to be declared a free agent. Henceforth, any player with at least ten years of major league experience, including five with the same club, could veto a proposed trade. By 1974, after salary arbitration had been ushered in but before free agency took effect, salaries accounted for 20.4 percent of revenues.[1]

Seitz's decision on the grievance filed by Andy Messersmith and Dave O'Malley did not overturn the reserve clause, but redefined it. The owners made an unsuccessful attempt to have the decision reversed in court, but Judge Oliver sustained Seitz's ruling. The owners' attention then shifted to negotiating the terms of free agency. The owners initially wanted a ten-year waiting period, even though A's owner Charley Finley had said, "Make 'em all free agents." Eventually, the owners and players negotiated a six-year waiting period as part of the 1976 CBA.

The economic impact of free agency, which the owners feared and the players anticipated, was dramatic. Between 1975 and 1980 the average major league salary grew from $44,676 to $143,756, and salaries as a percentage of revenue grew to 39.1 percent.[2] The owners did not take very well to their loss of control and the new world of baseball economics for two reasons. First, they were used to being "the lords of the realm"—a term that was the title of John Helyar's terrific book; and second, despite the success that many of the "the Lords" had had with other businesses, most owners could not envision how free agency would help create a new competitive model for baseball in which revenues and franchise values would grow so dramatically post–free agency.

Exhibiting the type of behavior that was to become characteristic, club owners decried the new reality, but at the same time, many of them rushed to sign free agents. George Steinbrenner's immediate success after signing Catfish Hunter and Reggie Jackson—an American League pennant in 1976 and World Championships in 1977 and 1978—clearly provided a model for other owners who hoped to achieve similar results. On one hand, owners seemingly couldn't control their impulse to spend money in the hopes of improving their clubs, and on the other hand, they sought remedies to slow the salary growth that such signings caused. Sports fans will note that in the thirty-eight years since baseball players gained free agency, this same situation has occurred repeatedly in every major U.S. professional sports league.

The rapid escalation of salaries during the late 1970s and early 1980s was caused by a combination of salary arbitration and free agency. By itself, free agency led to salary escalation created by bidding wars by owners in an open market. To compound the inflationary effects of free agency, arbitrators used comparative performance and salaries of similar players as salary reference points, and because free agency had driven up salaries, these reference points were also at higher levels. Arbitration created a situation whereby even if a player lost his case, he still dramatically increased his salary. As more than one player said when awaiting an arbitrator's decision, "I am going to be either rich or REALLY rich!"

Owners made offers to free agents, at big salaries and for many years, because they saw opportunities to both improve their ball clubs and demonstrate to the fans that the ownership wanted to build a winning team. No player or agent figuratively held a gun to an owner's head and demanded those big contracts. Many of the players who signed these big deals wound up playing at a level below, sometimes far below, expectations based on past performance. This reality exacerbated the resentment created among "the Lords" once the players dared to exert some economic influence. But despite the inconsistent and often disappointing performance of the free agents that they had signed, many owners simply could not resist putting in higher and higher bids for players on the open market, even players of marginal quality, in the hopes of winning that elusive championship. As Bill Giles explained, "Owners and team presidents were aware that many free agent signings did not make sense financially, but their egos and desire to win superseded their business sense."[3]

Free Agent Compensation

The architecture of free agency that was negotiated as part of the 1976 Basic Agreement following the Seitz decision contained a form of compensation to clubs that lost a player to another team. Once a club signed a free agent, that club was required to compensate the player's former club by assigning it a draft choice in the regular phase of the next year's amateur draft. However, owners ultimately did not consider this form of compensation adequate to make up for the loss of an accomplished major league player. Moreover, forfeiture of a draft pick, given the small percentage of amateur draft picks that actually became productive major league players, did not represent a sufficient limit on the owners' own impulses. So when talks commenced on a new CBA for 1980, the owners sought a remedy in the form of direct player compensation for lost free agents.

A model for this was already in use in another sport. After the merger between the National and American Football Leagues, which was announced in 1966 and completed in 1970, Pete Rozelle, long-time commissioner of the NFL, had instituted a rule that became known as "the Rozelle rule." This rule required any team that signed a player who was previously under contract to another team to offer a player as compensation for the lost free agent. The effect was to make signing a free agent a risky proposition because the signing team would only find out after the fact what type of compensation they would be required to make to the player's original team. As a result, NFL owners had little interest in signing free agents, and this led to minimal competition for free agents. No competition meant no bidding wars and therefore a negligible effect on salaries.

Thus was born the baseball owners' mandate to achieve direct player compensation for lost free agents. Miller and the players understood that direct compensation—whereby a team that signed a free agent would have to give up a player of similar ability—would result in less freedom to move to another club as well as lower free agent salaries. Therefore, they would not agree to any proposal that created limits on free agency beyond the six-year waiting period that was negotiated as part of the 1976 CBA.

No agreement on a plan for free agent compensation could be reached as the owners and players negotiated a new CBA in 1980 and into 1981. So the owners did what labor law permitted them to do, that is, unilaterally announce the implementation of the owners' new rules for compensation to teams who lose free agents. Marvin Miller responded, "I think one thing is clear. The owners have decided to instigate a strike."[4] The owners' insistence on direct compensation for free agency led directly to the fifty-day strike in 1981.

Free Agent Compensation in the New CBA

Pressure to find an acceptable compensation plan and an end to the strike grew dramatically once the owner's strike insurance was about to run out after a six-week interruption in the 1981 season. The strike was settled on July 31, 1981, although regular season games did not resume until August 10, after a rescheduled All-Star Game. The owners had demanded compensation in the form of players, while the players wanted any compensation to be in the form of draft picks. Over the course of the negotiations, the Players Association offered a compromise position based on a "player pool" concept. In other words, teams that lost free agents could choose from a pool of eligible players. Teams could protect a certain number of players on their rosters, similar to the concept of an expansion draft, and the rest of the players would be assigned to a pool from which players to be awarded as compensation would be selected. The "devil was in the details," but eventually the two sides agreed on a somewhat complex plan.

The plan worked as follows: compensation would be required for the top 30 percent of free agents, measured statistically, with players in the top 20 percent requiring compensation in the form of players and the remaining players requiring compensation in the form of draft picks. The rankings were based on a set of performance metrics relevant to the player's position, for example, batting average and on-base percentage for hitters and earned run average for pitchers. Teams signing a free agent could protect twenty-four players and other teams could protect twenty-six players. The unprotected players on the team's forty-man roster went into the pool. Teams that had lost a player who was ranked in the top 20 percent could choose a player from that pool as compensation. Teams losing a player rated between the top 20 percent and the top 30 percent received two amateur draft choices instead of a player.[5]

Almost immediately after the strike ended, the owners, the same owners who had caused the first significant strike in major league history through their insistence on direct free agent compensation as a way of controlling their own behavior, went right back to their spendthrift ways, continuing to bid up the price of free agents. By 1985, the average salary had grown to more than $426,000 and player payroll increased to approximately 40 percent of average club revenue.[6] So, as of the mid-1980s, the owners had tried to limit free agency through the courts as well as through collective bargaining. Neither attempt was successful.

Baseball's Financial Savior Arrives

Peter Ueberroth was a self-made millionaire who had completely changed the business model of the Olympic Games. For five years, he had served as organizer of the 1984 Los Angeles Olympic Games, and through tough negotiations with sponsors, the use of hundreds of unpaid volunteers doing much of the work, and revamping rights fees for televising the games, Ueberroth made the Los Angeles Olympics the most financially successful in history, with a surplus of $250 million.

The owners decided not to renew Commissioner Bowie Kuhn's contract in 1982; Kuhn was to stay on until the end of his term in March 1984. The first choice as the next commissioner, Yale president A. Bartlett Giamatti, was unavailable to succeed Kuhn because he was dealing with labor problems at Yale, so the owners turned to Ueberroth, whose effective management style and fiscal prowess had not escaped their attention. Ueberroth was named the sixth commissioner in the history of major league baseball. Though Kuhn was scheduled to leave office on March 1, Ueberroth's obligations in Los Angeles prevented him from assuming the commissioner's role until October 1, 1984. The owners were more than willing to wait.

It did not take long for Ueberroth to exert his influence, first settling an umpire's strike during the league championship rounds, then signing some large sponsorship deals. He also quickly reached the conclusion that the owners' spendthrift ways were hurting the baseball industry, and he saw this as the path to financial ruin for the sport. During the 1985 World Series, the owners met in St. Louis. During that and subsequent owners' meetings, Ueberroth called the owners on the carpet, lecturing them on their lack of fiscal responsibility and on the need to exercise discipline and discretion in free agent negotiations. This became a drumbeat.

Lee MacPhail, head of the owners' player relations committee and former American League president, had prepared a report that he delivered to the owners and general managers in fall 1985. This report showed that teams owed more than $40 million under guaranteed long-term contracts to players who were no longer in the league. The report also detailed the performance of free agents and players who had signed long-term contracts. Players who had signed long-term contracts spent more time on the disabled list than other players, and many of the players who had long contracts performed well below expectations based on their past performance.[7]

In addition, Ueberroth demanded that teams share their financial statements. As a result, the owners realized that many teams were losing money. Edward Bennett Williams, the owner of the Baltimore Orioles, said, "We opened the books to each other and realized we had an industry loss of $100 million one year, $80 million another year . . . owners realized we couldn't survive and we'd better get some fiscal responsibility."[8]

Ueberroth also required that the owners discuss salary and contract data that Ueberroth's staff prepared for presentation at the owners' quarterly meetings. He forced individual owners to stand up "and discuss the numbers and the outlook."[9] In revival meeting fashion, owners would admit to dubious free agent signings and long contracts that they had issued in the past and pledge to mend their ways.

Bill Giles, speaking about Ueberroth's style of leadership and approach as commissioner, said that once Ueberroth came aboard, the owners no longer met in conference room style and discussed issues as they had under Bowie Kuhn and earlier commissioners. Instead, Ueberroth had the meeting room set up in classroom style and, like a teacher, he lectured to the owners. These otherwise accomplished individuals were so desperate to find a solution to escalating salaries that they subjugated their sizable egos and accepted the not-so-gentle chastisement that the commissioner offered. In fact, characterization of the owners as "sheep," compliant with the commissioner's demands, would be accurate, according to Giles, who said that Ueberroth once told him, "Power is 20 percent given and 80 percent taken." And Ueberroth took it.

Giles has often told the story of the red button and the black button that Ueberroth used to raise the owners' self-awareness of their behavior. Ueberroth said, "The problem is that if I put a red button and a black button in front of you, and said, 'If you push the red button you would win the World Series but lose $10 million, and if you push the black button you would finish fourth and make a $4 million profit,' most of you would push the red button."[10] In other words, the owners would abdicate the sound business principles that made them successful in their other endeavors to have a chance at winning a pennant. As Ueberroth said, "You are so damned dumb. . . . Look in the mirror and go out and spend big if you want, but don't go out there whining that someone made you do it."[11]

At the conclusion of one of the owners' meetings, Ueberroth was quoted as saying, "Well, you are smart businessmen. You all agree we have a problem. Go solve it."[12] (Ueberroth later denied having said this.) At the 1985 meeting of the general managers in Florida, Ueberroth hectored the owners. "It's not smart to sign long-term contracts. They force clubs to want to make similar signings," he said. "Don't be dumb. We have a five-year agreement with labor."[13] After the January 1986 owners' meetings, Steinbrenner commented, "We didn't talk among each other. All Commissioner Ueberroth did was keep calling us together and tell us how stupid we have been."[14]

A Dark Chapter in Baseball History

Unfortunately for the owners, they had agreed to a provision in the CBA by which they would refrain from "acting in concert" with regard to negotiations with free agents. Article XVIII, Section H, of the 1976 Major League Baseball CBA states, "Players shall not act in concert with other Players, and Clubs shall not act in concert with other Clubs."[15] This clause originated from a memorable holdout by All-Star pitchers Sandy Koufax and Don Drysdale, who had led the Los Angeles Dodgers to a World Series win over Minnesota in 1965. The next spring, Koufax and Drysdale decided to band together and jointly demand a three-year contract for a total of $1 million combined. In addition, they had procured the services of an attorney to represent them in negotiations with Dodger owner Walter O'Malley. The year was 1966, a decade before free agency, and just a couple of years before the Players Association began to exert some economic influence. O'Malley was an old-line owner who took control of the Dodgers in 1950—and moved them from Brooklyn to Los Angeles after the 1957 season—and he did not approve of the players' approach. O'Malley would not tolerate negotiating with a third party and would not tolerate average annual salaries of $166,666 for his two pitchers.

After briefly holding out and flirting with a possible career in the movies—after all, they were in Los Angeles—Koufax and Drysdale signed individual contracts for substantial raises, but less than they had initially demanded. Remembering this episode a decade later, the owners demanded that collusion among the players be legally prohibited, a move readily agreed to by Marvin Miller as long as the owners agreed not to act in concert themselves. So, any evidence that owners were cooperating in an endeavor to avoid offering free agent contracts was in direct violation of the CBA.

Nevertheless, the owners decided to address the issue of escalating salaries by coming to an unwritten agreement not to compete with each other over free agents. Noting the report that Lee MacPhail had made about the performance of players who had long-term contracts, the owners also agreed to reduce significantly the length of contracts that they would offer. The owners complied with Ueberroth's "instruction." [*Note:* Ueberroth claims to this day that he never instructed the owners to collude or otherwise engage in behavior that ran contrary to the CBA.] They did so essentially without argument. In fact, Giles has said that the only owner other than himself who openly questioned Ueberroth's stern direction on signing free agents was Dodgers owner Peter O'Malley, who had taken over for his father. The younger O'Malley would later call the period "the low point in baseball for me by far."[16]

The owners went to work after Ueberroth's directives. As a result, for three seasons, starting in 1985, free agents were forced to re-sign with their original teams for little or no increase in pay, unless their team indicated that it was not interested in their services. Of the thirty-three free agents in the class of 1985–1986, all but four returned to their original teams and the four who did not return were not wanted by their clubs. By comparison, after the 1984 season, only twenty of forty-six free agents stayed with their original clubs. As a result of the low level of free agent activity, player salaries increased by only 5 percent from 1985 to 1986. In contrast, there was an average annual increase of 10 percent in the previous years that followed the advent of free agency.[17]

Players who should have been highly sought after, such as Detroit Tigers outfielder Kirk Gibson, who had hit twenty-nine home runs and driven in ninety-seven runs in 1985, and All-Star catcher Carlton Fisk of the White Sox, found little or no interest among the other twenty-five teams in baseball and had to return to their clubs. George Steinbrenner made an initial offer to Fisk, but after a call from White Sox Chairman Jerry Reinsdorf, Steinbrenner withdrew the offer.

Glen Macnow, now a commentator on sports talk radio in Philadelphia but formerly a baseball writer, wrote a column at the time in the *Houston Chronicle* that said:

> Things are different this year. Not only are conservative clubs such as the Tigers shunning big-name free agents, but once active clubs such as Texas, San Diego and Milwaukee are suddenly closing their wallets. Even notoriously high rollers Ted Turner and George Steinbrenner are praising the merits of "fiscal responsibility," which is sort of like Hugh Hefner praising the merits of abstinence.[18]

Realizing early on during the 1985–1986 off-season that teams were not moving on free agents, player agents began to complain about the seemingly frozen market. Don Fehr, a protégé of Marvin Miller who became executive director of the Players Association after a short and unsuccessful term by Kenneth Moffet following Miller's retirement, suspected collusion on the part of the owners and filed a grievance in February 1986. This became known as "Collusion I." None of the 1985 free agents received offers from teams other than their current club. According to Fehr, the union asked the arbitrator to award any free agent who was hurt by the alleged collusion damages and a remedy to the damages, which could take the form of a monetary award as well as freedom to move to another club.[19]

The owners did not exhibit a great deal of concern. Ueberroth had already said, "I've heard some talk of conspiracy. I can't take that seriously. Common sense has taken over. What has happened is the [economic] pot is dry." Meanwhile, Eddie Einhorn, co-owner of the White Sox along with Jerry Reinsdorf, said, "We've become cost-conscious. There are a lot of things we are not in control of. It's time we concentrate on things we are in control of."[20]

The market did not loosen up after the 1986 season. Eight prominent members of the free agent class of 1986, a group that became known as "baseball's big eight," included Rich Gedman, Lance Parrish, Bob Horner, Andre Dawson, Tim Raines, Bob Boone, Ron Guidry, and Doyle Alexander. None of these players had received any free agent offers after turning down offers from their own clubs. All of the free agents that year waited in vain for offers from other clubs that topped the offers from their own teams. No free agent had been offered more from a competing club than he received from his own club.[21] Those who did not sign with their original clubs before the January 8 contractual deadline were forced to sit out until May 1, even after they signed with their old clubs. Jack Morris, All-Star pitcher for Detroit and one of the vital cogs in their 1985 World Championship team (and later with the 1991 Minnesota Twins—he pitched one of the most memorable seventh games in World Series history, shutting out Atlanta 1–0 in ten innings), was forced to accept salary arbitration because no club was ready to make a legitimate offer. Morris had wanted to be a Yankee and his agent offered George Steinbrenner a one-year deal with salary decided by an arbitrator, but Steinbrenner did not take Morris up on his offer.

The case of Andre Dawson is particularly enlightening. An All-Star and one of the best right fielders in baseball, Dawson was desperate to get out of Montreal because his knees were taking a pounding from playing on the rock-hard artificial turf at Olympic Stadium. He thought he could find some relief by playing on the natural turf at Wrigley Field, but Cubs President Dallas Green was not interested. So Dick Moss, Dawson's agent who had previously worked with Marvin Miller at the Players Association, camped out at the Cubs' facility in Arizona during spring training 1987. Moss drew the attention of the writers and indicated that he was willing to agree to whatever offer the Cubs wanted to make, essentially offering to sign a blank contract. His hand was forced, but with the prospect of adding an All-Star to his outfield, Green filled in $500,000—and $200,000 in additional bonus money—a ridiculously low salary and less than one-third of what Dawson would have been worth in a functioning free agent market. Dawson signed the contract, hit forty-eight home runs, and became the most popular Cub and object of the Bleacherites' affection at Wrigley as well as the National League's Most Valuable Player.

Bill Giles Bucks the System

One owner made a legitimate attempt to sign a free agent after the 1986 season. That was Bill Giles. The Phillies had won the National League pennant in 1983, but their performance declined over the next three years. Giles thought that if he could sign a top-notch catcher, a position that was a weakness both offensively and defensively in 1986, his club could legitimately compete for a division crown in 1987. Lance Parrish had been one of the top catchers in the AL with Detroit, helping the Tigers win a World Championship in 1985, and was a free agent during the off-season of 1986–1987. Giles felt a great deal of tension about bidding for Parrish. On one hand, he had an obligation to be a "team player" along with the other owners, to "exercise fiscal responsibility" as it were. On the other hand, he felt he had an obligation to Phillies fans and his ownership partners to improve the team. He felt compelled to do what was right and believed that collusive behavior among the owners was wrong.

He was also getting pressure from players on the Phillies, including perhaps the greatest third baseman in the history of the game. According to Giles, "I was getting a lot of pressure from Mike Schmidt to sign Parrish. He would call and say, 'If we get Parrish, we can win this thing; you gotta sign Parrish!'"[22]

According to the rules of free agency at the time, the deadline for a free agent to sign with his original club was January 8, so Lance's Parrish's deadline to sign with the Tigers was January 8, 1987. If the player did not sign by the deadline, the club could not sign him until the following May 1. So, Giles decided not to approach Parrish until after January 8, explaining, "I'm sure that the union would say it's wrong, but I don't like going after a player when he has a chance to sign with his original club. It's a little bit like stealing, while trading for that player, even if he doesn't want to leave his club, is not stealing, it's just part of the game. I don't believe in stealing a player."[23] Giles decided and publicly announced that if Parrish did not sign with Detroit by the deadline, then the Tigers were not interested in re-signing him and he would pursue Parrish for the Phillies. During the last week of January, he met with Parrish and his agent, Tom Reich, to initiate talks.

But once he had opened negotiations with Reich, Giles was the subject of some pressure from fellow owners and executives, as he reports:

> Ueberroth was the leader, and there were two or three other owners and general managers. Jim Campbell of the Tigers was one, I remember, because he would call me periodically. There were four or five clubs really putting the pressure on everybody else not to sign a free agent if the club that had him wanted him. In other words, Lance Parrish was making a million or something with Detroit and I went after him. The unwritten rule was you cannot offer him any more than what Detroit has been offering. Not being sure what to do, I called my friend Peter O'Malley. I asked him for his advice, and his response was simple and sound: "Do what you think is right." I also called my friend Lou Hoynes, who was the attorney for the National League at the time, and he said, "I think we are on dangerous ground with this concept of not signing a Lance Parrish" or whoever, so I said, "What should I do?" He said, "I am not going to tell you what to do because I work for the commissioner's office, but I am not sure we are not going to get in trouble for this."[24]

Later on, it came out as part of the hearings with the arbitrator, George Nicolau, after a grievance was filed by the Players Association, that Dr. Bobby Brown, president of the AL, had called Giles. Brown urged him to reconsider because the Tigers still wanted Parrish and Brown did not want to have one of the star players in the AL skip to the rival NL. Bud Selig of the Brewers, and a member of the player relations committee, called and urged Giles to uphold his "fiscal responsibility," which could have been interpreted as code for "don't make any free agent bids higher than the player's club has offered him." Giles also was concerned that any free agent bids could potentially bring (deep-pocketed) George Steinbrenner and Ted Turner into the free agent market. Jerry Reinsdorf contacted Bill as well. According to Reinsdorf, he did not tell Bill to exercise fiscal responsibility nor did he tell him not to sign Parrish, as was reported at the time.

> I said to Bill Giles, "If you are going to bid on a guy, go ahead but don't win by a lot," because I always told people that. Why blow the market away? Texas paid A-Rod $250 million and the next bidder was at $160 million, and so I tell that to people all of the time. You're stupid if you win by a lot. So I told Bill, "If you go after Parrish, go after him, but don't win by a lot."[25]

Despite the pressure, subtle and not so subtle, from fellow owners and other baseball executives, Giles decided that his desire to improve his club trumped his desire to conform to the new, unwritten policy on free agent offers, so he continued negotiations with Tom Reich. Giles said, "Negotiations with Tom Reich were very difficult. I remember getting it done finally in a hotel in Tampa, Florida. I felt an obligation to the other owners, but I also felt an obligation to improve my ball club."[26]

By mid-February, the two sides appeared close to agreement on a one-year, $1 million contract, but negotiations broke down when the club insisted that Parrish waive all rights to future litigation. Reich believed that the owners were getting their signals from Ueberroth. He felt more strongly that this was the case when he seemed to have Parrish signed with the Phillies, only to have the club's lawyers insist that Reich agree to a clause prohibiting Parrish or himself from taking further legal action against the Phillies or baseball because of the way that Parrish had been treated as a free agent. Reich refused to agree to such a clause, angering and disappointing Bill Giles, who really wanted to sign Parrish. According to a newspaper report, the implication was that the club's lawyers, in demanding that Reich give up his legal rights, were acting on a directive from the owners' player relations committee, which took its orders from Ueberroth. However, Giles indicated that the idea came from Phillies' attorney Bill Webb. He said, "We wanted Parrish to sign a contract with a clause that would hold the Phillies harmless, but not baseball, and the Players Association agreed with us. The origin of this idea came from Bill Webb; I don't recall being pressured by the commissioner's office or the Player Relations Committee."[27]

Ultimately, the parties reached an agreement. In mid-March, Reich met with Giles and Webb and proposed a compromise. Negotiating throughout the morning and afternoon, they worked out language that would prevent Parrish from suing the Phillies but would not infringe on the union's right to take appropriate legal action, language that satisfied both the Phillies and the Players Association, which had filed a grievance over the matter. Parrish had reportedly retained the right to sue baseball officials or clubs other that the Phillies over alleged collusion.

Subsequently, Giles announced that Parrish had agreed to a one-year contract that paid him $1,000,000, plus $200,000 if Parrish did not experience any problems from a chronic back ailment. Parrish's offer also included financial incentives for making the All-Star team and for winning the league's Most Valuable Player award. Giles later said, "I certainly had mixed emotions in signing Parrish; it was the toughest decision I ever faced as an owner. I thought that collusion was wrong and I didn't go by the book. It turned out I made a mistake, not because of collusion but because Parrish didn't play well. And I was penalized by then-commissioner Peter Ueberroth."[28] To add injury to insult, the commissioner fined the Phillies $750,000 (in withheld central fund money) for signing Parrish against his and the other owners' wishes. This fact was not discussed publicly at the time.

Giles got his man; the Phillies did sign Lance Parrish. Unfortunately for both the Phillies and himself, Parrish did not prove to be a good signing because he did not play at a level that was anything close to his performance in Detroit. As a Tiger, he was a six-time All-Star who won five Silver Slugger Awards and a Gold Glove and averaged about twenty-five home runs per year, along with and just short of 100 runs batted in (RBI) per year his last five years with the Tigers. In two years with the Phillies, Parrish hit just thirty-nine home runs, had 127 total RBI, and hit just .245 and .215.[29]

Other owners and members of the baseball establishment considered Giles an independent thinker who would make his decisions based on what he felt was the right path, not necessarily following the party line. His decision to sign Parrish followed that approach. According to Giles:

> I made a lot of my peers very upset with me when I signed Parrish. It took me a few years to recover from that with a few of my peers, maybe three or four. I'm not too popular among some of the hard-line labor people, anyway. And now [after he announced during the spring of 1990 that he planned to carry 25 players on the Phillies roster as opposed to the 24 that the other owners had agreed to—as a way of punishing the union] I'm probably back on their list. . . . I didn't believe in the collusion thing. I thought it was wrong. I think we should be reasonable enough as owners to keep salaries under control without having to collude—or without resentment or lying or things like that. I just think we should have an honest industry. Agents don't trust ownership. Players don't trust ownership. There's a lot of mistrust in baseball. And that bothers me a lot.[30]

Collusion—Round 2

While the Giles-Parrish drama played out during the 1986–1987 off-season, the Players Association filed a second grievance over suspected collusion in February 1987. This became known as "Collusion II." By the time the union filed the Collusion II grievance, the owners had terminated Thomas Roberts as baseball's arbitrator. The new arbitrator was George Nicolau. In Collusion II, the Players Association argued that there was no real change in the owners' approach to the free agent market during the 1986–1987 off-season and that they were still in violation of the anti-collusion clause in the labor agreement.

Despite having been let go by the owners, Arbitrator Thomas Roberts was permitted by a federal judge, over the owners' objections, to rule on Collusion I. He delivered his decision late in the 1987 season, on September 21. The owners had alleged that the lack of interest in free agents was "nothing more than the culmination of a predictable evolution to a more sober and rational free agent market."[31] But Roberts found that the owners were guilty of collusion, restricting players' movement and weakening their bargaining position. Roberts determined that teams used a database and did not pursue free agents unless there was no interest by the original clubs, "in itself a strong indication of concerted action." He used the case of Kirk Gibson as an example. After Gibson had become a free agent, the Kansas City Royals approached him, indicating a strong interest in bringing him to Kansas City. According to evidence cited by Roberts, "The interest of the Royals in Kirk Gibson suddenly cooled . . . after meetings among owners and general managers." He ruled that those players who had re-signed with their original teams would be free agents . . . again, i.e., "new look free agents," if they preferred.[32] Roberts would also hear arguments from both sides regarding how much financial restitution the owners owed to the grieved players. The Players Association claimed that financial losses of the free agents affected by collusion were between $70 and $90 million.

In January 1988, Roberts granted immediate free agency to seven players, including Gibson and Carlton Fisk, both of whom were part of the 1985 class of free agents and did not receive any offers from other clubs. Gibson went on to sign with the Dodgers and, along with Orel Hershiser, led them to the 1988 pennant, and then, despite having been forced to the bench with two bad knees, hit one of the most dramatic home runs in World Series history off Oakland A's reliever Dennis Eckersley, a future Hall of Famer, to win Game 1 of the World Series. It was his only time at bat, but his one hit was enough to propel the Dodgers to an improbable World Series victory.

The Information Bank

After two years of collusion, the owners were aware that they had lost the Collusion I case and that the grievance in the Collusion II case was pending. After the 1987 season, instead of behaving as they had the previous two off-seasons and simply not bidding on free agents, the owners adopted what was called "the information bank." This was an idea crafted by Chuck O'Connor, an attorney for the player relations committee. Bill Giles explained the way that the information bank worked. Owners who were about to make free agent offers or offers of long-term contracts to other players to "lock them up" and prevent them from becoming free agents had to "deposit" information on what they planned to offer. Owners could "withdraw" information on offers intended by other clubs. According to Giles, this was done so that agents could not misrepresent or exaggerate offers that their players were getting, thereby artificially bidding up the price. According to Giles, "Larry Christensen's agent misrepresented an offer he was supposed to have from Montreal, but because of the information bank, I knew the correct amount of the offer."[33]

[*Note:* Fast forward to today. For a number of years, there has been a similar arrangement. According to Giles, club representatives are supposed to contact Major League Baseball to report on a proposed offer to a player. The practice was for Rob Manfred, now baseball's chief labor man, or Frank Coonelly, now president of the Pittsburgh Pirates who used to work in the commissioner's office, to take the call, listen to the details of the offer, then give advice like "That's too much money; it's going to hurt the industry," or "It's a fair deal; it's good for the industry."[34]]

While there was more movement after the 1987 season than during the previous two years, the players were still unhappy with the free agent market, so the Players Association filed a third grievance (Collusion III) in January 1988. The players' complaint was that the information bank that provided all clubs with detailed information about other clubs' free agent bids restrained the size of the bids. The union contended that while certain forms of information exchange among teams are legitimate, the information bank was not.[35]

Collusion II and III Rulings

The Collusion II grievance, which covered the crop of free agents after the 1986 season, was presented to baseball's new arbitrator, George Nicolau, who had replaced the deposed Thomas Roberts. Nicolau ruled on Collusion II on August 31, 1988, and found once again for the players, finding that club owners were guilty of colluding to stall the free agent market for a second consecutive year. Nicolau stated:

> What transpired in 1986 occurred because everyone "understood" what was to be done. By common consent, exclusive negotiating rights were, in effect, ceded to former clubs. There was no vestige of a free market, as that term is commonly understood. The object was to force players back to their former clubs and the expectation was that all would go back in a replication of 1985, requiring nothing more to be done.[36]

Two months later, twelve players who had been free agents in 1986 but could not find teams willing to bid for their services were freed by Nicolau, based on his decision in the Collusion II case. Included were Claudell Washington, Ron Guidry, Willie Randolph, Brian Downing, Bob Boone, Ernie Whitt, Rich Gedman, Alan Ashby, Jim Clancy, Doyle Alexander, Ken Dayley, and Roy Smith. Tim Raines would have been made a free agent again, but he had signed a contract with his old club, the Expos. These "new look" free agents were given until December 16 to sign with a new team, rejoin their old club, or remain free agents. Andre Dawson and Lance Parrish had already signed contracts for 1989 that waived their free agency rights.

Some of the most compelling evidence in the case was that of the pressure put on Bill Giles cautioning him not to sign Lance Parrish. Nicolau specifically found evidence to indicate that Bobby Brown as well as Bud Selig and Jerry Reinsdorf each separately requested that Giles not sign Parrish. Selig even suggested that failure to show restraint in the free agent market might lead other owners, such as Yankees owner George Steinbrenner, to jump into the free agent market. Each of these conversations evidenced, at a minimum, an attempt to collude.[37]

Nicolau did not rule on Collusion III until July 1990, but again found for the players who were members of the free agent group after the 1987 season. This ruling covered seventy-six players. The crux of the case was the information bank that was maintained by the owners' player relations committee. The owners took the position that the information bank did not violate the anti-collusion restriction in the CBA, an argument that fell on deaf ears.

The intended effect of the owners' behavior with respect to free agents during the "collusion years" was to eliminate or at least lessen the bidding wars for players, which drove up salaries. For that period, the strategy was a success. While eventually the owners paid the price for their collusive actions, over the four-year period beginning in 1985, collusion was quite effective in holding salaries in place. According to Zimbalist, player salaries comprised 17.6 percent of team revenues in 1974, before free agency, increased to 41.4 percent in 1983, and by 1989 had dropped to 31.6 percent, because of both increasing revenues and the depressed free agent market.[38]

Clearly, collusion depressed salaries and, as was ruled in three different sets of cases, did so illegally. The two arbitrators who ruled on the three grievances, Roberts and Nicolau, had to determine how much collusion had cost the players involved. Roberts ruled that owners had cost union members $10.5 million for Collusion I in 1986, and Nicolau arrived at figures of $38 million for Collusion II in 1987 and $64.5 million for Collusion III in 1988. It was not until September 1990 that Nicolau announced the $102.5 million in damages due to the affected players. In addition to these shortfalls, the owners had to compensate the players for ancillary losses related to multiyear contracts and various sorts of bonuses.[39]

The owners and players negotiated the final settlement, which was announced on November 4, 1990. Overall, $280 million was awarded, to be split among the players who had filed claims. These were only actual damages, that is, the difference between the value of the contracts that the players were forced to sign and what they would have been worth in a free market. There was nothing in the labor agreement about punitive damages, so no punitive damages were awarded.[40]

An Effect That Lasted for Years

Ultimately, the owners' decision to illegally—according to the CBA—manipulate the free agent market for three consecutive seasons had the following effects. One, while collusion took place, salaries grew much more slowly than they had previously. Two, the owners of the twenty-six major clubs agreed to pay $280 million (plus interest) in restitution to the players affected by collusion. This worked out to $11.7 million per team, a significant sum and a penalty that concurred with a steep decline in national television revenues. Many baseball insiders acknowledge that the decisions to expand baseball in 1993 and again in 1998—with the attendant franchise fees paid by the new club owners—were at least partially predicated on finding some means to pay the collusion bill.

Most importantly, collusion created a level of mistrust on the part of the players that had a dramatic effect on subsequent labor relations, at least until the 2002 labor agreement. This level of mistrust made all relationships between the owners and players more difficult and made the players that much more motivated not to make concessions to the owners.

Peter O'Malley said that collusion "set back our relations a full generation."[41] The severity of the 1994 strike and the close call again in 2002 likely were exacerbated by this mistrust, a fact acknowledged by Bill Giles, Fay Vincent, and others who were involved in player relations.

Bill Giles and Free Agents, After Collusion

After the 1991 season, collusion had ended but was still fresh in everyone's mind. That year, Kirby Puckett, the great outfielder of the Minnesota Twins, who had just led the Twins—along with Jack Morris—to their second World Series championship in four years, was a free agent. Giles wanted Kirby Puckett in Philadelphia, and Puckett was interested enough to listen to the offer. In December 1991, Puckett went to Philadelphia, met with Phillies general manager Lee Thomas, and took a tour of Veteran's Stadium. Giles than took Puckett and his agent to lunch at a restaurant in Wayne, Pennsylvania. During that luncheon meeting, Giles offered Puckett a $25 million, five-year deal that Puckett, unfortunately for the Phillies, turned down. How big was that number at the time? Darryl Strawberry had set the standard for superstars when he signed a five-year, $20.25 million contract with the Dodgers the previous year. Who knows what might have been if Puckett had been in the Phillies outfield during the 1993 World Series, which they lost to the Blue Jays? And had the Phillies been able to sign Puckett, would the fans in Philadelphia have continued to cling to their generally held belief that the Phillies had shallow pockets?

4

The Rise and Fall of Fay Vincent

Francis T. (Fay) Vincent, intelligent, educated, and accomplished in business, led a very successful life despite a significant injury suffered as an undergraduate at Williams College that ended his athletic career and made walking difficult. He demonstrated high moral standards and integrity. Given his wealth and experience as a senior business executive, one of his essential characteristics was independence in his thinking and actions.

Fay Vincent also had the misfortune of being called to action as commissioner of major league baseball at a time of great economic upheaval and a continuing storm of issues. His ideas about the appropriate commissioner's role did not jibe with the owners' view of the role. He wanted to be a commissioner for the owners, players, and fans, protecting "the best interests of baseball." What the owners wanted was a person who represented the owners' interests and helped them make money and increase the value of their franchises.

This chapter describes the rise and fall of Fay Vincent in his role as eighth commissioner of baseball by reviewing specific issues and decisions that defined his tenure. I explain how he went from being lauded and respected after his first two months on the job to being forced out of office less than three years later. To this day, Vincent has both admirers and detractors among the owners of the time, some of whom are still involved in baseball. As Peter O'Malley commented in an e-mail, the story has no villains. Vincent's biggest critics felt that they had legitimate interests that were at odds with Vincent's positions and decisions, but for the most part the conflicts were professional, not personal. The story of

Vincent's term as commissioner is enlightening and illustrates a great deal about the pressures surrounding the enterprise of baseball during a very difficult era and the key participants in that enterprise: the owners and their anointed commissioner.

From Sony to Major League Baseball

The story of Fay Vincent has been well chronicled. Educated at the Hotchkiss School and Williams College, then Yale Law School, he practiced corporate law, served on the Securities and Exchange Commission for a time, became CEO at Columbia Pictures, and was named executive vice president of Coca Cola after Coke acquired Columbia. He met and befriended Bart Giamatti, and they decided that if the opportunity presented itself they would work together. That opportunity came when Giamatti was elevated from National League president to commissioner effective March 1, 1989. Giamatti created the position of deputy commissioner and hired Vincent to handle certain aspects of the commissioner's job. Vincent, with his combination of legal and business experience, was uniquely qualified for this position.

Giamatti and Vincent worked together for six months. The Pete Rose gambling case, which Giamatti inherited from his predecessor, Peter Ueberroth, occupied much of their energy and focus and came to a head during this time. Vincent coordinated the investigative work on Rose, hiring Jon Dowd as special counsel who investigated the case and prepared the report. Giamatti suspended Rose indefinitely from baseball on August 23, 1989. Just nine days later, Giamatti passed away unexpectedly, leaving the commissioner's office vacant.

Bill Giles recalls Giamatti's sudden passing:

> Of course, I was shocked and saddened; he was such a romantic and loved the game; he was a great wordsmith about the attributes of baseball. He would have been such a great salesman for the traditions and beauty of the game of baseball. On the other hand, if he had remained commissioner for a long time, it is my belief that the business of the game would not have prospered and developed as it has under Bud Selig.[1]

Vincent's Appointment as Permanent Commissioner

When Giamatti died, baseball confronted a sudden and unexpected vacancy in the commissioner's office at a time when the game could not afford to be without a leader. In late 1989, baseball faced a possible strike, major litigation regarding the collusion issue, and a host of issues on the horizon. Thus, the owners moved quickly to make Vincent permanent commissioner. Referring to the upcoming negotiations with the players' union for a new CBA, one owner expressed an opinion held by the majority: "You can't walk into a labor negotiation with a commissioner *pro tem.* You can't have the guy looking over his shoulder." Giles said at the time, "I personally think it would be untimely to begin a search at this time with so many things coming up in the next few months."[2]

Some owners thought that Vincent might be a better candidate than his immediate predecessors. He had a better business background than Giamatti. He was more attuned to baseball than Ueberroth and was just as competent in legal matters as Kuhn. But some owners were not convinced at first and wanted to find out whether other viable prospects were available and might be a better choice for commissioner. And, given the benefit of twenty years' hindsight, Giles now says:

> When we [the owners] were considering Vincent, I did not know him [really] well. I knew of his corporate accomplishments and respected them, but I was really not in favor of him becoming commissioner. I did not see him as a vibrant leader who could stand publicly before the sports fans and sell the game of baseball. I thought it was time that we went outside baseball. Of course, Vincent was from outside baseball before he served as Giamatti's deputy. I liked George Mitchell, a guy who was in the minds of a number of people. But we had to move quickly, and so Vincent became the guy."[3]

After several days of discussion, the executive council voted to recommend to the owners that Francis T. (Fay) Vincent, Jr., serve as commissioner for the four-and-a-half years of the unexpired term of the late A. Bartlett Giamatti, through March 1994.

Vincent and Giamatti differed in a number of ways; they complemented one another in background and experience, but shared a number of perspectives, including how they perceived the proper domain of major league baseball's commissioner. This domain included preserving the integrity of the game, making decisions that supported the best interests of the game, and bringing the warring factions—the owners and the players—together. Students and practitioners of organizational behavior understand a concept called "domain dissensus," which occurs when individuals hold fundamentally different beliefs about the appropriate behaviors of people and offices within an organization. The commissionership of Fay Vincent represents a classic case of this phenomenon.

Certainly, many owners believed that the commissioner "overstepped his bounds" more than once, particularly regarding labor. Moreover, some of the owners, including Giles, had issues with his decision-making style as well as his independence.

I review the key issues and decisions that undermined Vincent's relationships with the owners in roughly chronological order.

The 1989 World Series

The new commissioner had been in office only a little more than a month when his first crisis struck. On October 17, 1989, at 5:04 P.M. on the West Coast, as Game 3 of the 1989 World Series was about to begin, a major earthquake hit the Bay Area. The Loma Prieta earthquake had a surface magnitude of 7.1 on the Richter scale. The violent movement of the earth collapsed part of the Bay Bridge between San Francisco and Oakland as well as highways in both cities. The toll was egregious: sixty-seven lives and between $6 and $7 billion in damage to property. People inside Candlestick Park in San Francisco knew that an earthquake had hit, but no one there, including Bill Giles, knew the extent of the loss of life and the horrific damage to bridges, highways, and buildings that had been caused by the earthquake. Once the scale of the disaster was understood, baseball was in a quandary about whether and when to continue the series, and Fay Vincent was the point man for the decision.

Giles spent time in a hotel suite with Vincent and some other baseball executives discussing options. Giles says:

> I did give Vincent high marks for handling the Bay Area earthquake. I spent a lot of time in his hotel room debating the merits of canceling the World Series, or postponing it, because of the tragedy in the Bay Area. We concluded that it would be good for the people [who] lived in that area to play the World Series. He used me as kind of a sounding board as to what to do about playing the World Series or not.[4]

Vincent described the World Series as "our modest little sporting event" and queried, "What was that next to the needs of a devastated community?" Ultimately, he made the call that Giles advocated, which was to wait a suitable time to ensure that Candlestick Park was structurally sound and for some of the damage and wounds in the community to heal and then resume the series to give the people in the Bay Area something to help get their minds off the trauma of the earthquake. Vincent handled this situation with empathy, sensitivity, and a clear sense of purpose.

The Series resumed, the Oakland A's swept the Giants, and Vincent had enjoyed his finest hour. His handling of the 1989 World Series gave him a national identity and a new level of confidence. Unfortunately, according to some, it also gave him an exaggerated sense of his power. As John Helyar observed, "It was the beginning of the transformation of his role. He started looking for issues."[5]

Vincent's Involvement in the 1990 Lockout and Labor Settlement

The labor agreement in effect when Vincent assumed the commissioner's role was set to expire at the end of 1989, so pressure was on both the owners and Vincent to move forward with negotiations on a new deal. The owners' Player Relations Committee had the primary responsibility for labor relations. Barry Rona held the position as lead negotiator and had served in that role since the Ueberroth days.

Vincent felt that Rona represented the "bad old days" of acrimony between the owners and the players. The new commissioner wanted to build a more harmonious relationship with Fehr and the Players Association and decided to relieve Rona of his duties. Vincent made this decision a month after the World Series and just three months before management's "deal-or-lockout" deadline of February 15, 1990.[6] Although Vincent recently said in an interview with Maury Brown that Player Relations Committee chair Bud Selig actually removed Barry Rona and that Vincent was merely the messenger, most accounts describe Vincent removing Rona.[7] Chuck O'Connor, an attorney with Morgan, Lewis & Bockius, the firm that served as baseball's legal counsel, replaced Rona. According to Bill Giles, O'Connor's performance did not meet the expectations of the owners, and this proved to be another issue that adversely affected the standing of the commissioner with the owners.

Another action that created concern among some of the hard-line owners was Vincent's hiring of Steve Greenberg as deputy commissioner. Greenberg was the son of Hall-of Famer Hank Greenberg, an attorney, a former players' agent, a Yale alumnus who had studied with Professor Bart Giamatti, and a friend of Don Fehr. In addition to Greenberg's skill set and experience, another ostensible motive for hiring Greenberg was to demonstrate to the Players Association that Vincent intended to handle labor relations differently than his predecessors and certainly much differently than the "hawks" among the owners. The new commissioner intended to adopt a conciliatory approach in an effort to create a more favorable bargaining environment. Unfortunately, at the time, nothing mattered in the bargaining but what the owners were willing to provide the players. Don Fehr wanted the best deal for the players that he could get without concern for whether negotiations were friendly or adversarial.

Several owners, particularly those from small markets, who increasingly found themselves in an untenable position relative to their large-market counterparts, did not want conciliation or reasonableness. They wanted someone to slow the rapid escalation of player salaries that was occurring once collusion had ended and the free agent market opened up. Bill Giles voiced what many of the owners thought, "Vincent appeared soft on labor matters, too much of a 'dove' when the owners wanted a 'hawk' to deal with Don Fehr."[8] Giles also provided the insight that the large-market owners tended to be doves because they had more to lose with lockouts or strikes, saying, "And I was probably more of a dove than a hawk. The small-market, low-revenue teams seemed to be more hawkish, as were the owners whose business had a lot of dealings with unions, like August Busch in St. Louis with Anheuser-Busch and Stan Cook of the Cubs with WGN. And Reinsdorf was very much a hawk in labor relations matters.[9]

The owners, fresh from the unsuccessful collusion gambit, tried to corral spiraling player salaries in the new round of negotiations. Chuck O'Connor, who had replaced Barry Rona, represented the owners and presented a new concept, a "partnership plan" by which the owners would provide 48 percent of all gate receipts and national and local broadcasting revenues for player salaries and ancillary benefits. In exchange, the owners asked for a salary cap that would prohibit teams from signing free agents once the cap was reached. In addition, the owners proposed a pay-for-performance system to replace salary arbitration that applied to players with less than six years of experience in the major leagues. The pay-for-performance scale plan used a statistical ranking system for players, according to position, as a basis for salaries.

The players felt that they had made significant concessions during the previous negotiations in 1985 by accepting an increase from two years to three years' service time for eligibility for salary arbitration. They did not want to seriously consider what they viewed as an attempt by the owners to control the player market, as had been done illegally after the 1985, 1986, and 1987 seasons. In addition, the bitterness that the players felt toward the owners, sown by the seeds of what Miller called "a collusive conspiracy," worsened the already acrimonious relationship between the owners and the players. The sides could not reach an agreement by the owners' deadline, and the owners decided to lock out the players and refused to open spring training camps in February 1990.

Bart Giamatti had pledged not to intervene and undercut the position of the Player Relations Committee in its dealings with the union.

However, his successor could not resist getting involved. Vincent's motives notwithstanding—one view is that he hoped to secure both labor peace and a legacy as the "labor relations commissioner"—he upset the small-market-owner majority by involving himself in the negotiation process, negotiating directly with Don Fehr and ultimately substituting what he perceived to be a more reasonable set of demands for those of the owners.

The great baseball writer Leonard Koppett asked, "How could the 'custodian of public interest' let a lockout happen?" With fans and media loudly calling for baseball to resume, a commissioner who said and believed that "my prime obligation is to the fans" could not sit idly by.[10] Some owners, including Fred Wilpon of the Mets, Peter O'Malley of the Dodgers, and Eli Jacobs of Baltimore, all high-revenue clubs, urged Vincent to settle the dispute, but the majority of owners wanted to keep the commissioner out of the negotiations. Nevertheless, Vincent decided to make "back-channel" overtures toward Fehr. He substituted his own, more moderate proposal for the Player Relations Committee's proposal.

Vincent tried to get the players to agree to a plan whereby the owners would end the lockout in return for a pledge by the players not to strike. Fehr scoffed at the proposal. Vincent's involvement forced the hand of the Player Relations Committee to give in on some key issues, including the concept of revenue participation coupled with a salary cap, the pay-for-performance plan for players with less than six years of service in the major leagues, and some givebacks in terms of eligibility for salary arbitration—and reach a compromise that most of the owners believed once again favored the players. The lockout that paralyzed baseball for thirty-two days ended on March 18, 1990, when the players and owners made a deal that included a compromise on the question of service time for eligibility for salary arbitration, the issue that bogged down the negotiations for more than five weeks once the owners had taken the other items off the table. The two sides agreed to grant eligibility to 17 percent of the players in the group with two to three years of major league service, beginning the next year. These players today are called "super twos." The settlement was crafted in time to play all 162 scheduled games. It is important to note that five of the six members of the Player Relations Committee endorsed the settlement that Vincent helped shape.

Unfortunately, many of the owners, especially those in smaller markets, considered Vincent's "triumph" nothing more than meddling in "their" business and a perceived softness in the critical area of labor relations. They felt strongly that Vincent, in getting directly involved in the negotiations, went beyond the role that the Player Relations Committee allowed. Further, Vincent had inserted himself too much into the negotiations and by doing so adversely affected the Player Relations Committee's bargaining position. Ultimately, the small-market owners believed, his involvement led to a much less favorable outcome that would have been the case otherwise. While he was trying to solve a thorny problem, Vincent's efforts undermined the owners' position, created a growing anti-Vincent faction, and prompted attempts by some hard-line owners to restrict the commissioner's role in labor negotiations.

Steinbrenner versus Vincent

George Steinbrenner signed future Hall-of-Famer Dave Winfield as a free agent in 1980, hoping to quickly get back to the World Series after the Yankees won championships in 1977 and 1978. Winfield's contract contained two provisions that later created significant problems. First, Steinbrenner agreed to an escalator clause based on inflation, apparently unaware of the effect of that clause, which has been estimated to have cost "the Boss" millions over the life of Winfield's contract. Steinbrenner was not happy about this, and he wasn't happy about failing to win another World Series. He began to refer to Winfield derisively as "Mr. May" after Winfield's less-than-stellar 1981 Series performance, a pointed reference to Winfield's inability to bring to the club what "Mr. October" Reggie Jackson had brought just a few years earlier during the days of "the Bronx Zoo."

In addition to the escalator clause, Winfield's deal mandated that Steinbrenner make annual contributions of $500,000 to the David M. Winfield Foundation. As the years went by, Steinbrenner became less and less enamored with Winfield because of both his performance on the field and Steinbrenner's continuing financial obligations to the foundation. The Boss began to suspect some irregularities in how the foundation's funds were managed. He eventually stopped his contributions, and the foundation sued for breach of contract. Ultimately, this led to a clandestine relationship between Steinbrenner and Howard Spira, a small-time gambler with mob connections, who had worked as a "go-fer" for the foundation.

Steinbrenner became involved with Spira because he wanted information about the foundation. Spira claimed that he knew the inside story and could provide information that Steinbrenner would find useful. Steinbrenner paid Spira $40,000 for his services. Then Spira attempted to extort an additional $110,000 from the Yankees owner, with the threat that unless he was paid this "hush money," he would divulge what he claimed to be damaging information about other Yankees as well as what had transpired between him and the Yankees owner. Steinbrenner refused to pay, opting instead to go the FBI. A Florida grand jury indicted

Spira on eight counts of extortion and for threatening to harm Steinbrenner and Dave Winfield.[11]

Vincent decided that Steinbrenner's behavior and his involvement with Spira constituted violation of rule 21 of the Major League Agreement, which covers "the best interests of baseball." Vincent appointed Jon Dowd, a former FBI agent whom Vincent had hired to look into the Pete Rose case, to investigate. This saga turned out to be Vincent's third crisis in less than a year on the job, although this one was limited primarily to the two parties, the Yankees owner and the commissioner. There was little discussion among the owners and especially with Steinbrenner. Giles said at the time, "As far as I know, there hasn't been much conversation. I only know what I read in the papers."[12]

Dowd's investigation confirmed the relationship between Steinbrenner and Spira, Steinbrenner's attempts to gather damaging information about Winfield and the foundation, and the payoffs. The matter came to a head in June 1990. After Vincent held a daylong conference with Steinbrenner and his attorneys, Steinbrenner agreed to resign, based on the finding that his 3½-year "undisclosed relationship" with Spira constituted conduct "not in the best interest of baseball."

As a result, Steinbrenner was permanently barred from day-to-day management and control of the Yankees. Vincent said that, as a limited partner, Steinbrenner would still be able to vote on major financial decisions, but the penalty prohibited the Boss from any involvement in the day-to-day activities of running the ball club, including hiring and firing managers. Steinbrenner was ordered to resign as general partner by August 20 and he agreed to sell at least 5 percent of his interest in the Yankees, which reduced his equity to less than 50 percent and made him a limited partner.

Vincent reiterated that Steinbrenner would be treated as if he had been placed on the permanently ineligible list. The commissioner saw the case and his decision as consistent with his role as protector of the game's integrity, saying, "My decision in this case and this result will serve, I trust, to vindicate once again the important responsibility of the commissioner to preserve and protect our noble game."[13]

Vincent intended to give Steinbrenner a two-year suspension, but Steinbrenner instead signed an agreement that amounted to a lifetime ban from running the club, seemingly a very curious decision. A Steinbrenner associate said that he had reasons for the decision. By avoiding being labeled as "suspended," Steinbrenner felt that he would be able to retain his coveted position as vice president of the U.S. Olympic Committee. And by accepting the penalty he did, Steinbrenner guaranteed that his son Hank would be permitted to replace him as general partner. But Steinbrenner's grand succession plans didn't come to fruition because Hank decided that he neither wanted the job nor wanted to move to New York City. After a series of moves and decisions, lawsuits, and other complications, eventually, Steinbrenner's son-in-law, thirty-one-year-old Joseph Molloy, took the reins as managing partner for the duration of Steinbrenner's banishment.

Bill Giles spoke for many of the owners when he said that "it is very unfortunate when any owner is penalized by the commissioner of baseball. I was surprised by the severity of Commissioner Vincent's decision, but I had no knowledge of the case other than what I learned through the news media."[14] After Vincent announced Steinbrenner's penalty, baseball officials mostly indicated support for the commissioner. Giles said, "I applaud Mr. Vincent for the strength, intellect and integrity he has shown since becoming commissioner. I do think it is imperative that any commissioner has the authority to make decisions such as Mr. Vincent's in the Steinbrenner case to uphold the integrity and image of our great game."[15] Peter O'Malley also spoke in favor of Vincent, saying, "There was never any doubt in my mind that Commissioner Vincent would give Mr. Steinbrenner a fair hearing and I support the commissioner's decision. The commissioner's ability to sanction those acting against the best interests of baseball is critical to maintain the integrity of the game."[16]

Orioles president Larry Lucchino concurred, saying, "We have complete confidence in the commissioner's judgment and action in this matter." The lone dissent came from former Yankees president Gabe Paul, who took over operation of the team when Steinbrenner was suspended by Commissioner Bowie Kuhn in 1974 for making illegal campaign contributions to Richard Nixon. "I think the commissioner gave in to pressure, pressure of the media," he said.[17]

Once the reality of the ban set in, Steinbrenner complained about "lack of due process" and an unfair sentence. Vincent replied, "Other than Saddam Hussein, I can't think of anyone I would rather have making these complaints."[18] It is safe to say that this comment did not play well either in the offices in Yankee Stadium or at the Steinbrenner household in Tampa.

In May 1992, Steinbrenner met with Vincent and asked to reassume active control of the Yankees. His banishment from baseball had lasted for almost the full two years Vincent had originally intended, since August 20, 1990. Vincent was expected to announce Steinbrenner's reinstatement in mid-June, but he delayed the decision after someone informed the commissioner's office that Steinbrenner had violated the terms of the ban on running the Yankees. An unnamed person alleged that Steinbrenner had made contact with members of the Yankees organization. Vincent called General Manager Gene Michael and Manager Stump Merrill to his office to query them about these allegations. That investigation was concluded when Merrill and Michael both testified that they had had no contact with Steinbrenner and had no direct knowledge of anyone else's contact with him. Not finding anything substantive, Vincent approved and announced Steinbrenner's return, which was scheduled for March 1, 1993.

Although Steinbrenner had few staunch allies among the owners, Vincent's handling of the Spira case not only alienated New York but also planted concerns about due process in other owners' minds. Vincent had acted to put the perceived "best interests of baseball" ahead of the best interests of a powerful owner. Did the Steinbrenner affair help undermine Vincent? Vincent later said, "I'm sure it did. I was having an awful lot of trouble on various fronts and I don't think it helped. I think Selig and Reinsdorf and others were way ahead of me. I didn't realize they were trying to push me out. I knew they were trying to cause trouble. It never occurred to me that Selig wanted to be commissioner."[19]

Vincent in the Middle of a League Dispute—Splitting Expansion Fees

After the National League agreed to expand for the 1993 season, the matter of divvying up the $190 million in franchise fees emerged as a major issue and was made more difficult because of the financial pressures mounting on the owners from a pending decline in television revenue as well as the collusion penalties. Up through the most recent expansion in 1977 in the American League, expansion revenue had previously stayed within the league, but earlier sums were diminutive compared with the 1991 total. The American League wanted what it considered an equitable piece of the pie, around 50 percent.

Giles, a member of the National League Expansion Committee, said that sharing expansion money with the American League was out and was nonnegotiable as far as he was concerned. He said, "We don't think they should get any. There's no rationale for it at all. We feel strongly as a group that it should be done as in the past. It's never been split before." Observing the lack of consensus on the issue, Vincent said, "They're meeting and I hope they can resolve it. It's been agreed that if it can't be resolved, it will come to me. I'm just quite hopeful that it doesn't come to me."[20]

Owners from the two leagues could not come to an agreement, and the matter came before the commissioner. Vincent said that he would make a binding ruling before the expansion process began. Vincent said, "People have painted this as a crisis, but I'm not really concerned about it being a problem. Maybe I'm naive. It's just money. There's nothing particularly complicated about it." When it was pointed out to him, though, that possibly twelve owners in the National League or fourteen owners in the American League wouldn't be happy with the decision, Vincent disagreed. "Twenty-six is more like it," he said.[21]

According to Zimbalist in *Baseball and Billions*:

> Vincent opted for a compromise, giving the AL teams 22 percent of the money but requiring them to provide players in the expansion draft. His middle-of-the-road solution, as he predicted, pleased no one. Twins' owner Carl Pohlad stated, "I haven't spoken to anyone who thinks it's a good decision." Jerry Reinsdorf affirmed the AL owners' point of view: "The commissioner made an incorrect decision; it should have been a 50–50 split."[22]

Bud Selig said, "I know that not everybody is happy about this decision."[23] Vincent reacted with some humor, saying, "I told George Bush [owner of the Texas Rangers at the time] that if he didn't stop yelling at me, I was going to tell his mother." Responded Bush, "That's the worst thing he could do."[24] Another unnamed owner was more threatening: "That's it. Fay Vincent is history. Every American League owner I've talked to . . . has serious doubts about reviewing Vincent's contract."[25]

Vincent had been put into a basically impossible position. His comment about making twenty-six owners unhappy was prescient. And his concern about the fallout from the decision, at such a difficult time in the baseball industry, was real. He admonished the owners of both leagues:

> I regret that this decision could, and perhaps will, damage the relationship between the leagues. One of my principal concerns as commissioner is the trend within ownership toward greater disunity. I am disturbed at the apparent unwillingness of some within baseball to rise above parochial interests and to think in terms of the greater good of the game. The squabbling with baseball, the finger-pointing, the tendency to see economic issues as moral ones . . . all of these are contributing to our joint fall from grace. If we in baseball seek the respect and loyalty of the fans who are the true owners of the game, we must be deserving in our actions. I suggest we start now.[26]

But more damage had been done in terms of Vincent's standing among the owners.

The Trouble with the Mariners

Jeff Smulyan and Michael Browning purchased the Seattle Mariners in August 1989 for $76 million from previous owner George Argyros. Smulyan, head of an Indianapolis-based media company, had taken out loans to finance the purchase. The Mariners had struggled both on the field and at the gate after they joined the American League as an expansion franchise in 1977. Smulyan thought he could make baseball successful in Seattle, but he walked into an unexpectedly difficult fiscal situation. First, the owners were on the hook for $280 million in collusion damages, $10.7 per club, which was roughly eleven times the $1 million assessment that Smulyan had estimated when he bought the team. Second, he bought the team right at the end of the collusion period, just when the free agent market reopened and salaries jumped dramatically. The Mariners' payroll was $8 million when he bought the team. Two years later, it was $23 million. In those two years, attendance had increased from 1.3 million to nearly 2.2 million, and in 1991, the Mariners finally had a winning season—after fourteen years of trying. But total revenues were far below the American League average.[27]

Facing a difficult financial situation, Smulyan announced on December 10, 1992, that the Mariners were for sale at an asking price of $100 million. Smulyan had a deal with the city that if the club's attendance and revenues didn't exceed a specific threshold, he could put the club up for sale, and if a local buyer was not found in 120 days, he could sell the club to owners in another city. The members of the Seattle business community had the impression that Smulyan did not expect a local buyer to come forward and that he therefore would sell the club to new owners who would take the club to the Tampa Bay area to play in the empty Suncoast Dome in St. Petersburg.

Washington State Attorney General Slade Gorton had filed a lawsuit that pressured the American League to award an expansion franchise to Seattle in the wake of the abandonment of the city by the ill-fated Seattle Pilots after their unsuccessful inaugural season in 1969. By 1992 Gorton was a member of the U.S. Senate, and he did not want the Mariners to get away. He started a campaign to locate buyers in the Seattle area. Minoru Arakawa, who had lived in Seattle for fifteen years, was president of Redmond-based Nintendo of North America. Arakawa told his father-in-law, Hiroshi Yamauchi, president of Nintendo in Japan, about the Mariners situation. Yamauchi offered to put up the entire $100 million, not because he cared about baseball—he didn't—but to thank the community for contributing to Nintendo's success as the world leader in video game production.[28]

Gorton correctly anticipated that a prospective owner from a foreign country would have trouble gaining Major League Baseball approval unless local people were involved. Gorton helped put together a group that included several Seattle business executives who represented key area companies, including Microsoft, McCaw Cellular Communications, Boeing, and Puget Power & Light Company. The group called itself the Baseball Club of Seattle and decided to offer $100 million for the team, plus $25 million in operating expenses to come from Yamauchi, whose portion of the purchase price dropped to $75 million. John Ellis, retiring CEO of Puget Power & Light, was picked to lead the group's effort to gain baseball's approval. As part of the deal, Ellis would acquire a small ownership interest. The Yamauchi offer presented baseball with a paradox: a strong local ownership group backed by foreign money.[29]

When the plan was first proposed, Vincent said that it would be "difficult" for the proposed sale of the team to be approved because the ownership committee had endorsed a resolution against foreign ownership. The committee presented the resolution to the other owners at the winter meetings in early December; however, no formal vote on the matter was taken. Vincent stood behind what he said was baseball's policy against selling franchises to non–North American ownership groups. He said that non–North American owners could create legal and logistical problems if they wanted to change the way baseball does business.

After a meeting with state and local officials in Seattle, Vincent said, "There is a policy, and there are principles. In light of those principles, it is my judgment that a transaction of this sort would not be approved. . . . We have thought about [foreign ownership] and we have found it difficult. The real concern was not for the game of baseball. It goes to the issue of the preference within the ownership of baseball, a strong preference, I think, for local ownership." Vincent did acknowledge, however, that Arakawa's longtime Seattle residence seemed to contradict the spirit of the resolution.[30]

As someone who did not hesitate to let people know his positions on issues, Bill Giles made some comments that were welcome in Seattle when he expressed an apparent change of heart on the issue. Giles, who at first declared staunch opposition to the planned sale, saying, "It's a patriotic issue for me," later said that he would vote to approve the bid if it is the only way to keep the Mariners in Seattle.[31]

To make the proposal more acceptable to major league baseball, the structure of the deal was altered. Originally, Yamauchi was to invest $75 million of the $125 million needed to buy and operate the team, giving him a 60 percent share, with the rest coming from the American investors. The offer was revised so that more of Yamauchi's money was devoted to operating capital, reducing his stake to less than 50 percent. The next biggest investors were Chris Lawson from Microsoft, at $27.5 million, and John McCaw, Jr., at $11.25 million. John Ellis indicated that the proposal included restrictions on the Japanese investors' rights to vote or sell their shares in the franchise and further increased American control of the Mariners. Yamauchi would act essentially as a silent partner. As a result of these changes that guaranteed that control of the club would rest in the hands of local people, baseball's owners approved the deal.[32]

Total authority was clearly the key, said Fred Kuhlmann of St. Louis, chairman of the ownership committee. "We had two principal goals, and both were accomplished as a result of our negotiations with the Seattle people. John Ellis has the kind of powers that any individual owner would have—to borrow money, change lease terms, find ways to raise additional revenues and establish [a] budget. That's a rather important power that should be lodged in one person."[33]

The commissioner faced heavy criticism for his early handling of the sale. He said early on that the owners' policy banned "off-shore" investors. Vincent thought that he had the twenty-six owners firmly behind him when he took the anti-Nintendo position, but according to Thomas Boswell, as soon as Vincent received criticism in the media for his perceived behavior as a Japan-basher, baseball's owners suddenly became silent.[34] John Ellis recalls the situation as it happened twenty years ago and said that he attributed the criticism of Vincent to a public relations campaign designed to create sympathy and public support for the group that wanted to purchase the club and keep it in Seattle. As a result, the campaign took on a "baseball versus Japan" theme. Given the amount of U.S. real estate being bought by Japanese interests during this period, this was not surprising. Ellis also stated that during the process, on all of the approximately six occasions when Ellis dealt directly with the commissioner, Vincent was invariably "nice and cooperative," although his position on the deal was neutral.[35]

Later, Vincent endorsed and encouraged the deal after the Japanese investors reduced their stake to less than 50 percent and agreed to allow a U.S. partner to operate the club. Even after the deal was approved, Vincent took some hits. "Vincent engineered a racist deal that permits Japanese to own, but not control, the Seattle Mariners," wrote *USA Today* founder Al Neuharth, echoing an opinion held by other newspaper columnists.[36]

[*Note:* In his interview, Ellis reported that after the deal was finally approved on July 1, 1992, he attended his first owners' meeting. Jerry

Reinsdorf was to introduce Ellis to the assembled group where, according to Ellis, they would applaud him, "probably for the last time." Reinsdorf walked with Ellis on the way to the meeting and remarked to him that they were planning to force the commissioner out that day. Ellis said that, since he had been concentrating on pulling together the deal to acquire the Mariners, going into the meeting, he had absolutely no inkling that Vincent was under such fire from the owners. He said that the meeting was both memorable and uncomfortable.]

Vincent Takes a Stand against the Superstations

Bill Giles long admired Ted Turner's vision and innovative ideas about televised sports. Turner created a new model for televised sports, the superstation. Turner was a visionary, turning his local Channel 17 in Atlanta into the first superstation by bouncing the signal off satellites and thus exporting his programming to cable markets throughout the United States. At first, there were no provisions to limit this incursion into local markets. The Tribune Company, owners of WGN, jumped on board and made WGN a superstation, giving Cubs' announcer Harry Caray a voice all over America, finally making him a national figure late in his broadcasting career. Similarly, WPIX (Yankee telecasts) and WOR (Mets) in New York became superstations. For a long time, depending on the local cable operator, people in areas throughout the United States could get Braves games, Cubs games, Yankees games, and Mets games in their local markets, along with the games of their local team. Clearly, the competition from these superstation telecasts could lower ratings for the local telecasts and in turn lower advertising rates and ultimately rights fees for the teams.

Giles helped broker a deal that led to agreements between the superstations and major league baseball by which the superstations would make payments to baseball's central fund as a way of reducing the negative financial impact of competing with individual teams' local telecasts. As a result, baseball had a copyright agreement with superstations that generated millions of dollars for the central fund, most of it coming from TBS and WGN.

Fay Vincent decided to go one step further and seek repeal of the compulsory license granted by Congress that lets cable channels pick games off the satellite without teams' permission and without direct compensation. His goal was to limit out-of-town games to counter the effect of superstation programming into local markets. He also wanted to help ESPN obtain larger audiences for its baseball telecasts and offset some of the losses it had experienced on its MLB contract in the early 1990s. Vincent's goal was to force the superstations to raise their annual payments.

According to Burk, "The commissioner intended to force the superstations to accept a new industry policy blacking out games when they conflicted with a local club's telecasts. But the superstations used their lobbying clout to kill the plan in Congress, a result that effectively wedded a hatred of Vincent for his failed gambit to emboldenment at his political weakness."[37] As a result, the commissioner had created more doubts about his performance and more enemies among the owners.

In response to Vincent's attempt to limit the superstations, Giles said:

> The superstations have been good for baseball. Since the superstations started broadcasting games several years ago, more people have been watching games on cable, and at the same time attendance at the parks has risen. The superstations are also providing about fifty million dollars to the central fund each year. Are we going to be able to replace that from our other television partners? I don't think so. Also, aren't we better off handling these problems ourselves and not getting the government involved?[38]

The Player Relations Committee Moves to Remove Vincent from Labor Relations

The CBA that was negotiated in 1990 ended after the 1993 season. The owners began preparing for the new round of labor negotiations early. In 1991, they hired Richard Ravitch as lead negotiator for the Player Relations Committee, which was chaired at the time by Bud Selig. Ravitch was experienced in dealing with unions, having served as head of the New York Transit Authority. He was given a salary of $750,000, which happened to be $100,000 more than Vincent's salary. This certainly was not a good sign for the commissioner and was a blow to his ego.

Most owners wanted Vincent to stay out of the new labor negotiations. Several powerful owners believed that Vincent's involvement during the 1990 lockout led to an agreement that was more favorable to the players. The owners agreed with a position that Ravitch took—that if Vincent stepped in and forced the owners' hands to avoid a work stoppage, the owners had lost their leverage. Ravitch, working through Selig, attempted to guarantee an unfettered hand by asking Vincent not to interfere in the upcoming negotiations. Vincent refused, citing "clear, irrevocable language in the Major League Agreement stating that the commissioner's powers could not be diminished while he was in office."[39]

Vincent did agree to three conditions: first, he would not independently discuss bargaining issues with the leaders of the Players Association; second, he would not comment to the media on matters related to collective bargaining; and, third, he would stay out of any labor action (i.e., a lockout) by the owners. However, at the June 1992 meeting of the Player Relations Committee, Vincent claimed that these conditions did not preclude his involvement in labor issues and bargaining. Vincent believed that the chief executive officer of any organization had the duty to be involved in such critical issues as labor deals.[40]

As the economic situation in baseball worsened, owners' dissatisfaction with their commissioner deepened. At an owners' meeting in Chicago on September 3, 1992, Doug Danforth of the Pirates, who turned out to one of Vincent's least favorite owners,[41] expressed the sentiment of the anti-Vincent owners:

> I personally have no confidence in Fay's leadership. Players' salaries are too high; clubs are on the verge of collapse; and there's no planning. Media leaks come out of his office, and he's intervened in areas he had no business getting involved in. The commissioner is the leader. He has to take the blame for how bad things are. Baseball cannot move forward under his leadership. The office is in disarray and he is not able to build consensus among owners.[42]

The owners who were leading the charge to eliminate the commissioner from labor negotiations, Jerry Reinsdorf and Bud Selig, proposed a change in the Major League Agreement that would accomplish their objective. The effort clearly indicated that some owners intended to take a hard line in negotiations with the union. This ran counter to Vincent's perspective. From the beginning of his term, the commissioner had chosen a more conciliatory approach, believing that improved relations with the union are necessary for the "best interests of baseball."

According to the Major League Agreement that was in place at the time, no change in the commissioner's powers could be made during a commissioner's term without his approval, and Vincent sternly rejected the proposal. Article IX stipulated that "no diminution of the compensation or the powers of the present or any succeeding commissioner shall be made during his term of office."[43] Vincent said, "I obviously made clear that I have no intention of changing my authority under the Major League Agreement. . . . I've said many times I know my role, but I also know under the Major League Agreement I have authority and I am not going to surrender it during my commissionership."[44] Vincent also said, "I understand there is concern the commissioner, whoever he is, will do something out of the blue like a bolt of lightning in the night and that could disrupt an orderly, seriously managed labor negotiation. I can tell you, as I can tell owners, I do not function that way."[45]

After a speech to the owners about the issue, Vincent had apparently turned the tide in his favor. He did have supporters among the owners, including Fred Wilpon of the Mets and George W. Bush of the Rangers. Giles, who always tended to take a positive view, said after Vincent's presentation, "I thought it was an excellent speech. He got a nice ovation. I thought it was very well received. I know I appreciated it."[46]

But the problem was far from solved. Jack Sands and Peter Gammons reported what happened:

> The next day, two story lines emerged [in the press]. The first was that Vincent had survived a surprise coup and was now in total control. The other was that Vincent had somehow saved the game for 1993. While some owners were furious, others could only laugh. "I kept wondering if I had been at the same meetings I read about," one owner said.[47]

The rift between commissioner and the owners had grown wider than Vincent was willing to admit. Between twenty-two and twenty-five owners had backed the Player Relations Committee's recommendation to keep Vincent out of the labor process. The next day, Vincent addressed the owners and his approach was more conciliatory, indicating that he understood that the Player Relations Committee had a job to do and that Ravitch would be handling the negotiations in which Vincent would not interfere. The owners came away with the impression that the one voice speaking for them in the negotiations would be that of Ravitch.

Unfortunately, after the meeting, Vincent made a tactical error when he summoned Hal Bodley of *USA Today* plus Murray Chass and Claire Smith of the *New York Times* to meet with him. He gave the writers his spin on both the meeting and the owners' reaction. He told the assembled reporters that he had held a meeting with the owners at which "I made it clear that I have no intention of changing my authority under the Major League Agreement."[48] The stories that followed claimed that Vincent had reasserted his authority and that "one owner after another approached Vincent, shook his hand, and congratulated him on his leadership of the past ten days."[49]

Bill Giles was incredulous at the reports. He said:

> That was a private dinner. Bodley wasn't there and I sure don't remember a row of owners coming up to the commissioner and

> congratulating him. As a matter of fact, the events that occurred that week were about a hundred eighty degrees different than what was reported. Except for two or three clubs, we all came away convinced more than ever that the commissioner has to be removed from the upcoming player negotiations.[50]

This episode solidified the strong majority of owners who were against the commissioner. His support was getting very thin.

The Steve Howe Issue

During mid-1992, the hits just kept on coming for the beleaguered commissioner. No one—except the Players Association—could argue with the notion that Vincent had the right and the authority to take a strong stand against player involvement in drugs and, like Ueberroth, Vincent did so. During his tenure, he suspended multiple players who were found to have been involved with illegal drugs. The last case proved to be one more controversy on the growing list of issues that ultimately sank Fay Vincent.

Steve Howe was a talented left-handed pitcher with a cocaine addiction. Before 1992, he had been suspended from baseball six times, starting when Bowie Kuhn was commissioner. In the latest incident, Howe had pleaded guilty to a charge of attempting to possess cocaine. On June 8, 1992, Vincent announced that he intended to suspend Howe "indefinitely." The Players Association filed a grievance. Arbitrator George Nicolau told Vincent that he needed to be more definite regarding the meaning of "indefinite," so Vincent changed the penalty to a permanent ban, making Howe the first player in history to be banned from baseball for a drug violation.

The Players Association immediately filed another grievance to reinstate Howe, which led to a hearing before the arbitrator, who called several witnesses, including Yankees manager Buck Showalter, general manager Gene Michael, and another front office person, Vice President Jack Lawn. All three testified that they would have preferred to have Steve Howe playing for the Yankees because he was a terrific competitor. The trouble started when baseball's lawyers, assigned by the commissioner and not the Player Relations Committee, as was the norm, cross-examined the three Yankees officials and got them to say that they felt that the punishment for Howe was too harsh under the circumstances. Their remarks were what one would have expected, given their roles, and none of the witnesses made a direct criticism of baseball's drug policy.

When Steve Greenberg reported back to Vincent about the hearing, Vincent became enraged and summoned the three to his office in midtown Manhattan the next day at 11:00 A.M., two hours before a scheduled Yankees home game. He lambasted the three because they had not stood forcefully behind baseball's drug policy and Vincent's decision to give Howe the lifetime banishment from baseball. The commissioner told the three that they were risking suspension from baseball for testifying against baseball's drug policy. According to one source, the commissioner used three phrases to emphasize his anger: "You've effectively resigned from baseball. . . . You've quit the game. . . . You're out of baseball."[51]

This time, the Players Association reacted and filed a charge with the National Labor Relations Board accusing Vincent of using his office to intimidate witnesses against testifying on behalf of the Players Association. The Players Association also filed another grievance with Nicolau. The focus of the case had shifted. Now the issue was the commissioner's actions against the three Yankees, not the merits of the decision to suspend Howe.

Vincent realized that he had overstepped this time, and he sent a memo to the owners saying that he would be more careful about involving himself in grievance hearings, but the damage was done. Vincent was the object of intense criticism and ridicule in the New York tabloids, and several columnists called on him to quit. The owners' wish to remove Vincent from office was about to come true.

Poking a Hornets' Nest—Moving the Cubs West

With both leagues preparing for expansion from ten to twelve teams in 1969, baseball decided to split both the National League and the American League into two six-team divisions. The Chicago Cubs consented to the split on the condition that they would play in the Eastern Division because of travel and game times and to preserve existing rivalries. And that is where the Cubs preferred to stay when the National League considered realignment in the early 1990s. With a new expansion about to take place, the time seemed right to align the divisions according to a logical geographical split. The idea was to take Atlanta and Cincinnati from the West to the East and to take the Cubs and the St. Louis Cardinals from the East to the West. Logical. The NL owners supported the realignment plan proposed by National League President Bill White by a vote of 10–2. The National League Constitution allowed one team to veto a plan for realignment, and the Cubs vetoed the plan.

Some of the owners who wanted the switch then petitioned Commissioner Vincent to step in. Vincent used his broad "best interests of baseball" powers to force realignment, ordering the Cubs and their longtime rivals, the Cardinals, to move to the National League's Western Division.

By taking this action, Vincent had in effect poked a hornets' nest with a stick.

The Tribune Company owned WGN (television and radio) and the Cubs. Stanton Cook, president of the Cubs, decided that it was better to sue than to switch. The Chicago Cubs filed a federal lawsuit in Illinois against the commissioner, charging that he illegally exceeded his authority by transferring the club from the Eastern Division to the Western Division. The suit branded Vincent's controversial Monday decision as "arbitrary and capricious" and said that it would result in "irreparable harm" to the Cubs and other National League teams.[52]

Meanwhile, both National League President Bill White and some of the owners expressed their displeasure at what they considered to be the commissioner's meddling in affairs that rightfully belonged to the league president and the owners. Los Angeles owner Peter O'Malley issued the most critical statement, saying:

> The Dodgers believe that the commissioner had exceeded his authority under the Major League Agreement by attempting to revoke what is, in effect, a business decision made by the National League clubs in accordance with the National League constitution. The Cubs have been in the Eastern Division since 1969. This alignment did not result from any "act, transaction or practice" that can be sanctioned by the commissioner pursuant to Article I of the Major League Agreement. This alignment was established by the National League clubs. Therefore, even though the Dodgers voted in favor of realignment and have traditionally been supportive of the office of the commissioner, the Dodgers do not concur with the commissioner's decision in this instance because it undermines the National League constitution. This decision could establish a dangerous precedent for the future of both the National and American Leagues.[53]

The Cubs, in an effort to forestall a move to the Western Division, had earlier suggested to Vincent that the National League be reformatted into three divisions. The Cubs strongly urged the commissioner to study the plan, knowing that it would take a year of analysis and discussion. While the process played out, the status quo would be maintained through the 1993 season. "The difficulty with it is that the decision would affect [national] television arrangements," Vincent said. "The idea of a wild card did not interest the networks."[54] Of course, after Vincent left office, three divisions is exactly the league structure that emerged.

In discussing these events, Bill Giles commented on the plan for realignment that embroiled Fay Vincent in yet another controversy, noting, "I was in favor of the realignment. I always thought the Cubs and Cardinals ought to be in the same division. It turned out to be a time zone issue for television reasons. Atlanta and Cincinnati are better for us, because both cities are in the Eastern Time Zone, from a television standpoint. So I was in favor of both the original plan for realignment and the way it eventually worked out [with three divisions]."[55]

The commissioner was trying to do what seemed right and appropriate and was consistent with the wishes of ten of twelve clubs in the National League. He made a decision, but it created discontent. Once again, he had gone against the interests of a powerful ball club. Too many issues had created too much discontent among the owners, many of whom increasingly had come to believe that the commissioner had to go.

Pressure Builds on the Commissioner

Mark Maske described the worsening environment in baseball on July 12, 1992, in the middle of the swirl of controversy surrounding Fay Vincent:

> Vincent has come under fire on virtually all fronts of late. He's been in the middle of the ongoing Steve Howe and George Steinbrenner controversies. He's drawn enraged responses for calling a trio of New York Yankees officials to his office two hours before an afternoon game to allegedly admonish them for testifying on Howe's behalf at the suspended pitcher's grievance hearing. And he's been assailed, not to mention sued, for overruling the [National League] bylaws to order realignment despite the Cubs' veto. These battles reflect the owners' growing dissatisfaction with Vincent. A petition calling for his resignation has circulated among them.[56]

Yet the bottom-line issue, as always, was money. One owner expressed this concern by saying, "There's enormous dissatisfaction and unhappiness among some owners caused by economics. As our industry continues to sink, there is a perception that Fay should be coming up with programs and ideas to alleviate the bad economic position we're in."[57]

In particular, the majority of owners were concerned about Vincent's possible role in labor negotiations with the players. These owners favored a hard-line approach. They considered Vincent too soft on the players' union during the 1990 negotiations. They were concerned that if the owners tried another lockout, he would likely order training camps reopened and thus hurt the owners' bargaining power. Vincent took a contrary position, saying:

> This is mostly a function of desperation. The owners are losing money and they're having trouble confronting the fact that they're the problem. They look for other people. They want to blame the union. They want to blame the commissioner. They'll blame anybody. The main reason clubs are losing money is because owners have made decisions and commitments [signing players] that exceed their resources. This is a business. And ownership has to decide whether they're going to be in business or in a hobby. Some are in a hobby.[58]

The commissioner, expressing his independence, also said, "I'm financially secure. I don't have to do this for a living. Any time I don't want to do it I can get on a plane and go to London and smoke some good cigars."[59]

One owner expressed some sympathy for the commissioner, noting, "It's really become a thankless job, with the current state of the game. He can't satisfy everyone, and lately it seems like he can't satisfy anyone. Even with the realignment decision—I mean, everyone but the Cubs wanted it. He orders it, and then he still gets criticized by half the league. . . . I certainly would not want that job, not in a thousand years."[60] One of the Vincent supporters said, "I don't quite understand the venomous feelings involved in this thing because it's not justified. Is the commissioner perfect? Of course he's not. But neither are the owners. You can't expect him to win a popularity contest."[61]

Newspaper reports late in the summer of 1992 indicated that it was unclear how many owners supported Vincent versus how many opposed him. The number of owners calling for the commissioner's ouster differed depending on whether the tally was reported by a Vincent supporter or a Vincent opponent. O'Malley and Giles said that they believed a majority of clubs no longer supported the commissioner.[62]

Expressing the viewpoint of the majority of owners at the time, Giles said, "I just feel we have so many critical issues facing us because people don't have confidence in him anymore. I don't think it's healthy for the industry and that it's in the best interests of baseball that he remains as commissioner."[63] Furthermore, he commented, "We have some difficult economic issues to deal with over the next few years, namely TV and player compensation. Due to that, the majority of clubs have lost confidence in the commissioner."[64] Though Giles said that he agreed with Vincent on "many" issues, he also said, "I think baseball is best served if he would resign."[65]

Regarding the "gold watch" labor issue, Giles said, "I feel it's better for a future commissioner to stay out of labor relations. It's better for him personally, better for the office, to let three quarters of the owners make decisions as far as the compensation system is concerned."[66] Giles stressed that, for the next labor agreement, he wanted a fair, reasonable, and collusion-free plan, saying, "Historically, commissioners have been put in tough positions. If there is a work stoppage this spring or the spring after that, the commissioner is in a difficult position. Therefore, it's best to stay out of the labor process. Media, fans and some owners have pressed commissioners to make decisions contrary to the wishes of a majority of owners."[67]

Summarizing his perspective, Giles said, "I don't feel any commissioner should overrule the voting process, unless it involves the integrity of the game. The voting process is set up for business decisions. I don't like to see any commissioner overrule voting procedures and I don't believe he should try to make unilateral, dictatorial decisions."[68]

Vincent Resigns

The issue came to a head when the league presidents called a special meeting of the owners on September 3, 1992, to discuss the commissioner's status. Bill White had asked Vincent for a meeting on August 17, but the commissioner had refused the request, saying that the purpose of the session would be "unlawful and contrary to the Major League Agreement."[69] The commissioner also sent a five-page letter to owners in which he vowed never to resign and to fight any effort to remove him in court. The letter said:

> Even if there is a meeting and a vote to remove me from office or an attempt to limit my powers, all in contravention of the Major League Agreement and my employment agreement, I will not leave. I will continue to carry out my responsibilities until such time as the highest court of this land tells me otherwise. I have concluded that any action to terminate is unlawful and I will oppose with extraordinary zeal any effort to harm the office of the commissioner.[70]

Article V, Section 3, of the agreement allowed the league presidents to call such a meeting if the commissioner did not, and so National League President Bill White called the meeting. As the day of reckoning approached, opponents of Vincent backed away from the original plan to fire Vincent. The goal switched to putting enough pressure on the commissioner to convince him to resign. Giles said that the anti-Vincent owners would attempt to build enough of a coalition so that Vincent would bow to the wishes of a majority of owners and resign. "If we tried to fire him, there would be some legal problems. I don't think they have the stomachs to do more than tell him a number of owners have no confidence in him and wish him to resign."[71]

Giles and Doug Myers wrote in *Pouring Six Beers at a Time* that Selig, Reinsdorf, O'Malley, and Cook "started a coup to oust Vincent from the commissioner's post. Selig and Reinsdorf worked the phones to find out which owners favored dumping the commissioner." At the owners' meeting of September 3, 1992, the agenda focused on Vincent's future. Giles recalls that the "conspirators" arranged the seating to put an anti-Vincent owner next to any owner who was on the fence so that they could persuade enough owners to join the coup.[72]

In the absence of the commissioner, who refused to attend a meeting he considered illegal, Toronto president Paul Beeston chaired the meeting. Doug Danforth of the Pirates introduced the resolution:

> The major league clubs do not have confidence in the ability of the present commissioner, Fay Vincent, to carry out the responsibilities of the office of the commissioner, and that under his direction it is impossible for baseball to move forward effectively and constructively.
>
> Those clubs voting in favor of this resolution will not vote in favor of the re-election of Commissioner Fay Vincent to another term of office when such matter is presented to the major league clubs for vote.
>
> [It is] further resolved, that Commissioner Fay Vincent be requested to resign effective immediately and that the commissioner be offered in the event of his immediate resignation a severance agreement consistent with his employment agreement of Dec. 13, 1989.[73]

The plan worked, and the owners voted 18–9–1 (Marge Schott left the meeting early and abstained) to call for Vincent's resignation. Giles voted with the majority.

Vincent's first response to the owners' action was one of defiance. He released a statement that said, in part, "In my letter of Aug. 20, 1992, I informed the owners that I would not resign and I affirm that decision today. I believe strongly that a baseball commissioner should serve a full term as contemplated by the Major League Agreement."[74] But after a weekend at his summer home in Cape Cod, he decided to give up the fight. He sent the owners a letter of resignation that expressed his feelings:

> A fight based solely on principle does not justify the disruption when there is not greater support among the ownership for my views. While I would receive personal gratification by demonstrating that the legal position set out in my August 20 letter is correct, litigation does nothing to address the serious problems of baseball. I cannot govern as commissioner without the consent of owners to be governed. I do not believe that consent is now available to me. Simply put, I've concluded resignation—not litigation—should be my final act as Commissioner "in the best interests" of Baseball.
>
> I can only hope owners will realize that a strong Commissioner, a person of experience and stature in the community, is integral to baseball. I hope they learn this lesson before too much damage is done to the game, to the players, umpires and others who work in the game, and most importantly, to the fans.[75]

One baseball executive said, "I think Fay's friends finally got to him and convinced him that he didn't need this kind of aggravation. They advised him to get out and let someone else deal with the enormous task ahead of trying to restore fiscal sanity to the game without damaging it in the near and distant future."[76]

Giles expressed his relief at the news:

> I personally am relieved. I'm happy that he did resign. It was in the best interest of baseball that he did. He didn't have the confidence of ownership. I think baseball can go on from here. We have some economic problems that we have to solve in the next 12 to 18 months and it is most critical that we get a man in the commissioner's position that we have confidence in, and that we go forward in a positive way. We immediately have to restructure baseball, not only the responsibility of the commissioner's office but the league presidents also. In my opinion, the league presidents should have more responsibility, have more to do that affects baseball in a more positive way.[77]

Giles said that it was important to have a new commissioner in office by mid-November 1992 because of major issues that were approaching, including negotiations for a new national television package.

The next decision that the owners made turned out to be crucial: to let the Executive Council of twelve owners run the commissioner's office until a new commissioner could be found. The owners named Selig president of the council and voted Giles in as a member. Now the owners had what many wanted: a CEO type of leader who would advocate for the owners' economic interests as well as "the best interests of baseball."

In Summary: Why Fay Vincent's Tenure as Commissioner Came to an Early End

As commissioner of baseball, Fay Vincent may have been the right person, but for his style of governing, it was clearly the wrong time. Baseball was on the verge of a sea change, and Vincent marked the end of an era in which the commissioner could operate as an independent voice in MLB. As he stated, "Guys like me tried to be independent but we ran into trouble because of it."[78] Only a commissioner whose primary concern focused on the economic interests of the owners could have succeeded during the late 1980s and early 1990s. Clearly, in retrospect, that is why Bud Selig—an owner who understood issues from an owner's point of view—was able to oversee a period of prosperity unprecedented in the history of baseball and has now served as commissioner (1992–2014) longer than anyone except Landis (1920–1944).

But clearly other factors were at play in Vincent's forced resignation, including his style of governing. One lawyer involved in baseball said that many in the game viewed Vincent as "too haughty, too dictatorial, he doesn't know his place, he's arbitrary, he's too big for his britches, he doesn't know who he works for."[79] Helyar had good reason to title his book on the business of baseball *Lords of the Realm.*

One way of characterizing Fay Vincent's decision-making style is to say that he was independent. Another way is to say that he didn't want anyone telling him what to do. Bill Giles said that his impression of Vincent's thought process was along the lines of this: "I am the commissioner. I am smarter than you are and I am going to do it my way, come hell or high water." Giles also says of the owners' move to oust Vincent, "I think it was a culmination of various things. Almost anything he did upset somebody. When you upset as many people as he did with various decisions, he is not going to last very long."[80]

At the beginning of the chapter, I discuss how Vincent's perception of the appropriate role of the commissioner diverged from that of many of the owners, particularly those in small markets, owners who were at an economic disadvantage, who were struggling to succeed financially as salaries skyrocketed and the disparity in revenue between large-market and small-market teams increased. In discussing the Vincent situation twenty years after the fact, Giles said of the role of the commissioner:

> The players are baseball; the players are the people that people pay money to see play. I would argue, if I was commissioner, that I should have some control over players, but the union does not look at it that way and I understand why. I was always in favor of a two-headed monster: the commissioner, who would look out for the game in general and the popularity of the game, and then the Chairman of the Executive Council, who would be kind of the [chief operating officer] and would handle all of the business of the game, like realignment and so forth. I always believed that. Looking back at it, I am not sure it could have worked very well, but I argued for that many times in meetings.
>
> My job, and this is Selig talking, is to make the franchise values go up; that was his main goal. And he has. I bought the Phillies for $31 million [in 1981], and if we put the club up for sale [in 2012], we would probably get over $1 billion for it.[81]

5

Era of Unrest

The Strike of 1994 and the 1996 Collective Bargaining Agreement

The Owners versus the Players Association, 1966–1990

Before the advent of free agency in 1976, the owners held the power in their economic relationship with the players. A few stories from the earlier annals of baseball speak to that power. In the early 1950s, future Hall of Famer and longtime Mets broadcaster Ralph Kiner regularly led the National League in home runs for the Pittsburgh Pirates and just as regularly had salary disputes with the famously penurious Branch Rickey, who had moved to Pittsburgh after selling his interest in the Dodgers. Rickey reportedly dismissed Kiner's protests about salary cuts, saying, "We finished in last place with you; we can finish in last place without you."[1] In 1957, Mickey Mantle hit .365 with thirty-four home runs and ninety-four RBI, but didn't win the Triple Crown as he had done in 1956. Mantle won his second consecutive Most Valuable Player Award in 1957, finishing ahead of Ted Williams, who hit .388. George Weiss cut Mantle's salary by $17,000, saying, "It's what you're worth."[2] The next year, Phillies center fielder Richie Ashburn, another future Hall of Famer, won the 1958 National League batting championship, after which John Quinn, Philadelphia's general manager, offered him less money, saying that his singles did not go far enough. To that Ashburn replied, "Well, if I hit them any farther, they'd be outs."[3]

Background

That power began to even out—and labor issues began to emerge—when Marvin Miller became executive director of the Players Association in 1966 and negotiated baseball's first collective bargaining agreement in

1968. The owners and players reached a second labor agreement in 1970. In 1972, the owners decided to battle with the players over pension issues; the players staged their first-ever strike as a result. Beginning in 1972, each time a CBA ended, there was either a lockout by the owners or a strike by the players before an agreement was reached, for a total of seven labor stoppages in all through spring 1990.

The balance of power swung significantly when Peter Seitz found for the players in the Messersmith-McNally grievance in December 1975, thereby establishing the free agent system. The owners locked the players out of training camp in 1976 before agreeing on a plan for free agency in the new CBA. The first major strike took place in 1981 after the owners and players could not agree on compensation for free agents signed by other clubs. A two-day midseason strike in 1985 over the issue of pension contributions by the owners was settled quickly through the efforts of Lee MacPhail, on behalf of Peter Ueberroth, and as part of that deal the players ended up giving back service time for arbitration eligibility to the owners, going from a requirement of two years of service to three years.

Collusion

The owners' collective inability to restrain their spending on free agents, combined with the scolding that the owners received from Ueberroth about their profligate ways, spawned the collusion era, which extended from 1985 to 1988. Collusion had three major effects. The first was to put restraints on salary increases. Financial results for the 1989 major league season showed revenues of $1.2 billion, a 23 percent increase over the 1988 season. Operating expenses increased 16 percent for 1989, leaving record profits for the industry of $214 million, an average of $8.3 million per team. It was the sixth consecutive year that baseball operating profits had increased. Chuck O'Connor, head of the Player Relations Committee, tempered the news that baseball was doing very well overall by saying, "The difficulty is that they have to get below the aggregate figures to determine the health of the individual parts that make up the game, the 26 clubs. There, there's a different story. You can't look at the overall industry profits and say, 'Therefore my team in Pittsburgh is in great shape.'" O'Connor reported that four teams lost money in 1988, but that number would grow to nine once the bill for collusion came due.[4]

The second effect of collusion was that the owners were forced to pay damages amounting to $280 million for violating the anticollusion provision of the CBA. Baseball's 1990 season showed profits that had declined 33 percent to $142.9 million on record revenues of $1.34 billion. This decline did not include costs related to the collusion settlement. The disturbing news for the industry was that revenues had increased 7.7 percent while expenses had increased 16.2 percent. More disturbing was the news on player salaries, which increased 20.2 percent between 1989 and 1990 and another 32 percent in 1991. O'Connor said, "We've got to do something to bring the total salary bill into line with revenue growth. The bottom eight clubs are losing as much as the top eight are making."[5]

The third effect of collusion was a significant worsening of player-owner relationships due to the distrust and bitterness spawned by the owners' collusive behavior. When asked about the state of labor relations in the late 1980s, Bill Giles responded that they were "the worst ever."[6] By the end of the decade, the players' resentment and mistrust of the owners had solidified them. When the 1985 CBA ended in 1990, the union was in no mood for any more givebacks, while the owners sought to accomplish via a labor agreement what they could not through collusion, that is, restraining salaries. These conditions set the stage for the 1990 spring training lockout, which was ended, to several owners' chagrin, by Commissioner Vincent.

The story of labor relations from the mid-1970s until the end of the 1980s was a story of massive gains by the players. Salaries and payrolls took off in the wake of the availability of salary arbitration in 1973 and free agency in 1976. The collusion era put a brake on players' salary gains, but once collusion had ended, the owners went right back to their free-spending ways. Rapidly increasing salaries were one of the critical economic challenges facing the baseball industry; the other was the increasing disparity in revenues for individual franchises. These two issues fueled the labor wars as baseball entered the 1990s.

The 1990 Lockout and Settlement

The 1990 lockout occurred because owners realized that control of runaway salary growth was an economic necessity. The owners could not make any agreement to restrain their offers for free agents—alleged collusive behavior had cost them $280 million in damages. They could not rely on individual restraint because at least one owner would always try to gain an advantage over the others by signing "that one player who will put my team over the top." Heading into the 1990 negotiations, the owners decided to exercise another option—a salary cap that would limit their excessive spending. The owners proposed a revenue sharing plan—in essence, a salary cap—by which the players would receive 48 percent of the money from tickets and broadcast contracts, plus elimination of salary arbitration in return for a pay-for-performance plan for players with less than six years of major league experience.

Given the intransigence of the union, the owners eventually had to back away from the salary cap and the pay-for-performance plan to reach a labor agreement. They also accepted a negotiated adjustment to arbitration eligibility, expanding the pool of players who were eligible arbitration to include one-sixth of the two-year players plus the three-year players. Fay Vincent's role, as we have seen, was important in ending the impasse but also significant in his eventual demise as commissioner. A number of owners blamed the commissioner's unwelcome involvement in the negotiations for the resulting CBA, one that did not achieve a significant change in the economic model that would control salaries. The owners prepared for war in the next round of negotiations. As it turned out, there would be two parallel wars: owners versus players and owners versus other owners.

Individual Club Revenue Disparity Emerges as an Issue

Of the four major team sports in the United States, baseball historically has had the smallest percentage of "national" revenues and the highest percentage of local—mostly unshared—revenues. In December 1988, the Yankees signed a huge local cable deal with Madison Square Garden worth approximately $500 million over twelve years. The Yankees were making $50 million a year from local television while the Mariners were making $3.5 million.[7] In 1992, the Orioles opened Oriole Park at Camden Yards. These two seminal events signaled significant acceleration in the local revenue gap among the clubs. More and more clubs signed lucrative local TV deals, and the success of Camden Yards set off a ballpark building boom. Revenue disparity continued to grow. The frustration felt by low-revenue teams created increasing pressure for greater revenue sharing, which didn't amount to much in the early 1990s, when American League teams shared 20 percent of their gate receipts with visiting clubs, while the National League clubs shared less than 5 percent.

The increasing attention to the need for more sharing of local revenues did not originate in the late 1980s. In 1982, after the owners had approved a proposal to restructure the commissioner's office, A's owner Roy Eisenhardt indicated that another major issue facing baseball at the time was the sharing of television revenues between teams in lucrative markets and those in lesser markets. Eisenhardt was quoted as follows: "It isn't that we're only talking about money. But we're talking about whether baseball can survive as a national sport."[8] Over the rest of the decade and into the 1990s, the problem only worsened.

Added to the increasing disparity in local revenues was the prospect of a significant reduction in national television revenues after 1993, with the end of the lucrative CBS television deal. Soon after the CBS deal commenced in 1990, the owners realized that the network was losing a ton of money and a new contract would be much less remunerative. According to Helyar, that made "small-market interests more hawkish than ever."[9]

The Winds of War

The 1990 CBA, settled after the thirty-two-day spring training lockout, had an expiration date of December 31, 1993, but it contained a clause that allowed either side to reopen contract negotiations on major economic issues after three years. Near the end of year three, in December 1992, the owners decided to reopen negotiations on salaries and the free agency system by a narrow vote of 15–13. The narrow vote reflected divisions among the owners that foreshadowed the difficult battles on revenue sharing and a new labor deal that lay ahead. The owners' chief negotiator, Dick Ravitch, said, "I want to emphasize that we are not seeking a confrontation. We would like to move toward some change in the player compensation system. We want to do it rationally, constructively and optimistically."[10]

Given the forced resignation of Fay Vincent and the owners' move to reopen the labor deal, Don Fehr expressed concern that the owners would lock the players out before the 1993 season, a strategy that had been publicly discussed by hard-line owners. The owners notified government agencies that a lockout was possible, so Fehr's concern was well grounded. Ultimately, Ravitch assured the players that a spring training lockout would not occur in 1993, but the owners continued to harden their bargaining position for the new round of negotiations.

By 1993, the average major league salary, which had more than doubled in the four years since collusion had ended, grew to $1.12 million. On one hand, the owners girded for a battle to control salaries, while on the other, they continued their pursuit of free agents and continued to drive salaries ever higher. In light of some ominous economic signs—declining attendance for the 1992 season and CBS's public pronouncements regarding losses on its TV contract—labor hard liners such as Jerry Reinsdorf and Bud Selig began to exert more and more influence within the ranks of the owners.

A few days after the announcement was made that the owners would reopen negotiations with the players' union, Ravitch, participating in a roundtable discussion of baseball, indicated that the owners should release their financial records to the public to prove that "most clubs are losing money." The idea was part of an attempt to convince the players that the owners were in somewhat dire financial circumstances. The players did not believe the owners' claims because several years earlier the Players Association had hired economist Roger Noll of Stanford University to "decode the books," and Noll's interpretation of the fiscal health of baseball had had little in common with the owners' assessment.

Bill Giles was one of the few owners to respond publicly to Ravitch's suggestion, saying, "My first blush is that it is a good idea. I wouldn't mind doing it. I can't speak for other clubs. My thought is that there are a number who would oppose it, especially the ones who are making money."[11] Other owners who commented were less sanguine, including Stanton Cook of the Tribune Company, owners of the Cubs, who said that the Tribune Company does not release financial information about individual parts of the company.

The Owners Battle over Revenue Sharing

Giles expressed the typical attitude of large-market franchise owners regarding revenue sharing some years earlier, well before the Orioles opened Camden Yards, when he said, in response to a proposal from then-Orioles owner Edward Bennett Williams for increased revenue sharing, "Well, of course, if I were Edward Bennett Williams I would feel that way, too. But I have a responsibility to the people who invested $30 million in this ball club and we would not have paid so much if we had to share our TV revenue to a greater degree."[12]

After the owners decided to reopen labor negotiations in late 1992, some meetings involving the owners and players took place during the first half of 1993. However, no tangible offers were made by either side, in part because the owners had to deal with revenue sharing. Ravitch, who had been hired to replace the departed Barry Rona as the owners' labor negotiator, came up with a plan to jointly address both runaway salaries and revenue disparity. This plan involved revenue transfers from the top to the bottom clubs, tied to a salary cap to control payrolls. In essence, savings that the big-market clubs could generate through a salary cap would be used to transfer money to the low-revenue clubs, ostensibly putting the low-revenue teams on a more even economic plane with the high-revenue teams. Ravitch's plan was to be the centerpiece of the owners' proposal to the Players Association. When Ravitch unveiled his plan, one baseball official said, "There is no way the big markets will vote for revenue-sharing without a salary cap attached. Why would the Cubs or the White Sox want to share money with Pittsburgh or Seattle unless there is something in it for them?"[13] During early 1993, Ravitch lobbied the owners to accept the philosophy of revenue sharing tied to a salary cap, stressing that the costs of player compensation as a percentage of industry revenues [that would reach 58 percent in 1993 and 60 percent in 1994] were unsustainable.[14] To the Players Association, Ravitch stressed the notion of a player-owner partnership based on the sharing of revenue.

To bring about agreement on a revenue sharing plan, Ravitch arranged an owners' meeting for three days in Kohler, Wisconsin, in August 1993. A few days before the meeting, Bill Giles indicated his support for the basic concept. He said, "My position is that there should be increased revenue-sharing, but I'm not in favor of just television [revenues]. All elements should be shared."[15] Ravitch needed twenty-one votes, a three-fourths majority of the twenty-eight clubs, to pass his proposal, which he said was very complicated, having "legal issues, conceptual issues, arithmetical issues."[16]

The gap between the large-market teams and the small-market teams widened during the meeting, and the two groups ended up meeting in separate caucuses. After meeting for nearly thirty-one hours over three days, the meeting adjourned without an agreement. The effort to reach an agreement was scuttled by a ten-team group of richer teams: the Yankees, the Mets, Los Angeles, Toronto, Boston, Baltimore, Colorado, Florida, Texas, and St. Louis. George Steinbrenner decried revenue sharing as socialism and began several of his comments to the other owners with "Comrades . . ." The small-market teams included the Padres, Brewers, Astros, Pirates, Expos, Cardinals, Indians, Twins, and Mariners, plus the Reds and Royals, clubs concerned about economics because of limited local broadcasting revenues that were low compared with those of the Yankees, Dodgers, and Cubs.

Several participants described the Kohler meeting as a low point in the history of relationships among baseball's owners, with a great deal of anger, significant disagreement among the owners in the different cohorts, and real vitriol. In a 2005 interview with Andrew Zimbalist, Selig gave his impression of the Kohler meeting:

> I've never seen anger like that. It wasn't just bad. It was vile. Kohler, Wisconsin, was probably the most painful three days I've ever been through. Everybody else who was there, including George W. Bush, had never seen anything like it. It was worse than terrible. People said things to each other that were awful.[17]

The large-market and small-market segments hardly spoke with each other, with some of the more moderate owners moving between the meetings almost as couriers. Giles recalls that the managing partner of the Rangers, George W. Bush, was very instrumental in mediating the battle between the haves and the have-nots, but ultimately to no avail. Jerry Reinsdorf's take on the meeting, eighteen years after the fact, was:

> It was very ugly. Ravitch said that you had to share revenues. We had to go to them with a revenue sharing plan. There were twenty-six teams at the time, and ten were inalterably opposed to revenue sharing and sixteen were in favor of it. Kohler degenerated to the point where the ten guys were meeting by themselves and the sixteen guys were meeting by themselves. I was going back and forth because I was theoretically a big-market team, but I was in favor of revenue sharing . . . I thought it was good for the game. Bill Giles wasn't one of the ten. The funny thing is some of the ten became revenue sharing payees eventually. Like Toronto was dead set against revenue sharing and they were in the group of ten. For the last—I don't know how many years—they have been receiving revenue sharing.[18]

Former Red Sox chairman John Harrington also commented on the Kohler meetings:

> We [the Red Sox] weren't against revenue sharing *per se* because we already had it. It was in existence and the concept was accepted that you had to share some revenue, ticket revenue, cable money, with the visiting teams, but we felt that some of the things that were being proposed were going to go too far and would create a disincentive for teams to find ways to raise revenues. We also felt that there had to be proper controls and restrictions on whatever you passed down or shared. We felt that welfare states never work anywhere. We believed that you had to have a salary cap and you had to have a salary minimum. If you were going to give money to small-market teams, they had to spend a certain amount on players' salaries to produce a competitive team. You didn't want money going into owners' pockets and things of that nature. So in Kohler we were talking about all of those things. And so that is where the bitterness came out of Kohler. Some club owners simply wanted revenue sharing with no strings attached, no controls, no restrictions, and we felt that was just not going to work. So we left Kohler in a terrible state, if you will.[19]

Despite the emotion and the lack of agreement, the owners tried to put the best face on their failed efforts. Giles said, "It was a good meeting. We're close."[20]

After passions had cooled, Ravitch summoned the owners once more. Five months later, in early January 1994, the owners met in Rosemont, Illinois. At the Rosemont meeting, the owners managed to agree to make any revenue sharing plan contingent on the earlier implementation of a salary cap, but could not agree on the plan itself. Acting commissioner Bud Selig characterized the Rosemont meeting as another step closer to expanded revenue sharing, but the opposition to the Player Relations Committee plan was solid enough to keep the situation in limbo until the owners met in Fort Lauderdale, Florida, later that month. Selig reported, "I believe that this was just part of a process that continues toward a very satisfactory conclusion. Bill Giles told me to make sure I tell you that all 28 teams voted for revenue-sharing in some form today."[21]

Reaching a consensus on revenue sharing presented the owners with a thorny problem, complicated by other significant issues, the resolution of which depended on a revenue sharing agreement. Clearly, labor negotiations with the Players Association depended on this, but so did realignment as well as the naming of a permanent commissioner and the restructuring of the commissioner's office. Giles said, "The revenue-sharing issue is the trigger event."[22] There was, in fact, a running joke about revenue sharing: An agent first asks God when we will see another .400 hitter and then when we will see another thirty-game winner. Both times, God says, "Not in your lifetime." Then the agent asks about revenue sharing. "When will the big-city owners agree to help the teams in the smaller cities?" God smiles and says, "Not in My lifetime."[23]

The small-revenue owners decided to play hardball in the revenue sharing battle. Baseball had an agreement that allowed visiting teams to televise games to the visiting team's home market, even though under U.S. copyright law, the home team owns the rights to that telecast (i.e., performance). The small-market owners used this as leverage, threatening to scuttle the agreement when it came up for renewal at the end of 1993.[24]

At one of the January 1994 owners' meetings, Steinbrenner said that he was not against revenue sharing per se, but stated, "I am against revenue-sharing in its present form, which is neither proper nor fair. The way things are being presented today is that we have large-market franchises against small-market franchises."[25] The Boss went on to explain that he was against taking the Yankees' money, which could be used to improve the club, and giving it to Detroit so that they could sign players. Someone needed to bridge the large-market versus small-market gap. Stuart Meyer of St. Louis, a club that had been a staunch opponent of revenue sharing, broke the logjam by suggesting a sharing plan involving three levels of clubs rather than two levels. The top-revenue markets would be net contributors; the middle-revenue clubs would be in a neutral position, neither paying nor receiving funds; and the small-market, low-revenue clubs would qualify for aid on a sliding scale, with a maximum of about $9 million going to the poorest teams.[26] Triumph! The owners supported the revised plan unanimously, by a vote of 28–0.

Donald Fehr's reaction to the news was muted. He said, with a sarcastic tone, "I don't really have any reaction. It's taken Dick [Ravitch] a long time, but he's entitled to a big raise. He's deliberately kept us in the dark and excluded us from this process. At some point, if he cares, I suppose they'll let us in on the details." Fehr had consistently maintained that if the owners had revenue sharing so that every club was on relatively sound, equal financial footing, they would not need a salary cap. "We didn't care [about what the owners wanted to do with revenue sharing] as long as it did not adversely affect the free market. Now they want the union to cooperate in adversely affecting the market. That's what a salary cap is."[27] Fehr believed that tying a salary cap to significant revenue sharing had the effect of making the players fund the revenue sharing program, and there was little indication that he would consider such a deal acceptable.

Bill Conlin of the *Philadelphia Inquirer* wrote the following about how Giles viewed the financial situation in baseball from the perspective of his Philadelphia Phillies: "[Giles] said the Phillies were going to lose somewhere in the neighborhood of $1 million this season. He presented a concise outline of his fiscal woes: With attendance basically the same as last year's record 3.1 million, with the payroll up and national TV revenue sharply down it would take a return to the World Series to nudge into the black." Giles also told Stan Hochman of the *Philadelphia Daily News* that the Phillies could survive a continuation of the current economic system of arbitration and free agency, but he also said, "There are nineteen teams losing money this year." Conlin wrote, "Giles is fighting the good fight on behalf of his lodge brothers, he said, because his family has been in major league baseball 74 years, because he doesn't want the fans of Pittsburgh and San Diego to lose their ball clubs."[28]

At Last the Owners Propose a Deal

As part of the restructuring of the commissioner's office that was announced in January 1994, the hard-line owners took advantage of the absence of a permanent commissioner and stripped authority over labor issues from the commissioner's "best interests of baseball" powers. Inspired by Jerry Reinsdorf, one of the leading "hawks," the owners made a change in the voting procedure regarding labor issues. Instead of requiring a simple majority of owners to approve settlement of a strike or a lockout, it would now take a three-quarters "supermajority," meaning that as few as eight clubs could veto a proposed settlement.

During the spring of 1994, as camps opened and the players prepared for the season, the drumbeats of war sounded throughout baseball. The union set aside one-third of their licensing income of $100 million to set up a strike fund. Fehr lobbied Congress to lift baseball's antitrust exemption, and the union announced its intention to vote on a strike date at the All-Star break.

In retrospect, one of the questions one might ask about the owners' approach in presenting a salary cap to the union was very simply, "Why?" Ravitch explained the owners' position as follows: "Our objective is to produce a system to provide ownership with cost certainty, the right to bargain for the aggregate cost of playing baseball and to achieve a system to enhance competitive balance."[29] While Zimbalist maintains in *May the Best Team Win* that "the Players Association had never categorically ruled out a cap,"[30] the union had regarded a salary cap as a non-starter whenever the owners mentioned it in negotiations, and former union head Marvin Miller had taken the position of "not in this lifetime, not in the next" regarding a salary cap in baseball. The union did not want to seriously entertain any mechanism that placed a significant brake on salaries, starting with a cap. Since both the NFL and the NBA had instituted caps at the time, and although the NBA featured a "soft cap" with numerous exceptions, the players understood how caps worked. They also did not trust the owners, especially after collusion, and this certainly played a role in the difficulties the owners encountered.

Fehr made it clear to the owners that if a salary cap was to be part of a serious proposal, certain conditions had to be met. First, the owners would need to share more revenue. Second, the owners would have to provide audited financial statements to the Players Association so that the players could verify the actual amount of owners' revenues, a share of which would be allocated to the players. Third, since players' salaries would vary with baseball's revenues, the players would have a stake and a specific role in major financial decisions that affected revenues, for example, negotiation of television deals with the networks. Finally, both sides would have to agree to an appropriate cap level, that is, the percentage of revenue that would go to compensating the players.[31]

Ravitch finally unveiled the owners' salary cap and revenue sharing proposal to the players in mid-June 1994, eighteen months after deciding to reopen negotiations. The proposal specified a $1 billion payroll minimum and a maximum limit of 50 percent of revenues. The definition of revenues was expanded to include the players' licensing income.

Each club's payroll would have a ceiling of 110 percent of the previous year's major league mean payroll, and no club could have a payroll that amounted to less than 84 percent of the mean. The players stood to gain through expanding free agency to fifth and sixth year players (the waiting period had always been six years of service time since the original deal on free agency was struck in 1976), but with teams holding the player's contract given the right of first refusal for those two additional years. The players stood to lose by having the owners replace salary arbitration, long thought by the owners to be a major source of salary escalation and a focal point of the owners in labor negotiations since 1985, with a sliding salary scale tied to years of service in the major leagues. In addition, players' pensions, health coverage, and other benefits would be funded out of their 50 percent share of revenues.

Fehr responded to the owners' specification of a limit of 50 percent of revenues for players' salaries by noting that the current share was 58 percent of a total that did not include players' licensing income. From the start, the idea of a salary cap created an insurmountable barrier to a labor deal. Fehr's calculations put the cost to the players of at least $1.5 billion over the seven-year term of the new agreement.[32] Only four days passed before Fehr formally rejected the offer, presenting a counterproposal from the players that included lowering the threshold for qualifying for salary arbitration to its pre 1985 level of two years, eliminating the restriction on repeat free agency within five years, and raising minimum salaries to $175,000 and later to $200,000. Within a few days, the owners rejected the players' offer. At this point, no bargaining was taking place.

The Players and Owners Head for a Cliff

At the All-Star break, the players voted to set a strike deadline of August 12. The players chose the date to accomplish two objectives. The first objective was to inflict maximum financial damage on the owners because the bulk of television revenues came during the late season and the postseason. The second objective was to leave some time for negotiations in case a deal could be reached without having to cancel the rest of the season.

With the strike deadline approaching, the owners escalated the battle when they decided to withhold a scheduled $7.8 million contribution to the players' pension fund, proceeds from the All-Star Game broadcast revenues. The players participated in the All-Star Game strictly because the owners were contractually bound to make the contribution to the pension fund. The owners claimed that because the CBA had expired, they were under no obligation to make a payment that had been specified in the previous CBA. The players' response to this apparently intentional provocation was predictable outrage. Some players wanted to strike immediately, but union officers convinced them that the owners' move was designed to elicit an early strike that would cost the players more in lost salary, so the union stuck with the August 12 deadline.

Reinsdorf continued to maintain that baseball had serious economic problems that could only be addressed through stringent cost controls. He said that Fehr had "seen the books" and was misleading the players, essentially coaxing them into a job action. The players made some suggestions to the owners for enhancing revenues and distributing them more efficiently, but these suggestions went nowhere. Talks broke off on August 10. In the last few days before the strike deadline, some owners expressed frustration with their peers. George Steinbrenner told a reporter that the owners' main argument for a salary cap—competitive balance—"doesn't wash" and that individual owners, who had been restricted from doing so, should sit in on the negotiations. Peter Angelos suggested to his fellow owners that they agree not to impose the cap unilaterally if the players agree not to strike. Both Jerry McMorris of Colorado and Marge Schott of Cincinnati expressed doubts about the owners' strategy. Giles, however, characterized the attitude of most of the owners, who themselves were frustrated by the seeming intransigence of the players, saying, "The only way is to play hardball right now."[33]

Van Dyck characterized the stalled negotiations as largely the fault of the owners, citing several factors:

> The claim that 19 teams are losing money, laughed at so hard that caretaker commissioner Bud Selig had to amend it to 12 to 14 teams. The truth, according to the respected magazine *Financial World*, says as few as five teams might be losing money. Proof that teams are going broke never has been given, although owners have claimed doom-and-gloom for two decades. The players keep asking: If things are so bad, how come franchises keep selling for record prices? An owner press release that said, among other things, that the players want ". . . one thing more—more." In fact, the players only want a continuation of the present system. Owners have cried poor, but they have shown a strange way of begging for help. And the real question is whether they should be crying poor at all.[34]

Another complication for the entire scenario—and more reason for the players' lack of trust in the owners—was an analysis by Roger Noll, who was again hired by the Players Association to review the Player Relations Committee's financial information that had been provided to the players. While the owners claimed a type of financial exigency, with projected losses of $100 million for the baseball industry in 1994, Noll reported that the owners had understated expected revenues by between $50 and $140 million. In addition, baseball's reported administrative costs exceeded reasonable levels by at least $100 million. Noll concluded that baseball would actually have a 1994 profit of between $50 million and $140 million. Noll, who had performed a similar analysis for the Players Association in 1985, wrote, "The prophecy of impending doom is far more implausible in 1994 than it was nine years ago."[35] Of course, the owners, citing Noll's status as a paid consultant to the union, attacked his analysis as biased, factually inaccurate, and based on faulty assumptions. As Rudyard Kipling had written 100 years earlier, "Never the twain shall meet."[36]

Giles expressed his concern about the situation while alluding to owner solidarity, saying, "I know we've cried about this [being poor] for a hundred years. There's no question the owners are partly to blame. Collusion was wrong. I think the owners have been as wrong as the players. In the past, we said we wanted to change the system. But we were not as serious as we are now."[37]

Stee-rike!

The players walked on August 12, in the middle of one of the most exciting baseball seasons in anyone's memory, with the Expos in first place, Tony Gwynn hitting close to .400, Matt Williams and Ken Griffey, Jr., challenging Roger Maris's home run record, and Greg Maddux enjoying the best pitching season since Bob Gibson posted an earned run average of 1.12 in 1968. What promised to be a special season died in the arms of an industry that simply could not get all of the key participants on the same economic page.

Given that only six weeks remained in the regular season when the players struck, the owners had to quickly discuss the date they believed negotiations must be concluded if the season was to resume. Giles thought that the point of no return for the 1994 season would arrive in less than a month. He said, "I think we'd have to be playing by the middle of September to have any integrity to the season and the playoffs. I'm frustrated we're not playing ball, and frustrated we're not making progress. I hope eventually the players will listen to our proposal in a serious manner."[38]

With bargaining going nowhere, and given the terrible relationship between the owners and the players, many expressed real concern about the possibility of resuming play at all in 1994. The question asked by *Philadelphia Inquirer* columnist Frank Dolson in early September was,

"What will happen this time if there is no resumption of play, as seems so likely? If there is no final chapter to the '94 season, no playoffs, no World Series, no guarantee of a full season of big-league baseball in '95?" Dolson spoke with Giles and reported, "Even Phillies president Bill Giles, a confirmed optimist by nature, fears the impact if this season truly ended in the second week of August. Giles said, 'If we have a postseason, I think it will be forgotten about by spring training. But if we don't have a postseason, I think it's going to hurt.'"[39]

Just after the strike, Colorado Rockies owner Jerry McMorris said, "I think we could negotiate a settlement that did not include a salary cap. I feel the salary cap is a negotiable issue because, let's be realistic, this is all about simple economics. There has to be a change in the economic system and some sanity."[40] Selig attempted to put some life in the talks before the drop-dead date for canceling the season by forming a six-person owner negotiating panel, then appointing some moderate owners, including McMorris. In mid-August, McMorris and Chuck O'Connor, the owners' legal counsel, suggested a new idea, replacing the salary cap with a graduated tax on teams that spent more than the mean payroll figure, coupled with a minimum salary to ensure that teams could not simply let revenue sharing dollars drop to the bottom line. If a club's payroll exceeded a certain level, that club would pay a tax, with the proceeds of the tax going into a pool to be distributed among the low-revenue teams. McMorris recognized that to get the necessary support, that is, twenty-one affirmative votes, the proposal "has to be something that slows the percentage of revenues going to salaries."[41]

While the Players Association recognized that a tax on excess payroll served as a drag on salaries, Fehr did not reject the idea out of hand. The players responded on September 8 with a counteroffer that included a small (1.5 percent) tax on the revenues and payrolls of the sixteen richest clubs that would shift funds to clubs with the smallest revenues. The owners considered the magnitude of the tax rate insignificant, with minimal impact on salaries, and rejected the terms of the deal. Some owners, such as John Harrington of the Red Sox, professed that they saw merit in the concept. But with no chance at achieving the three-quarters majority required to pass the deal, Selig abandoned the process. Giles said, "The feeling of the Executive Council is that if nothing meaningful has happened, then we should call the rest of the season off."[42] Selig, the chair of the executive council, announced after a September 14 conference call that the rest of the season and the entire postseason were canceled.

The strike of 1994 led to significant financial losses, amounting for the owners to an estimated $376 million in lost revenue net of savings in player and administrative salaries, ballpark maintenance, and other expenses. The players lost 29 percent of their pay, $352 million plus the players' share of the postseason revenue.[43] Fans and the baseball industry lost the conclusion of the regular season plus the entire postseason. The World Series had been played every year since 1904, when the New York Giants refused to play the American League champion Boston Red Sox, even through two world wars and the Great Depression, but the 1994 Series became a victim of acrimonious relations and an unwillingness to compromise by both parties. The networks lost substantial revenue via lost postseason telecasts. Licensing sales dropped precipitously, and Major League Baseball Properties saw declines of 15 percent in 1994, with expectations of a 25 percent drop the next season. Peripheral businesses fed by crowds attending ballparks lost revenues, and ballpark employees lost jobs. Front office employees of some clubs lost pay and bonuses, and several teams laid off staff.[44]

Just about the only part of baseball that benefited from the strike was minor league baseball. Attendance at minor league games, which had been growing since the late 1980s, jumped 14 percent because of the strike.[45] I recall that the day after the strike started, the *Philadelphia Inquirer* sports section included schedules, ticket information, and ballpark locations and directions for all of the minor league teams in the area.

The Long and Winding Road toward Resumption of Baseball

An entire book would be required to delve into a detailed review of the process, involving owners, the Player Relations Committee, players, the MLB Players Association, the White House, Congress, federal mediators, the National Labor Relations Board, and the courts, that eventually led to a resumption of major league play in April 1995. The scope of this book allows only a cursory review of the highlights, or as we might characterize them, the lowlights. This certainly was not a pretty time in the history of major league baseball.

In what has become a recurring theme in baseball history, Congress jumped into the fray, with several members calling for an end to baseball's antitrust exemption. Representatives Mike Synar of Oklahoma, Major Owens of New York, and Jim Bunning of Kentucky—the former major league player who once pitched a perfect game for the Phillies against the Mets in Shea Stadium on Father's Day in 1964—introduced a bill that would strip baseball of its exemption if owners unilaterally impose working conditions, such as a salary cap. Bunning said, "The courts have been saying we should do something about the antitrust exemption for years."[46]

Expressing a common sentiment on Capitol Hill, Representative Jack Brooks, a Texas Democrat, said that the exemption "has contributed to a recurring pattern of strikes, lockouts and bad faith collective bargaining that makes labor disputes in the auto, steel or coal industries look like the epitome of harmonious dialogue."[47] Some owners, at least, appeared to have gotten the message. The chairman of the Atlanta Braves, Bill Bartholomay, said, "The message I read is that we'd better make every attempt to seek a resolution prior to Congress's return in January."[48]

No owner was more perplexed, disappointed, and hurt by the 1994 strike than Bill Giles. On one hand, he wanted nothing more than to get baseball going again. On the other hand, he understood the situation and empathized with owners of small-market teams, who found it difficult to compete in the economic milieu that baseball had created for itself. Giles was asked in late October 1994 whether he had concerns about the ability of small-market franchises to survive a strike that extends far into the next season. He answered, "Yes, I do. I know the condition we're [the Phillies] in—which is not good—and we're in a lot better shape than some other teams."[49]

In December, the owners met to discuss the perilous state of baseball. A financial report indicated that the combined debt of the twenty-eight major league teams had reached approximately $600 million, an average of over $21 million per club, with about 20 percent of that debt attributable to teams borrowing from baseball's central line of credit. When asked about the report, Giles would not confirm any specific numbers, but said that the amount of money the clubs had borrowed from the central line of credit is "by far the largest number we've ever had in baseball."[50] Clearly, despite the numbers claimed by Professor Noll, some major league clubs were struggling financially.

From Negotiation to Litigation

Baseball had fallen behind football in terms of overall popularity and fan interest, but it still held an important role in American culture. Therefore, much political pressure arose in the halls of Congress and in the White House to get a labor deal done. President Clinton lacked the power to force a deal, but he wanted to move the negotiations along, and in October, the president appointed William J. Usery, a noted and experienced mediator, to bring the sides together. Usery did make progress in eliciting some new ideas and getting some modest compromises on both sides, but he also lacked the power of law to force a settlement, and the sides could not agree to engage in binding arbitration of the dispute. The parties were so polarized and relationships between them were so acrimonious that none of the mediators had any success in bringing the sides together. Part of the problem was that the owners themselves were split into different camps—those who were dead set against a deal without a salary cap, those who wanted to settle at almost any cost, and moderates in the middle. Owners such as Angelos, Peter O'Malley, and Fred Wilpon were key members of the group that wanted to settle because their clubs had more to lose as a result of a long strike. Owners from small-market teams, such as Kansas City, Milwaukee, Montreal, Pittsburgh, and Seattle, were committed to radical change. Giles was clearly one of the moderates. These divisions had prevented a quick resolution of the revenue sharing issue and now prevented effective bargaining on a new CBA.

Both sides continued to engage in what Burk termed "mutually destructive vendettas."[51] The owners planned to declare an impasse in labor negotiations if a settlement was not reached by November 1994 and then unilaterally impose the salary cap plan. The players anticipated the owners' tactics and planned to file charges of unfair labor practices with the National Labor Relations Board to obtain a federal court ruling enjoining the owners from implementing their new proposal. The players had already filed an unfair labor practices complaint against the owners for nonpayment of the pension contribution after the All-Star break, a complaint that was later sustained by the National Labor Relations Board. In mid-December, Angelos, who did not favor the strategy unilaterally imposing a cap, said "It would exacerbate feelings on both sides and take us back to square one." With legal counsel advising the owners that implementing the cap would not withstand a legal challenge, Selig announced that the owners had voted 25–3 to delay implementation of the cap for a week to allow negotiations to continue, but that the deadline the next week was firm.[52]

When last-gasp negotiations collapsed, the owners declared a bargaining impasse on December 23, 1994. If the December 23 date in the annals of baseball labor relations sounds familiar, that's because nineteen years to the day earlier, Peter Seitz had "set the players free" with his decision on the reserve clause in the Messersmith and McNally case. After an impasse was declared, the owners unilaterally imposed their plan that incorporated a salary cap and elimination of salary arbitration. The Players Association responded by filing another unfair labor practices complaint, claiming that negotiations were active and not at an impasse. The dispute had thus moved from negotiation to litigation.

Right after the New Year, Congress opened its 104th session with more talk of lifting the antitrust exemption. Daniel Patrick Moynihan, a

Democrat from New York, initiated action in the Senate. Moynihan previously had been silent on the antitrust exemption. He introduced legislation entitled the "National Pastime Preservation Act" that called for full repeal of the antitrust exemption. Moynihan explained, "Major league baseball is in grave peril. The antitrust exemption allows the owners to act as a cartel. The exemption gives the owners substantial power over wages and work rules." Repealing the exemption, according to Moynihan, would "help equalize bargaining power between the two sides and will permit unfair labor practices to be challenged in U.S. court."[53] In February, the bill was reconstituted as the "Professional Baseball Antitrust Reform Act" and was narrowed to cover only the labor question—not franchise relocation or minor league baseball—thereby permitting players to sue if the owners impose unilateral contract terms. Don Fehr responded in a letter to Orrin Hatch, "If the bill becomes law, I will recommend to the members of the Major League Baseball Players Association that we end the strike."[54]

Replacement Players

Meanwhile, the owners had to plan for the 1995 season. In mid-January, amid all of the turmoil, the team owners put a plan in motion to open the 1995 season with replacement players if the regular players continued to strike, similar to what the NFL had done for three weeks during a players' strike in 1987. The owners decided to open spring training camps as scheduled in February, with replacement players if necessary. The owners' operations committee worked on guidelines for assembling replacement teams. According to Giles, the Phillies had a list of about twenty potential replacement players. He recalled, "I think that's probably the direction we're headed. The [operations] committee has done a lot of work on it. I was opposed to it initially. [But] we played around with it [yesterday]. The more you get into it, the more fun it could be."[55]

In mid-January, at the annual luncheon to kick off the Phillies preseason promotional efforts, Giles expressed his utter devastation at what had happened to his beloved game.

> I do not believe in my heart that the union leaders care about the game. I really do not. I believe they have other agendas . . .
>
> The union has spent most of its time in Washington, attacking our antitrust exemption, instead of trying to reach a settlement.
>
> I believe in my heart that a lot of our players believe that the game is more important than some ideological stance. And every day that passes, I want to emphasize that, every day that passes

> means more revenue is drained from the system. I believe they realize they are very fortunate to be able to play this game and that their union leader's goal is not to bring the game to the highest point possible.

Giles also repeated his firm intention to use "hungry replacement players" while admitting that he hopes that tactic will "persuade" the regular players to report back to work. "It's not a pleasant option, but it's the best one we have right now and it's one we will go forward with," he promised.[56]

Everyone acknowledged that the quality of baseball would not approach true major league standards, but the owners needed their own leverage to move the negotiating process along. A threat to start the season without the real players and the fact that players would continue to sacrifice paychecks were important bargaining chips for the owners. Two teams refused to use replacement players, the Orioles and the Blue Jays. In Toronto, Canadian labor law prohibited the use of "strikebreakers" in place of regular workers. Baltimore owner Peter Angelos was a labor lawyer by trade, and he rejected the practice of using a substitute labor force. Moreover, his star player, Cal Ripken, was on the verge of breaking Lou Gehrig's sacred record of 2,130 consecutive games, and that record would be sacrificed if the Orioles played league games without Ripken in the lineup. Mercifully, American League President Gene Budig canceled the Orioles games, preserving Ripken's streak in the event that the season started with replacement players. Tigers manager Sparky Anderson refused to manage the replacements and took an unpaid leave of absence from the club. But most managers shared the perspective of Tommy Lasorda of the Dodgers, who decided that it was right and proper to manage whichever players wore Dodger uniforms.

With the strike keeping the regular players out and replacement baseball on the agenda, one of the problems facing the owners was selling tickets. Several teams announced plans to entice fans to attend games they knew would not replicate the quality of regular baseball. Texas and St. Louis announced plans to tie ticket price reductions to the size of the opening day payroll. Other clubs announced percentage discounts. Giles announced that ticket prices for the Phillies' first twenty home games of the regular season had been reduced, even if the regular players returned by opening day. Tickets that regularly went for $12 and $14 would be discounted by $5, with lower-priced tickets discounted proportionally. Giles, who said that season ticket holders would receive an appropriate adjustment, acknowledged that "the prolonged unrest in the labor situation has been very trying on our fans."[57]

Toward a Settlement

The process moved ahead. In late January, with spring training in doubt, not to mention the 1995 season, President Clinton ordered Usery to bring the parties back to the bargaining table. Giles responded to the president's involvement, saying, "I'm optimistic. It seems Clinton's pressure is helping." But Giles also said that he did not think the strike would be settled quickly, that in his experience, strikes usually are settled "when two chief negotiators on opposite sides go for a long walk down a street and say to each other, 'What do you really want?' That hasn't happened yet. Mostly, it's been group meetings. Not much happens in rooms with lots of people in them."[58]

Talks resumed on February 1, and the owners substituted the proposal of a luxury tax on high payrolls for a salary cap. The plan incorporated a 75 percent tax on payrolls between $35 and $42 million and a 100 percent tax on payrolls above $42 million. By comparison, the median team payroll in the major leagues in 1994 was $32 million. In addition, the owners unilaterally revoked the authority of clubs to sign player contracts, eliminated salary arbitration, and ended the anti-collusion clause.[59] Facing a National Labor Relations Board unfair labor practices complaint because of the December imposition of the salary cap, the owners withdrew the cap.

The labor negotiations caused some concern over progress on other key baseball issues, such as the timing of future expansion. Giles, a member of the expansion committee, indicated that the rollback of the salary cap and the latest breakdown in talks could affect team owners' plans to add two clubs in 1997 or 1998 and another pair of teams two to three years later, saying, "This is just my personal view, but I think it would be hard to come up with a logical price [to charge for expansion franchises] until we know what the labor costs are going to be."[60]

The president called the owners and players to the White House on February 7 and asked the sides to engage in binding arbitration, which the players accepted but the owners rejected. The next day, the Players Association filed yet another unfair labor practices suit in response to the owners' imposition of new conditions two weeks earlier, that is, revocation of the authority of clubs to sign player contracts, the elimination of salary arbitration, and termination of the anti-collusion clause.

In early March, the news brightened a bit. The union submitted a proposal that accepted the owners' revenue sharing plan and expressed a willingness to be flexible in formulating a system for a tax on payrolls. While the payroll threshold and tax rates remained significant issues, Chuck O'Connor acknowledged a "forward direction" in the talks.[61] Unfortunately, only a day passed before the situation worsened once again as the owners argued that the players' numbers would simply not provide the cost containment the owners needed. The issues of payroll threshold and tax rates would continue to be sticking points for the next eighteen months, long after other issues had been resolved.

The National Labor Relations Board agreed with the players' unfair labor practices claims, informing the owners in mid-March that it would file an unfair labor practices charge against them. The National Labor Relations Board complaint accused the owners of illegally eliminating salary arbitration and other terms of baseball's old economic system in February. The union announced that if the National Labor Relations Board obtained an injunction restoring the old system, the players would call off the strike and either return to work or force the owners to lock them out.[62]

At the Phillies camp in Clearwater, Florida, Giles was so stung by baseball's bleak prospects that he said he was on the verge of issuing a public plea to Phillies players to cross the picket line. He said, "If this thing goes past the weekend, I'm thinking about trying to encourage our players to come back and play with the replacement players, or replace the replacement players." Giles said that he "would want to see a minimum of 15 [Phillies returning]. If you get less than 15, I don't think it would be a good idea." He also stated that he would do so only with the blessing of the executive council. Don Fehr responded that Giles' remarks were "unfortunate," but he also said, "Bill will do what Bill will do."[63] Giles went on to say:

> I've gone through more hell in the last six months than I ever have before in my life. I just wake up every day wondering what I can do to solve this awful mess. We have no choice but to play hardball in these negotiations. We've always given in before and after all the damage that's been done, we have to come out of this with something meaningful. I'm just trying to find the solution, find the trigger event that will get the real game back on the field.[64]

A week later, still in Florida, Giles spoke out again:

> I'm no longer angry. I'm no longer frustrated. I just shake my head and say, "How sad." Until a few days ago, I was trying to plan for every scenario. But as of now, I'm not making any more plans for anything—because I have no idea what's going to happen. I don't know if we're going to have replacement players. I don't know if there'll be a lockout. As of Friday [St. Patrick's Day], I just gave up. I'm just waiting for somebody to tell me what's going to happen.

Giles also said that the overall economic situation would hurt the players, at least in the short run. "Free agents are going to get clobbered. If they want to play, they're going to have to take a big hit. A lot of them are not even going to get offers. I suspect a lot of clubs will play with minor leaguers who really aren't ready, just to save money."[65]

In late March, the National Labor Relations Board went to court to obtain an injunction against the owners that would force them to restore the key parts of the expired labor agreement. The case went before Judge Sonia Sotomayor in federal district court in New York. She took arguments and ruled on the case in short order. On March 31, Judge Sotomayor, who some now recognize as the "savior" of baseball in 1995, ruled for the players. She issued the requested injunction and ordered the owners to restore the terms and conditions, including free agent bidding, salary arbitration, and the anti-collusion provisions of the previous CBA, which had expired at the end of 1993. She also ordered the owners to continue bargaining.

The players had previously stipulated that one of the conditions for not striking was such a move, and therefore they announced the end of the strike. This put the ball in the owners' court, so to speak, and the owners had to decide whether to lock the players out or live with the old CBA. Although the owners did mount what proved to be an unsuccessful court challenge to Judge Sotomayor's ruling, they decided that they risked too much in continued financial losses and fan support if they extended the labor stoppage. The lockout question was resolved by the owners by consensus and did not even come to a vote. On April 2, the owners and players reached a tentative agreement to open spring training and start the season. The teams cut their replacement players.

Baseball Is (Sort of) Back

The strike, at long last, had ended. But there was still no labor agreement, and the prospect of another walkout by the players still loomed. Bret Saberhagen of the Mets said, "I'm happy to be back at work, but there's still no basic agreement yet. There's still a long way to go. We're playing baseball, but we're still in the same situation as last year." Giles spoke for the owners when he said, "I think we need a no-strike pledge, but I understand the players don't want to do it."[66] After an abbreviated spring training period, the season began, with regular players, on April 26. The late start date meant that the regular season would have to be shortened, and so the 1995 season lasted 144 games and ushered in the expanded playoffs, originally scheduled to be introduced in 1994, which included three division winners and a wild card team in each league.

Because the owners and players were required to resume bargaining by Judge Sotomayor, negotiations took place throughout the 1995 season without an agreement. Meetings between attorneys from both sides and some players took place on a regular basis, but no formal negotiation sessions were held after Judge Sotomayor granted the injunction. In September, Richard Ravitch left his post as labor negotiator for the Player Relations Committee, and the owners named New York City Commissioner of Labor Relations Randy Levine to head the negotiations.

Negotiations took a turn for the better, primarily because Fehr did not intensely dislike Levine as he had Ravitch, so the bargaining was cordial and professional. Some vexing issues remained, however, including the specifics associated with the luxury tax, plus the players' demand that the owners grant them service time for games lost due to the strike. This issue raised a lot of emotions on both sides. From the players' point of view, it was nonnegotiable; the owners had always granted service time for past stoppages, and the issue had significant implications in terms of eligibility for arbitration and free agency. Some owners were willing to give in, but others, such as Andy MacPhail of the Cubs, drew a line in the sand over service time and were adamant that they would not accede to this demand, which they considered outrageous.

Despite the appointment of Levine, no real negotiating took place for several months; 1995 became 1996 and still no agreement was in the works. The players still did not like the terms proposed by the owners, seeing the luxury tax as a salary cap in disguise. Giles said that there was no urgency to produce a deal because teams prepared for the 1996 season under the old labor rules. "There's no pressure point until next November." When asked whether fans would return to baseball in 1996 after two seasons shortened by a strike and the threat of replacement baseball, Giles responded, "There is reason for optimism. There's not going to be any strike[;] there's not going to be any lockout. Both sides have seen the damage that can be done."[67] The owners approved interleague play for 1997, predicated on reaching a labor agreement since interleague play was a bargaining issue.

Levine and Fehr kept at it, and in March 1996, the owners presented a proposal to the players that Fehr found much more acceptable than previous proposals regarding the luxury tax as well as some elements of the arbitration process that the players did not want. The owners finally and officially approved a revenue sharing plan by a vote of 26–1 with one abstention, which Astros owner Drayton McLane characterized as "a giant step for baseball."[68] In April, the Commissioner's Office released financial and attendance figures for 1994 and 1995 that showed a combined loss by the clubs of $702 million, significant declines in revenues and attendance, and large losses, even for typically profitable clubs.

With negotiations still sputtering in June, some team owners threatened to return to court to once again impose a new economic system unilaterally if the talks continued to languish. In July, negotiations ceased once again, driven by players' concerns about an overly regressive luxury tax and owners' concerns about lack of cost containment. This time it was the players' turn to rattle sabers, and signals indicated that the union would once again consider going out on strike. The mutual threats spurred more bargaining, and Mark Maske of the *Washington Post* reported on August 11 that a settlement appeared near.[69] David Cone, the American League player representative, said, "Finally, we may be getting some conclusion to this nightmare."[70]

Then the talks hit a snag because of the service time issue as well as an owners' demand that the Players Association agree not to seek legal damages for any action taken by the owners during the dispute. Giles, however, said that owners should give in on service time. "Philosophically it's wrong because they went out on strike, but I'd be willing to do it if it would get things settled."[71]

Other owners, however, were not so sanguine. Talks continued in an attempt to resolve the latest issues, with another one added for good measure—some hard-line owners did not want the players to get two consecutive years at the end of the deal (2000 and 2001) without a luxury tax because they thought it would be difficult to reinstitute the tax for the next CBA. Levine said, "I can't predict when the train is going to arrive at the station, but it's on the track."[72]

Peace at Last

Levine continued to tweak the details of the owners' proposal in an attempt to mollify the hard-liners, who kept scuttling the process into late October. Ultimately, MacPhail and others with similar sentiments let the service time issue go for the greater good, and Levine and Fehr reached a tentative agreement on October 24. Selig, however, did not publicly support or advocate the agreement, and the hawks among the owners drove a negative vote of 18–12 to reject the new deal. Reinsdorf held firm to his position against a settlement without a salary cap. He continued to exert significant influence among his fellow owners. Levine threatened to resign his post in total frustration.

Then, the White Sox owner went out and signed the talented but obstreperous Albert Belle to a five-year, $55 million contract. The deal was announced on November 19. Almost immediately, Selig called the owners together for another vote on the same deal that the owners had defeated a month earlier, and on November 26, 1996, the October 24 terms were approved with only two negative votes. One negative vote came from Reinsdorf, who stuck to his "no deal without a cap" guns and also claimed that he believed his signing of Belle had little or nothing to do with the owners' change of heart. "The Belle signing had nothing to do with [owners changing votes]. I'm convinced votes changed before the Belle signing."[73]

That view was backed, at least publicly, by Bill Giles, who said, "I don't know that it did change anything. I was in favor of the deal before. I'm in favor of it now. Every club has the right to do what it thinks is best."[74]

Reinsdorf attributed the owners' mood change to the persuasive powers of acting commissioner Bud Selig, saying, "People changed their votes because Bud Selig told them to. He's very persuasive. He ought to be the majority whip in the House."[75]

Giles said that the owners came to realize that "we couldn't change the deal" and that an attempt to gain more concessions probably would have provoked another work stoppage.[76] Some owners decided that a deal they didn't like was better than no deal at all. "We wish we would have gotten a better system, but you're not going to conquer the world in one negotiation," Giles said.[77] Andy MacPhail commented, "I think it was just time to put this to an end and try to move the industry forward. That's hopefully what we did today. There just comes a time when you have to do what you think is best for the game." Even Reinsdorf expressed relief at the outcome, saying, "My friend [Padres owner] Larry Lucchino has a saying, 'All's well that ends.' I think that works."[78]

The 1996 CBA contained significant elements, including major league baseball's first significant sharing of local revenues plus a luxury tax on high team payrolls. In addition, the owners and players agreed to create and jointly support an "industry growth fund" to promote the game not only in North America but also throughout the world. A fourth part of the new agreement contained a two-year experiment with interleague play that not only created a great deal of fan interest but also was a step on the way toward eliminating the leagues as decision-making entities and centralizing all of the business of baseball into the commissioner's office.

The Final Act in the Drama: The Curt Flood Act

The players had long argued that the antitrust exemption contributed to the labor difficulties that had been endemic to the game since the first CBA in 1968. According to Andrew Zimbalist, the exemption made it impossible for the Players Association to defend itself in court if the owners unilaterally imposed restrictions on the operation of the player market, for example, a salary cap.[79] Before the strike, Fehr announced that he would not recommend a strike to the players if the owners pledged not to impose unilateral terms during the off-season or if Congress passed a partial lifting of the exemption so that the players could defend themselves against such ownership moves with antitrust litigation (similar to what the NFL Players Association did during the 2012 NFL lockout). Because the owners refused to guarantee that there would be no unilateral terms and conditions and because Congress did not act before August 12, 1994, the players believed that a late-season strike represented the most effective way to defend themselves against new, limiting labor market restrictions.[80]

After the strike, and as part of the 1996 CBA, the owners and players agreed that it was in the best interests of the game to have the exemption lifted. With the support of both players and owners, Congress acted. The Curt Flood Act of 1998 ended baseball's antitrust exemption as it applied to labor negotiations. The measure added a new section to the Clayton Act. This provision mandated that major league baseball players would be covered under the federal antitrust laws to the same extent as other professional athletes and defined "major league baseball players" as persons who are or were parties to major league players' contracts. The principal purpose of the law was to make sure that federal antitrust laws apply to the relationships between major league baseball owners, teams, and players, "that major league baseball players will have the same rights under the antitrust laws as do other professional athletes, along with a provision that makes it clear that the passage of this Act does not change the application of the antitrust laws in any other context or with respect to any other person or entity."[81]

Conclusion

The long nightmare for baseball had finally ended with a deal that may have been far from ideal but at least brought back the game. The new CBA, which was set to expire on December 19, 2002, unfortunately did not address all of baseball's economic maladies, and as a new strike date of August 30, 2002, approached, most observers thought that baseball was going on a labor-enforced hiatus again. Fans feared that they would lose baseball once again and were out of patience with baseball's ongoing labor woes.

In remembering what for him was the worst time he has ever spent in baseball, Bill Giles says, "The labor strike in 1994 was the most frustrating time in my career, but it did teach the owners and players alike that there should never again be a work stoppage that affects postseason baseball. Baseball was fortunate that the home run race between Mark McGwire and Sammy Sosa happened on the heels of the shutdown so that fan interest in baseball rebounded nicely."[82]

6

Expansion, Realignment, and Interleague Play

Bringing Baseball into the 1990s

No decade ushered more change into the structure of major league baseball than the 1990s. The last expansion had occurred in 1977, when the American League added two teams, but baseball had maintained the same twenty-six franchises since then. After much outside pressure from Congress, and threatened with possible loss of its anti-trust exemption, baseball became serious about further expansion, adding two franchises to the National League in 1993. With expansion arose the issue of how teams were aligned in their respective divisions in the National League. Commissioner Fay Vincent made some decisions about expansion and league alignment that proved to be very unpopular with the owners. As a result of these decisions and the owners' perception that Vincent was soft on labor issues, he was forced from office in September 1992. This move created a vacancy in the commissioner's office that was filled by the owner of the Milwaukee Brewers, Bud Selig, who as chair of the owners' executive council, became *de facto* acting commissioner, but for close to six years, baseball operated without a permanent commissioner.

Eventually, the owners decided to align the leagues into three divisions within each league and created an expanded postseason, including a wild card team in each league. Once the baseball enterprise had reached twenty-eight teams, talk emerged about further expansion to thirty teams. After extensive discussion of numerous alternative models, this new round of expansion in 1998 brought with it another round of realignment, along with a revised schedule format. Owners continued to dilute the power of the individual leagues as baseball centralized its business operations and adopted what amounted to a CEO model in the commissioner's office. Baseball changed a ninety-four-year-old tradition and began interleague play. All the while, owners negotiated with each other about competitive balance and revenue sharing and with the players about the economic structure of baseball. After three years of negotiations over a new labor deal, a period that included the devastating strike of 1994–1995, a new labor deal was reached. Selig, after saying consistently that he had no interest in being permanent commissioner, finally accepted the job in 1998.

In this decade of significant upheaval and change, Bill Giles was not only a participant but also one of the chief architects of the structure of Major League Baseball that emerged after baseball centralized following Selig's appointment.

Looking Back: Expansion of Baseball from Sixteen to Twenty-six Teams, 1961–1977

From 1901, when the American League began play, through the end of the 1960 season, which culminated with Bill Mazeroski's walk-off World Series home run against the Yankees, baseball had just sixteen teams. Franchise relocations during the 1950s included movement of the Boston Braves to Milwaukee, the St. Louis Browns to Baltimore, the Philadelphia Athletics to Kansas City, the New York Giants to San Francisco, and the Brooklyn Dodgers to Los Angeles. These moves opened up new markets and took baseball to the West Coast. By the end of the decade, Calvin Griffith was anxious to flee Washington, D.C., for the greener pastures of Minnesota, which he did after the 1960 season. During this time, despite population growth and significant population movement to the South and West, baseball held to sixteen teams.

Once Horace Stoneham and Walter O'Malley took their clubs out of New York City, leaving the largest city in the country and the financial capital of the world to the Yankees and without a National League team, a vacuum was created that was bound to be filled. Mayor Robert Wagner's appointment of Bill Shea to head a movement to bring a National League team to New York and Shea's ensuing inability to attract an existing club to the Big Apple resulted ultimately in the initiative to start a new league, the Continental League. The pressure from both Congress and an incipient new league moved the major league owners to finally agree to expand baseball, and shortly thereafter four new franchises, two in each league, came into existence. In 1961 the American League added Los Angeles and Washington, D.C., with the latter move designed to preempt any Congressional pressure by filling the void in the nation's capital once Griffith had fled to the Twin Cities. The National League added New York and Houston. Like all subsequent expansions, the first expansions happened not so much because major league owners proactively sought to expand baseball's footprint but because outside forces exerted pressure and threatened baseball's comfortable legislative status quo.

As the tumultuous decade of the 1960s came to a close, the baseball establishment decided once again to expand. In 1967, when Athletics owner Charlie Finley announced that he was moving the A's to Oakland, Kansas City officials asked major league baseball for an expansion team to replace the American League club, similar to what happened when the Senators left Washington, D.C. The people of Kansas City were told to wait a few years. With that, city officials called on Stuart Symington, then a senator from Missouri, who announced that he was opening hearings on revoking the anti-trust exemption. Very quickly, American League owners held an emergency meeting by telephone and awarded Kansas City an expansion team. In what proved to be a mistake, the Seattle Pilots, later made infamous by Jim Bouton's *Ball Four*, became the twelfth American League team. However, it was a bad team and sparked almost no interest among Seattle baseball fans. Meanwhile, the National League added a franchise in San Diego and one in Montreal. By adding Montreal, the city in which Jackie Robinson began his career in organized baseball in 1946 with the Triple-A Royals, baseball had made its first official move toward internationalizing the major leagues.

Major league owners knew that twelve-team leagues did not make any sense. Certainly, they understood the difficulty of keeping fans interested in—and selling tickets for—a club in 11th or 12th place. They also knew that a championship series in each league meant more television money. The owners decided to split each league into two six-team divisions, creating two pennant races in each league, and to introduce a five-game League Championship Series in both the American League and the National League.

That structure did not last through the 1970s. The decision to expand the American League by two teams in 1977 occurred as a direct result of an anti-trust lawsuit by Slade Gorton, then attorney general of Washington. The lawsuit had been winding its way through the courts since his Pilots had declared bankruptcy after just one season and had been sold to a group led by Bud Selig, who moved the club to Milwaukee. Threatened with treble damages and the loss of anti-trust protection, the American League acceded to the demand and awarded Seattle another franchise. Because Montreal was part of major league baseball, Toronto became very interested in becoming a major league baseball city. So the American League expanded, adding the Seattle Mariners and the Toronto Blue Jays in 1977.

The National League at the time decided not to expand. This left major league baseball with twelve teams in the National League and fourteen teams in the American League. This imbalance created some issues with the division of national TV money, which always had been split evenly between the two leagues. With two fewer National League teams, each National League team received more than each American League team, so the formula was adjusted to divide TV revenue twenty-six ways. A fourteen-team league is unwieldy from several perspectives, including scheduling. Through the rest of Bowie Kuhn's term as commissioner and into the term of Peter Ueberroth, there was off-and-on pressure to expand again, both internally and from legislators representing cities and states that wanted major league baseball. In the face of this pressure, neither the owners nor the commissioner took definitive action to add more clubs. Some movement on the issue became inevitable, though, when the basic agreement negotiated between the owners and players early in 1985, during Ueberroth's tenure, gave approval for expanding the National League by two clubs.

More Attention to Expanding Major League Baseball

If demand exists for additional major league baseball franchises and if cities have sufficient size and offer adequate potential fan support and facilities, why would baseball be hesitant to expand? According to an analysis by Ronald Cox, baseball sought to delay and limit expansion to maintain a high level of competition for potential new franchises, thereby driving up new franchise fees. At the same time, the baseball hierarchy maintains "believable threat locations," that is, cities without clubs that give teams the ability to threaten to relocate if their current cities do not approve public subsidies for ballpark construction or renovation.[1]

One additional argument for not expanding baseball has always been that expansion leads to dilution of talent because the talent pool is not sufficient to bring fifty or 100 new players into the league and maintain the same level of pitching, hitting, and defense. Bill Giles talks about asking his dad, National League President Warren Giles, where the players for the expansion teams would come from. The elder Giles responded:

> Mr. Wrigley [Philip K. Wrigley, CEO of Wrigley's Gum and at the time the owner of the Cubs] always votes against expansion and he always says the same thing in the meetings. He says, "If I want to sell more chewing gum, I don't put water in the chewing gum."

> And he said, "Expansion is watering down the quality of play and we are in trouble because there are not enough players and the quality will go down."[2]

According to one unnamed owner, "The main question is talent. You're not doing these cities a favor if there's not a well-conceived plan. Have you ever seen pitching worse than it is now? What happens when you add six more clubs?"[3]

Another key factor, according to baseball executives including Bill Giles, Former Red Sox CEO John Harrington, and former MLB chief operating officer (COO) Bob DuPuy, is a concern that expansion dilutes central fund money, which comes mostly from national television contracts, into smaller shares for individual clubs. According to Giles, "Some club owners felt that the expansion money they received was good for them. I never agreed with that, and I don't agree with it today because the more teams you have, the more you split up the central fund, and over a long period of time, you really don't make that much money from expansion."[4]

In May 1987, Commissioner Ueberroth commented:

> I have a sense, a real sense, that they [the owners] are moving forward. Baseball's no different than any institution. With all the teams losing money, expansion could not even be considered. But that's turning around quickly [teams' finances]. I think [expansion] is much more in the forefront. I'm not bringing it up [now]. It's being brought up in general by other baseball people, which is a good sign.

American League President Dr. Bobby Brown indicated that expansion had been discussed at a spring meeting of baseball's long-range planning committee. "With our current 14 teams, scheduling problems are monumental. They'd be eliminated with 16 teams," said Brown. "Expansion, in that light, is always being looked at. . . . I believe there'll come a day with 32 teams, 16 in each league. That number is certainly more magic than 26."[5] Ueberroth later commented that major league baseball would expand "sooner than later" and said that he believed that having thirty-two teams "makes the most sense, long-term."[6] Having thirty-two teams opens up the possibility of four eight-team divisions, and that prospect creates interest in interleague play. In fact, Giles said at the time that he wouldn't favor expansion until interleague play was considered.[7]

On October 31, 1987, the U.S. Senate established a task force, officially named the Senate Task Force on the Expansion of Major League Baseball, led by Senator Tim Wirth of Colorado and including senators from eight states. The task force's stated goal was expediting the expansion process by putting political pressure on major league baseball. "We hope that our presence and our joint interest will help to encourage Major League Baseball to move more rapidly than they have on expansion," said Wirth.[8] Other powerful senators on the task force included Howard Metzenbaum of Ohio, chairman of the Antitrust, Monopoly and Business Rights Subcommittee of the Senate Judiciary Committee, and Dennis DeConcini of Arizona, the ranking Democrat behind Metzenbaum on that committee. Florida's two senators, Democrats Lawton Chiles and Robert Graham, joined the task force, intent on seeking a franchise for South Florida in Tampa–St. Petersburg. "We look forward in Florida to having that major league expansion come our way," said Chiles.[9]

The next spring, when Ueberroth still had not indicated definitive plans for expansion, the senators were not pleased. Senator Wirth said, "We operated in good faith and have not gotten a sufficient response. We don't like to be stiffed that way." John Warner, Republican Senator from Virginia, used a baseball metaphor to warn the owners that "[baseball] better gets its act together, because if Congress gets into the batter's box, we'll hit the ball and we have no idea where it will go."[10] Other interested observers also expressed skepticism, including Steve Katich, executive director of the Denver Baseball Commission, who said, "In 1984, Commissioner Ueberroth called expansion a front-burner issue. In 1985, thirteen cities made presentations to a committee in New York. We thought baseball was ready to move. The last couple of years have proved very frustrating. If major league baseball is addressing the issue, it's difficult to see the process. It doesn't seem to be very high on anyone's priority list."[11]

During the owners' meetings in December of that year, Giles, after hearing the commissioner indicate his support for expansion, said, "I'm sure there's going to be expansion. I just don't know when it's going to be. Right now, there's just no momentum for it. That could change, but I don't know when."[12] National League President Bart Giamatti, citing two of the barriers to specific plans for expansion, noted, "There is no time schedule. Until the TV agreement and the labor agreement are reached, it would be a senseless act to go faster."[13]

The hammer that members of Congress could wield against baseball results from baseball's anomalous anti-trust exemption, originally granted by a Supreme Court decision in 1922 and never overturned, despite repeated opportunities to do so, including the celebrated Curt Flood case. Every time baseball has acted in a manner that members of Congress do not like, one or more legislators will trot out the old idea of looking at baseball's anti-trust exemption as a not-so-thinly-veiled threat that baseball had better do what Congress wants. These Congressional threats have continued to today, most recently regarding baseball's response to its steroid problem.

Baseball clearly values its special status as the only major spectator sport with such an exemption because it allows for control over the number and location of franchises as well as the structure of the minor leagues, two "gold watch" issues for baseball. As a result, the creation of the Senate committee and its threat to introduce legislation to revoke the exemption forced Peter Ueberroth's hand, and he responded by at least engaging in some discussion about the logistics of expansion. Bart Giamatti and his deputy and then successor, Fay Vincent, had the same message for the legislators who demanded expansion: baseball will decide when it is right to expand, and baseball will expand on the timetable of its choosing, initially by two teams in the National League. The commissioner's office offered more specifics with an announcement on June 15, 1989, that baseball would establish a timetable for expansion of the National League by two teams, not six, as the members of Congress wanted, within ninety days after the completion of a new Basic Agreement, because the CBA in place at the time was due to expire at the end of that year.[14]

According to Jerry Reinsdorf, "It was basically political pressure to expand. Baseball has always been concerned about the loss of its anti-trust exemption, and so there were cities that could support baseball and they got their senators involved and created a lot of pressure to expand."[15] Sports commentator Evan Weiner proclaimed that the 1990s expansions came about partly because Senators Tim Wirth of Colorado and Connie Mack (grandson of the legendary A's manager and owner) put heat on baseball to expand or risk losing its anti-trust exemption.[16]

Only four weeks before his sudden and unexpected death, Giamatti met with the task force and two congressmen. They pressed the commissioner for a commitment to expand the American League by at least two teams and the National League by at least four, for a total of thirty-two teams. Senator John McCain from Arizona, a supporter of an expansion franchise in Phoenix, commented, "In our view, there are six or eight cities which are very strongly qualified" for a major league team. Giamatti's response was simply to repeat the National League owners' commitment to add two teams at some point in the 1990s. The commissioner said, "It is a fact that two is not six. It is not eight. It is not ten," he told reporters after the meeting. "Our disagreement is about the pace and about the number."[17]

On assuming the job of commissioner after Giamatti's death, Fay Vincent said that he supported Giamatti on the expansion issue and that the previously announced timetable would not change. "I think the expansion process is right. We will stay the course." National League owners said that the league would expand by two teams within ninety days of signing a new CBA with the players.[18]

On March 1, 1990, nineteen senators from the Western Plains and Rocky Mountains regions signed a letter to Commissioner Vincent, pushing Denver as the next expansion city. The letter created the final push that it took to get the owners and the commissioner to establish a specific timetable for expansion.[19] After the spring 1990 lockout ended and the owners and players reached a new labor agreement, Vincent reported, "It is clear the National League is going to announce a timetable for expansion . . . some time before the middle of June. Then will come an announcement as to when the expansion will take place."[20] The National League agreed to expand by two teams, and Vincent indicated that at the time there were no plans to expand beyond twenty-eight teams in the two major leagues. Vincent articulated baseball's position as follows:

> I'm not saying expansion beyond two teams is unlikely. I'm saying it is unlikely that baseball will expand by four additional teams by the year 2000. My sense is that as we begin to look at the process and evaluate the expansion of these two teams, we will find that the markets that we might have evaluated might not be as strong, that the complexities of expansion are going to be more considerable than we'd anticipated and, given the economics of baseball and the pricing that will be involved here, there are not going to be as many candidates with the kinds of resources and local support as we might otherwise have expected.[21]

Several factors created the motivation to expand in 1993 (and again in 1998), including the pressure from Congress on baseball's anti-trust exemption and the advantages enjoyed by baseball due to that exemption. However, other factors were at work, including "political mobilization by cities and ownership groups that had long lobbied for inclusion in baseball's exclusive club and along the way had established an important connection to baseball's power brokers, giving them an edge in the politics of expansion."[22] In addition, as we have discussed in the chapter on collusion, baseball's owners were on the hook for $280 million, the total amount of the penalties assessed by arbitrators Thomas Roberts and George Nicolau in the three rounds of collusion grievances brought by the Players Association. Moreover, the owners faced a precipitous decline in national television revenue once the sweetheart CBS contract ended in 1993.

The Expansion Plan Comes Together: Round One

The National League expansion committee initially consisted of Pittsburgh Pirates Chairman Doug Danfort, New York Mets president Fred Wilpon, and Houston Astros owner John McMullen, plus National League President Bill White. In January 1991, Bill Giles, who had been a member of Peter Ueberroth's long-range planning committee, replaced McMullen, who had announced his intention to sell the Houston franchise. As public relations director and traveling secretary of the Houston Colt .45s at their beginning, Giles had experience. "I've gone through the expansion thing from both sides. I know what's necessary from the expansion end. Plus I've built a number of stadiums."[23]

The National League expansion committee received eighteen applications, each accompanied by a $100,000 fee, from prospective owners in Buffalo, Charlotte, Denver, Miami, Nashville, Orlando, Phoenix, Sacramento, Tampa–St. Petersburg, and Washington. From the beginning, the bid from the nation's capital was problematic for some baseball leaders. While Orioles owner Eli Jacobs said that he had no position on a Washington, D.C., franchise, Giles said, "I'm partial to putting teams in areas where there's not a close proximity" to existing franchises.[24] After initial review of the applications, the committee chose Washington, Buffalo, Denver, Miami, Orlando, and Tampa–St. Petersburg as the six finalists.

The baseball hierarchy considered multiple factors in evaluating proposals from different cities and different ownership groups. Peter Ueberroth had said that the three most important criteria in deciding on an expansion city are: (1) the stadium being owned or controlled by the baseball team; (2) local ownership with roots in the community; and (3) long-term political support in the community.[25] Expansion committee Chairman Douglas Danforth said that in addition to the quality of stadium facilities and location, the cities are judged on capital structure (who the investors are, the amount of debt the team will be carrying, probability of economic success), quality of ownership (whether the prospective owners are the type of people baseball's current owners want as partners), public support (government and fans), and demographics (population density, media market size, projected television and radio revenues, the area's economic profile, and climate).[26]

Similarly, Giles identified the major factors as the following: (1) the quality of the ownership group; (2) adequate capital of the ownership group to invest in the initial franchise fee as well as other start-up costs because baseball does not like to bring in owners who have to borrow a large portion of the up-front investment; (3) an adequate facility or the promise of one; and (4) the size of the city, that is, the size of the television market, the number of potential fans, and the number of corporations that can sponsor the club. He also said that baseball has to consider geography. For example, a potential Washington, D.C., franchise would not make sense in the American League because of the proximity to Baltimore. Early in the process, Giles said, "I just don't see giving out a new franchise when it's going to hurt an existing one."[27] Giles says today:

> I was head of the expansion committee and we went to Miami, we went to Orlando, we went to Tampa Bay, and to Denver. Washington was in the mix somehow. Those were the five candidates. [Buffalo had been eliminated from consideration before the expansion committee visited the candidate cities.] We needed to have number one, a good market; number two, a facility to play in; and number three, good ownership. Washington never came up with any good ownership. So we didn't really study that too hard because there was not a candidate to own the team, which always kind of disappointed me in particular and everybody [else as well] because I always felt that major league baseball should be in the capitol of the United States, but they never had a viable ownership there.[28]

While some observers speculated that Giles might be partial to Tampa–St. Petersburg due to the relationship he had built with that area because the Phillies train in nearby Clearwater, he denied that this factor would have any impact on the committee's decision. "I have no connections with anybody. The selection process is going to be a close call."[29] The expansion committee visited each of the finalist cities and carefully reviewed the ownership groups. Being a baseball lifer, the son of a former club president and league president, and someone who from his youth had wanted to run a baseball club, Giles was particularly concerned about the quality of the ownership group. "I think I can usually analyze people rather quickly, whether they have integrity and whether they have intelligence. And I'm usually right on it." As for the prospective owners, "They're going to be a partner, a brother so to speak. And the way this industry is going, it's important to have people of integrity and the right kind of philosophy. . . . I think it's kind of bad sometimes to have owners that have baseball as a hobby, because if we don't have owners that think of the other partners—meaning the other owners—then we're going to have more financial problems."[30]

The National League expansion committee recommended which two groups should have teams, but the process required the ownership committee to approve the selections. Criteria for evaluation, according to ownership committee Chair Fred Kuhlmann of the Cardinals, included the prospective ownership groups' finances, partnership agreements, personal backgrounds, and ties to the communities they represent. Kuhlmann's committee endorsed the expansion committee's choices unanimously.

On June 10, 1991, the expansion committee recommended Denver and Miami as the two new expansion cities, but the official announcement did not come until July 5, after the National League owners had approved the committee's recommendation. One of the disappointed cities was Phoenix. Fay Vincent said, "Everyone looks at this as a competition among cities. It is not that. It is a competition among ownership groups. I think that has been overlooked. It wasn't that Phoenix was a bad city. It's just that they didn't have the ownership in place."[31] Giles had changed his mind about the potential for Washington, D.C., as an expansion franchise, citing RFK Stadium and parking as positive factors. Nevertheless, the D.C. bid failed due at least in part to undercapitalization. Some equity commitments disappeared during the process, leaving the D.C. group short of the total initial capital requirements for the expansion fee plus start-up costs.

The awarding of a franchise to Denver was based on a good deal of political lobbying, legislation, and taxpayer support. Interestingly, Tim Wirth called no more meetings of the expansion task force once Denver became an expansion city. A strong ownership group headed by John Antonucci, an Ohio beverage distributor, and Michael I. Monus, head of the Phar-Mor drugstore chain, added to the attractiveness of the Denver proposal. Local and regional companies completed the group.

Miami's choice as the other 1993 expansion club was due in large part to its prospective owner, Wayne Huizenga, who had built a huge business empire, first with Waste Management and then with Blockbuster. His wealth meant that he did not have to borrow any of the franchise fee or upfront investment requirements. Huizenga also was a close friend of Carl Barger, a longtime and well-respected baseball executive who was president of the Pittsburgh Pirates and a member of the board of directors of Blockbuster Entertainment Corporation. Shortly after making his successful bid, Huizenga named Barger president of the Marlins. Huizenga had a controlling interest in a suitable facility, Joe Robbie Stadium, which had been constructed as a multipurpose facility and would get the requisite modification in seating arrangements to render it suitable for baseball. A few years later, Huizenga's Marlins won the 1997 World Championship. In the following off-season, he gutted his team, claiming—somewhat disingenuously, according to an analysis by Andrew Zimbalist[32]—that he had lost $34 million. He sold his club once his five-year tax benefit of writing off the value of player contracts had expired; at that point, Huizenga was considered much less of an asset to baseball.

The selection of Miami and Denver ended a six-year contest among six finalists and left several losers, including Washington, D.C., Buffalo, Tampa–St. Petersburg, and Orlando. Having already lost the prospect of a team—the White Sox had flirted with moving to St. Petersburg—the decision was especially galling because St. Petersburg had built a domed stadium specifically to lure a franchise. Citizens of St. Petersburg would have to wait a few more years and endure one more failed courtship, when National League owners refused to let Bob Lurie sell the San Francisco Giants to a Florida-based group in 1992, for their entry into the big leagues.

A New Issue in Baseball Arises: How to Split Expansion Fees between the Leagues

National League President Bill White led a four-person committee that set the entry fees for the new expansion clubs at $95 million, a figure higher than the selling price of any franchise in history, save for the New York Mets in 1986, and reflected the trend of rapidly increasing franchise values after free agency. Previous expansions (1961 and 1962, and 1969, when both leagues expanded, and 1977, when only the American League expanded) were league-only affairs, and each league handled the expansion separately. New clubs stocked their rosters with players in a one-league expansion draft, and each league kept the money from the entry fees.

The franchise fees in 1977 had been only $7 million (which included $175,000 for each of thirty players drafted in the expansion draft), so $95 million represented, as characterized by former Red Sox president John Harrington, "real money." All previous bets on sharing expansion fees were off. In 1993, American League owners pressed for a liberal share of the new dollars coming from Denver and Miami. The American League owners believed that a windfall of nearly $16 million apiece for the twelve National League teams could create competitive imbalance, while funds generated by national television, radio, and licensing rights would be cut twenty-eight ways instead of twenty-six. Moreover, the American League owners were on the hook for the collusion damages, just as the National League owners were. Giles articulated the initial response of the National League owners, "As far as I'm concerned it isn't negotiable. But certainly the American League has the right to speak their piece. I just feel that there's no precedent or logic for it. It's always been kept within the leagues. The league in which you expand is always going to be hurt initially because attendance will suffer some because the expansion cities will not draw well."[33]

According to league statutes, National League owners had to approve the new teams by a three-quarters vote, while American League owners had to approve the new franchises by a majority vote. Commissioner Vincent, aware that the American League owners, unhappy over the prospective split of the new franchise fees, could block the expansion altogether, announced that if the dispute could not be resolved through negotiations, he would make a binding ruling.

Eventually, the National League offered the American League 30 percent of the total of $190 million in expansion fees, but the American League owners thought that they could get a better deal from Vincent. After considering the request, the commissioner announced the deal: American League owners would get 22 percent of the total, while each of the fourteen American League teams would contribute three players to the pool of players joining the new National League clubs. This amounted to 54 percent of the players. He also announced that in the future, expansion fees would be split 50–50 between the leagues. This decision did little to mollify American League owners, who clearly understood that with twenty-eight teams split evenly between the two leagues, future expansion would have to include both leagues to maintain parity.

One of the baseball executives who complained most vociferously about Vincent's decision was Twins General Manager Andy MacPhail. This small-market club had its revenue constrained by the size of the Minneapolis–St. Paul market. MacPhail expressed his position clearly:

> What is equitable about this? We provide 54 percent of the players and get $1 million a player. The National League clubs get $6 million a player to replenish their coffers and make up for the cost. We spend $6 million a year in scouting and development, and if we produce two good players a year, we are doing our job. Losing three players in a small market and not getting compensated is a major loss. The Dodgers or Red Sox can eat the losses. We can't. We couldn't afford to gamble $800,000 on a John Candelaria; we wanted him, but we couldn't afford $800,000. Texas has had to juggle its roster and payroll to keep at $20 million. Fay has polarized the leagues and the conflicts within the leagues. But maybe he doesn't understand the cost of replacing the players.[34]

Vincent made his decision, which, based on the 22 percent allocated to the American League, awarded $12.8 million to each National League team and $3 million to each American League team. As a result, American League owners were unhappy with both the commissioner and their National League counterparts. American League owners had concerns about the expansion draft, specifically, about the quality of players the American League stood to lose by placing them on the unprotected list for draft in November 1992. Each team stood to lose three players. The format specified that a team could protect fifteen players in the first round, three more in the second round, and three more in the third; technically, a team would lose its 16th, 20th, and 24th players.

According to Giles, "I think that there is some concern in the American League that if they're going to give up three players for $3 million, the guidelines for the quality of those players should be readjusted. I'm assuming, reading between the lines, that the 16th, 20th and 24th players are probably worth more than 3 million bucks. I can see their logic."[35] Jerry Reinsdorf said, "I think people would rather have no money than give up three players for $3 million.[36]

Realignment of the National League

In 1992, after the decision to add Miami and Denver, talk of realigning the National League emerged. Having Chicago and St. Louis in the East and Atlanta and Cincinnati in the West made little geographic sense. A league committee proposed that the Cubs and Cardinals move to the West, exchanging places with the Braves and Reds, who would go to the East. Such a move made perfect geographical sense because the position of those in the respective divisions was a remnant of the initial placement of clubs, mainly based on rivalries, when the National League went from ten to twelve teams in 1969. Atlanta and Cincinnati were both quite pleased with the move because they would play more games closer to home in the eastern and central time zones, taking advantage of earlier start times. St. Louis agreed to the move, provided that the Cubs, their number one National League rival, went with them. The trouble rested with the Cubs, owned by the Tribune Company, also owner of WGN, a local Chicago television station turned superstation, which broadcast many of the Cubs games. The proposed move to the Western Division threatened the size of WGN's broadcast audiences because many more games would start at 9:00 P.M. or 10:00 P.M. central time, leading to smaller audiences, lower ratings, and a consequent decline in advertising revenue. The issue came to a vote, which was 10–2 in favor of realignment, but was blocked by a negative vote from the Cubs, which was all it took.[37]

Subsequently, six clubs asked Vincent to order the teams to move. Shortly before the 1992 All-Star Game, Vincent, using his "bests interests of baseball" power, announced his decision to move Chicago and St.

Louis from the National League East to the West, flip-flopping with Atlanta and Cincinnati, which were bound for the East. Stanton Cook, a Tribune Company executive and president of the Cubs, expressed strong reservations. Before Vincent's pronouncement, National League President Bill White had been trying for months to persuade the Cubs to move. According to Sands and Gammons, he had been working on a flexible schedule for the 1993 season that would have allowed WGN to continue to broadcast most of the Cubs games early enough to lead into the station's lucrative late-evening news show.[38] Vincent said that he determined that "the best interests of baseball have not been served in this instance by the National League's stringent voting requirement, which thwarts the preferences of the great majority of National League clubs."[39]

Vincent's decision, as previously indicated, outraged White. Heretofore, the leagues had handled these types of decisions internally, according to their respective league constitutions. Now, Vincent had appropriated what White believed to the purview of the league—the owners and president. The feeling was that Vincent's decision could create a slippery slope that resulted in the loss of the independence of the two leagues. While the owners of the other clubs in the National League may have favored the moves ultimately ordered by Vincent, they absolutely did not approve of the commissioner usurping—in their minds, at least—the league's authority, under its constitution, to make such alignment decisions. White released a statement, saying, "I am very disappointed with the commissioner's extraordinary decision to override the National League constitution. By this act the commissioner has jeopardized a longstanding working document which has governed the National League for decades. Although we worked to attain realignment, we did so within the guidelines of the constitution."[40]

The Cubs filed suit to block the move, on the basis that Vincent was exceeding his authority, as limited by Article VII of the Major League Agreement, which limited the commissioner's latitude in resolving disputes that were covered by either the Agreement or by collective bargaining. The Cubs found a favorable ruling with District Judge Suzanne Conlon in the northern district of Illinois that concluded that the Agreement superseded the commissioner's "best interests" authority.[41] The commissioner appealed Judge Conlon's decision, but before a ruling could be made on the appeal, Vincent, under extreme pressure from the owners for a series of unpopular actions and decisions, announced his resignation on September 8, 1992. Later in September, baseball's executive council, chaired by Bud Selig, rescinded the realignment order.

After Vincent stepped down and Bud Selig assumed his new role, Selig announced the formation of a new schedule format committee whose task was to examine "all aspects of divisional alignment, scheduling and possible new formats," which could include interleague play, an increase in the number of divisions, and the number of teams in the postseason. The committee consisted of John Harrington of the Red Sox as chair, Stanton Cook of the Cubs, Eddie Einhorn of the White Sox, Richard Jacobs of the Indians, Stan Kasten of the Braves, and Giles, plus the league presidents, Bobby Brown and Bill White.[42]

Mark Maske wrote in February 1993 that the game's decision makers were concerned about baseball's dwindling popularity, not to mention its shrinking revenues due to the end of the CBS TV deal. As a result, some radical proposals saw the light of day. These included a realignment that created East, West, and Central Divisions in each league, thus creating another round of playoffs with a wild card team joining the three division winners. Postseason playoffs would include a best-of-five first-round series in each league to precede the best-of-seven league championship series. Interleague play could be adopted, with American League and National League clubs playing a limited number of regular season games against one another.[43] Giles, also a member of the committee negotiating the next television contract—which ultimately created the Baseball Network—confirmed in early 1993 that network officials had expressed a desire for interleague play. He said, "Everybody is interested in interleague play."[44]

As part of the new TV deal, the owners approved expanding the playoffs by adding an additional round for the 1994 season, but without deciding on how the additional playoff teams would be selected. With two divisions in each league, the options included the second-place teams in each division and the first-place teams plus the two teams with the next best records. During summer 1993, pressured by a deadline to submit the 1994 schedule to the union, the owners decided to postpone the split into three divisions until 1995. Then Donald Fehr announced that the players were in favor of going to three divisions in each league. Fehr said that the players opposed expanded playoffs that would include two non-championship teams, but would consider an additional round in the postseason if the four postseason teams consisted of three division winners and a wild card team, the team with the next best record overall. After much discussion and deliberation, and having been pushed by the Players Association, the owners voted 26–2 in favor of three divisions in each league and adding a wild card team to the postseason, thereby doubling the number of playoff teams in each league from two to four.

Bob Costas, for one, hated the idea of what he considered watering down the postseason and ostensibly devaluing the pennant races. In his 2000 book, *Fair Ball: A Fan's Case for Baseball,* he decried the fact that the Atlanta versus San Francisco race in the National League West in 1993 was, for him, at least, the last great pennant race. When asked about whether three divisions and expanded playoffs somehow hurt baseball, Giles, a champion of three divisions and expanded playoffs, voiced the opinion that the expanded playoffs would help baseball by giving more fans hope that their team could reach the World Series, or at least the postseason. He went on say that fan surveys had all indicated that fans wanted more teams in the playoffs. He was a strong believer in the notion that more spots in the postseason meant more fans engaged in the pennant races as the season approached its climax, leading to more interest in the game and better attendance and television ratings.[45]

In defending the new plan, Giles told Frank Dolson of the *Philadelphia Inquirer*, "I did not like the idea of second-place teams in two divisions [qualifying for the postseason play], but I do believe in expanded playoffs." One of the fears associated with the original owners' plan was the possibility that a team that finishes a distant second, with a poor won-lost record, will land in the playoffs. "This way, I don't think you'll ever have a team below .500 with a chance to be in the playoffs."[46] Giles also advocated both an unbalanced schedule—"The real way to do it in my opinion is to have an unbalanced schedule"[47]—and the use of a best-of-seven format in all postseason series. However, several teams refused to support the expanded divisional alignment without retention of a balanced schedule, and the use of "best of seven" in the divisional series proved to be problematic because of the length of the season and the potential for playing World Series games in November.

A couple of issues regarding placement of teams delayed the final resolution. Atlanta preferred the East to the Central and could reasonably trade places with Pittsburgh, although Pittsburgh preferred to stay in the East to maintain its rivalry with Philadelphia. Giles said, "The Pirates feel very, very strongly—Atlanta does, too—but Pittsburgh has been in the East for 104 years and they have rivalries with us in Philadelphia and the Mets and they didn't want to go Central."[48] As owner of the Phillies, Giles "wanted to have Pittsburgh and Cincinnati in our division. The Braves were fine, but we wanted the older, more established teams" with which the Phillies had had rivalries for 100 years. He continued, "We didn't care about Florida and Montreal." But the Pirates finally consented to go to the National League Central.[49]

Giles pointed out, "There were a lot of arguments about who went where. Time zones were a big part of it, to get better TV ratings." Detroit is in the Eastern Time zone, and "we thought they should be in the East." According to Giles, "when the Tigers saw that they were going to be in the same division as the Red Sox and Yankees, they volunteered to go to the Central Division. They looked at the White Sox and Minnesota and said, 'We can beat these guys because they have about the same money that we do.'"[50] The Texas Rangers, for reasons similar to those underlying the hesitancy of the Cubs to be placed in the National League West, objected to being placed in the American League West. George W. Bush, future president and at that time managing partner of the Rangers, said, "I don't want to be in the American League West, where most of our games are in the middle of the night and most of our fans are asleep." Bush also expressed reservations about the extra round of playoffs, saying that, as a traditionalist, "I think they're bad for baseball."[51] Former Red Sox CEO John Harrington explained how Bush finally agreed to be placed in the AL West:

> George Bush didn't want to take Texas into the Western Division because of the time zone difference. He knew that we were looking at unbalanced schedules at the time as well, where you played more games within your division than outside your division. To get his vote, and he was the very last vote to come across on the three divisions, whereby he would go into the four-team American League West Division, we had to agree that we would play a balanced schedule. He didn't want to have to play more games on the West Coast than he was playing already. So that is the way we resolved that issue. Once you studied everything and talked to the owners, it kind of fell into place and George held out, and understandably, because he was very concerned about the impact on radio and TV [ratings].[52]

Reaching a Conclusion

Finally, in January 1994, at the owners' meetings in Fort Lauderdale, Florida, Major League Baseball announced adoption of the realignment plan and expanded postseason, with fourteen teams and three divisions in each league. The Players Association approved the plan after reaching an agreement on how the revenue from the additional round of playoffs would be distributed between the owners and players. The plan was approved for the 1994 season only. The strike of 1994, however, caused a delay in implementing the new plan until the 1995 season.

Some owners, as we have seen, did not like the alignment of the divisions. In addition, the Players Association had a stake in divisional alignments and the structure of the postseason, and any deal required union approval. Coincident to the discussions on realignment and the postseason, the owners and players were at loggerheads over the terms of the new

CBA. To avoid an inevitable logjam, the owners and players agreed to discuss the realignment and postseason questions separately. The two sides were stuck on how much money the players would receive from the additional round of playoffs. After a series of proposals and counterproposals, the owners accepted a proposal from the Players Association that the players be granted 80 percent of the revenues from the first three games of the best-of-five first-round playoffs. The formats for the league championship series and World Series that gave 60 percent of the revenue for the first four games of each series to the players remained unchanged.[53]

The job was only half completed. Already, owners had been discussing another round of expansion to take baseball to thirty teams and introduce interleague play.

Expansion, Round Two: From Twenty-Eight to Thirty

Realignment into six divisions directly led to a second round of expansion in the 1990s, since baseball could add two teams and have six divisions of five clubs apiece. Early on, as the owners considered a new alignment with twenty-eight teams and an expanded postseason, the matter was under discussion. Giles was one of the owners who commented on the situation, saying, "Unofficially, there's been some talk. We're not going to do anything drastic until we have a new labor agreement [with the players] in place. I personally am in favor of three divisions [in each league] with five teams apiece, along with the expanded playoffs and interleague play."[54]

After delaying expansion for a decade and a half, why did baseball decide to expand again so quickly? The owners missed out on more than $500 million in potential revenues in 1994 and 1995 because of the players' strike, and the addition of two teams that each pay a franchise fee in the vicinity of $140 million would generate $10 million for each of the twenty-eight existing clubs. The owners also still wanted to preserve their exemption from federal anti-trust laws. It just so happened that the representatives from Florida and Arizona had been leading the effort to get the exemption repealed or limited.

Another factor was the Players Association. Donald Fehr long had been a vocal proponent of further expansion. Mark Maske reported that the union would approve expanded playoffs if the owners agreed to expand from twenty-eight to thirty-two teams in a "reasonable" amount of time—perhaps five years. With thirty-two teams, baseball could have four eight-team divisions, with the division winners qualifying for the playoffs, as well as an undetermined number of runners-up.[55]

From the start, Tampa–St. Petersburg and Phoenix were solid front-runners for the two new franchises. One owner speculated that there might be no need for the "public beauty contests" that preceded the 1991 expansion announcement. With franchise values continuing to rise, insiders speculated that the next round of new clubs would have to pay $140–200 million for the privilege of joining the major leagues. Nevertheless, the owners knew that there would be cities hoping for the opportunity to join their exclusive club. Despite its continuing efforts, most owners apparently did not consider Washington, D.C., a serious player, saying privately that if Tampa Bay and Phoenix didn't get the nod, then Orlando, Charlotte, and perhaps even Mexico City would be next in line.[56] Buffalo, Sacramento, Memphis, and Nashville were also considered early in the process.

In March 1994, there was further evidence that Phoenix and Tampa–St. Petersburg were in line to receive franchises when the Executive Council appointed six owners to an expansion committee, chaired by John Harrington of the Boston Red Sox and joined by George Steinbrenner of the Yankees, Jerry Reinsdorf of the White Sox, Richard Jacobs of Cleveland, Stan Kasten of Atlanta, Stanton Cook of the Cubs, and Giles. Although he claimed that his friendship with Jerry Colangelo, a Chicagoan and a fellow NBA owner, had nothing to do with the selection process, at the time it was thought that the Reinsdorf-Colangelo friendship could only be good news for Phoenix. In addition, some thought that Reinsdorf owed a debt to the Tampa Bay area because it was his threatened move of the White Sox to that area that prompted the Illinois Legislature to approve construction of a new Comiskey Park in Chicago. Another committee member was connected to a candidate city; Steinbrenner lived in Tampa, the site of the Yankees spring training base. "This isn't a committee just to study cities," said Harrington. "It will cover all aspects, but especially the economics. We want to judge the impact it has on the future and present major leagues."[57]

The expansion committee made its recommendation to award new franchises to Phoenix and Tampa–St. Petersburg on March 7, 1995, and Major League Baseball Properties quickly placed officially licensed Diamondback and Devil Ray merchandise on store shelves. The turnaround time from franchise announcement to the arrival of product in stores was testament to the fact that Phoenix and Tampa Bay were the apples of baseball's eye long before the decision was announced. Sales of baseball merchandise had slowed significantly due to the players' strike and was down by 20 percent for the 1994 season. Baseball hoped that new merchandise with contemporary, nontraditional color schemes would boost sales.

The off-and-on romance between baseball and the Tampa Bay area had started well before the spring 1994 decision to add the Devil Rays to the ranks of major league baseball. Despite Commissioner Ueberroth's admonition that a new stadium would not necessarily lead to a major league franchise, the St. Petersburg local government approved and built a taxpayer-financed domed stadium for more than $234 million, a project that commenced in 1986 and concluded in 1990. In 1988, during the construction phase, the Chicago White Sox used the threat of relocating to Tampa Bay to secure public funding and favorable lease terms for the new Comiskey Park, now U.S. Cellular Field, which required a last-minute appropriation by the Illinois State Legislature. Tampa Bay's continuing efforts to secure a franchise via either expansion or relocation included a long-running lawsuit against major league baseball on anti-trust grounds filed by Tampa Bay businessman Frank Morsani over the failure to secure a franchise, a case that was not settled until 2003, and another flirtation when Bob Lurie wanted to sell the San Francisco Giants to a St. Petersburg–based group in 1992, but was turned down by the National League owners.[58]

Once the owners placed the Diamondbacks in the National League and the Devil Rays in the American League, both baseball insiders and observers speculated that an additional realignment of the leagues would be necessary, including perhaps the radical idea that some teams would switch leagues. A group of eight American League teams threatened to block the expansion assignments, but six of them changed their minds when the owners agreed to establish a committee to examine realignment and the schedule format for 1998 and beyond. Some American League teams were concerned that they would have additional games out of their time zone, causing early and late television starts that could decrease ratings and revenue. The committee, chaired by John Harrington, who had also chaired the expansion committee, was given a charge to make a set of recommendations to the owners by June 30, 1997. A full owners' vote was scheduled to take place by the end of September to allow enough time to put together a schedule for the 1998 season, when Phoenix and Tampa were due to start play.

The 1998 expansion left major league baseball with thirty teams, two fewer than the Senate committee had mandated a decade earlier. In addition, Washington, D.C., was still without a team. Baseball, however, was still struggling financially as a result of the 1994–1995 strike and its aftermath, in addition to the rapid increase in salaries in the years after collusion, and as a result, more expansion made little economic sense. Giles said at the time that he "personally favors a moratorium on expansion after 1998." The *Kiplinger Letter* reported that the next major league baseball expansion would be pushed back to 2002.[59] As we know now, that final expansion to thirty-two teams never took place; instead, Commissioner Selig advanced what turned out to be a failed attempt to contract to twenty-eight teams right after the end of the 2001 World Series.

Interleague Baseball

Interleague play was not a new idea in the mid-1990s. During the 1930s, William Veeck, father of Bill (as in Wreck) and at the time president of the Chicago Cubs, had advocated interleague play as a way to help baseball overcome financial woes brought on by the Great Depression. Later, as owner of the struggling St. Louis Browns in 1953, the younger Veeck proposed a thirty-two-game interleague schedule, but the other owners defeated the proposal, in large part because of Veeck's unpopularity with his peers. According to Leonard Koppett, the American League proposed various plans calling for interleague play in 1960, 1962, 1973, and 1976, but these proposals were always defeated by the National League owners.[60]

Giles became the banner carrier for interleague play. He announced early in the process of the 1993 expansion that he wanted to see each team play about ten interleague games per season, meaning two against each of the clubs in the same division of the other league (e.g., East versus East, West versus West).

As the talk about divisional alignment proceeded, the owners discussed interleague play, understanding its potential for fueling fan interest and driving attendance and TV ratings. Jerry Reinsdorf recalled:

> Selig had always been a proponent of three divisions and a wild card. He wanted to have an extra round of playoffs. So I think we started with that first. Sometime in that period serious talk about interleague play began. I was always opposed to it, but I was opposed as a baseball purist. The fact is that the consumer loves it. The numbers are clear; average attendance at interleague games is higher than average attendance at regular games.[61]

Serious discussions about interleague play commenced along with the decision to expand a second time in the 1990s, from twenty-eight teams to thirty teams. Bill Giles, a strong supporter of any innovation that helped to promote baseball, said, "I'm a big proponent of 15 and 15 [teams in each league]. I don't like four-team divisions [as the American League West and National League West now are]. I'm also a big proponent of interleague play. If you go 15 and 15, you have to have interleague play."[62]

According to Giles, "We've done a lot of research among fans. I think it was 63 percent who favored interleague play. We haven't done research on the economic impact, but my gut feeling is that it will improve attendance, television ratings and interest. There are definitely a few drawbacks, but I think if you weigh the pluses and minuses, it's a positive thing to do."[63] When asked about opposition to the concept, Giles replied, "I don't know of any."[64] He acknowledged that the owners had not conducted any in-depth studies about the effects of interleague play, but he became a strong and outspoken advocate. George Steinbrenner, another member of the executive council at the time, said, "We have to look at anything that could make the game more attractive, and that [interleague play] is certainly a possibility."[65]

By early January, the press reported that the "most talked-about plan on the table is the brainchild of Phillies owner Bill Giles." Under Giles' proposal, teams from the corresponding divisions of the two leagues would play a three- or four-game series, with home fields alternating each year.[66]

Official authorization of interleague games required the approval of both the owners and the Players Association. As part of the 1996 CBA, the players agreed to limited interleague play in 1997 and 1998 only, with approval needed for extending interleague play into the future. Fehr said about interleague play, "This is an idea that obviously merits serious consideration and we will give it that. We have to take a hard look at anything that will be beneficial to the game." In reply, Jerry Reinsdorf said, "The purpose of interleague play would be to increase the revenues of the game, which is good for everybody. So I would hope they wouldn't make it an issue."[67]

Weighing in on the matter, Gene Orza, Fehr's lieutenant, said, "I think interleague play will be here for 1997. The case for interleague play is strong. . . . Not seeing Ken Griffey and Barry Bonds on the same field—forget economics, but from a standpoint of pure entertainment value—is hard to justify."[68] Later, Don Fehr reflected on the Players Association's position on interleague play:

> We thought on its face it was a good idea. We thought that you had all kinds of natural rivalries that would have the advantage of both novelty and staying power, and it wasn't just the Yankees and the Mets and the Cubs and the White Sox. Things like . . . Cleveland and Cincinnati and Kansas City and St. Louis or Dallas [Texas] versus Houston, and later on [Miami] Florida versus Tampa Bay. And so you could create these rivalries. It would have some novelty.

> It would allow fans in all cities to see players from everywhere, and the people that we always thought would have the most problems with it would be the baseball traditionalists, the baseball purists. And the reason they would have a problem with this was mostly because it was different and anything that is different is suspect, and I don't mean that in a negative way, but that's how they view it. The hardest thing to do in baseball is anything that no one has ever done before, and that is like moving a mountain. And so you had it there; we always thought it would be good.[69]

The Designated Hitter

The American League (AL) adopted the use of the designated hitter (DH) in 1973, at a time when the leagues were separate and made their own decisions on rules. The National League (NL) owners voted on implementing the DH in August 1980, but did not approve the measure. Giles turned out to be a central figure in the drama. The Phillies management felt that the DH would serve the team well because the Phillies had a couple of players, in particular Greg "the Bull" Luzinski, who were perfectly suited to be DHs. So Phillies owner Ruly Carpenter told Giles, who as executive vice-president often represented Carpenter at owners' meetings, to vote in favor. However, as Giles tells the story, he learned that the implementation of the rule would be delayed until the Players Association approved the measure. Not knowing what to do under that circumstance, Giles tried to reach Carpenter, who was out to sea fishing and could not be reached. Giles therefore decided to abstain, and when the Pirates, instructed to follow the Phillies lead, did the same, the vote did not carry. No DH in the NL then, now, or presumably, ever.

With the advent of interleague play, the NL was dead set against adopting the DH and the majority of AL owners expressed a desire to eliminate the rule as well. Jerry Reinsdorf said that, despite his forty-one-year ownership of the Chicago White Sox, as a Brooklyn native and an intense Brooklyn Dodgers fan, he considered himself "an NL guy" and preferred the NL style of play, without the DH.[70] As an economic issue, however, the Players Association expressed unwillingness to dump the DH. The association's position was that a DH is, on average, paid substantially more than the 25th player on the roster, who ostensibly would replace a DH if the position were eliminated. After much discussion, the owners decided to use the DH in interleague games in exactly the same way it had been used in the All-Star and postseason games, that is, a DH is used in AL parks, but there is no DH in NL parks. This decision fell short of the stated goal of the Players Association to expand the DH to the NL, but did not reduce the role of the DH for AL clubs.

According to Reinsdorf, this "is backwards from what it should be. We should use the DH in the NL parks so NL fans could see a DH game. They should not use the DH in the AL parks so that AL fans can get to see a game with pitchers up to bat. I just think it is backward." Regarding the economic issue, Reinsdorf reflected:

> The DH came into play before I was in baseball, and I think it is not as good a game [with the DH]. I think that there is less strategy involved. If we could change it on our own, we would change it. The Players Association won't agree to it because they say that if you eliminate the DH you are eliminating a high-priced player and theoretically replacing him with the 25th man on your roster [who will be paid substantially less, and payroll records verify this notion]. I say that they are overlooking the fact that we spend all of the money that we have to spend. So if I didn't have to pay a DH, I would have more money to spend on somebody else. So I don't think it is [really] a money issue, but the union believes it is.[71]

Interleague Play Approved

In January 1996, the owners approved interleague play. The Players Association approved the concept for the 1997 and 1998 seasons, subject to renewal, as part of the 1996 CBA settled later that year. Each team would play fifteen interleague games, except for the NL West and AL West clubs, which would play sixteen games each. In the first year, at least, the NL East would play three games against each of the five teams in the AL East, the NL Central would do the same against the AL Central, and the NL West would play four games apiece against the four AL West clubs. Instead of playing interleague games all season, as would have been the case with two fifteen-team leagues, baseball's hierarchy decided to highlight the innovation by creating two interleague play blocks, the first right after Memorial Day and the other around Labor Day (which was later changed). The designated hitter would continue to be used in AL parks, but not those in the NL.

Some observers noted two potential weaknesses in the initial plan. First, the idea to play against teams from the "matching" (i.e., East versus East) division left fans in other divisions without access to certain teams. For example, no one in Kansas City would ever see the Yankees or Red Sox play. Giles, referred to by Jayson Stark as the "No. 1 member of the Interleague Play Booster Club," said that this problem could be solved by rotating which division plays which in future seasons. "In the long run, a lot of people feel that's the best way to do it, so people in Philadelphia would get to see Ken Griffey play. And I, personally, favor that."[72] A second drawback involved the balanced schedule. Teams in five-team divisions play their division opponents only twelve times per year. Hence, only forty-eight of 162 games would be head-to-head division contests. But Giles pointed out that it would be possible to amend the schedule so that teams play more games against division foes and fewer against the rest of the league.[73]

In retrospect, interleague play has achieved its objectives of hyping fan interest and raising attendance and TV ratings, phenomena that commenced immediately with the first year of interleague games. Overall, interleague games in 1997 attracted an average attendance of 33,407, a figure 18 percent higher than regular games.[74]

One issue that Reinsdorf has with interleague games to this day is the fact that different teams in the same division play different interleague opponents. Potentially, this scheduling issue could give a club a significant advantage over an intradivision rival. The Cubs play six games against the White Sox every year, and these are wars. The Cardinals play six games against the Royals every year. In most recent years, the Sox have proved to be a tougher opponent for the Cubs than are the Royals for the Cardinals. According to Reinsdorf:

> Playing the Cubs [as a natural rival] means three sell-outs for us. What I don't like is that the original concept was for every team in a division to play the same teams in the other division. The AL Central [teams] would all play their interleague games against the same teams from the NL, all from one division. Then we added so-called natural rivals, and then it got perverted. I really don't like it where you [i.e., teams in the same division] play different teams.[75]

Realignment: Was Baseball Ready for Radical?

As the baseball enterprise prepared to welcome the Arizona Diamondbacks and the Tampa Bay Devil Rays, with interleague play already approved, a second realignment of the major leagues began to be considered. The owners had to resolve whether to divide the expansion teams and go to two fifteen-team leagues or have a sixteen-team league and a fourteen-team league. With two fifteen-team leagues, interleague play had to be every day. While the 16–14 model allowed interleague games to be played simultaneously during specific schedule intervals during the season (allowing the two "extra teams" to play each other in an intraleague series), questions remained about the specific league alignments. Assigning Tampa Bay to the AL West made little geographic sense. As a result, a major realignment was put on the discussion agenda, including the possibility that some teams might even switch leagues.

Bill Giles clearly articulated his desire for a more "radical" realignment that would place teams in divisions based on geography and likely require teams to switch leagues, an idea that was anathema to baseball "traditionalists." For example, he said, it made sense to have the Texas Rangers, Houston Astros, Kansas City Royals, and Colorado Rockies in the same division.

Bud Selig, chair of the executive council, and John Harrington, chair of a new committee on realignment, a successor to the expansion committee, agreed that major realignment was necessary to fix baseball's scheduling problems. In preparation for a possible major realignment, the owners proposed a plan to the Players Association by which the designated hitter rule would be eliminated in exchange for adding a 26th roster spot to each club. Union officials responded that they had no intention of permitting the owners to get rid of the designated hitter. Harrington and Angels President Tony Tavares, another member of the realignment committee, acknowledged that a major realignment could be approved without a change to the designated hitter rule. "The real goal isn't to realign. The real goal is to come up with very efficient scheduling which would make the season more meaningful," said Harrington. "Due to the complexities of scheduling . . . 16–14 is probably what we would come out with. And all of our teams want unbalanced scheduling."[76]

From a revenue perspective, geographical realignment provided benefits such as reduced travel and more fan-friendly television schedules. Harrington said:

> Eighty-five percent of all games will be played within the same time zone for fans to be able to watch and listen to games at reasonable times. The benefits are in the schedule-making. We're trying to get back to the way it was in the old days, with the eight-team leagues. Every game meant two games in the standings, and your fans knew everyone on the opposing teams because they saw them all the time.[77]

Harrington indicated that the owners preferred to accomplish realignment in one step in time for the 1998 season, instead of in stages. The committee faced a time deadline because of the requirement to present the 1998 schedule to the Players Association well in advance of the season. At this point, a radical idea emerged. Giles said that most owners favor placing all Pacific Time Zone teams in the NL as part of one large division or two smaller ones. Under that scenario, he said, "many clubs will play 150 of their 162 games in their time zone, and there would be more young people seeing games."[78]

Support was growing among owners to adopt a "16–14 plan"—favored by Selig—that would involve realignment of teams into geographical areas built around time zones, requiring between thirteen and fifteen teams to change leagues and putting the Cubs and White Sox and Yankees and Mets in the same divisions. The specifics of the "16–14" concept included two seven-team divisions in the AL and two eight-team divisions in the NL, with one league including the fourteen teams east of Chicago. The other league included the two Chicago teams and all other teams westward to California.

Chicago's teams were split on the idea. Andy MacPhail, having moved to the Cubs as president, said, "My personal bias is that I see no point in the same teams coming to the same city [to play both teams]. I don't see any magic in that. It could get to the point where Kansas City might come in and play the Sox, then go play the Cubs. I see some good in two-team cities having different teams come through." How about Ken Griffey, Jr., on the South Side and Barry Bonds on the North at Wrigley? But Reinsdorf, a member of the realignment committee, disagreed, saying, "I think rivalries are a fabulous thing. Let's get 'em going and keep 'em going. We'll be able to keep our Brewers rivalry while adding the Cubs and even the Cardinals. The Brewers can get one going with the Cubs. The two Texas teams will start meeting. That will be great for the people there." In addition, Reinsdorf stated:

> I really like the time-zone idea. There won't be as many games with three time zones in between. Those cause severe TV problems, location-wise as well as expense-wise. You've got East Coast games starting at 4 P.M. in California when people are still working and West Coast games starting at 10 P.M. in the East when people are going to bed. One of my concerns is that as a team in a two-team market, we and the Cubs will both be selling the same product to our fans. On the other hand, getting to play the Cubs 14 times, seven at home, ought to make up for it.[79]

Selig had originally pushed for radical realignment, but was open to alternatives, saying, "As much as I believe in three divisions and the wild-card format and interleague play, I believe in significant realignment. I'm just not sure to what extent."[80] Jerry Colangelo, owner of the expansion

Arizona club, steadfastly refused a simple realignment that would move his team from the NL West to the AL West. Colangelo felt that a minor realignment doesn't address what needs to be done and that baseball needs thorough and full realignment.

Several of the NL executives expressed varying degrees of dislike for the "16–14 plan." San Francisco Giants President Peter Magowan did not want the Giants and neighboring Oakland Athletics in the same league. "When you buy a team, you buy assets, which include exclusive monopoly rights to promoting games within your own league in your area on an exclusive basis. We would be asked to give that up. . . ."[81]

The Cincinnati Reds, who would have been assigned to a division that included the Braves, Marlins, and Cleveland Indians, objected to the "16–14 plan," based on both the tradition of being the oldest team in the NL and the need to compete directly with teams in larger markets with big payrolls. Cincinnati Reds Managing Executive John Allen said:

> We feel very strongly about the oldest team in baseball staying in the NL, and from the fans I've talked to, they are passionate, avid and hard-core traditionalists, like me, who don't want the Reds in the AL. The plan puts us in with some big-market teams with big payrolls. While that's not a guarantee that a team will win, recent history tells us it's a huge advantage. And then there is the [designated hitter]. We're dead-set against it.

The Pittsburgh Pirates had similar sentiments. However, the Phillies, a member of the NL since the team's founding in 1883, faced the prospect of going to the AL East and "reluctantly" approved of the plan. Giles cited the advantages of being in the same division with the Red Sox, Yankees, and Orioles, a team that was in the midst of a long string of sellouts after Camden Yards opened in 1992. He said, "I think it could be very, very exciting. I think it would increase attendance, general interest and TV ratings. I think there will be more electricity in the crowds." As a baseball lifer whose dad was president of the NL for nineteen years, he acknowledged that it would be very hard for any of the original eight teams in the NL to switch. "It could be rather earth-shattering. But I still think there are a lot more pluses than minuses."[82]

Selig's ultimate concern was how baseball's divisional and league structure would affect revenue. The *de facto* commissioner was a firm believer in "16–14." He said, "I think there is no question, having pushed through three divisions, the wild-card and interleague play, where I stand. Baseball hasn't grown its revenues. Scheduling is the most important marketing tool we have. A lot of people don't understand that. He went on, "We have to be aggressive. But we also have a magnificent history and tradition in baseball. We're trying to balance one against the other. But at the same time, it's a new era."[83]

The strongest opposition to radical realignment came from New York and Chicago. The two franchises in each city believed that the benefits of additional intracity games if they were in the same league would be offset by the lack of variety in visiting teams. Andy MacPhail, president of the Cubs, wondered, "How does it help the Chicago baseball fan if all the same teams come into Wrigley Field and then they go play 9 miles south [at Comiskey Park]? You reduce the number of teams that come through the city from 30 to 23. How many times can you bring the [Kansas City] Royals in here?"[84]

As the controversy brewed, the Cubs released a survey of season ticket holders that indicated that 76.9 percent did not want the NL to introduce the designated hitter. Asked if the Cubs and Sox should play in different leagues, 65.4 percent of the approximately 1,700 season ticket holders strongly agreed. Only 10.6 percent of Cubs fans strongly wanted to be in the same division as the Sox. Asked if baseball should realign geographically, Cubs fans showed their traditional leanings, with two-thirds strongly wanting to keep the leagues the way they were. Other teams surveyed fan preferences, including the San Francisco Giants, whose season ticket holders opposed radical realignment 6–1. Based on that, "I don't see any circumstance where we'd support [radical realignment]," Giants Executive Vice President Larry Baer said.[85]

As opposition to the radical plan grew, other, less draconian plans were advanced. One was a "moderate" or "modified" plan that required a minimum of seven and a maximum of nine league changes, depending on whether Houston and Kansas City were to switch. The proposal called for an unbalanced schedule in which teams would play more than half their games against division rivals, including home-and-away series with teams from the other division in their league and one of the divisions from the other league. This variation addressed two major concerns—travel and television—but avoided league changes for teams opposed to the more radical plan. Not surprisingly, several of baseball's executives concluded that the plan was flawed, as were most of the others (Giles said at one point that he had created or looked at something like eighty different plans) the realignment committee had studied.

The moderate plan had sixteen teams in the new NL, with four divisions of four teams each, and fourteen teams in the new AL, with two divisions of five teams and one division of four. This alignment would have created separate rules for the NL and AL. The NL would have had four division winners in the playoffs, while the AL would have had three winners and a wild card. However, the plan had the benefit of keeping dissenting clubs (the Cubs, Giants, Pirates, Reds, and Mets) in the NL, which would still not have a designated hitter. In fact, the only century-old team to move would have been the Phillies, who at that juncture did not actively oppose realignment.

Another alternative was a "simplified" plan that had been in the background while radical realignment was discussed. This plan kept the leagues and divisions intact, with the Arizona Diamondbacks joining the NL West, the Tampa Bay Devil Rays joining the AL East, and either the Milwaukee Brewers or the Detroit Tigers switching leagues and joining the NL Central to create room for the Devil Rays and avoid "15–15."

As the discussion continued, moving inexorably away from a more radical approach, Bill Giles concluded:

> I think the odds are better that we'll end up in the NL than in the AL. If we were going to do the real radical realignment, with 14 teams shifting leagues, we were in favor of it. But it doesn't appear that's going to happen. And under the current plans, there are not enough positives to make us want to do what I didn't want to do in the first place—which is move to the AL.

He continued, "If we could have been in a division with Baltimore, the Yankees, Boston and the Mets—and with no [designated hitter]—we were willing to bite the bullet and switch leagues. But it doesn't appear as if any of those is going to happen. So now we're not in favor of switching."[86]

At one point, Selig said that "the owners had looked at more maps than Magellan." The *Chicago Sun-Times* reported that while many teams favored realignment, teams are willing to vote for certain plans, while threatening to block others, and views were very parochial (imagine that!).[87] Ultimately, the owners basically decided to punt. To keep a 16–14 league structure for scheduling purposes and to ensure that Tampa Bay was placed in the East, where the team belonged, one AL Central team was asked to switch to the NL Central. The owners decided to give Kansas City the right of first refusal, but after considering the proposal, the Royals refused to jump leagues. All along, Bud Selig had wanted his Brewers to be in the NL Central, to stir up a rivalry with the Cubs, just ninety miles to the south of Milwaukee. After Kansas City opted to stay put, the Brewers jumped at the chance and became the 16th NL team. The Detroit Tigers could then switch from the AL East to the AL Central, with the Devil Rays replacing the Tigers. Selig said that the most pressing concerns were resolved, finding a spot for Tampa Bay and creating a sixteen-team NL and a fourteen-team AL.[88]

And the rest, as they say, is history. Baseball did not revisit realignment until 2012, when the Houston Astros consented to switch from the NL to the AL, join the Texas Rangers in the AL West, and create two fifteen-team leagues. Clearly, baseball wasn't ready for this move in 1997, but by 2012, times had changed. The 2013 season welcomed interleague play every day and further weakened the identity of the leagues. Ban Johnson must be rolling over in his grave.

Concluding Comment

Realignment was all about marketing the game and generating fan interest. It was about new ballparks, superstations, and cable rights. It was about selling tickets, suites, and sponsorships. According to Bill Giles, "The whole deal on realignment and wild cards and interleague play and everything was to generate more revenue. Period."[89]

7

The Evolution of Baseball's Governance System

Professional baseball's governance structure first emerged during its early days and has continued to evolve as baseball's circumstances have changed and its footprint has continued to expand. The importance of the changes in baseball's governance lies in their effect on baseball as an enterprise. How baseball governs itself, along with labor peace and attention to addressing issues of competitive balance, together have helped usher in an era of unprecedented growth and development of our national game.

In this chapter, I look at the history of governance and how it has both adapted to and led changes in the business of baseball. I provide a context by reviewing governance up to 1982, when, a year after Bill Giles bought the Phillies, the owners restructured the commissioner's office. Over the next eighteen years, governance continued to adapt to baseball's emerging economic, political, and legal circumstances, culminating in the end of the American and National Leagues as we knew them and the centralization of power in the office of the commissioner. I believe that it is significant that the owners did not approve such a landmark change until the person in the commissioner's chair was a former owner.

Baseball has faced numerous judicial challenges since its anti-trust exemption by the landmark Supreme Court ruling in the Federal Baseball case in 1922. The anti-trust exemption gave baseball a unique legal status and at the same time made it easy for members of Congress to threaten baseball with the removal of its exemption on numerous occasions when the owners did not comply with congressional demands. Baseball's hesitancy to expand led to significant congressional pressure to add franchises in cities within the districts or states of powerful legislators. In addition to the demands of owners and fans and the significant changes in baseball's economic environment, the continuing political and legal pressure on baseball's anti-trust exemption has contributed to the evolution of baseball's governance system over the last century.

Through its first forty years or so, baseball developed league by league. For most of its subsequent history, the business of major league baseball had been run by the leagues. Until the 1980s, the league presidents held the power and authority for most baseball decisions and issues. Warren Giles and Ford Frick were the two candidates for the commissioner's post in 1951. Frick took the commissioner's post and Giles took second prize, became National League president, and served until 1969 in a position that had substantially more authority over the day-to-day business of baseball than that of the commissioner. Today, Bill Giles is "honorary" president of the National League. His only real duty is presenting the Warren Giles trophy, named for his dad, to the National League pennant winner each year (which in both 2008 and 2009 was the Phillies). I discuss how and why the influence and authority of the leagues and their presidents declined so precipitously from the time of Warren Giles to baseball's centralization at the end of the twentieth century.

A Brief History of Baseball's Governance from the Beginning to 1982

In the spring of 1857, just eleven years after Alexander Cartwright and his Knickerbocker club played in the first recorded baseball game on the Elysian Fields, members of the club invited several neighboring groups of players in New York City to meet for the purpose of developing a standard set of rules. Ultimately, this fledgling effort led to the creation of baseball's first attempt at governance, the National Association of Base Ball Players. As professionalism emerged along with the post–Civil War growth of "our national game," baseball split into amateur and professional factions and a new organization was created in 1871, the National Association of Professional Base Ball Players. With neither the power to control the rampant gambling and bribery in the game nor a solid business foundation, the association ceased operations after the 1875 season. A coal magnate from Chicago, William Hulbert, recognized the economic opportunity in creating an organized league of clubs—not players, as had been the case with the National Association of Professional Base Ball Players—run by business professionals. Hulbert organized a group of other businessmen with an interest in baseball, and the group created the National League of Professional Base Ball Clubs, which started play in 1876.

The increasing popularity of baseball and the consequent potential for profit encouraged new teams to emerge, but the National League held tight to its monopoly, forcing additional leagues to form. One of those leagues was the American Association, founded when the original Cincinnati Reds were expelled from the National League for daring to sell beer during games. The American Association prospered and was eventually recognized as a major league. Rival teams and leagues engaged in economically destructive behavior in hopes of recruiting players to help them win and draw fan interest—and revenues. Players jumped from team to team, salaries escalated to unprofitable levels, and generally the game was in economic chaos. In an attempt to gain some control over their growing but chaotic enterprise, the "magnates" of the National League, the American Association, and a third league, the Northwestern League, met and negotiated the "Tripartite Agreement" (later to be called the first National Agreement) in 1883. The National Agreement, along with the reserve clause, brought some order to early professional baseball. Additional leagues, such as the Union League and the Players League, came and went quickly. By the late 1890s, the other major leagues had folded and the National League owners once again achieved monopoly status as the only major professional baseball league.

Ban Johnson's new American League outdrew the National League in 1902, and the competition for players between the owners of the two leagues dramatically increased salaries and lowered the owners' profits. This economic pressure forced the National League owners to negotiate peace with their American League counterparts, and the two groups of owners forged the National Agreement of 1903, an agreement that created the structure of major league baseball that has lasted for more than a century.

The 1903 National Agreement ushered in a system of governance for baseball. Henceforth, baseball would be administered by a three-person national commission, consisting of the presidents of the two leagues and a third person of their choosing. This system was rife with conflicts of interest and perceptions of favoritism, and owner dissatisfaction with the system meant that the National Commission was on its way to oblivion, even before the scandal surrounding during the 1919 World Series. The final straw for the National Commission proved to be the willingness of a group of Chicago White Sox players to accept money from gamblers to "throw" the World Series. The enmity between White Sox owner Charles Comiskey and Ban Johnson, who had once been close friends and allies, contributed to the inability of baseball to deal with the emerging scandal properly. While subsequent research has shown the endemic nature of gambling during the early years of baseball, the fact that gamblers could cause ballplayers to throw the World Series created a crisis that baseball could solve only by creation of a strong central governor in the form of an independent commissioner, someone who could restore, in the eyes of the public on which baseball depended, the "integrity" of the game. In recasting the governance of baseball, the owners passed the first Major League Agreement in 1921.

The Major League Agreement (later amended to the "Major League Constitution" when baseball centralized its operations in 1999) has served as baseball's governing constitution since its inception. The 1921 Major League Agreement created the office of commissioner and defined the power of the office, especially with regard to establishing virtually absolute authority to investigate and address "any act, transaction, or practice charged, alleged, or suspected to be detrimental to the best interests of the national game of baseball. . . ."[1] For almost 100 years, the baseball industry has recognized the authority of the commissioner to take actions "in the best interests of the game." The Major League Agreement also expressly provided that the commissioner's decisions would be final and could not be challenged by clubs in court.[2]

Every baseball fan knows that Judge Kenesaw Mountain Landis became baseball's first commissioner. Landis, a federal judge from Illinois and a big fan of the Chicago Cubs, had come to baseball's attention several years earlier. Landis was the presiding judge for an anti-trust lawsuit by owners of the Federal League. The Federal League owners claimed that actions by the American and National Leagues to prevent Federal League owners from signing players—who were held to their clubs only by the reserve clause—represented restraint of trade. Landis, surmising that a ruling in favor of the plaintiff could hurt his Cubs and the rest of organized baseball, sat on his ruling long enough so that the Federal League disbanded. Landis thus became attractive to baseball's owners when the idea of creating a strong commissionership emerged in the wake of the Black Sox Scandal.

Landis knew that the owners were desperate to find someone who could restore baseball's image and mandated that his new post would have absolute authority, a nonnegotiable condition of his acceptance of the job. Granted that power, Landis first moved to purge baseball of its "original sin" by banning the eight White Sox players who were suspected of taking money in the Series fix (along with some others). Subsequently, he ruled baseball with an iron fist from his appointment in 1921 until his death in 1944, although certain owners regarded some of his decisions as capricious and unwarranted.

After the death of Landis in 1944, the owners, with the integrity of baseball no longer an issue (despite continued resistance to opening the game to African Americans), and somewhat frustrated by the judge's unchecked authority, took the opportunity to restrict the commissioner's powers by redrafting sections of the Major League Agreement. In particular, the wording in the revised Major League Agreement prevented the commissioner from exercising his "best interests" power against an "act or procedure" that complied with any "Major League rule or joint action of the two Major Leagues" and gave clubs the right to challenge the commissioner's decisions in court.[3]

The owners appointed Albert "Happy" Chandler, former senator from Kentucky, as baseball's second commissioner to succeed Landis. Chandler, despite the reduction in the power of his office, exercised a good deal of independence in his position and made some unpopular decisions during his term. The owners forced Chandler from office in 1951. Chandler's successor was a much more docile Ford Frick, the president of the National League and a former sportswriter and ghostwriter for Babe Ruth—whose loyalty to Ruth swayed his decision to place the infamous "asterisk" next to Roger Maris's sixty-one home runs as the new home run record. Ford had served as president of the National League for seventeen years. According to Bill Giles, not much happened during Frick's administration, although "the Commissioner did play a lot of Gin Rummy in the conference room."[4]

As Frick prepared to leave office in 1964, he encouraged the owners to restore the commissioner's "best interests" powers and the owners responded by reversing the changes to the office that they had made twenty years earlier. As part of the revision of the Major League Agreement in 1964, the owners changed the wording of the best interests clause from "detrimental to the best interests of" to "not in the best interests of." This change expanded the commissioner's authority and the commissioner could now invoke the best interests power without having to prove that an action was actually detrimental to baseball, but only that it was not in baseball's best interests.[5] In addition, the owners reinstituted the provision waiving any right of recourse in the courts to challenge a commissioner's decision.

General William Eckert, described as "the unknown soldier" at the time of his surprise appointment in 1965, succeeded Ford Frick. Bill Giles, who was working in Houston at the time, tells a funny story about Eckert (also recounted in Larry Moffi's *The Conscience of the Game*). Some evidence suggests that the owners became confused about the identity of the Air Force General whom they wanted to be fourth commissioner of baseball. General Eugene Zuckert, former secretary of the Air Force, was on the original short list of candidates. Somehow, General William Eckert was voted into office by the owners. Fay Vincent, with no love lost for the owners after he was forced out of office, said, "The owners went to get Zuckert and they got Eckert. They couldn't spell."[6] While Eckert knew little about baseball, he is often credited with making baseball a more efficient organization by streamlining business methods, developing a more effective committee structure, and stabilizing some franchises with bigger stadiums and longer leases. However, Eckert never really fit into his new role and was let go in 1968, after only three years.

Bowie Kuhn, an attorney for the National League for nineteen years, became successor to Eckert in 1969 as a compromise candidate when the owners could not decide between long-time executive Chub Feeney (who wound up succeeding Warren Giles as National League president) and Mike Burke, president of the Yankees. Using his office's "best interests" powers, Kuhn stepped in to end a lockout imposed by the owners during spring training in 1976 after the Seitz decision granting free agency. Kuhn negated the June 1976 attempt by Oakland A's owner Charles Finley to sell three of his star players, Joe Rudi, Rollie Fingers, and Vida Blue, to the Yankees and Red Sox for a total of $3.5 million. Kuhn nullified the sales, having decided that Finley's attempt to derive value from players that the A's would inevitably have lost to free agency was not in baseball's best interests, despite the fact that Finley purportedly planned to use the money from the sale of these players to bolster his club's farm system. Kuhn also suspended Braves owner Ted Turner for violating guidelines issued by Kuhn regarding tampering with free agents. These actions led to lawsuits against Kuhn, but in both instances, the courts ruled that the commissioner had acted within his authority.

Evolution of the Commissioner's Office, 1982–1994

In the first several decades after baseball established the office of the commissioner, before television, the Players Association, free agency, expansion, public funding of ballparks, corporate sponsorship, licensing, and the other changes that affected the landscape of baseball so dramatically, commissioners acted to represent jointly the interests of the owners, the players, and the fans. Moreover, the primary focus of the commissioner's job was to maintain the public's confidence in the integrity of the "National Game of Baseball."

Especially after Landis, baseball's commissioners' view of their duties and responsibilities, although specified in the Major League Agreement, often proved to be at odds with what the owners wanted. Commissioners who did not accommodate the needs of the game, as defined by the owners, were forced out, as in the case of Fay Vincent. Once Marvin Miller assumed leadership of the Players Association and molded it into a powerful union representing strictly the interest of players, the role of the commissioner representing the interests of both owners and players became an anachronism. Miller frequently scoffed at the notion that his counterpart, Bowie Kuhn, who was hired by the owners and essentially worked at their bidding, could represent the players as well. Miller, a labor leader in the classic tradition, saw his role as representing the players and the commissioner's role as representing the owners—and he maintained a hard line between the two sides.

Changing Circumstances Create the Need for a Change in the Commissioner's Role

Shortly after Giles completed his ownership group's purchase of the Phillies in fall 1981, baseball's owners, smarting from the fifty-day strike of the previous season and cognizant of the changing economic landscape of baseball, established a restructuring committee at the winter meetings to address the issues that had emerged. Although he had been attending owners' meetings regularly as Ruly Carpenter's representative, Giles adopted a philosophy recommended by his father and left the heavy lifting to his more experienced colleagues.

In April 1982, the owners endorsed a restructuring proposal that called for a merger of the two league offices into the commissioner's office and a more centralized business operation. This involved placing the American and National Leagues as well as the Player Relations Committee—which had been formed in 1967 to act as owners' representative in dealings with the Players Association—and various business ventures directly under the authority of the commissioner in a new chain of command. As a result, the owners of the twenty-six clubs would operate "like a board of directors" while the commissioner's office acted as a CEO. The other changes included:

- Shortening the commissioner's term to five years from seven years
- Increasing the number of owners' meetings each year from two to four
- Creating an owners' executive council with the authority to oversee the operation of baseball between the owners' meetings

- Building closer relations between the promotion and player relations departments of the commissioner's office
- Changing the way in which votes were tallied: eliminating the unanimous rule and adopting a new voting procedure so that both leagues vote as a single entity on major issues "while at the same time having a three-quarters vote rule in effect"[7]

The voting change created a straight twenty-six-team vote on major issues; previously, the vote was split by league. A vote by three-quarters of the teams in both leagues would be sufficient to move franchises or change rules, and one club could not scuttle a decision with a negative vote, as had been the case in the National League.

Bowie Kuhn said at the time, "The administrative structure was good until we got to the modern era, where telecasts, marketing and other factors began to have a more profound impact on the game."[8]

Roy Eisenhardt of the Oakland A's, acting as spokesperson for the owners, said that the restructuring was designed mainly to get all twenty-six clubs to act as a unit. Eisenhardt and Kuhn agreed that the shoring up of the commissioner's authority was at least partly a result of the previous summer's fifty-day strike, which exposed how little power the commissioner actually possessed.[9]

Once the owners approved the restructuring proposal, baseball's lawyers had to revise the Major League Agreement. Changes would not be implemented until the new agreement was ratified. Kuhn was up for reelection in 1982 and faced many problems. A minority of owners had indicated dissatisfaction with Kuhn's performance. Much of the owners' criticism of Kuhn had focused on his business acumen, for instance, not obtaining sufficient television revenues, as well as his low profile during the 1981 strike. A compromise was proposed whereby Kuhn would retain his current powers and financial and other business matters would be handled by a COO, business affairs (COOBA), who was technically to be under the authority of the commissioner. This new position would handle network television contracts, marketing, promotion, films, licensing, long-range planning, revenue sharing, and office administration.[10]

If Kuhn decided to accept this solution, his term would be extended for four more years, including the year remaining on his contract. Since the American League had expanded to fourteen teams, the three-quarters rule meant that five negative votes in the American League or four negative votes in the National League would terminate his employment. In November 1982, the final vote was 7–5 in the National League and 11–3 in the American League, both in favor of Kuhn. Yet the rule requiring a three-quarters vote in each league meant that he was defeated.[11] Kuhn would serve out his term and even extend it until his successor was able to take office, but his days as a baseball power broker had ended.

Peter Ueberroth Takes Control

Peter Ueberroth came to the attention of major league owners based on his success in serving as organizer of the 1984 Olympic Games in Los Angeles. Even before the Olympics took place, he had demonstrated his ability to galvanize, organize, and lead a successful effort to recruit sponsors, monetize the operation, and accomplish goals. The owners elected Ueberroth in March 1984. To entice Ueberroth to accept the position, the restructuring proposal of 1982 was implemented and other concessions were granted. The owners scuttled the COOBA proposal and recognized the commissioner as baseball's CEO, with all departments reporting to him. Reelection would no longer require a three-quarters majority; instead, a simple majority would be necessary, provided that there was approval from at least five clubs in each league. Also, the commissioner's authority to fine clubs was increased to $250,000; the previous limit had been $5,000. The owners also granted Ueberroth expanded authority in both marketing and labor relations.[12] Ueberroth began his term on October 1, 1984, and immediately used his "best interests" powers to settle an umpire strike that was marring the postseason.

Ueberroth changed the dynamics of the commissioner's office. The new Major League Agreement specified four plenary owners' meetings per year, and he ran those meetings in classroom style as opposed to the boardroom style that had been used in the past. He disbanded the owners' committees that had been set up by his predecessor and acted like a CEO. He kept his own counsel instead of relying on influential owners, such as Kuhn had done with Walter O'Malley, who essentially served as "shadow commissioner" during much of Kuhn's tenure. Baseball had set up the MLB Promotions Corporation in 1968; Ueberroth brought the marketing arm of baseball in-house under the commissioner's control. He placed a much greater emphasis than any previous commissioner on marketing, licensing—raising licensing and merchandising revenue from less than $40,000 per club in 1984 to more than $36 million annually by 1989—and television revenues.[13] As we know from our discussion of collusion, Ueberroth "suggested" to the owners that they refrain from what he considered profligate spending on free agents, which ultimately cost the owners the tidy sum of $280 million. Although he put baseball on a stronger financial footing, by the time he stepped down, he had lost much of the goodwill that accompanied his initial appointment.

Giamatti and Vincent

When Ueberroth refused to be considered for a second term, the owners once again had to find a commissioner. This time, they did not have to look far and they strongly supported the candidacy of Bart Giamatti, former English literature professor and president of Yale, who had been serving as the president of the National League since December 1986—an ironic situation, given his New England upbringing and devotion to the Boston Red Sox. The owners elected Giamatti unanimously, and he took office as baseball's seventh commissioner on March 1, 1989. His term as commissioner was tragically short; he died suddenly on September 1, 1989, just a week after rendering a judgment in the Pete Rose gambling case, a situation that consumed much of his commissionership. Giamatti did accomplish one significant governance change during his tenure by creating the position of deputy commissioner and hiring his friend Fay Vincent to serve in that role. Giamatti oversaw baseball operations, public relations, and player issues. He put Vincent in charge of broadcasting, special events, corporate sponsorship, licensing, and publishing.[14] After Giamatti passed away and the owners elected Vincent, the new commissioner hired Steve Greenberg to serve as deputy commissioner to fill what had been Vincent's job, plus another set of responsibilities—for legal, financial, and security affairs.

Baseball's Executive Council

The Executive Council was created and defined in Article II of the Major League Agreement. Originally, the council was composed of the commissioner, the president of each league, and four club owners from each league. Bowie Kuhn met with the council regularly and relied heavily on some of its members for guidance and counsel, in particular, Walter O'Malley while the elder O'Malley was still active as the owner of the Dodgers. However, Peter Ueberroth, who acted much more autocratically than his predecessor, had little use for the Executive Council. Most often, Ueberroth told the council's members what he had decided rather than soliciting advice. Giamatti, given his academic background and comfort with governance systems based more on discussion and consensus, had reverted more to the Kuhn approach.

After Giamatti's untimely passing, the Executive Council, of which Bill Giles was a member, held a critical position because by statute (the Major League Agreement), the council assumed the powers and duties of the commissioner in the commissioner's absence. Although the major league agreement didn't specifically spell it out, the council also had the authority to move to fill the vacancy. Giles said at the time that he had spoken with two other owners, and "they and myself are in favor of continuing with Mr. Vincent for that three-year term. My dad convinced me a long time ago how important it is to have a commissioner. It's a strong power, but it's important. We allow any commissioner to judge as he sees fit, as long as he's fair."[15]

Restructuring the Commissioner's Job, 1992–1994

As controversy swirled around Fay Vincent during summer 1992, there was a good deal of discussion about what league presidents and the commissioner should be doing in their respective roles to advance baseball. Former Phillies All-Star center fielder Garry Maddox, readying himself as a possible candidate for National League presidency after Bill White's resignation, discussed Giles' view of the role of league presidents. "Bill says that the main thing they're interested in is having the National League president be an ambassador, someone who will promote the game, the league and its interests. They also want someone who is capable of receiving instructions from the owners and [can] go about carrying out the decisions made."[16]

Meanwhile, Jerry Reinsdorf, one of the commissioner's leading critics as well as one of the hardliners in labor negotiations, expressed his opinion that it was time to rewrite the governing Major League Agreement. Reinsdorf wanted the commissioner to become the CEO of baseball business, essentially the same role that had been specified by the 1982 restructuring proposal but had never really been implemented. The board of directors would be the twenty-eight franchise owners. Like any other business, the CEO would report directly to his board and to no one else, especially the employees.

Reinsdorf said, "We would announce him as the CEO—of the owners, not the players or the umpires." Agreeing with Marvin Miller's perspective, Reinsdorf said that the players don't need a commissioner to protect them. "Once we establish [that] his job is to run the business [for] the owners, not the players, umpires or fans, then that would give power to [management]."[17]

Vincent, who clearly did not share Reinsdorf's position, responded, "Unfortunately, some want the commissioner to put aside the responsibility to act 'in the best interests of baseball'; some want the commissioner to represent only owners, and to do their bidding in all matters. I haven't done that, and I could not do so, because I accepted the position believing the commissioner has a higher duty."[18]

Vincent eventually resigned under pressure in early September. Following the turbulence of Vincent's three-year tenure as commissioner, the Executive Council once again took the reins of baseball's governance. But this time, no obvious successor stood in the wings, as had been the case with Vincent three years earlier. The owners were so fractured at the time that it would have been difficult to find a candidate who could hold the three-quarters majority that was necessary for election to the office. At the same time, Reinsdorf's model of the commissioner's office was gaining support among his peers.

After the news of Vincent's resignation became public, Giles said, "We immediately have to restructure baseball, not only the responsibility of the commissioner's office but the league presidents also. In my opinion, the league presidents should have more responsibility, have more to do that affects baseball in a more positive way." Given Bill's lineage and background, his belief in the need for strong league presidents came as no surprise. Giles also said that having a new commissioner in office by mid-November was important because of major matters that were approaching, including negotiations for a new national television package.[19]

The owners needed someone to serve as their leader in the absence of a permanent commissioner. The members of the executive council elected the consummate consensus builder, Bud Selig, as chair and *de facto* commissioner. The council gave Selig the title of "chairman," as opposed to "acting" or "interim" commissioner, to avoid a vote that would have required three-quarters approval of the twenty-eight owners. Selig said that deputy commissioner Steve Greenberg, who was appointed by Vincent, would remain on the job for an undetermined period to handle the daily business of the commissioner's office.[20]

At the same time, the owners decided that the office of the commissioner needed an overhaul. Clearly, their rationale included preventing recurrence of some of the problems that the owners believed Vincent had created because he believed in the "old model" of commissioner as serving owners, players, and fans. A majority of the owners on the Executive Council who could be considered "hawks" in the ongoing battles with the Players Association could no longer tolerate an independent commissioner who could derail the owners' labor negotiations tactics. A ten-member restructuring committee was formed to redraft the Major League Agreement.

The biggest issue facing the restructuring committee involved the commissioner's position with respect to labor negotiations. Richard Ravitch, the owners' labor negotiator, favored an arrangement whereby the commissioner would be removed from labor. Others saw the situation differently. Selig suggested that the matter could be resolved by either putting the commissioner in complete charge of labor, as the 1982 restructuring committee proposed, or removing the commissioner from labor completely, as Ravitch wanted. Speaking on the Bob Costas radio show, *Costas Coast to Coast,* Giles said that he wanted baseball's "labor man" to be under the authority of the commissioner.[21]

In addition, the sometimes contentious relationship between the league presidents and the commissioner was on the committee's agenda. One member of the restructuring committee said that all concerned would be left with "a clearer understanding of who [the league presidents] work for and how they are hired, etc." Such a clarification was contained in a restructuring report in 1982, but never implemented. Now, the official said, such rules are being underlined and implemented.[22]

Steve Greenberg stayed in his deputy commissioner's post for only a few months after Vincent's resignation. He planned to step down on April 1, 1993. Because Selig was not running day-to-day operations in baseball, the owners approved a proposal that would put the daily operation of the commissioner's office in the hands of two people. Dick Wagner, who had served as general manager with Cincinnati and Houston and had spent the previous six years working as a special assistant in the commission's office, was named office administrator, assisted by Pete Widdrington, chairman of the Toronto Blue Jays.

Over a fifteen-month period from September 1992 to January 1994, each time the owners met, there was speculation about the release of the restructuring report and discussion of the naming of a new commissioner. The delay in the decision on restructuring was attributable to lack agreement on both revenue sharing and the role and responsibilities of the commissioner.

In the months after Vincent's resignation, Selig denied that there was disagreement over the strength of the commissioner's position. "Whatever the basis of the discussions, everybody wants a strong commissioner in the context that you and I know it today. I don't think that's a question. People obviously have different views on some parts of the job. But there is no one advocating a weakened commissioner. Everybody understands the need for a strong commissioner. That is not a debatable point." Some owners, supporting Reinsdorf's model, wanted the office structured so that the commissioner is a CEO reporting to the owners as a board of directors, but other owners expressed concern about weakening the office.[23]

In 1993, as spring turned into summer, still without a restructuring report, Selig said:

> Owners have spent a lot of time on restructuring. It's a 72-year-old agreement. The fact is that the office will be strengthened. But it's more sensitive to 1993. That agreement was written in 1921. There was no television then. There certainly was no Players Association. Nothing. There are gaps in it. What I say about the next commissioner is that he will be stronger, he will have a road map in every area of our business, [and] he'll hopefully have the courage to do what owners should have done, and that's address the economic problems and not leave them to somebody else. Dick Ravitch is right. He says, "In the end, there are things only ownership can do." Don't bring a guy in and suggest he's going to solve the fact that you have $42 million of revenue and I have $114 million. But yet our labor costs are the same. Nobody wants to confront those problems, because they're not pleasant.[24]

The January 1994 owners' meeting in Ft. Lauderdale, Florida, proved to be a blockbuster. First, Bill Bartholomay of the Atlanta Braves, head of the commissioner search committee, reported that a coalition of sixteen to seventeen clubs had made it clear that they would not vote on a commissioner at a time when management was about to begin labor negotiations with the Players Association. So the process of picking baseball's ninth commissioner was delayed, and Selig would remain the game's reluctant leader (at least, that is what he kept saying) for a period that wound up extending all the way until summer 1998, a year-and-a-half after the agreement on a CBA in November 1996.

At the Fort Lauderdale meeting, the owners voted unanimously, 28–0, to adopt revenue sharing, a landmark event in the history of baseball. This agreement set the stage for the owners' position entering the negotiation of a new labor deal—revenue sharing tied to a salary cap—which we know now didn't fly and precipitated a strike the next summer. The important thing was that revenue sharing—increasingly critical to baseball's economic success because increases in local revenue had widened the income disparity between clubs—had been established.

Finally, the owners announced a restructuring plan at the January 1994 meeting in Ft. Lauderdale, dramatically revising baseball's governance system. The effects of the plan "indicated a desire by the owners to shift MLB governance towards a corporate-style system."[25] The owners recast the Major League Agreement, amending the best interests clause, and preventing the commissioner from invoking the best interests clause except in any matter that "involves the integrity of, or public confidence in, the national game of Baseball."[26] The owners clarified the commissioner's role in labor negotiations by introducing a clause in the Major

League Agreement that read, "The powers of the Commissioner to act in the best interests of Baseball shall be inapplicable to any matter relating to a subject of collective bargaining between the Clubs and the Major League Baseball Players Association."[27]

The owners removed the best interests authority from collective bargaining even while giving the commissioner "exclusive responsibility for labor matters." In the next sentence, though, the report says, "The clubs, as the employers of the players, are ultimately responsible for the obligations imposed by federal labor law." The report did not acknowledge the dilution of the commissioner's authority. Instead it termed the changes "clarifications" that would enable the commissioner "to serve baseball more effectively."[28]

While placing labor relations and the owners' labor committee under the authority of the commissioner, the report noted that, ten years previously, the owners, acting on a previous restructuring report, placed the "operations and functions of the Player Relations Committee under the jurisdiction of the commissioner." According to Murray Chass, "that step turned out to be illusory."[29]

The changes to the Major League Agreement strengthened the role of the commissioner in some respects, but weakened the position in other areas. On the plus side, the commissioner was given singular control over hiring league presidents and appointing members of all committees. Once a permanent commissioner was named, he would become the chief negotiator in labor relations. The owners dissolved the Player Relations Committee, but Selig said that the group of owners who oversaw labor issues would remain unchanged except for its name. The plan was that, when a permanent commissioner was named, he would become the chief negotiator in labor relations. In the meantime, Richard Ravitch, who headed the PRC, handled the negotiations.[30] The owners voted to change their bylaws so that the ratification of a new labor agreement would require a three-quarters approval vote rather than a majority, strengthening the owners' position vis à vis the commissioner.[31]

The amendments to the Major League Agreement were intended to prevent the commissioner from using those powers to circumvent the owners in player relations and negotiations, as had happened with Kuhn, when he ended the 1976 spring training lockout over the issue of free agency, and with Vincent, when he used his best interests powers to end the 1990 lockout. The commissioner officially was placed in charge of negotiating labor agreements with the players' union for the owners, giving him substantial control over labor negotiations, but he could no longer overturn a decision by the owners to stage a lockout of the players.

Previously, commissioners had virtually unlimited power to take actions "in the best interests of baseball." With the revisions, the commissioner could no longer invoke the best interests clause in matters covered by club votes in leagues jointly or individually. Amendments contained in the restructuring report prevented commissioners from using their "best interests" power to affect World Series and postseason play, scheduling, interleague play, divisional alignment, expansion, the sale of teams, the relocation of teams, revenue sharing, or broadcasting agreements.[32]

Both Peter Ueberroth and Fay Vincent characterized the restructuring as substantially weakening the commissioner's office. Ueberroth said, "Basically, the commissioner seems to have no portfolio, power or job. That's what it looks like from a distance. I think the changes dramatically change the position. There will be the appearance of more responsibility, but [there will be] substantially less authority. That's the recipe for a non-job." Vincent commented, "They are wrong, but time will correct it. Eventually, it changes back."[33]

Selig disagreed with the view that the commissioner's powers were being eroded. "On all integrity issues, there's no change. On business issues, there's more accountability. By clearing up the ambiguities, I really believe the commissioner, in total, is as powerful as he ever was, and one could make a case for his being more powerful." He went on to say, "I think overall the office is clearly strengthened. This brings the whole structure and office into this decade and gets ready for the 21st century."[34]

Dodgers President Peter O'Malley, a member of the restructuring committee and an advocate of a strong, independent commissioner, said that the work of the committee "identified, clarified, and removed ambiguities" that previously existed in the seventy-three-year-old Major League Agreement under which the commissioner operated. "If anything," he said, "the powers of the commissioner and league presidents have been strengthened, not weakened." New York Mets President Fred Wilpon, co-chairman of the restructuring committee, defended the changes, saying they made the commissioner's job more attractive because the role was more defined. "He's involved in the integrity of the game, as well as [being] the chief person running the game. He's the chairman of all the major committees. That's a very powerful position."[35]

According to Jonathan Reinsdorf, the 1994 restructuring changed the role of commissioner from that of "umpire of baseball" to "CEO of baseball" in that the commissioner "no longer protects the status quo, but leads the business into the future."[36]

Baseball Appoints a Chief Operating Officer

In June 1997, despite the continued reduction in the authority of the league presidents, owners gave American League President Gene Budig and National League President Leonard Coleman, whose terms were set to expire in 1999, three-year contract extensions. At the same time, several owners expressed a strong sentiment to have Bud Selig stay in office and accept the role of permanent commissioner.

Selig, in his dual role as *de facto* commissioner and owner of the Brewers, continued to operate out of Milwaukee, leaving a leadership void in the commissioner's office in New York City. Baseball resolved that problem when Paul Beeston moved to New York and accepted an appointment as COO of baseball. Beeston, president of the Toronto Blue Jays and one of the most influential owners, assumed day-to-day operating responsibility for baseball, a move widely seen at the time as clearing the way for Selig to accept an appointment as permanent commissioner. Before Beeston's appointment, department heads reported directly to Selig, as they had done since deputy commissioner Steve Greenberg left the commissioner's office. As COO, Beeston became Commissioner Bud Selig's lone direct report, with major department heads reporting to Beeston. Tracy Ringolsby reported, "While Beeston takes care of the daily chores, baseball now can have a commissioner who concentrates on the big picture instead of daily details."[37]

Baseball's Owners Convince Bud Selig to Become Permanent Commissioner

During his service as *de facto* commissioner, Selig consistently maintained that he did not wish to be permanent commissioner. However, many of his fellow owners wanted Selig in that role, and on June 19, 1998, the Associated Press reported that "Bud Selig intends to become baseball commissioner and will call an owners' meeting in the next few weeks for a formal vote."[38] At their meeting in July, the owners voted unanimously to offer Selig a five-year term as permanent commissioner. Selig accepted the offer, and on August 1, he became the ninth commissioner of baseball. To avoid an obvious conflict of interest, Selig announced that he would step down as president of the Brewers, place his ownership share in trust, and appoint his daughter, Wendy Selig-Prieb, to run the team.[39]

As he accepted his post on a permanent basis, Selig predicted, "By the turn of the century, if we keep moving in the right direction, you will see the greatest renaissance in baseball history. People talk about the so-called golden era of baseball, but we know in the golden era of baseball in the '40s and '50s, the average attendance was 13,000. This year, it'll be over 29,000."[40] Selig said he believed that an improved marketing campaign would boost baseball's resurgence after the damage wrought by the strike of 1994–1995.[41]

Within a year, Selig had established a strong central administration for baseball. Tim Brosnan, who had been in charge of MLB International, picked up most of the league's business responsibilities and added MLB Properties (which included sponsorship, licensing, and marketing) and broadcasting to his portfolio. He was named executive vice president of business. The only major revenue stream that did not fall under Brosnan was the Internet, which became the pet project of Bob DuPuy, promoted from his role as legal counsel to executive vice president of administration. In addition to Brosnan and DuPuy, other direct reports to Beeston included Rob Manfred, executive vice president of labor and human resources, and Sandy Alderson, executive vice president of baseball operations.[42]

The League Presidents

The 1982 restructuring proposal and the resulting revisions to the Major League Agreement indicated a significant reduction in the power of the league presidents as more and more of the operational aspects of baseball reported to the commissioner. By the 1990s, the responsibilities of the league presidents included the power to interpret and enforce the league's rules; authority to suspend or fine players for on- and off-field infractions; approval of player contracts; responsibility for scheduling; responsibility for hiring, firing, and disciplining umpires; and approval of the contracts to supply baseballs and other equipment.

Bill White, former All-Star first baseman and long-time Yankees broadcaster, became National League president in 1989, when Bart Giamatti stepped down to become commissioner. White was a vociferous defender of the power of the league presidencies and the league constitutions, as indicated by his protest against Fay Vincent when Vincent unilaterally moved the Cubs to the Western Division over the authority of the league constitution. He chafed at the continued erosion of his authority.

At the 1994 Ft. Lauderdale meeting, White proposed an amendment to the restructuring report that would have delineated the responsibilities of the league offices. The report, as presented, said that the leagues would carry on their traditional responsibilities. The amendment was defeated.[43] The power of the league presidents was vastly reduced under the restructuring report. Instead of being solely responsible to owners in their leagues, league presidents would henceforth be responsible to the commissioner, who had the power to hire them. Just after the meeting, White, who had stayed in office ten months beyond his intended departure so that a successor could be found, announced his intention to resign immediately. He left office and was replaced by Leonard Coleman.

Baseball Centralizes

At the time of Selig's election, it was already understood that he would merge the two leagues into a centralized operation, push the idea of a World Cup for baseball, work with the Players Association to improve baseball's marketing and promotional operations (baseball did not have a full-time marketing executive until 1996, which Bill Giles always found confounding), move to make interleague play permanent, and push for realignment.

At an owners' meeting in September 1999, club owners voted unanimously to abandon the traditional league organization and consolidate all operating functions in the commissioner's office. The restructuring transferred umpires, player discipline, and scheduling to the commissioner's office. Selig assigned Sandy Alderson supervisory power over umpires in both leagues. At the same time, owners voted to merge the administrative operations of the American and National Leagues. The owners unanimously approved a resolution calling on their lawyers to redraft the Major League Agreement, which governs baseball, to merge the American League and National League in all areas but on the field, where the leagues and divisions would remain unchanged pending further realignment. Since the origin of the National League in 1876 and the origin of the American League in 1900, each league had run its own affairs. But the commissioner's office had taken an increasingly active role after the restructuring report of 1982, the decision by Peter Ueberroth to move the leagues to New York City, and the restructuring report of 1994. Interleague play, which began in 1997, provided further impetus to merging the leagues into a centralized administration of baseball.[44]

Selig said, "This is an historic moment that many have felt was long overdue. Baseball took a very historical step that it had to do. It is imperative that we conduct ourselves as a single entity. Frankly, the system was an anachronism."[45]

Bill King of *Sports Business Journal* wrote the following in September 1999:

> You'd think that it would be simple for Major League Baseball to buy baseballs. After all, one company, Rawlings, supplies all the balls that are used in big league games. But because baseball's his-

> tory is one of competing leagues that gradually have consolidated, Rawlings Sporting Goods Co. has separate contracts with three entities that operate as one—the American League, the National League and the Office of the Commissioner. AL balls are used in AL parks. NL balls are used in NL parks. Commissioner's office balls are used in the All-Star Game and World Series. The only difference is the signature between the seams. Yet there are three separate contracts with the ball maker, an example of the duplication and confusion that MLB owners were trying to eliminate by consolidating leagues . . .[46]

The merger of the American and National Leagues and the centralization of the administration of major league baseball was, by September 1999, a *fait accompli.* The increasingly complex legal and economic environment for baseball was exacerbated by two leagues with different rules, practices, and protocols. For example, as long-term contracts for free agents and the financing of new ballparks created increasing franchise debt, the two leagues handled this problem differently. In the National League, any incurring of debt by a club had to be voted on by all sixteen clubs. In the American League, only a transfer of controlling shares came to an open vote.[47]

Over a period of almost thirty years, virtually all of the duties and responsibilities that had been league responsibilities for most of baseball's history had gradually been shifted to baseball's central administration. As a result, league presidents lost their portfolio and league offices became redundant. Selig commented, "We're getting ready for the 21st century. We need to be efficient in our structure. This is a structure spawned by 100-plus years of history that quite frankly was not serving us in the best way as we move forward. This system was an anachronism. There's no other way to articulate it."[48]

Bob DuPuy said at the time, "I really do think this is about efficiency, both in terms of business and in terms of operations and operational control. If you look back at our history, which is more than 100 years old, we started as 16 individual clubs and two competing leagues that really were competing business entities. Over time, the distinctions of the operations of the leagues had blurred dramatically. The business became more centralized. It was probably time for this 20 years ago."[49]

DuPuy also explained that centralizing decision-making would make the process much more efficient. "We've had meetings where the Executive Council received a presentation, and then we'd break into the two league meetings and have same presentation, and then go back into joint meetings and see the presentation again before voting on it jointly. It just didn't make sense to have that separate and run the risk of politics interfering with the efficient operation of the clubs."[50]

Thirteen years later, DuPuy reflected on baseball's centralization:

> Baseball was created before radio, before television, before national sponsorships, before any of that sort of thing. You had a commissioner who was in charge of discipline, who was in charge of the integrity of the game, who was in charge of refereeing fights among owners, who was in charge of refereeing fights between the leagues. That was really the commissioner's role. The league presidents really ran the game. The leagues were separate businesses. They had nothing to do with each other, other than the All-Star Game and the World Series. There were no playoffs. They really had absolutely nothing do with each other.
>
> Bill Bartholomay [of the Atlanta Braves] and I talked to Bud about blowing up the leagues and converting to a single business structure as early as fall 1992. We thought that it would allow baseball to be brought not necessarily into the 21st century but at least the 20th century in terms of the business operation. The leagues were wonderful, but they were an anachronism. They didn't allow us to sell from one place; they didn't allow us to sell national sponsorships. They hurt us in terms of the broadcasting agreements. Once you went to interleague play and once you decided you were going to combine the umpiring staff, having separate leagues as business structures didn't make any sense at all; all they had was the baseball contract. That was it; it was the National League baseball and the American League baseball [and the postseason baseball], and really there were no other significant distinctions between the two leagues, other than the one thing we did give up, which was the rivalry between the leagues. I mean Bill Giles is a true blue; he bleeds National League. But for the most part, those distinctions are not the same as they were twenty years ago or thirty years ago. Take the All-Star Game. The competition between leagues is not as cut-throat in terms of people caring about which league wins.[51]

John Harrington, former CEO of the Red Sox, also commented on the decision to centralize baseball:

> My baseball career began at the league level, working for American League President Joe Cronin for three years before I moved to the Red Sox. During Kuhn's era, we wanted to assimilate the league functions under the commissioner's office and move the

league presidents to New York City. The league offices were in different cities. You could see at the time how traditional the thinking was and how separate the leagues were. But Lee [MacPhail] didn't want to leave Boston and Chub [Feeney] didn't want to leave San Francisco.

I saw the deterioration of the power of the league under Kuhn and Ueberroth. And so it was inevitable that the power was going to shift to a central office, the commissioner's office. It was also necessary, except for some perfunctory things like making up the schedule for each league and things like that. So when it started happening, it was acceptable to me and it was a route to keep the leagues and the natural rivalry between the leagues intact. Originally, I didn't think that [the centralization] would go that far but it went all the way to where even the schedule making was done by the commissioner's office. Ultimately, and especially with the advent of interleague play, I felt it was the right approach to have one coordinated schedule.

I wondered at that time how Bud Selig's role was going to be accepted by the public. Many sportswriters and fans still held to the belief that the commissioner represented all of baseball, both players and owners. But we knew that was not and could not be the case once the union emerged. The commissioner couldn't be the commissioner of the players. He couldn't even discipline them without having an appeal from the union regarding fines and suspensions and everything else. So it was sort of natural that the commissioner became the owners' commissioner. And the centralization was needed because the league offices were so provincial in their thinking that it created all sorts of factions and frictions. You couldn't have one league president going at the other and the commissioner sitting at the table saying, "How do I get these guys together?"

The owners recognized that, to operate efficiently, we would have to eliminate the power of the league presidents. With all of the difficult issues faced by Fay Vincent, it was clear that we had to make some changes. I believe that one of the reasons for getting rid of Fay and going to Selig was that the transition was going to be a lot easier to accomplish. So I think it was in the minds of everybody at that time. And our former president, George Bush [at the time managing partner of the Texas Rangers], was very active in the process. He was involved in the committee to design the rules of governance, the new constitution, and he was very outspoken, articulate, and hard-working in that process.

> The results show that the changes we made have worked out for the better. You can see the increase in revenues brought about by having one voice for the governance of baseball, the commissioner's voice.[52]

Mr. Harrington also had some interesting comments about the All-Star Game:

> Joe Cronin and Mr. [Warren] Giles really instilled a competitive motivation to the players elected and selected for the All-Star Game. In those days, the league president took great pride in beating the other league, so the conduct of the All-Star Game in those days was just not a perfunctory thing. Giles and Cronin really went at it. They liked each other and really respected each other, but it was like a golf match; they wanted to win. It was just a matter of pride. In order to instill some meaning into the All-Star Game today, we have to award the winner of the All-Star Game the home field advantage in the World Series. But you didn't need any motivation like that when you had league presidents who were very active and involved.[53]

The Owners Expand Selig's Power

Fay Vincent said, at the time of the 1994 restructuring, "They are wrong, but time will correct it. Eventually, it changes back."[54]

Proving Vincent to be a good prognosticator, the owners strengthened the office of commissioner with baseball's new constitution, adopted on January 19, 2000. In addition to merging the governance of the American League and the National League, the 2000 constitution added two crucial sentences to Article II, Section 4, that defined the commissioner's best interests powers as they apply to integrity:

> Integrity shall include without limitation, as determined by the Commissioner, the ability of, and the public perception that, players and Clubs perform and compete at all times to the best of their abilities. Public confidence shall include without limitation the public perception, as determined by the Commissioner, that there is an appropriate level of long-term competitive balance among Clubs.[55]

With the formal merging of the leagues, the governing document was renamed the "Major League Constitution" instead of the "Major League Agreement." The term "agreement" dated back to 1903, when two leagues agreed to work together. Professor Zimbalist commented, "Now, for the first time, they were formally acknowledging that they were in the same boat. . . . The interleague rivalry was just one more division that impeded effective coordination and governance in baseball."[56]

The metamorphosis of baseball's governance system had been completed. From the absolute authority granted to Kenesaw Mountain Landis to the expanded authority granted to Bud Selig, the commissioner's office had come full circle. Of course, Landis's authority was given to restore and uphold the integrity of the game. Selig certainly has a responsibility to the game's integrity, as his fight to usher in a strong drug testing program attests, but his powers were really all about addressing baseball's economic issues, something that he has done very successfully.

Giles Appointed Honorary National League President

On June 14, 2001, the commissioner named Bill Giles and Jackie Autry (widow of the late Gene Autry) of the California Angels as honorary league presidents. Giles had already stepped down from his position as general partner of the Phillies and had ceased involvement in the day-to-day responsibilities of running the ball club. His appointment as honorary league president paid homage to the long, honorable service of his father as president of the National League from 1951 to 1969, as well as the younger Giles' lifetime of dedicated service to baseball with the Reds, Astros, and Phillies, and as a very influential owner until his resignation in 1997.

Certainly, Giles' best moments as honorary league president were the two occasions on which he awarded the Warren Giles Trophy, symbolizing the winning of the National League pennant, to his beloved Phillies in 2008 and again in 2009. Nothing could have honored his father's memory more than that.

8

Toward a New Era of Labor Peace

The 2002 Collective Bargaining Agreement

The 1990s represented an era of increasing economic difficulty for baseball, despite its growth in overall revenue. As the calendar turned to "Y2K," baseball's labor situation once again emerged as a major issue. The talks that were about to take place on a new CBA would occur within a framework of fresh memories of the damaging strike of 1994–1995 but also after a period of dramatic growth in the game after the strike, helped significantly by Cal Ripken's march to surpass Lou Gehrig's consecutive games record in 1995 and the stirring McGwire-Sosa home run battle of 1998. The owners and players alike wished to avoid a labor stoppage, understanding that another strike or lockout on top of what had occurred in the previous decade could permanently damage the game.

Efforts to curb salaries with a tax on high payrolls that was part of the 1996 CBA had little effect as salaries tripled from the end of collusion in 1989 to 2000 and team payrolls grew rapidly but unevenly. The players understood that competitive balance is important, but they also steadfastly resisted efforts to take away the free labor market that had been so beneficial to them in terms of increasing compensation. The owners first had to agree among themselves how to find solutions to financial and competitive balance issues and then had to get the players to agree to changes that would inevitably put a brake on salaries, a challenging task, to say the least.

The State of Baseball as the 21st Century Approached

Baseball's economic and competitive situation leading up to 2002 can be characterized by: (1) increasing industry revenue; (2) player salaries increasing at a substantially higher rate than industry revenue; (3) increasing revenue disparity among teams; (4) increasing disparity in club payrolls; and (5) substantial lessening of competitive balance. In combination, these elements represented a major threat to the economic health of the game.

Local television deals in the large markets, fueled by regional networks such as Fox Sports, began to create large differences in the deals available to large-market versus small-market teams. The most extreme example involved George Steinbrenner, who in 1988 had negotiated a twelve-year, $488 million contract with Madison Square Garden for local telecasts, a contract that produced more than $40 million per year on average. Second, new ballparks in places such as Baltimore, Cleveland, and Seattle created new revenue from higher attendance because of the ambience and charm of the new facilities, higher ticket prices, more premium seating, and stadium revenue from signage, concessions, and parking. In 1992 the Orioles opened Camden Yards and their revenue jumped by $40 million in the first year and kept rising. With central fund money falling as a result of lower TV revenue and local revenue for certain teams increasing dramatically, the revenue disparity between the richest and poorest clubs exploded. In 1989, the revenue difference between the top and bottom teams was $30 million, and by 1999, it was $163 million.[1]

Player salaries, which took off in the wake of free agency and then moderated during the mid- to late 1980s, had accelerated again. It is instructive to note just how much salaries had grown since Marvin Miller had become head of the Players Association in 1966. The average salary in baseball was $19,000 in 1967. By 1976, the year before free agency became a factor, but after salary arbitration had been in effect for three years, the average salary reached $51,501. By 1988, it had grown by roughly a factor of ten to $512,804. After collusion ended, the average salary jumped to $1,168,203 in 1994 and reached $2.38 million in 2002. From 1976 to 2001, baseball's average salary increased by 4,200 percent, while revenue grew 1,900 percent, from $182 million to $3.5 billion.[2] As of spring 2002, baseball's average salary had risen 71 percent, from $1.4 million to $2.38 million, in the past four years alone.[3]

In 1994 national television revenue plummeted with the end of the 1990–1993 CBS contract. That year, the ratio of the highest team payroll to the lowest was 3.3–1, with the Yankees at $45 million and the Padres at $13.5 million. By 1999 that discrepancy had grown to a ratio of more than 6–1, with the Yankees at the top and the Expos at the bottom.[4] In 1998, the Baltimore Orioles, playing in Camden Yards since 1992 and generating revenue hand-over-fist, had the highest payroll, approximately $71.9 million, while the Montreal Expos, a team that never recovered from the

1994 strike, suffering in a bad stadium in a city in which baseball was not part of the culture, had a payroll of only $8.3 million.[5]

The Effect of the 1996 CBA

Before the CBA that was negotiated in late 1996, the owners shared less than 20 percent of gate receipts, and a small fraction of pay television money—cable and superstation—but nothing from local television and radio contracts. The key "competitive balance" and "curb salaries" provisions of the 1996 CBA were the revenue sharing plan and the luxury tax. The revenue sharing plan called for each club to contribute 20 percent of its local revenue (net of stadium expenses) into a pool, from which 75 percent was divided equally among the clubs (via a straight-pool approach) and 25 percent was divided among the clubs that fell below the average for club revenue (the split-pool approach). The plan was at 60 percent of full effect in 1996 and 1997, 80 percent in 1998, 85 percent in 1999, and 100 percent in 2000 and 2001. The luxury tax required owners of the clubs with the top five payrolls to contribute 35 percent of payroll over $55 million in 1998 and 34 percent of payroll over $58.9 in 1999 to a general fund that was distributed to low-payroll teams. The tax was not in effect in 2000 or 2001.[6]

The effect of the 1996 revenue sharing plan was negligible. In 1998 the Yankees contributed the most, $11 million, while the Expos received the most, about $12.5 million. But that reallocation did little to address a $135 million difference ($170 million at the top and $35 million at the bottom) between the teams' revenue.[7] The amount of money transferred from the top to the bottom clubs, $13 million in 1999, even when combined with luxury tax, was not nearly enough to offset the growing disparities. In 1999, the top-to-bottom disparity was between the Yankees at $176 million and the Expos at less than $12 million.[8]

What about Competitive Balance?

Before the advent of free agency, competitive balance in Major League Baseball was largely a myth. The Yankees won four consecutive World Championships from 1936 to 1939, and between 1949 and 1964 the Bronx Bombers won all but two American League pennants. Between 1947 and 1959 the only teams to win National League Pennants were the Dodgers (seven), Braves (three), Giants (two) and Phillies (one, which was only the second pennant in history for a team that began play in 1883). The twenty years after free agency introduced an extended period of competitive balance in baseball. In the seasons from 1977 through 1990, thirteen different teams won the World Series.

With the increasing discrepancy in local revenue and payrolls during the 1990s, lack of competitive balance became a critical issue in the wake of the 1994 strike. The Yankees won four more World Championships in five years (1996, 1998, 1999, and 2000). From 1995 through the end of 2001, there were thirty-one playoff series, with none won by teams in the bottom half of payrolls. Of the 227 postseason games played from 1995 to 2001, teams in the bottom half of payrolls won exactly five.[9] In 1998 all of the eight teams that made the postseason were among the top twelve teams in payroll. Among the twelve clubs with the highest payrolls, all had records above .500, except for the Baltimore Orioles, who finished at .488. Of the bottom eighteen teams in payroll, only two teams finished with records above .500, and of the bottom ten in payroll, none finished above .475.[10] At the December 1998 meeting of baseball's owners, management estimated that "18 teams will enter the 1999 season with no chance of making the playoffs."[11] During the same month, Rosentraub wrote, "All the teams now dominating MLB are either owned by a large media organization, playing in a subsidized ballpark in a market with more than 4 million people, or situated in one of the nation's most populous areas."[12]

Paul Beeston, MLB president, said, "Some teams simply don't have a chance. That doesn't mean if you spend money you win. If you start looking at higher market clubs and higher payrolls, you'll see those teams will be contending in September and playing in October."[13] Sandy Alderson, MLB's vice president for baseball operations and former Oakland A's executive, said, "Not only are payrolls going up, but they're also going down. We lose sight of the fact that there are some clubs that are giving up." Alderson also stated, "Payroll disparity results from revenue disparity and leads to competitive disparity."[14]

Braves General Manager John Schuerholz explained baseball's dilemma. "The economic reality is that teams that operate in large markets generate more revenue, sell more tickets, sell more skyboxes, sell more executive suites, and get better support from corporate sponsors who have more money to spend. Teams that operate in the bulk of our markets, the mediocre-size markets or small markets, aren't going to have that revenue." Cleveland transformed from a low-revenue team to a high-revenue team after moving in to new Jacobs Field, but eventually reverted to midmarket levels of revenue. The Brewers, the Pirates, and other clubs in small markets enjoyed only a short-lived, usually one year, burst of attendance and revenue from their new parks. As Doug Melvin of the Texas

Rangers expressed, a new park "is a short-tem solution, but in the long term you'll just be losing in a prettier ball park."[15]

Signing Players to Big Contracts While Complaining about Rising Salaries: The Owners' Dilemma

During the late 1990s and into the new century, at the same time the owners and their commissioner were moaning about baseball's economic problems, clubs continued to sign free agents at ever-escalating salaries. The Mets signed Mike Piazza for $91 million. The escalation continued with Kevin Brown's $105 million contract with the Dodgers and A-Rod's unprecedented $252 million contract with Tom Hicks of the Rangers. These and like signings did little to bolster the argument that baseball was bleeding money and needed relief in the form of a constraint on salaries. But more than signaling that baseball had money to spend, the $1 billion spent on free agents during the 1999–2000 off-season mortgaged the future of baseball, according to Hal Bodley of *USA Today,* to the tune of $3.7 billion on guaranteed players' salaries contained in multiyear deals.[16]

Baseball also had difficulty crying wolf about its finances when the value of franchises continued to escalate. Rupert Murdoch's Fox Group paid $311 million for the Dodgers in early 1998. The question that could be asked by the Players Association was, "If all of those clubs are losing so much, how is it that the value of the franchises continues to rise?"

Selig's Blue Ribbon Panel

In early 1999, with the end of the 1996 CBA still at least two years away, Selig formed a special Blue Ribbon Panel to study the economics of baseball and make recommendations that would become a key part of the owners' position on entering negotiations for a new CBA. Selig appointed to his Blue Ribbon Panel, along with twelve owners, columnist and noted Cubs fan George Will; economist and former head of the Federal Reserve Paul Volker; former senate majority leader and onetime candidate for commissioner George Mitchell; and Yale University President Richard Levin. His charge to the panel was to evaluate and recommend solutions for the significant economic problems faced by baseball. Selig chose not to invite anyone from the Players Association, a curious move in view of the labor strife that had characterized baseball during the decade.

The commissioner's major objective in forming the panel was to create a platform for negotiation of the next CBA. The panel met and studied the baseball business for fifteen months before releasing a report in July 2000 that focused on baseball's key economic issues. The findings were as follows. First, large and growing revenue disparities between clubs were causing problems of "chronic competitive imbalance." Second, problems of revenue disparities and competitive imbalance had worsened considerably since the 1994 strike. Third, the limited revenue sharing and payroll tax provisions in the 1996 CBA had not addressed the issues of competitive imbalance and rising payrolls, both of which continued to increase instead of decrease. Fourth, "some low-revenue clubs, believing the amount of their proceeds from revenue sharing insufficient to enable them to become competitive, used these proceeds to become moderately profitable."[17] In sum, the 1996 CBA had not had the intended effect of creating a significant drag on salaries, nor had competitive balance been enhanced.

The central theme of the report was that revenue disparity was increasing, leading to increasing payroll disparity and decreasing competitive balance, while exploding payrolls had created what amounted to financial exigency in the industry. The panel's major recommendations were in the areas of revenue sharing and a payroll tax, designed to both address revenue imbalances and curb rapidly increasing club payrolls. The panel recommended allocating between 40 percent and 50 percent of each club's net local revenue to a pool that would be distributed evenly across the thirty clubs using a straight-pool format, with the rationale that local revenue is really industry money, not club money. The panel's other main recommendation was to establish a 50 percent tax on team payrolls above a fixed $84 million threshold, thereby creating a strong disincentive for teams to operate above the payroll limit. The panel noted that the payroll tax currently in effect "failed to moderate the rapid escalation of club payrolls."[18]

The report encouraged clubs to have a minimum payroll of $40 million and for the commissioner to withhold central fund money from clubs that did not reach the minimum. High-revenue clubs wanted a minimum payroll that would help ensure that recipients of revenue sharing spent their funds on players in an attempt to compete instead of simply dropping those funds to the bottom line. The report also recommended that baseball use some of its central fund revenue, amounting to about $500 million annually from national television deals, licensing, and sponsorships, to assist low-revenue teams in meeting the minimum payroll.

The panel also recommended a competitive balance draft whereby the bottom eight clubs (as measured by a three-year winning percentage) could draft one player each from the top clubs each year, with the top clubs being able to protect twenty-five players in their respective systems. The downside of this proposal is easy to see: potentially, well-managed clubs that draft well and develop their young players would be penalized, while other, less successful clubs would be rewarded. The owners approved this concept in their January 2001 meeting. Nelson Doubleday, co-owner of the Mets along with Fred Wilpon, took an opposite view and lambasted the proposal, "I personally think it's an outrage. It's a sham. It's everything baseball shouldn't be for. What you're saying is that you don't have to scout. We'll do that for you. Why spend money on scouting when you can take eight of our best players, or four of them or two of them?"[19]

The Phillies were one of the teams in favor of the draft. General Manager Ed Wade commented, "Our position is that some fundamental changes need to be made to provide more competitive balance in the game. Although a lot of them will revolve around economics, it's worth exploring other ways of accomplishing that. There's some sensibility to this [proposal]."[20]

The committee advocated a worldwide draft, including all amateur players. Clearly, this recommendation was a response to the huge contracts commanded by Japanese free agents, Cuban defectors, and some other young Latino players. In particular, small-market clubs had simply lacked the funds to compete for established stars such as Cuba's Orlando Hernandez, who inevitably wound up with big-market, high-spending clubs such as the Yankees, further exacerbating competitive imbalance.

Another recommendation was that college players would be eligible after senior year instead of junior year, which would have the effect of reducing leverage for players who threatened to return to school, in addition to a signing deadline of July 15 for all draft picks. The committee also recommended allowing clubs to trade draft choices and eliminating compensation picks for lost free agents. The panel specified that baseball could solve its problems without necessarily having to contract, but indicated that franchise relocation would be important in addressing the financial woes of some clubs in very limited markets.

Shortly after the panel reported its findings, Zimbalist wrote an article for *Sports Business Journal* in which he claimed that "The Blue Ribbon report unquestionably loses some credibility by uncritically regurgitating owners' claims of ubiquitous financial woes" but acknowledged the fact that "these and other shortcomings have little to do with the main thrust of the report's analysis. The great bulk of the eighty-seven-page report concerns baseball's growing competitive imbalance and what to do about it."[21]

Another problem with the panel's findings was its failure to distinguish between small-market and small-payroll teams; there has never been a perfect correlation between market size and revenue, between market size and payrolls, or between payrolls and performance. A year after the panel's report, the "Moneyball" Oakland Athletics went on a historic twenty-game winning streak and won 102 games during the regular season, making the postseason as a wild card team before losing in five games to the Yankees.

In November 2000 the commissioner told a Senate panel that baseball needed "sweeping changes" in its economics, citing the contention that "at the start of spring training, there no longer exists hope and faith for the fans of more than half our 30 clubs. It is my job to restore hope and faith." Without balance, baseball cannot thrive; even Yankees fans don't want to see the Yankees bludgeon the other teams every game. The satisfaction of watching the Yankees play ball is ultimately dependent on the quality of the opposition. Selig cited statistics that only three of 189 postseason games since the 1994–1995 strike were won by teams that didn't have payrolls among the top half. Finally, he claimed that between eighteen and twenty clubs would lose money in the coming year.[22]

Bargaining Begins

Baseball's latest CBA was due to expire at the end of 2000, with an option for the Players Association to extend the deadline for a year, which the union exercised. On January 20, 2001, George W. Bush, former managing partner of the Texas Rangers, was inaugurated as president. From his unique perspective, Bush commented on baseball's economic dilemma, acknowledging that increased revenue sharing posed a problem for the owners. "It gets harder as the value of the franchises, the equity in each franchise, differs. But the truth of the matter is, I always felt the long term solution was to share revenue, as much revenue as possible, particularly the media contracts because, you know, you're no good in the big market unless the small market teams come to play."[23] On several occasions during the discussions, the president indicated that baseball should negotiate a peaceful solution to its problems and that his office would not get involved as his predecessor, Bill Clinton, did during the strike of 1994–1995.

Just before spring training in 2001, Red Sox CEO John Harrington, a member of the Executive Council and vice chairman of the Blue Ribbon Panel, commented on the labor situation facing baseball:

> You're not going to see [a work stoppage] happen again. Sure, the drums will start beating during the season. This is posturing; part of the negotiating process. But we, as an industry, got hurt the last time and we're not going to let it happen again. The players want

> to keep [the CBA] status quo. Why not? Who could blame them? They've got a great thing going. But the owners need more. We need more revenue-sharing, more luxury taxes, and more things that would restrain the rapid growth of player salaries. Both sides have to know that we had to do something to make the non-competitive clubs [lower end of the revenue scale] more competitive. In my opinion, nothing will happen at the end of this season. I think we will agree to extend the agreement one more year, and continue to talk. Then the next year [after the 2002 season] it will be the same way. No one gained when we had the labor problem in '94 and '95. Our industry can't take another hit like that. The image of the players was hurt. The game as a whole suffered. But, we have brought it back. Baseball is popular again. Both sides just have to keep talking until something happens to give all teams a chance.[24]

As the players met during spring 2001 to discuss the labor situation, players such as young Paul Konerko and veteran Harold Baines of the White Sox speculated on the prospects for labor peace or another stoppage and expressed their concerns. Don Fehr indicated that the bargaining climate in early 2001 was substantially more positive than that of 1994, saying, "If you'll notice, there is no open hostility between the two parties now. The atmosphere is not as poisoned."[25] Fehr also said that, from his perspective, the game was healthy, noting that "there are a lot of new stadiums, a lot of attendance, a lot of revenue coming in and records are being set left and right."[26]

The commissioner introduced a positive element to the bargaining early on by assigning Paul Beeston, appointed as MLB's COO in 1997, and Rob Manfred, one of MLB's labor attorneys, to try to find a peaceful solution with the players. The manner in which Beeston and Manfred interacted with Fehr and the Players Association stood in stark contrast to the likes of Ray Grebey (in the 1980s) and Richard Ravitch, labor negotiators for the owners who had established anti-labor reputations and were viewed by the Players Association, rightly or wrongly, as union busters.[27]

The Blue Ribbon Panel had suggested that contraction was not an economic necessity, noting that "if the recommendations outlined in this report are implemented, there should be no immediate need for contraction."[28] Instead, baseball should consider relocation of problematic franchises. Unfortunately, potential markets for relocation—including Portland, Oregon; Charlotte, North Carolina; Las Vegas; and Northern Virginia—were not considered to possess adequate potential. Jerry

McMorris of Colorado first proposed contraction. In 2000, several owners and economists began to discuss reducing the number of franchises as a last-resort option to fix the problems in some markets. Notably, the last contraction in major league baseball had been in 1899, when National League owners bought out franchises in Cleveland, Washington, Louisville, and Baltimore to shrink from twelve to eight teams as they faced a challenge from Ban Johnson's new American League, and the last professional team in any sport to be eliminated was the original edition of the Washington Bullets of the NBA in 1954.

Selig commented in early March 2001 that, although he had a different perspective a year earlier, contraction was now being considered as a possible option in addressing baseball's economic situation. "I will tell you today that the economic situation is so significant, and as I would call it, pervasive, that I wouldn't take contraction off the table. It's one of the options out there that we are considering."[29]

Early Talks Look Promising—Go Nowhere

Paul Beeston had been appointed the COO of Major League Baseball as part of the restructuring of baseball's central administration. Selig assigned Beeston and Rob Manfred, an attorney in baseball's central office, the task of beginning negotiations with the union in February 2001, with the CBA due to expire in November of that year. According to Zimbalist, the two sides held twenty-three meetings between February and June 2001. At the close of the meeting on June 20, 2001, the Players Association thought that they had an agreement with Beeston and Manfred, but never heard back from Beeston. Selig pulled Beeston from the bargaining sessions, presumably because Selig believed the owners could not support the offer to the players. Apparently, Selig, who had been kept informed of the progress that Beeston and Manfred had been making, had misread the owners' willingness to deal. No further formal negotiations took place during the rest of the season. Having had the proverbial rug pulled out from under him, Beeston later resigned his post.[30]

One owner, who remained anonymous less he face a stiff fine from the commissioner, indicated his dissatisfaction with the process. He said: "We thought we had reached the point where there was a deal to be made with the players, in terms of lowering costs, dragging salaries, and increasing significantly the sharing of revenues. We were making progress with guys like Beeston and Sandy Alderson . . . management guys who had made deals in the past. But the small-market owners started screaming at the commissioner and that stopped everything right there."[31]

The 2001 Season

The 2001 season created a lot of fan interest. Barry Bonds chased Mark McGwire's new home run record and smashed it with seventy-three home runs. The Oakland A's had a historic winning streak. The Seattle Mariners won 116 regular season games. With less than three weeks left in the regular season, the United States was jarred by the September 11 terrorist attacks on New York and Washington, D.C. Baseball took a hiatus to let the nation's wounds heal a bit and returned on September 16. During the first Cubs game after the hiatus, against Houston, Sammy Sosa hit a home run into the right field bleachers at Wrigley Field, then circled the bases with a small American flag in his hand. It was a magic moment. More magic occurred in late October and early November during a classic seven-game World Series between the four-year-old Arizona Diamondbacks and the defending champion Yankees that was played against the backdrop of the horror that had devastated Lower Manhattan several weeks earlier. Mariano Rivera, the greatest relief pitcher of them all, could not hold a lead in the ninth inning of game 7, and the Diamondbacks won the Series with a bloop hit by Luis Gonzalez over a drawn-in Derek Jeter.

Contraction

The good feeling about the state of baseball was not to last. In the immediate wake of the World Series, Twins owner Carl Pohlad, weary of fighting a losing battle to secure public funding to help build a new ballpark, told the press that he would not stand in the way of the Twins ceasing to exist, saying, "I've furnished a team here for 15 years and put $150 million of cash into it, and I'm not going to do it anymore. I'm tired of it. A business has to pay for itself."[32]

Shortly after the World Series ended, in early November, Selig dropped a virtual bomb by announcing that baseball planned to contract two teams, not named but widely speculated to be Minnesota and Montreal. The "contraction gambit," as Zimbalist called it, created a significant amount of negative reaction. The union, faced with the loss of eighty jobs, filed a grievance that claimed that neither the commissioner nor anyone else could unilaterally reduce the number of major league clubs, that it was an issue that had to be bargained. Pohlad likely would have been glad to receive the payout from MLB if his club had been eliminated via contraction, but the Minnesota Sports Facility Commission thought differently. The commission filed for an injunction to stop MLB from contracting the Twins, arguing before a judge in Minnesota that the Twins had an obligation, based on their Metrodome lease, to play during the 2002 season. The court agreed, an appeals court upheld the lower court's ruling, and the Minnesota Supreme Court refused to hear the case.[33]

Certain of baseball's smaller-market franchises were plagued by ownership or stadium problems that made it very difficult to earn enough revenue to compete with large-revenue clubs in free agency and player development. Montreal's poor attendance, only about 9,000 per game, along with the lack of an English-speaking television contract and stadium problems, made it the top relocation or contraction candidate. Although Minnesota had reached first place in the American League Central in early 2001, the Twins had the smallest payroll in baseball. Pohlad had tried to move the club to North Carolina in the late 1990s, but could not secure a stadium deal. His efforts to secure public funding for a downtown, open-air stadium in Minneapolis continued to be unsuccessful. With lagging attendance (28th in baseball) and the lack of a stadium deal, the Florida Marlins were considered a prime candidate for relocation or contraction. Tampa Bay's management situation (no team CEO), a bad facility, and declining attendance—ranked 29th of 30 clubs—made the Devil Rays another contraction option.[34]

Selig's "contraction gambit" faced challenges on multiple fronts. These included: (1) local and state governments in cities identified as contraction candidates would stage a legal fight to keep teams playing in publicly owned and funded facilities; (2) the union would attempt to block efforts to eliminate jobs; (3) the National Association of Professional Baseball Leagues, the minor leagues, had a contract with Major League Baseball that obligated the big leagues to provide each minor league team in the association with a major league affiliate; (4) existing owners would be on the hook for the cost of buying out the contracted franchises, plus their minor league affiliates, plus the cost of contracts for the players contracted and potentially not transferred to other teams; (5) other entities, such as sponsors and concessionaires, might take legal action against baseball for potential violation of contracts; (6) the public relations impact of cutting existing baseball clubs could be severe on top of the continuing labor problems plaguing baseball; and (7) Congress would be sure to react by once again threatening to remove baseball's anti-trust exemption.

While the strategy of contracting teams faced a variety of hurdles, reports indicated that the owners had set a $250 million buyout price for the teams that were folded. Baseball writer Tracy Ringolsby reported in late September 2001 that the Players Association might be agreeable to eliminating two teams if the active rosters of the remaining teams were expanded to twenty-seven players, a move that could be justified by a trend to expanded pitching staffs. That move could be a win-win situation, with more roster spots overall for the players and fewer franchises to share national revenue and participate in revenue sharing for the owners.[35]

The owners met right after the World Series and voted 29–1 in favor of contraction. Selig pronounced, "It makes no sense for major league baseball to be in markets that generate insufficient local revenues to justify the investment in the franchise. The teams to be contracted have a long record of failing to generate enough revenues to operate a viable major league franchise." The commissioner also reported that the owners had not yet picked the teams to be consolidated, indicating that there were "more than two candidates" and noting "a lot of people in the game who were in favor of four-team contraction." In reaction to questions about possible franchise relocation as an alternative solution, Selig said, "Merely transferring existing problems to another ownership group or another city would only exacerbate the problem, not resolve it."[36]

Reaction to the commissioner's announcement was both swift and predictable. Don Fehr said, "This is the worst manner in which to begin the process of negotiating a new collective bargaining agreement" and that the owners' announcement was a "severe blow" to the hopes of ushering in a more positive relationship between the owners and players.[37] On the public side, Congress opened up with what might be called "both barrels": Senator Paul Wellstone from Minnesota said that he would introduce legislation immediately that would revoke baseball's anti-trust exemption, while John Conyers, the ranking minority of member of the House Judiciary Committee, announced that he planned to introduce legislation to limit the exemption. The proposed limitation would allow injured parties, such as a government entity, a stadium authority, or even a player, to sue for anti-trust violations, essentially preventing the league from moving or shutting down teams. Other elements of the exemption, including minor league baseball, licensing deals, and intellectual property rights, would remain intact.[38]

Within two days the Players Association filed a grievance that claimed that the labor contract had been violated. The union claimed that the owners had violated the terms of the CBA by unilaterally deciding to cut teams. The owners claimed that baseball had the right to eliminate teams, but that the "particulars," such as how to disperse players from the folded clubs, had to be bargained. Shyam Das, baseball's permanent arbitrator, would hear the case. Even if Das ruled in the owners' favor, contraction in time for the 2002 season was unlikely because the players could take the case before the National Labor Relations Board. In addition, the municipalities that stood to lose their franchises could file lawsuits, further delaying the process. With all of these complications, it was easy to see why many thought that the contraction announcement was much more a negotiating ploy, an attempt to extract concessions from the union in return for not contracting, then a serious strategy designed to address baseball's economic problems.

In mid-November a judge in Hennepin County, Minnesota, responding to a suit filed by the Minnesota Sports Facilities Commission, issued a temporary injunction barring baseball from disbanding the Twins until the team fulfilled the terms of its lease and completed its 2002 home schedule in the Metrodome. This ruling effectively ended serious discussion of contraction.

The Rocky Road to Labor Peace

Not until September 2001 did the owners formally send notice to the union that they planned to seek changes in the CBA. The 1996 CBA was due to expire on October 31, 2001, or the day after the World Series ended, whichever came later. With a delay in the season caused by the events of 9/11, the deadline turned out to be November 7. Owners could lock out the players the next day, and this would put a stop to free agent negotiations and leave many players wondering where they would play the following year. However, the terror attacks had an impact on the baseball negotiations. In the aftermath of 9/11, there could be little talk of a lockout. "Baseball's squalid little squabbles,"[39] as they were called by Yale President Bart Giamatti during the 1981 strike twenty years earlier, became insignificant in comparison to the nation's suffering. Moreover, the U.S. economy, already headed into a slowdown in late summer 2001, had been hit hard by the terrorist attacks. Discretionary spending, which was the source of revenue for professional sports, was likely to take a hit, at least in the near term. The Lords of Baseball had to tread carefully.

Against the backdrop of public posturing and legal maneuvering on the labor front, the owners extended the commissioner's contract for three years to 2006, thereby making the statement that they were in full support of the commissioner in baseball's relationship with the Players Association. Meanwhile, a game of musical chairs began among owners that involved the purchases of the Boston Red Sox and the Florida Marlins and the sale of the Montreal Expos. Five groups submitted bids to buy the Red Sox, with various groups including Tom Werner, former owner of the San Diego Padres, Larry Lucchino, former president of the Padres and Baltimore Orioles, and John Henry, owner of the Marlins. Jeff Loria, owner of the Expos, wanted to sell his languishing franchise but remain in baseball, and Henry's purchase of the Red Sox involved Loria selling the Expos and buying the Marlins.[40]

In January 2002 the owners approved a series of transactions. Henry sold the Marlins to Loria for $158 million. Henry's investor group, including Lucchino, who would serve as president, and Werner, bought the Red Sox and 80 percent of the New England Sports Network (NESN) from the Yawkey Trust for a price of $700 million, despite not being the highest bidder. Major League Baseball took the Expos off of Loria's hands for $120 million, and MLB ran the club until it eventually moved, under new ownership, to Washington, D.C., in 2005.

The Commissioner's Report to Congress

The commissioner testified before the House Judiciary Committee in the fall of 2001 and laid out baseball's economic disaster by opening up baseball's books. Selig claimed that the industry had lost $511 million on revenue of more than $3 billion in 2001, which amounted to a $232 million operating loss after interest and depreciation had been factored out. The union dismissed these numbers, as they had done in the past, claiming that history proved that there are many ways for a baseball team to both underreport revenue and overstate expenses.

Much skepticism followed Selig's claims, not only from the union but also from Congress, *Forbes* Magazine, and economists who studied baseball, among others. Some writers repeated the famous statement by Paul Beeston, then Toronto Blue Jays vice president, who said, "Under generally accepted accounting principles, I can turn a $4 million profit into a $2 million loss, and I can get every national accounting firm to agree with me."[41] Andrew Zimbalist explains a concept called "related party transactions," which can occur when club owners also owned related businesses, such as the WGN and the Chicago Cubs, both part of the Tribune Company. This allowed the Cubs to legally understate the true value of their TV deal with WGN by booking less revenue for the Cubs and more revenue for its sister company, turning a profit into a stated loss, but having no effect on the Tribune Company's financial statements. The same thing happened in Atlanta with Ted Turner and WTBS.[42] Zimbalist pointed out that Wayne Huizenga had used related party transactions when he owned both the stadium and the Marlins in 1997, claiming huge losses when in fact he understated revenue significantly, instead attributing them to the stadium that he also owned. This allowed Huizenga to "cry poor" as a rationale for unloading almost all of the Marlins' highly paid stars after they won the World Series in 1997. In addition, related party transactions allow clubs to reduce the amount of revenue taxed by baseball's revenue sharing program.[43]

However, while Selig's numbers most likely overstated baseball's economic problems in the aggregate, one could not argue with the fact that some low-revenue teams had significant economic problems and simply could not afford to compete with high-revenue clubs as the disparity in revenue continued to grow. Blum reported that "officially, eleven MLB teams showed operating profits in 2001, a number reduced to nine after revenue sharing. Some clubs, including the World Champion Arizona Diamondbacks, showed significant losses. Jerry Colangelo's club booked a $32.2 million loss and had to tap every possible source of short-term credit, both from Major League Baseball and from the banks, to meet obligations." Montreal, a leading candidate for contraction, had an operating loss of $38.5 million.[44]

The Phillies, according to unaudited MLB figures, made $81.5 million in revenue in 2001, with operating costs of $102.3 million, for a deficit of $20.8 million. A little more than half of that loss was recouped through revenue sharing, from which the Phillies were given $11.7 million. Even after revenue sharing, the Phillies ownership partners had to contribute more than $9 million to meet the financial obligations for the year.[45]

The Owners Make a Labor Proposal

In early January 2002 the commissioner made a specific contract proposal to the union, asking for a 50 percent luxury tax on the amounts of payrolls in excess of $98 million, a figure $14 million higher than that recommended by the Blue Ribbon Panel. In addition, the commissioner asked for a $100 million annual discretionary fund from which he could dispense funds to teams as he thought necessary. In terms of revenue sharing, Selig proposed that teams place 50 percent of their net local revenue into a pool that would be distributed equally to all thirty clubs, using a "straight-pool" format. Selig also proposed including all international players in the draft as well as other changes, as recommended by the Blue Ribbon Panel. Other elements of the owners' proposal focused on an old bugaboo, salary arbitration. The owners proposed eliminating salary arbitration for currently eligible players with two to three years of major league service and allowing teams to release players after the exchange of proposed arbitration figures without having to give them any termination pay or salary.[46]

Zimbalist explained the straight-pool versus split-pool issue as follows:

> Under the split pool, every team's local net revenue is taxed at the same rate. Of the resulting collection of funds, 75 percent is distributed equally across all the teams, and 25 percent is distributed to

> teams only with below-average revenues. Under the straight pool, 100 percent of the collected funds is distributed equally across all the teams. Because the split-pool system disproportionately redistributes to lower-revenue clubs, it does considerable more to equalize revenues than the straight-pool system.[47]

The big-market clubs did not necessarily support expanded revenue sharing. However, George Steinbrenner, who had been a leading opponent of the concept when it first surfaced in the early 1990s, indicated a willingness to accept increased revenue sharing with one qualifier, that is, assurance that franchises on the receiving end must use the money to improve their clubs. His comment was, "When I see owners putting it into their own pocket, that's not right for fans. They're not paying their hard-earned money to see us play so we can pay it to someone else."[48]

The players viewed the owners' attempt to share up to 50 percent of local revenue more as a limit on salaries than as a way to achieve competitive balance. The union was reluctant to raise the rate much beyond existing levels because, as Zimbalist pointed out, "higher tax rates undermine an owner's incentive to win and to pay salaries commensurate with a player's value. That is, revenue sharing has two effects: it equalizes team revenues and it depresses player salaries."[49]

When the union responded, Fehr indicated a willingness to increase revenue sharing from its current level of 20 percent to 22.5 percent, a move in the right direction but far short of the figure proposed by the owners. The difference in dollars between the owners' proposal of 50 percent and the players' proposal, based on 2001 revenue, amounted to $66 million ($253 million versus $187 million). The players, however, favored retaining the split pool as a means of distributing the revenue sharing fund, with 75 percent of the funds divided equally and 25 percent going to teams with revenue below the industry average. Compared with the effects of the straight-pool approach, the split-pool plan makes a given amount of revenue sharing go further in helping to address revenue imbalance. Fehr maintained that the difference in the two proposals was therefore less than it appeared.

The owners' change in their characterization of the excess payroll tax from a "luxury" tax to a "competitive balance" tax did little to assuage players' concern that the tax was nothing more than a back door salary cap. In fact, Rob Manfred freely admitted that the purpose of the tax was to put a brake on the explosion of salaries that had occurred since the players returned to work in early 1995. The players' position on the luxury tax was voiced by Fehr, who said, "Our simple view is that players are not luxury items. This is a difficult issue for us."[50]

On top of everything else that was cooking in baseball's economic and legal circles, it came to light that Selig had borrowed $3 million from a company controlled by Carl Pohlad in 1995. The funds were paid back in full in a matter of weeks, but the lack of disclosure of the loan violated baseball rules for such transactions and appeared to represent a major conflict of interest since Pohlad wanted to be contracted out to the tune of $250 million and Selig stood to benefit if no major league franchise existed 300 miles to the west. Representative Conyers, in what amounted to a grandstand play, called on Selig to resign. Selig respectfully declined the invitation.

In late January the Minnesota Court of Appeals upheld an injunction by the lower court requiring the Twins to play their entire 2002 schedule in the Metrodome. At about the same time, Paul Beeston, who had had his negotiations with the union stopped by Selig when seemingly on the verge of a deal the previous June, announced his decision to step down from his post. In early February, the Minnesota Supreme Court declined to hear baseball's appeal of the lower court decisions in the Metropolitan Sports Facilities Commission case, basically putting an end to contraction plans for the 2002 season. Shortly thereafter, Selig announced that baseball had delayed its plans to shrink until 2003. The Players Association, however, continued pressing its grievance against the owners for announcing plans to contract, citing some agents' claims that the uncertainty surrounding contraction had negatively affected the free agent market.

On a more positive note, Fehr, testifying before the Senate Judiciary Committee in mid-February, indicated that he favored "significant" increased sharing of the clubs' local revenue, a position he had not previously articulated. Bob DuPuy, MLB's executive vice president for administration and chief legal officer—shortly to be named the successor to Beeston as president and COO—called the union's willingness to negotiate the revenue sharing issue "the most positive" aspect of the committee's hearings on baseball's anti-trust exemption. However, Fehr also reiterated the union's position opposing any kind of player payroll constraints, including a salary cap or a "competitive balance" tax on high-payroll teams.[51]

The "60–40" Debt Limit Rule

Selig dropped another bombshell in early March, when he notified the owners that baseball would enforce a long-standing rule that limited the amount of debt a team could carry. The debt limit rule was known as the "60–40" rule and had been created in 1975—by Selig—but had not been enforced in recent years. The commissioner's letter informed clubs that beginning in June 2002 they had to be in compliance with a rule that debt cannot be higher than 40 percent of a team's asset value. Penalties for noncompliance could include forfeiture of central fund revenue or possibly being placed in trusteeship. The formula measured franchise value as two times the most recent year's gross revenue and included loans from banks or other private lenders and from MLB plus the current value of long-term player contracts as liabilities. Interestingly, the current value of future television revenue would not count on the asset side, while revenue sharing money contributed by high-revenue teams would be counted as a liability.

Selig had originally crafted the "60–40" rule in 1975. The players filed a grievance with arbitrator Richard Bloch over the rule in 1983, but Bloch found for the owners in 1985, indicating in his ruling that no evidence suggested that the debt limits affected player compensation. The "60–40" rule was, according to Zimbalist, "long dormant" when Selig "dusted it off" in March 2002.[52] Since the value of long-term player contracts was to be treated as a liability, the union, as expected, considered the threat of imposition of debt limits another backdoor approach to limiting salaries. Along with the threat of contraction, the debt limit issue added to the suspicion and mistrust affecting the negotiations. Whether intentionally or not, along with the threat to contract two teams and reduce the number of union jobs, Selig had put on the table yet another significant bargaining chip.

Toward the end of March, Selig announced a pledge not to lock out the players or unilaterally impose new bargaining terms through the end of the 2002 World Series. The commissioner's press release said, "Our fans deserve to know that the 2002 season will be played to completion. . . . I pledge that we will not take any economic action in the form of a lockout or unilateral implementation against the players association throughout the course of the season and postseason."[53] In the context of the mistrust between the owners and the union, Fehr interpreted Selig's promise as a veiled threat to lock out the players and impose changes as soon as the World Series ended, calling Selig's statement, "a tacit acknowledgement of the clubs' continuing intention" to make changes after the postseason.[54] Instead of calming the situation, Selig's pledge actually raised the specter of a possible players' strike during the season. The fact that the union had been withholding licensing money from the players to bolster a strike fund of $100 million added to the likelihood of another long and bitter labor war.

Forbes released its annual report on the finances of major league baseball in late March 2002. The magazine's figures reported the same revenue for the industry that MLB had reported ($3.57 billion versus $3.55 billion) but indicated that baseball had significantly lower expenses ($3.495 billion versus $4.378 billion) than Selig had indicated. This difference turned a claimed loss of $232 million to a reported profit of $75 million. Selig and MLB executives immediately criticized the Forbes numbers as "dishonest" and "fiction" and not subject to audit, as MLB's numbers had been. *Forbes* stood by its figures.[55]

Throughout the 2002 season, as talks started, stopped, and then started again, discussions centered on finding the acceptable middle ground between the owners' and the players' positions, much like any other labor negotiations. The players accepted revenue sharing in principle, but not at the amounts proposed by the owners, expressing concern that too much revenue sharing would drain money from high-revenue clubs that would then cut spending on player salaries. The players resisted the imposition of a payroll tax because such a levy discourages teams with the highest payrolls from spending money on players. The players understood the notion that "a rising tide lifts all boats." The owners' position was voiced by Manfred, who said, "We need a direct form of payroll regulation to promote competitive balance. Revenue sharing alone is not enough."[56]

In mid-May, reports began to circulate that attendance in 2002 was down appreciably from the previous year, and if the decline held, attendance was projected to take its biggest drop since the strike. While MLB officials attributed the decline to poor weather during the early season, other observers were less sanguine. One sports analyst said, "There's a growing sentiment that baseball just doesn't have its act together. And for a lot of fans, it's just not worth their allegiance." The president of a fan advocacy organization agreed, saying, "Baseball's overall problem is that people just see it in turmoil. From contraction, to the labor problems, to the small-market-big-market thing, they have a lot of problems."[57] MLB's Sandy Alderson acknowledged that the lack of hope in small-revenue cities reduced fan interest in those clubs, "People in certain cities are going to stop going to games if they think their team doesn't have a chance to win. Or, they're going to go less frequently. It's reflected in season tickets as well as walk-up attendance."[58] Clearly, baseball needed to solve its competitive balance and labor problems and let fans focus on the games on the field, not the gamesmanship off the field.

Also in mid-May, talk in the Players Association turned toward the possibility of setting a strike date, designed primarily to put urgency in the negotiations and pressure on the owners. DuPuy called the strike talk "counterproductive," and Fehr indicated that the players were not yet moving toward a strike.[59] However, a strike represented the players' "hammer," as Claire Smith called it, because a strike during the season could preempt a management move after the season to impose a lockout, enforce new working conditions, possibly eliminate some franchises, and "tax high spending teams to such an extent that they won't ever pay A-Rod-type money again."[60] Tom Glavine, the National League's player representative, explained the players' position regarding a possible strike, saying, "If we don't do something right now, then probably the day after the World Series, [the owners] will do something. If we don't do something now, then we won't have any leverage until next season."[61]

Glavine also made a statement that infuriated fans who were disgusted with the situation and could not understand how "billionaire owners" and "millionaire players" could not figure out a way to share $3.6 billion in revenue. Glavine commented on the players' opposition to the luxury tax, saying, "It's a luxury tax[;] it's a salary cap. Call it what you want. It's still designed to keep players from making money."[62] Fans did not appreciate that comment when the average salary of players has reached more than $2 million per year and Americans were struggling in the post-9/11 economy.

The Action Heats Up

Another key issue in the talks emerged in May: the discussion of steroids and testing of players for illegal drugs. Until this point, the position of the union had been that any testing for drugs was a violation of the players' right to privacy. However, after revelations from both 1996 National League Most Valuable Player Ken Caminitti—in a 2002 *Sports Illustrated* cover story—and former All-Star Jose Canseco that they and a majority of players used performance-enhancing drugs, some players began to request testing so that they would not be lumped in with the "cheaters."

Once again, the commissioner added fuel to the fire when, in late May, he pronounced that up to eight baseball clubs were in danger of going out of business if baseball's broken economic system was not fixed. Selig argued that this was old news, but it was the first time he publicly indicated that a specific number of teams were in financial distress. Not surprisingly, the union's position was that once again, the owners, through their mouthpiece, the commissioner, were "crying wolf" in an attempt to force favorable terms with the players.

In June, the owners began to move on their offer, reducing the the initial percentage of the luxury tax to less than 50 percent and cutting the amount of money in the commissioner's discretionary fund to $85 million. A couple of weeks later, the union, which had proposed a discretionary fund of $30 million for "supplemental sharing," raised that figure to

$40 million. Selig continued to insist that baseball needed to change its economic system, and Fehr continued to insist that the players would not accept any changes that would restrict salaries.

On July 10, while declining to identify any club, Selig announced that one team was in danger of not meeting its next payroll and another had so much debt that it would likely be forced out of business. He also claimed that baseball clubs in total had amassed debt of between $3.5 and $3.6 billion and that twenty teams had reached the limit of $72 million from baseball's credit line. By making these announcements, Selig was essentially declaring a type of "financial exigency" for major league baseball. On the issue of competitive balance, as of the halfway point in the season, projections for the pennant races in 2002 indicated that, of the eight teams to make the postseason, six would be in the top ten in payrolls and seven would be in the upper half. Five teams were on a pace to finish the season with at least ninety-eight losses; all five were in the bottom eleven in payrolls.[63] Given all that had transpired on baseball's labor, economic, and competitive fronts, in midsummer 2002, baseball could be said to have a negative prognosis.

As the July bargaining sessions continued into August, progress occurred in small steps. The difference in the revenue sharing proposals was reduced to $70 million, but there was no significant movement on the threshold and percentage for the luxury tax. The owners' plan called for a tax rate of 37.5 percent initially that would move up to 50 percent, while the players countered with a 15 percent tax rate. The union agreed to include international players in the amateur draft, but only if the draft was cut to sixteen rounds (the draft included fifty rounds at the time). Owners moved from fifty rounds to forty to thirty-eight, but would not go any lower, maintaining that a sixteen-round draft, when there are six minor league teams, is not adequate. The owners proposed a $45 million minimum payroll, but the players consistently opposed both a payroll minimum and a payroll ceiling, preferring to maintain a free market. The sides drew closer on the minimum player salary and reached a tentative agreement at $300,000. They also reached agreement on shortening the time to fund deferred compensation as well as an increase in owners' contributions to the players' benefit plan and an increase in the minimum salary for minor league players appearing on forty-man rosters for two or more seasons.

A key breakthrough occurred when the players agreed to steroid testing. Under the union's proposal, players would be subjected to one or more unannounced tests in 2003 to determine the level of steroid use. If the survey showed "insignificant" use, then a second round of tests would be set up in 2004 to verify the results. If more than 5 percent of the test results were positive in either survey, then players would be randomly tested for two years. The union did not specify penalties to be levied against players who tested positive for steroids. Don Fehr, who had long resisted any drug testing, explained his change of heart, saying, "We had an obligation to bargain on it. It was a serious issue. It took a lot of time and effort and thought." A Players Association survey on independent testing for steroid use in July showed that almost four of five respondents favored testing. While the owners wanted a more stringent program than that proposed by the union, Rob Manfred, attorney for the owners, characterized the proposal as "very significant. It is the kind of proposal that will put us very easily on the path to a very timely agreement."[64]

Movement continued, with the owners presenting a revised tax proposal that would raise the payroll threshold to $100 million, with a phase-in of the tax over the life of the new deal, and then raise the threshold again to $102 million on August 15, but the players stuck to an initial threshold of $130 million, with increases during the life of the agreement to $150 million, plus a much overall lower marginal tax rate and a phase-out of the tax after three years.

The Players Set a Strike Date

On August 16, the union set a strike date of August 30, pushing both sides to accelerate negotiations. Neither side wanted a labor stoppage; the stakes were simply too high in terms of potential lost revenue and salaries. As Zimbalist pointed out, the situation in 2002 was quite different from that of the mid-1990s, a time of a booming stock market, several new ballpark projects, and compelling events on the field. A strike in September 2002—during the first anniversary of 9/11, when the economy was in recession, when the stadium building boom had slowed, and when increasing evidence of rampant use of performance-enhancing drugs was surfacing—could have been catastrophic. The enterprise of baseball simply could not expect the confluence of factors that brought baseball back in the late 1990s to occur again in 2002, so cooler heads among the owners and players prevailed.[65]

President Bush reacted to the announcement by saying that he would be "furious" if the players walked, and he sternly urged the players and owners to come to an agreement. Don Fehr claimed that the idea of a luxury tax represented "a wholesale attack on salaries," and Rob Manfred countered that he found Fehr's comment to be "a baffling characterization." To the entire world, a strike seemed imminent. Jerry McMorris told the Associated Press, "The hawks are circling."[66] A management lawyer sent a nine-page letter to team executives to prepare them for a strike, urging them to make plans to cut expenses.

Suddenly, the winds seemed to shift. The press reported a "good day" for the talks, using words such as "progress" and "optimism." The owners reduced the revenue sharing numbers, further narrowing the gap with the players to $33 million. The players had moved on the percentage for the revenue sharing plan to 33.3 percent and agreed with the owners to use a straight-pool format. While the luxury tax still represented a significant barrier, both sides expressed optimism about a possible settlement.

With less than a week remaining before the August 30 strike date, the owners raised their threshold—to $107 million in 2003 and $111 million in 2006—and lowered the proposed luxury tax rate by 2.5 percentage points, with higher rates for teams that exceeded the cap an increasing number of times. Players had proposed thresholds of $125 million next year, $135 million in 2004, $145 million in 2005, and no tax in the final season of the deal. The owners also slightly decreased the amount of local revenue to be shared. The owners were now at 36 percent and the players at 33.3 percent, so most thought that the small gap could be bridged. Mike Stanton, player representative for the Yankees, said, "The deal is there. It's just a matter of getting it done. There have been concessions made on both sides and we're still meeting. That's a reason why I'm cautiously optimistic."[67] However, not everyone agreed. Red Sox pitcher John Burkett said that the players had already given too much to the owners and that he expected to strike, for a long time, based on his experience in 1994.

Talks intensified during the last few days before the strike deadline, and the sides continued to make progress. On drug testing, Los Angeles Dodgers catcher Paul Lo Duca, the team's player representative, said, "The drug testing is a done deal. We agreed on that, and that's great. They're getting closer and closer."[68] However, there was still a great deal of uncertainty about the outcome. The commissioner flew from his Milwaukee home to New York to be on hand for the outcome, either a last-minute settlement or a strike on August 30. Only a majority vote of owners was needed to approve a deal, but a three-quarters vote, twenty-two of thirty, was required to approve the revenue sharing plan.

At the Deadline, a Deal Gets Done

On August 30, all major league games were night games except for an afternoon contest in Chicago between the Cardinals and the Cubs. The owners and players, after an all-night bargaining session, finally reached an agreement on the morning of August 30, just a few hours before the afternoon (3:20 P.M. Central Daylight Time) contest at Wrigley Field. Literally, players on the Cardinals team did not know until almost the last minute whether they were going to take a bus from their hotel to the ballpark or scatter to catch planes to go to their various homes. The owners and players reached an agreement in the nick of time and the game went on as scheduled, as did all MLB games that night. Finally, baseball had achieved "peace in our time," as the sides reached a settlement without a labor stoppage for the first time in thirty-two years. The deal was set through the 2006 season, so baseball could enjoy at least twelve seasons of baseball uninterrupted by a labor stoppage since Judge Sotomayor's decision had put the players back to work in April 1995.

The deal was done, without a strike or lockout and without the rancor that had characterized previous breakdowns in the talks. The 2002 season, as well as baseball through 2006, was saved. The efforts of Cubs President Andy MacPhail, a third-generation baseball man, and Peter Angelos, Bob DuPuy, and Rob Manfred, on the owners' side, and Michael Weiner and Steve Fehr, on the players' side, resulted in a deal that many thought earlier in the summer would never get done.

The owners had two professed goals for the new CBA, enhanced competitive balance and a restraint on payrolls. The elements of the CBA that contributed to this outcome included significantly higher tax rates on local revenue (34 percent versus 20 percent in the old CBA), a luxury tax on excessive payrolls, a new rule that deferred salary must be fully funded within eighteen months of the year in which it is earned, and the new debt limit regulation that states that a club's debt cannot exceed ten times earnings before interest, taxes, depreciation, and amortization (EBITDA) in 2006, adjusted to fifteen times for clubs with new facilities.[69]

The final revenue sharing formula was a compromise between the owners' preference for a straight pool and the players' preference for a split pool. The central fund amount, 25 percent of the redistribution, was to be done on a split-pool basis, while 75 percent was to be allocated via a straight-pool system. The new CBA increased the minimum salary to $300,000 in 2003 and 2004, with cost-of-living adjustments thereafter. For the first time, random testing for steroids was authorized. First-time offenders were given drug treatment, and second-time offenders were suspended. The question of including international players in the amateur draft was not resolved; instead, the CBA established a committee to evaluate the idea.

When baseball announced the final terms of the deal, it was clear that both sides had continued to adjust their positions until the deal could be accepted. Like all CBAs, the final agreement was complex. The agreement specified the following:

- Length: The agreement starts retroactively with the 2002 season and runs through December 19, 2006.
- Luxury Tax: Teams whose payrolls exceed set thresholds will be taxed on the portions above the thresholds, with the money to be used for player benefits, including [the] player benefit plan, or the industry growth fund, or developing baseball players in countries lacking organized high school baseball. The thresholds are as follows: 2002, no tax; 2003, $117 million; 2004, $120.5 million; 2005, $128 million; 2006, $136.5 million.
- The following tax rates apply: 1st time over threshold: 17.5 percent in 2003, 22.5 percent in 2004 and 2005, no tax in 2006. 2nd time over threshold: 30 percent. 3rd and 4th times over threshold: 40 percent.
- Luxury taxes expire on the final day of the 2006 season, meaning that if the sides play under the status quo in 2007, there would be no tax.
- Payrolls are for 40-man rosters and include averages of multiyear contracts; health and pension benefits; clubs' medical costs; insurance; workman's compensation, payroll, unemployment and Social Security taxes; spring training allowances; meal and tip money; All-Star game expenses; travel and moving expenses; postseason pay; and college scholarships.
- Revenue Sharing: Base plan—Each team contributes 34 percent of its net local revenue, after deductions for ballpark expenses, to a pool that is redistributed equally to all 30 teams.
- Central Fund Component: $72.2 million annually, taken from those teams that are net payers in [the] base plan and redistributed to teams that are net receivers in [the] base plan. The central fund component phases in at 60 percent in 2003, 80 percent in 2004, and 100 percent in 2005 and 2006. It is collected by taking a figure in which the numerator is $72.2 million and the denominator is total net local revenue after ballpark expenses of all payer clubs, and multiplying the figure by a payer club's total net local revenue after ballpark expenses. It is redistributed on a split-pool basis based on distance from the average.
- Commissioner's Discretionary Fund: A total of $10 million—$333,333 from each team—is taken from the central fund and may be redistributed by the commissioner.
- Drug Testing: All players will be randomly tested for illegal steroids in 2003 as a survey. If 5 percent or more test positive in any survey year, mandatory random testing for illegal steroids shall take place during the following two years. If 2.5 percent or

fewer test positive in consecutive years, mandatory random testing shall cease. In any year in which there is not mandatory random testing, there shall be survey testing. The first time a player tests positive during mandatory random testing, he is placed in a treatment program. For subsequent positive tests, penalties range from a 30-day suspension to a two-year suspension.

- Amateur Draft: The sides shall establish a committee to establish rules for a worldwide amateur draft, which it will try to have in place for June 2003. Clubs have proposed 38 rounds, players 20. The committee will make the determination. The committee will consider, among other issues, whether teams should be allowed to trade draft picks and the negotiating rights to selected players. If a team fails to sign a first-round draft pick, it will receive a corresponding pick in the first round of the following year's amateur draft (example: if a team fails to sign the No. 2 overall pick, it would be awarded an extra pick immediately following the No. 2 pick in the following draft). If a team fails to sign a second-round draft selection, it will receive a pick in the sandwich round between the second and third rounds of the following year's amateur draft.
- Contraction: Teams may not be eliminated through the 2006 season. The clubs may elect to eliminate two teams for the 2007 season, but must notify players by July 1, 2006. If the clubs elect to contract for 2007, the union would not contest before the National Labor Relations Board that contraction is a mandatory subject of bargaining.
- Minimum Salary: First figure is for major leagues, second is minor league rate for players with split contracts appearing on a 40-man roster for two or more years: 2002, \$200,000/\$40,500; 2003, \$300,000/\$50,000; 2004, \$300,000/\$50,000; 2005, \$300,000/\$50,000 plus two-year cost-of-living adjustments; 2006, 2005 minimums, plus one-year cost-of-living adjustment.
- Debt: A team may not have more debt than 10 times EBITDA (earnings before interest, taxes, depreciation, and amortization), except that a team that has moved into a newly constructed ballpark within the past 10 years may not have more debt than 15 times EBIDTA. There will be a three-year grace period, during which the commissioner has the right to retain the debt service rule, fully implemented. If he so elects, the commissioner must revoke the 60–40 assets-to-debt ratio rule. If he doesn't want to revoke the 60–40 rule, the debt-service rule becomes fully implemented.

- Interleague Play: Interleague play, which had been agreed to on a test basis in the 1997–2001 agreement, is agreed to for the length of the contract.
- Free Agent Draft Pick Compensation: Draft-pick compensation for losing Type A and Type B free agents is eliminated.
- Benefits Plan: The clubs' contribution will be $114 million to $115 million annually, up from $70 million in 2002.
- Allowances: Spring training and in-season allowances will be increased at the rate of the Consumer Price Index.
- Waivers: Each year will be divided into four waiver periods instead of three. The current periods are Nov. 11 to day 30 of the season, day 31 to July 31, and Aug. 1 to Nov. 10. The first period will be divided into Nov. 11 to Feb. 15, and Feb. 16 to day 30.
- Tenders: All contract tenders to unsigned players on 40-man rosters will be made by the commissioner's office instead of individual teams.[70]

Conclusion

With a season in the balance, the players and owners displayed rationality, reason, even goodwill. Clearly, the lessons from 1994–1996 were not lost on either side, despite the emotion and rhetoric. The 2002 CBA was critical in setting the stage for the current situation in major league baseball, which is labor peace through at least the end of 2016. Management and labor reached agreements without fanfare in 2006 and 2011. Thus we now have an industry that continues to grow in revenue, franchise values, and player compensation, and an industry ready to be injected with new rounds of cash from both local and national television contracts, not to mention digital media. Competitive imbalance has not been eradicated, but it has been addressed. Adjustments to subsequent CBAs addressed some of the flaws in the 2002 CBA, including a marginal tax on revenue that actually penalized small-market clubs when they increased revenue and little control over whether revenue sharing recipients used the money to try to improve their teams.

Bud Selig, now seventy-nine, continues to lead the major leagues because, like Hyman Roth in *The Godfather: Part II*, he always makes his partners money. Selig has announced he will retire when his current terms is up, on January 24, 2015. Don Fehr these days is plying his trade for the NHL Players Association, which was subject to a lockout by the owners that shortened the 2012–2013 season to forty-eight games. Fehr was replaced by Michael Weiner, which was good for baseball because of the positive relationship between Weiner and Rob Manfred. Unfortunately,

Weiner passed away recently after a fifteen-month battle with brain cancer. Mr. Weiner will be sorely missed by baseball.

Owners continue to shower money on free agents; Albert Pujols, Josh Hamilton, and most recently Robinson Cano are among the players taking advantage of baseball's increasing revenues. The average major league salary has reached $3.44 million, as reported by CBSsports.com. Baseball is in a truly prosperous mode as we approach the 2014 season, despite the continuing effects of the 2008 recession, and much of the credit goes to the individuals who worked hard to complete a deal in 2002.

9

Bill Giles and His Baseball Team

The Lifelong Dream of Running a Baseball Team

Once Bill Giles discovered at an early age that he loved baseball and wanted to be part of it like his dad, it didn't take long for him to realize that he lacked the talent to play the game professionally. He decided that the next best option to being a major league player was to be the guy in charge of the players, a major league general manager. He established the goal of becoming the general manager of a major league team by the time he was forty-two years old. As it turned out, he was able to exceed his dream by becoming an owner . . . and then became his own general manager.

The experience Giles gained from his time working with the Cincinnati Reds, Houston Colt .45s—Astros, and Phillies, rising from traveling secretary and publicity director to executive vice president, prepared him for the day when he would have the opportunity to buy a baseball team. That day came on November 15, 1980, only three weeks after the Phillies had beaten Kansas City to win their first-ever World Championship. That fateful day, the announcement came that a ballplayer named Claudell Washington accepted a five-year free agent deal with Ted Turner's Atlanta Braves for the astounding total of $3.5 million for five seasons. Turner was about to pay an average of $700,000 per season to a player who had averaged ten home runs and fifty-nine RBIs in his six full seasons for four different teams and who played such an indifferent brand of outfield for the White Sox that fans in Comiskey Park hung a sign in the outfield stands that said "Washington slept here."[1] For Phillies owner Ruly Carpenter, Claudell Washington's deal was the culmination of all that was going wrong in baseball; for Bill Giles, that same deal opened the door for him to achieve and far surpass his dream of being general manager.

Ruly Carpenter, who succeeded his father, Bob Carpenter, as head of the Phillies organization, basked in the glow of the 1980 World Series win, but since the advent of free agency four years earlier, the younger Carpenter had become more and more dissatisfied with the exploding salaries and the direction of baseball's economics. He resented the salary increase, but he also was uncomfortable with what he saw as the increasing gamesmanship plus the loss of camaraderie and loss of integrity among the owners. The Washington signing was the "straw that broke the camel's back" for Carpenter, and he decided that he could no longer be an owner of a major league baseball team. He announced his plan to sell the Phillies during spring training in 1981. Over a period of several months after Carpenter's announcement, Bill Giles recruited a group of investors, put together a deal that met Carpenter's demands, and purchased the Phillies. That started a career as part-owner, president, CEO, and general partner that lasted until 1997, when Giles stepped down but continued in his new role as chairman.

In this chapter, I explore some highlights and important accomplishments of Bill Giles' time running the Philadelphia Phillies, from the purchase of the club through his retirement. Like all major league owners, Giles played a dual role. Each owner serves, in effect, as a member of baseball's board of directors, making decisions about how major league baseball will be run. Each owner also runs his own club, trying to assemble a winning team, compete successfully with other clubs, and run a successful business as the leader of his ownership group. So far, I have focused on Giles as part of baseball's management hierarchy, but in the next two chapters, I look at Bill Giles as the owner and architect of a baseball club.

Buying the Phillies

After winning the National League pennant in a thrilling five-game series with Giles' former team, the Houston Astros, the Phillies defeated the Kansas City Royals, four games to two, to win the team's first-ever World Championship in fall 1980. Philadelphians who are old enough can still remember the police dogs ringing the field as the Royals batted in the top of the ninth inning of Game 6 and Tug McGraw jumping triumphantly with both hands in the air after he struck out Willie Wilson to clinch the championship. The Phillies organization was on cloud nine during the winter of 1980–1981. Players, coaches, and broadcasters were all in demand as speakers at banquets and meetings throughout the Delaware Valley and beyond. Even Executive Vice President Bill Giles was getting in on the action. As Giles said at the time, "What happens generally is that when someone calls and gets the price of the players, they'll say, 'Well, do you have anybody for less money?' So then we'll give them Harry Kalas or Richie Ashburn or Chris Wheeler [the Phillies television announcers at the time], because they get less than the players. Then some of them will say, 'Well do you have anybody that goes for free?' These people get me."[2] In less than a year, the guy who had been speaking for free would be part owner, general partner, and president of the team.

Ruly Carpenter announced to the world that he planned to sell the Phillies and exit baseball on March 6, 1981. He said that his decision was based on "some deeply ingrained philosophical differences between the Carpenter family and some of the other owners as to how baseball should be conducted. . . . It's been a dramatic escalation in salaries and what I'm saying now [is] enough is enough."[3]

Bill Giles reacted almost immediately to the news and announced that he planned to assemble a group of investors to buy the team. He said, "I'm doing it because I love baseball, I love Philadelphia[,] and I just feel that this is one of the three or four best franchises in baseball." Giles was aware that the National League preferred that there be one strong individual putting up a large chunk of money so that the purchasing group would have greater financial stability, but he did not possess the financial resources to go it alone. He knew he could find money but "I don't know whether it will be enough money or the right kind of money."[4]

Gene McCurdy served as president and general manager of WPHL-Channel 17 in Philadelphia, the Phillies' local television outlet. Before the 1979 season, WPHL had been instrumental in helping to bring Pete Rose to Philadelphia by chipping in $600,000 to allow the Phillies to sign the future "Hit King." When McCurdy heard that Ruly Carpenter planned to sell the club, he said, "Under Ruly's ownership the team was tremendously cooperative in all areas, such as promotion and production. A key part of that cooperation has been Bill Giles, who is the number one baseball promoter and merchandiser. If Bill remains in the picture, the odds are better that things won't change."[5]

Carpenter's decision to sell the club reflected his belief that in the new economic environment of baseball, with owners making all sorts of what he considered outlandish free agent deals, it was no longer financially feasible to own a ball club, even for an heir to the DuPont fortune. Giles had a different viewpoint at the time, remarking that "the financial outlook was not good, but I thought we could survive. I didn't view the future of baseball as being that bleak."[6]

Giles said that the one negative factor in purchasing the Phillies would be the lease with the city for playing in Veterans Stadium, according to Giles, by far the most expensive lease in baseball. "Very few people realize that the city takes in $2 for every customer who comes to a Phillies game." He compared the Phillies lease with that of the Yankees, noting, "The city of New York took in $400 or $500 thousand from Yankees games last year. The city of Philadelphia took in $6 million off Phillies games. And it cost them about $4 million to operate the stadium." As it turned out, the lease at Veterans Stadium would continue to vex Bill Giles and the Phillies until the advent of Citizens Bank Park.[7]

Giles worked for several months to assemble a group of investors that met the criteria specified by himself, the National League owners, and Carpenter. Giles wanted his group to be small and as well financed as possible. He said: "I'm just interested in getting good people who are going to let me, Paul Owens, Dallas Green and Dave Montgomery run the club, and I want them to be people who will operate with the same Phillies philosophy of trying to win as many ball games as possible without going broke in the process. I don't want somebody who will operate like some other clubs operate—say we're going to finish third or fourth and just try to make money."[8]

Giles said, "The National League requires that you have twice as much equity as you have debt. In other words, say you were spending $30 million [Giles' early estimate of what it would take to buy the club]; you would have to have $20 million in cash and you could borrow the other $10 million."[9]

The Carpenter family specified that there could be no more than five partners in the group because Pennsylvania law dictated that if there are more than five purchasers of partnership interest, all financial statements of the selling party would be made public. The family did not wish to disclose either the financials of the Phillies under their ownership or the family's net worth. This meant that Giles had to find partners who were willing to put up at least $5 million. Giles worked with Phillies' attorney Bill Webb to identify and make calls on prospects. It was easy to find people who would put up $1 million, but much more difficult to find partners willing to go for $5 million. In typical Giles fashion, he reported in March 1981 that he had received hard cash from one potential investor, saying, "Yep, I've got one 13-year-old kid. He sent me a dollar. Only 29,999,999 to go."[10]

Giles and Webb contacted a large number of business leaders and other wealthy people. Eugene (Fitz) Dixon, a prominent local businessperson and philanthropist, announced that he had agreed to sell the NBA's Philadelphia 76ers and become part of the investment group assembled by Giles in a partnership with Bob Levy, who owned racehorses and racetracks. This news heartened Giles and significantly enhanced the chances of a successful bid by his group. He found Jim, Bill, and Alexander Buck, who had a family partnership in the venture capital business. The Buck Brothers were Phillies season ticket holders and big baseball fans and joined the partnership with a $5 million commitment.

Another big-money person was Jack Betz, an Eagles fan who owned Betz Laboratories, an industrial water treatment firm based in Trevose, Pennsylvania. Giles tells a story about his attempt to recruit Jack Betz. Giles and Webb had gone to the office of Bob Hedberg, who represented Betz, and presented the case for him to consider. Hedberg called Betz with the proposal. Fortunately for Giles, Jack's wife, Claire Betz, a big Phillies fan, overheard the conversation and prevailed on her husband to invest the $5 million because she loved Tug McGraw and the Phillie Phanatic and wanted a better parking pass for the Eagles [at the Vet]. Chalk up another investor.

In June 1981 the players went on strike. One potential bidding group that included Don Meredith, former Dallas Cowboys quarterback and color analyst on *Monday Night Football*, dropped out at that point, turned off by labor difficulties in the game. Ever the optimist, Giles said, "I think it will be a long time before there is another strike. I think everyone realizes that everybody loses in this type of deal. The players lose. We're losing. The fans are losing. It's not a good thing, but no matter how many problems arise, the game is going to survive. It has survived many problems before."[11]

At that point, five groups remained in the running to buy the team. Some of the groups had already asked Giles to run the team if their group won the bid. Giles was making progress assembling his group, but still faced a significant gap between available funding and what Carpenter was likely to ask for the team. At the same time, in his capacity as executive vice president of the Phillies, Giles was looking to sell the radio rights to the club. Local news station KYW had owned the rights since 1977, but was facing strong opposition from WCAU, which hoped to leverage Phillies' broadcasts to raise its low ratings. Giles' TV and radio experience and relationships would prove to be crucial in his quest to buy the Phillies.

The Taft Broadcasting Company was headquartered in Cincinnati, where Giles had grown up. The Taft family had a long history with the Giles family because of the relationship between Taft and the Reds when Warren Giles ran the Cincinnati club. Taft Broadcasting had a local affiliate in Philadelphia, WTAF-TV, Channel 29, a UHF station. In his memoirs,

"*Pouring Six Beers at a Time and Other Stories from a Lifetime in Baseball,*" Giles said, "On June 15, 1981, I received the most important phone call of my financial, and perhaps my baseball, life. It was from Dudley Taft, the president of Taft, which was headquartered in my hometown of Cincinnati, Ohio." Taft told Giles that his board had decided to invest up to $30 million to help him purchase the team, and he thought, "Hallelujah! My dream of running a baseball team was now much closer to becoming a reality."[12]

The partnership was complete once Taft had made its offer to put up whatever amount Giles needed to close the deal, which amounted to just under half of the purchase price. Once the Taft money was included in the deal, Giles met with the other partners to discuss the details. He had $13.5 million from the Buck Brothers, Dixon and Levy, and Jack and Claire Betz. They decided to take $15 million from Taft to give Giles $28.5 million in equity. Giles took $3 million in up-front payments from CBS Radio (WCAU Radio 1210) from a deal to broadcast Phillies game, using half for working capital and half to make up the rest of the offer. It took some time to negotiate the TV deal with Taft, and by August, Giles made a formal offer to buy the Phillies.

The strike-split 1981 season ended on a disappointing note for the Phillies, although Giles thought it was clearly the best team in the National League. The Phillies were crowned "first half" division champions, but baseball decided to have the division leaders from both the first and second halves of the season meet in a preliminary playoff round to decide which team would get to the National League Championship Series. The Phillies wound up losing to the Montreal Expos, and as a result, the team's promising 1981 season was over. At the end of October Carpenter announced that the Giles group was the successful bidder, and the Carpenter family's tenure as Phillies owner, which started in 1943, also ended. Bill Giles' season had a better ending, at least for him. On October 28, 1981, at the age of forty-seven, Bill Giles had a baseball team. And one of the responsibilities he took on very early was to function as general manager, handling player decisions, which he had always wanted to do.

Ruly Carpenter's family had owned the Phillies for thirty-eight years, so the day he announced the sale was emotional. Carpenter said, "I like baseball, at least the balls and bats part of it. I have not enjoyed some of the other things that have been happening in this game the last five years. You all know that's why I'm selling." Carpenter said he was very happy to be able to sell the club to the group headed by Giles, citing a great relationship between Ruly and Bill and between Ruly's father, Bob Carpenter, and Bill's father, Warren Giles. Carpenter said, "It's been a great relationship, and the Giles name is probably even more a part of the National League than the Carpenter name."[13]

Giles put up $50,000 of his own money for a 10 percent ownership stake in return for running the club as managing partner. Jayson Stark reported the ownership group as consisting of:

- Taft Broadcasting Co., a Cincinnati-based firm that owned seven television stations, including WTAF-TV (Channel 29) in Philadelphia; six AM and FM radio stations; five amusement parks, and various entertainment production and distribution companies. Taft was the largest single investor, contributing close to 50 percent of the total bid.
- J. D. B. Associates, consisting of a partnership between John Drew Betz, and Robert D. Hedberg. Betz was chairman emeritus of Betz Laboratories Inc., a company that specialized in industrial water treatment; Hedberg was a financial-investments consultant and a director of Betz Laboratories.
- Tri-Play Associates, a partnership among three brothers—Alexander, James and William C. Buck, executive officers of TDH Inc. and TDH Capital Corp., private venture capital investment companies.
- Fitz Eugene Dixon Jr., former owner of the 76ers, chairman of the board of Temple University and Widener College, and local philanthropist.
- Rochelle Levy, Philadelphia artist, the wife of Bob Levy, chief executive officer of DRT Industries and owner of Atlantic City Race Course. Giles said that Mrs. Levy had agreed to sell her interests in the race track as per a directive from Commissioner Bowie Kuhn prohibiting any involvement by baseball people with gambling interests.[14]

The price of the deal was $30.175 million, at the time, the largest price that had ever been paid for a baseball team. The Mets had sold for $21.1 million to Nelson Doubleday and Fred Wilpon in 1980. The Tribune Company purchased the Cubs from longtime owner Philip K. Wrigley for $20.5 million earlier in 1981. Giles noted that the main reason for the premium he had to pay for the Phillies was that both the Cubs and the Mets, although in larger markets than Philadelphia, shared those markets with other clubs. The Phillies had the fourth largest media market in the country to themselves.

At the same time that the Phillies announced the sale of the club, Giles announced a television package with WTAF-TV that he characterized as the largest television rights package in baseball history, due to take effect after the existing contract with WPHL-TV ended after the 1983 season. The deal with WTAF called for a revenue sharing arrangement instead of a pure "rights" deal whereby each party would take a portion of the revenues from advertising sales for the broadcasts. This deal foreshadowed the novel arrangement, led by Giles and Eddie Einhorn, that baseball made to create The Baseball Network in 1993.

Now that he had the responsibility to run the club, Giles had a couple of immediate items on his plate. One was to find a manager to replace Dallas Green, who left the Phillies to become president of the Chicago Cubs after the 1980 season ended. The other was to sign All-Star third baseman Mike Schmidt to a contract extension. In the post–free agency era, Schmidt commanded a salary of at least $1.5 million a year on a long-term deal. Giles said, "Ruly and I are working on that together. Unfortunately, it's now my money, not his."[15]

In 1986, Taft Broadcasting announced plans to sell its Philadelphia affiliate, Channel 29, to TVX Broadcast Group. At the same time, Taft announced that it wished to sell its 47 percent share of the Phillies. The sale and purchase of Channel 29 did not affect its broadcast contract with the Phillies, which was scheduled to run through the 1992 season. However, Taft's plan to sell its share of the Phillies was music to the ears of Bill Giles. Giles and his partners negotiated with Taft to acquire Taft's shares, roughly doubling the interest of each of the other ownership partners. The deal carried a risk and a large expense because since Giles' group had paid $30 million for the Phillies, franchise values had increased significantly. The recent transfer of ownership of the Mets valued the franchise at roughly $90 million (compared with just $21 million only six years earlier) and provided a benchmark for a valuation of the Phillies. Giles said that, despite the numbers, his partners remained interested in purchasing Taft's share of the team.

On December 9, the deal was announced and Giles had increased his share of the team to 19.5 percent. The shares of the other partners were not disclosed, but each partnership share, except for that of Rochelle Levy, who did not participate in the Taft deal, roughly doubled. Giles said, "I'm gambling my financial life on this transaction. It's a great gamble on my part but I believe in the Phillies and in baseball. There is the possibility that perhaps we couldn't run the club, or a catastrophe like a long strike. But if everything goes the way it has the last five years, I feel it will be a great investment." The sale price was not announced, but Giles said, "The Carpenters bought the club in 1943 for $460,000 and sold it in 1981 for $30 million. It's now worth about $65 million and that's a good investment."[16]

Bill Giles and Television

As a student at Denison University in Ohio, Bill Giles wrote a senior thesis on the economics of baseball. He had a bit of an advantage in that he had access to the financial records of the National League through his "connection," his dad, president of the league. In that thesis, Giles talked about television and baseball, circa the mid-1950s, and discussed his father's fear that placing too many games on television would hurt attendance and that baseball risked becoming a "studio game." But the son didn't agree with the father in this instance, and Bill's feeling was that televising a game provided a significant source of revenue to the club. He also thought that showing fans cheering and having a great time supporting their team at the ballpark would entice people to come to the game and enjoy a similar experience.

By the time Giles bought the Phillies, he had already negotiated local television and radio deals for the Phillies. As of October 1981, the Phillies had the richest radio agreement in baseball with WCAU (an affiliate of CBS Radio) to the tune of $18 million over eleven years. After negotiating the Taft deal as part of the purchase of the club, the Phillies would have the richest television deal in baseball, starting in 1983, a package worth more than $30 million for nine years.[17]

The inclusion of Taft Broadcasting among the partners that bought the Phillies created some interesting dynamics in Philadelphia's local broadcast community. WTAF-TV, Taft's Philadelphia affiliate, naturally did not want its valuable Phillies product carried by a competitor. WPHL-TV had the rights to the Phillies through 1983 via its previous agreement and had provided the cash necessary to swing the Pete Rose deal—and help the Phillies win the team's first World Championship—just three years before. WPHL generated more advertising revenue with the Phillies than with any other property, so the station's executives were loath to give up their contract early. Ultimately, Taft had to come up with a financial offer to convince WPHL to terminate the contract early.

At the time Giles became owner, the Phillies had the best radio deal in baseball and were about to negotiate the best local TV deal in baseball. Giles, though, had even bigger dollar signs in his eyes regarding the future of television and baseball. Giles understood the revenue potential of cable television at an early stage of cable's life cycle. Writing from the perspective of today, it is fascinating to look back more than thirty years to a time when most of the Philadelphia area, including the city itself, was not yet wired for cable. ESPN was in its very early stages, still televising Australian rules football and rodeo, among other programming. Yet Giles saw the future, saying, "My basic philosophy on TV is to have all your road games on free TV, and have your home games on pay TV. We'll continue PRISM, which shows 30 home games, but the other 51 games will be available on a pay-per-view basis. If that develops, there are pretty good dollars to be derived from that."[18] Giles was familiar with pay TV and cable TV by 1981, having been part of the groundbreaking venture called PRISM, along with Ed Snider, the guy who helped bring the Flyers to Philadelphia.

Founding PRISM

Bill Giles played a significant role in major league baseball's national television deals in the 1980s and 1990s. The commissioners from Kuhn to Selig appointed Giles to the television committee because by the time he joined baseball's ownership group, he had already established a reputation as a savvy "TV guy." One of his major accomplishments, while still working for the Carpenters as executive vice president, was helping to found PRISM (the acronym initially stood for "Philadelphia Regional In-home Sports and Movies"), a local premium cable channel featuring sports and movies. In this venture, he worked with Flyers founder and owner Ed Snider, who had formed a company called Spectacor, which owned the Flyers and their original home, the Spectrum, among other holdings.

In 1976, as he did on a fairly regular basis, Giles attended a Flyers game at the Spectrum. Snider invited Giles to have dinner with him before the game in the executive suite. Over dinner, Snider told Giles that he had an idea to create a pay sports channel featuring three of the four major league franchises in Philadelphia: the Flyers of the NHL, the 76ers of the NBA, and the Phillies. The Eagles would not be part of the concept because the NFL has no local contracts to televise football games; all games are part of the league's national broadcasting contracts.

On hearing Snider's idea, Giles affirmed that it was a sound concept: a premium channel, distributed by cable television systems, charging households a monthly fee for programming, including live games and events, plus first-run and popular movies. PRISM's programming would be exclusive, not available on free TV, either via the network or local affiliates. The differentiator between PRISM and other services available at the time was the extensive sports programming, including the three Philadelphia professional franchises plus Big 5 college basketball (Villanova, Temple, Penn, La Salle, and St. Joseph's), live World Wrestling Federation events, and studio shows, such as the *Great Sports Debate,* which proved to be the forerunner of the sports talk shows that populate national and regional sports networks today.

Once Giles and Snider agreed on the concept, the next step was to negotiate details regarding programming, rights fees, carriage fees, and so on. PRISM was founded in a matter of months and became a significant part of the Philadelphia television landscape over a twenty-year period. Snider's Spectacor was the majority owner. Later, Snider sold PRISM to Rainbow Media, which launched SportsChannel Philadelphia, an affiliate of its SportsChannel American network. PRISM was one of the pioneering ideas in cable television as one of the first sports-oriented premium channels. Initially, the Phillies televised thirty home games a year on PRISM and increased that number to forty over the years.

The Economics of the Phillies, 1982

One of the issues facing all major league owners in spring 1982 was baseball's lack of a significant national television contract. Baseball lagged the NFL in terms of national TV revenues, and as a result, owners lacked the "safety net" that their NFL counterparts enjoyed and depended more heavily on the current popularity of their teams, which drove attendance at games. Giles said, "I don't think this will be a gold mine, but I expect to make a decent profit. We're not in it to make a lot of money. We want to keep our heads above water, have fun and satisfy millions of Phillies fans."[19]

Giles reported to the press that the team's general operating budget was about $21 million (less than Ryan Howard makes each season now), with revenues at about the same level, based on an attendance projection of between 2.6 and 2.7 million at the Vet. There were three categories of revenue: gate receipts, radio and television income, and miscellaneous. Gate receipts were projected to total approximately $11 million, an amount that was net of shares paid to the visiting team (seventy-two cents per ticket, which represented National League revenue sharing at the time) and rent paid to the city of Philadelphia for the use of Veterans Stadium, plus the Phillies' share of gate receipts for road games.

In 1982, the average ticket price for a Phillies game was $4.90 (it is unbelievable how ticket prices have grown in thirty-three years; by comparison, single game tickets in the lower bowl behind the Diamond Club at Citizens Bank Park were priced at $75 per game for the 2012 season). At the time, the Phillies had the fourth-lowest average ticket prices in the National League. The Phillies had $6 million in TV revenue from WPHL and PRISM, $1 million from the club's share of baseball's network contracts, plus $1.3 million from WCAU radio. The $2 million miscellaneous revenue was made up of concessions revenue (approximately $1 million net of the city's share), with the rest including scorebook advertising, sales of yearbooks, souvenirs and Phillie Phanatic paraphernalia, and rent from city-owned luxury suites.

Expenses included $11.5 million in team expenses (mainly players' and coaches' salaries); $4 million for scouting, player development, and signing bonuses; $2 million in stadium operations; $2 million for marketing, ticket sales, and public relations; and $1.5 million for general and administrative expenses. In 1982, just to demonstrate how the economics of clubs have gone full circle in thirty years, the Phillies had the fourth-highest player payroll in baseball, at just over $8 million. Only the Angels and Yankees had higher payrolls. To show how things have changed since 1982, Houston and Montreal had payrolls that were at about the same level as the Phillies.

More than a decade later, Giles would lament that the Phillies were in essence a "small-market team," a statement for which he was soundly criticized. But the fact is that the Phillies had a poor lease (the club gained no revenue from parking plus paid an 18 percent assessment on ticket revenues) and netted less revenue on a per capita fan basis than other clubs. In terms of the ability to generate revenues, therefore, the Phillies were virtually a small-market club. Of course, Giles was aware of this situation as he prepared his offer to buy the club, the market value of which likely was lessened by the revenue-generating limitations of the club's lease with the city.

The Yankees would not land a big-money cable contract with Madison Square Garden for another six years, but even in 1982, Giles, a member of baseball's revenue sharing committee, had concerns about revenue disparity among the teams in major league baseball. Though hard to believe now, based on what happened to the Expos after the 1994 strike, Montreal had television revenue of $10 million per year, while the Phillies had $7.3 million and small-market Milwaukee had $3 million. Giles accurately predicted baseball's coming explosion in revenues:

> Broadcast revenues will continue to grow at a more rapid pace than ticket revenue grows, which will benefit the big markets more than the small markets. The Yankees, Dodgers and Phillies of the world will continue to grow, while the Seattles, the San Diegos and the Minnesotas will not grow as fast. The Yankees will survive with a $14 million payroll, while San Diego will struggle with a $3 to $4 million payroll.[20]

Giles took the opportunity to recommend that baseball create a central fund to pool money from national television, the All-Star game and World Series, and sales from the commissioner's office, money that would be distributed equally to all clubs. However, he stopped short of saying that a percentage of local TV and radio revenues should also be put into the fund and shared. He said, "We've worked hard getting our TV and radio rights up to where they are, and I don't feel that it is right for me to give a large portion away to a visiting team."[21]

A Lull in the Sports Landscape of Philadelphia

The period before and just after Bill Giles purchased the Phillies represented a true "golden age" in Philadelphia professional sports. Starting with back-to-back Stanley Cups by the Flyers in 1974 and 1975, along with the sustained success of the Phillies from 1976 through 1983, when they won five division titles, two National League pennants, and a World Series, the Eagles made it to the Super Bowl in 1980. While the 76ers of Dr. J. experienced the frustration of losing the NBA finals in 1977, 1980, and 1982, they acquired Moses Malone and won the World Championship in 1983. Philadelphia basketball fans who are at least forty years old will remember Malone's famous prediction for the playoffs that year: "Four, Four and Four!" However, success seemed to spoil the fans of Philadelphia, and by early 1984, Jayson Stark wrote an analysis of the case of the dwindling crowds. He cited several reasons. First, all four teams had jacked up the price of tickets. For example, the Phillies raised 200 level ticket prices by 60 percent between 1977 and 1983. To put the situation in perspective, the Phillies still had the cheapest ticket in town, only $3 for general admission, but people still complained about the price of tickets. Giles commented, "It's interesting that people don't seem to worry that much about the price of quality tickets. If you have good tickets, people are willing to pay good prices for them. It's once you get to the 700 level in the outfield that people start getting price-conscious."[22]

Stark cited television as a factor, bringing to mind Warren Giles' concerns expressed more than thirty years earlier about the potential negative effect of too many televised games on attendance. Bill Giles repeated his vision for the Phillies and TV:

> My thoughts seven or eight years ago—and they haven't changed a whole lot—were that you should still have all your road games on regular TV. That not only brings in revenue, but people get to see you, they get interested and they come out to watch you when you're home. Then I think you put 30 home games on subscription TV with PRISM. And then you put the remaining games on a pay-per-view basis, where people have the option to buy a game on a game-by-game basis for, say, three, four or five bucks.[23]

In early 1984, the technology for pay-per-view as Giles envisioned it did not yet exist. However, Giles was considering an offer to develop a Phillies-only cable network would offer Phillies games, movies, and some college sports and would have the capacity to handle the pay-per-view option that Giles viewed as the big TV trend on the horizon.

Without that option available, Giles expressed satisfaction with PRISM, despite survey results that showed that the Phillies were losing 1,000 people at the gate for every 100,000 subscribers:

> But even though the research shows that, the facts have not shown our research to be true. For example, say we have a Monday-Tuesday-Wednesday series with Cincinnati. All three games are equally attractive, and we're on PRISM Tuesday night but not Monday or Wednesday. Our studies show attendance on the middle night hasn't fluctuated at all. So if the history we've seen so far is true, we're not going to be hurt by it. But even if we did lose maybe 4,000 fans, as the research shows we should, we make $60,000 a game from PRISM, against the $20,000 we'd lose in attendance money after taxes. So we still come out ahead.[24]

By 1986 attendance at the Vet had declined precipitously from the high-water mark of 2.78 million in 1979, Pete Rose's first year with the club, to 1.83 million in 1985. The team was languishing in the standings, finishing fifth in the six-team National League East, and club officials expected a further decline in the coming season. By this time, revenues had increased to $32 million despite the drop-off in attendance, because of baseball's new national TV deals, which generated $10 million annually per club. Because of the TV and radio deals in effect at the time, by 1988 the Phillies still ranked behind only the Yankees and Mets in local broadcast revenue.

The situation was about to change—dramatically. In December 1988 George Steinbrenner signed his landmark deal with Madison Square Garden network, and the annual rights fee ballooned to $42 million per year. A rising tide would eventually prove to lift all boats, but at the time this deal shook the very foundations of the business of baseball. Asked if the Yankees' prospective television deal had come up at the most recent owners' meeting, Giles said, "It came up a lot, mostly in terms of other peoples' amazement and jealousy." Giles said that other teams have always been concerned about the financial advantages held by the big-market clubs, the Yankees, Mets, and Los Angeles Dodgers, noting, "Those teams have always had more money. If you're asking me whether George having more means he'll spend more on salaries, I have to think things won't be different than they are now."[25]

Would Steinbrenner's deal create a new market for local rights fees? Giles did not think so and said, "I can't see the Phillies ever getting that close. They have three different cable companies bidding for the rights, getting the price way up there. We don't have the TV competition here to fuel a bidding war. I've already met with the PRISM people and told them about the Yankees' deal, but I don't think we'll be seeing those numbers around here."[26]

The Cable World Keeps Advancing

In 1987 Cablevision became the sole owner of PRISM, and in 1989 Cablevision and NBC became equal partners in PRISM when they cut a deal that led to the launching of CNBC, a new national cable channel. In late 1989, NBC and Cablevision announced a plan to launch a new cable sports channel to be named, fittingly enough, SportsChannel. This new local cable network would combine national SportsChannel America programming with that of local clubs, including the Phillies and Flyers. His plans to put Phillies home games on pay-per-view were never realized, so Giles planned for SportsChannel Philadelphia to carry twenty-five Phillies games that were not available on other channels in addition to forty two games on PRISM. Channel 29, in the middle of a ten-year deal with the Phillies, planned to carry eighty-six games, mostly road contests.

This new deal, signed in January 1990, combined with the existing PRISM and Channel 29 deals and the Phillies' share of the new national TV deal with CBS, would raise the team's broadcast income by 40 percent over 1989, reaching a total of $26 million in revenue in 1990. Giles commented, "The money will help us compete, and we plan to use it in that direction." He also said, "I don't really think [the increased television exposure] will hurt us at the gate, because, watching the game on television, you get a feel for the stadium and that may entice the fan to come out."[27]

During spring training in 1991, word leaked out that the Phillies were considering televising their home opener against the St. Louis Cardinals on pay-per-view. The idea was not completely novel because the Cardinals had tried their own plan the previous three years. The San Diego Padres also had some games on pay-per-view that generated revenue, but not enough to create a great deal of interest in pay-per-view among other clubs. The plan that was being devised by the Phillies called for households to pay $10 each to watch the opener, which would be available to most households that subscribed to PRISM. Projections indicated that after sharing the revenue with its cable partners, the Phillies could reap about $200,000. However, only a few days after the plan was reported, the Phillies canceled the deal because of negative fan reaction. Commenting on what had transpired, David Montgomery, then executive vice president, said, "I think it's fair to say, clearly, there was some consumer fear out there. And we did not want to embellish that fear. It's just something for another day, I guess."[28]

The following year, in early January 1992, Bill Giles and Randy Smith, executive vice president and general manager of WPHL-TV, announced that after the expiration of the contract with Channel 29, WTXF-TV (new call letters for a new owner, TVX Broadcasting), which started in 1983, the Phillies would return to Channel 17. The new agreement would extend five years, through the 1997 season, and would be a revenue sharing instead of a rights deal, as was the case with the Channel 29 contract. Giles commented, "We enjoyed our relationship with Channel 29 and look forward to working with Channel 17 again. The new contract calls for approximately the same number of telecasts . . . five in spring training, 85 during the season . . . and selected pre-game shows. Other programming commitments have made it more difficult for Channel 29 to deliver this many dates the last two–three seasons."[29]

Ed Snider, Comcast, and the Phillies

Philadelphia sports mogul Ed Snider brought the NHL Flyers and the Spectrum to Philadelphia, created Spectacor, and built an empire. By the mid-1990s, he had built Spectacor into a major player on the sports scene, with his ownership interest in the Spectrum and Flyers, plus his new arena, the CoreStates Center. Ralph Roberts created the Comcast Corporation, which by 1996, through a series of acquisitions, was the third-largest cable television distributor in the United States. In March 1996, Snider, who was already in negotiations with Comcast regarding the acquisition of Spectacor, developer Ron Rubin, and fitness guru Pat Croce convinced Harold Katz to sell the Philadelphia 76ers. Snider and Comcast then concluded a deal by which Snider then sold a 66 percent share of his holdings to the cable company. This deal created Comcast-Spectacor. The newly merged company owned two-thirds of the Flyers, the 76ers, and the two arenas.

The formation of Comcast-Spectacor eventually completely changed the landscape of sports and sports television in Philadelphia. After Snider sold PRISM, he and Giles had some conversations about forming a new all-sports station for the Philadelphia region. Giles had also been engaged in conversations with Comcast about putting the Phillies on a cable channel with the 76ers and Flyers. After Comcast acquired Spectacor, discussions heated up. Comcast had both the financial resources and the media capability to create such a network, and the Phillies were involved from the beginning. Giles had extensive discussions with executives at Comcast-Spectacor about a range of issues, including possible sale of the team, potential new cable TV deals, and even the funding of a new, baseball-only ballpark, which had been Giles' dream since he saw Camden Yards four years earlier.

Giles and his partners discussed selling the Phillies to Comcast, but the group agreed that they would remain in control of the club. In early spring 1996, Giles reported, "I brought it [selling the club to Comcast] up at our last partners' meeting and we are not interested in selling part or all of the team right now."[30]

Twenty-four years later, Giles reflected on the events leading up to his deal with Comcast:

> We had many discussions with Ralph Roberts way back when we were struggling. We lost $30 million during that '94 strike and the ownership was not particularly strong during that period, and very conservative in their philosophies. I had several meetings with different people, including Ralph Roberts, sometimes his son, Brian Roberts, and Snider, about buying the Phillies. I kept using the term "Comcast." This was after they bought the 76ers and they made a deal with Snider to buy Spectacor. I kept saying "you really ought to buy the Phillies," and you can call it "Comcast Country," this whole complex of sports[;] it is all Comcast. They thought long and hard about it; they were on the verge of making an offer a couple of times and then changed their minds.[31]

[*Note:* Go into the Wells Fargo Center in Philadelphia today, the arena originally built by Snider, and you will see signs greeting you with the words, "Welcome to Comcast Country."]

Although the sale of the club never received serious consideration, Giles had significant interest in a television partnership with Comcast and its new subsidiary, Comcast-Spectacor. Giles understood that a new, regional all-sports network would require baseball. The hockey and basketball teams gave a network plenty of fall through early to mid-spring programming, but that left a huge gap in the spring and summer, into early fall. Baseball was a critical component, and Giles understood that.[32]

Another consideration was funding for a new ballpark. Local politician and financial consultant Sam Katz observed that involvement with

Comcast-Spectacor "would certainly strengthen the capacity of the Phillies to bring money to the table for a new stadium."[33] Comcast had a need for the Phillies as "programming inventory." The company also had deep pockets and could potentially fund a new ballpark. Giles said, "If we are a partner rather than just a holder of rights money, then they have a long-term arrangement which would be beneficial to them."[34]

Comcast had the cash that Bill Giles needed to make his vision of a new ballpark a reality. The six months of programming that Giles could offer to a new all-sports network put the team in an advantageous position. PRISM and SportsChannel could survive only if they had the Phillies, and the team was also a key element of any new all-sports station. Giles told the press:

> If you are going to form a joint venture, or a partnership, everybody has to look at it as if they're improving their business. I think Comcast would be much better off if they had a partnership with the three sports. Then they'd have guaranteed programming forever and ever. It knocks out the third party. Right now for them to get sports programming they have to deal with [a competitor, Cablevision chairman Charles] Dolan's people all the time.[35]

Once Comcast-Spectacor became a reality, Comcast had several options. First, the company could maintain the status quo, negotiating new deals with PRISM and SportsChannel to carry Flyers and 76ers games. Second, Comcast could purchase PRISM and SportsChannel. Third, Comcast could form its own network. According to Giles, "I've felt for some time, and I've talked to Ed Snider about it, that it would be a very good idea for the sports teams to have their own cable channel. To form a partnership with Comcast and the Spectacor people and the Phillies makes a lot of sense to me."[36] The Phillies' deal with PRISM and SportsChannel extended through the 1997 season, so discussions were at a critical juncture.

Giles and Comcast continued to discuss the prospects for a Phillies-Comcast partnership. Talks centered on a possible arrangement whereby the Phillies would give Comcast television broadcast rights in exchange for financial help to build the new ballpark. The negotiations concluded, however, with no arrangement. "We asked Comcast if they were interested in building a stadium and they said, 'No, we want to do a cable deal.'" Giles went on say that the Phillies and Comcast had jointly decided to end talks about stadium financing and that any new stadium would have to be built with a majority of state money.[37]

Plans materialized quickly for Comcast and its plans for a sports channel. In mid-April, the *Philadelphia Business Journal* published an article that disclosed "a preliminary plan" for content in addition to the broadcasts of Flyers, Phillies, and (eventually) 76ers games. "Plans call for 'extensive' news coverage, profile shows focusing on local athletes, team highlights and background magazine-type shows, as well as minor league games, college games and 'extreme' sports' plus lifestyle issues related to sports, such as nutrition and exercise. Another interesting angle would be a focus on women's sports."[38]

Just two days after Giles and Comcast decided to end discussions about financing a new ballpark, the trade press reported on April 25, 1996, that the Phillies, Comcast, and Spectacor announced that they had formed a new venture involving cable TV rights for the Phillies, Flyers, and 76ers. Brian Roberts, president of Comcast, announced, "We will launch a super-regional all-sports channel in October 1997."[39]

Comcast SportsNet (CSN), as the new station came to be called, offered much wider distribution than predecessors PRISM and SportsChannel because CSN would be available on basic cable. PRISM was a premium channel and carried a much higher monthly cost than a basic cable channel. CSN would debut with distribution to 2.0 million of 2.5 million potential households. Snider specifically mentioned that pay TV would not be part of the package. Giles commented, "Our goal is to make this channel available to as many people as possible through broad cable distribution at a lower cost to sports fans."[40] According to Giles, the Phillies' investment amounted to 30 percent of the venture (which the club sold after opening Citizens Bank Park to pay down some of the debt; the Phillies still owned 1 percent of CSN in 2012), and CSN would pay a rights fee for the team's appearances on the new network. As it prepared to launch Comcast SportsNet the following year, Comcast purchased PRISM along with some other Cablevision properties. PRISM (1976–1997) was put to rest with the launch of CSN on October 1, 1997.

Three months later, in January 1998, the Phillies announced a new television package, effective for the 1998 season. CSN replaced the combination of PRISM and SportsChannel and would carry seventy-seven games. WPHL retained its rights on free TV, signing a one-year deal to broadcast seventy games. In the new deals, the Phillies opted to give up traditional rights fees in exchange for the right to control all advertising, a riskier proposition, but one that provided an opportunity for much higher revenues if the Phillies suddenly became a hot property. The club would get between \$7 and \$8 million from its CSN deal while continuing to control advertising in a revenue sharing agreement.[41]

Stepping Down and Stepping Up

After a surprise National League title and trip to the World Series in 1993, the fortunes of the Phillies lagged both competitively and economically in the mid-1990s. Similar to what had happened in 1980–1981, the year after the 1993 pennant was a strike year. The 1994 strike extended into April of the following year and delayed the start of the 1995 season. The Phillies suffered from the "split season" in 1981 when Giles considered the team better than it had been the year before, when it won the World Series. The team was not as good in 1994 as it had been in 1993, but the strike really hurt the club economically. Giles estimated that it lost $30 million due to the effects of the strike. And the team did not recover quickly; in fact, the opposite occurred and the team went into a slide. Interest in the club and attendance sagged.

In May 1996 Phillies beat writer Jayson Stark examined the "staggering" drop in attendance and its possible causes. The team's 22 percent drop was the largest decrease of any National League team. Giles said, "I've got to be honest. I'm concerned." According to Stark, "There is a feeling for baseball that used to be present in this town, and suddenly it's missing. At times, in fact, it has been replaced by a feeling that borders on hostility." Stark advanced a number of possible reasons for the decline in the Phillies game attendance, including weather, the strike, the injuries, and the Flyers, but also noted the team's lack of a marquee player and the perception that Giles was more "committed to pinching pennies that to winning." Giles also said that talk of a new ballpark stigmatized the Vet as a bad facility.[42]

By September attendance was down more than 350,000 from 1995. Giles was pained, to say the least, saying, "It's no secret that it's been a bad year. We haven't won many games. We've had such a turnover, 53 different players, that there's no fan identity. Our marquee players are not here. There's just not much interest in our team." Giles admitted that the club's group sales "really got demolished" due to the strike and that the "first battle" over the off-season will be to try to maintain "as much of the season ticket base as possible." Giles added in jest that the club's new marketing slogan could be, "We Can't Possibly Be This Terrible Again."[43]

New promotions and a new marketing plan did not turn things around. Interleague play, which began in 1997, created some excitement, but the most exciting thing to happen in interleague play for the Phillies in 1997 was Curt Schilling's sixteen-strikeout masterpiece against the Yankees on Labor Day. By then, it was far too late to save the season, both on and off the field. By mid-June 1997 the Phillies averaged only 17,000 in per-game attendance and the team was on pace to lose more than 100 games. Giles was in a state of anguish over his ball club.

After meeting with his partners about the state of the team, and much soul-searching, Giles decided that he had had enough. On June 20, 1997, Giles relinquished his post as president and CEO of the Phillies. David Montgomery, the protégé and right-hand man whom Giles had hired for the sales staff in 1971 was now serving as executive vice president. He was named to fill the position. Montgomery immediately assumed day-to-day operating responsibility, with all department heads reporting to him. Giles transitioned to the position of chairman, retained his ownership interest, and announced that he would henceforth "concentrate on making a new, natural-surface, baseball-only stadium a reality in Philadelphia."[44] Giles was too emotional to speak, but a press release quoted him as saying, "Handing over the duties of running the ball club will allow me to focus my energy on realizing my dream of getting a new ballpark built for our team in the city."[45]

A few days later, after he gave his emotions some time to subside, Giles spoke publicly about his decision:

> It's been like a Chinese water torture since the [1994] strike. I never believed there should have been a strike. . . . Replacement players. Agents who don't tell the truth. Injuries to key people. Losses. Not making people happy. Major league owners suing other owners. An industry that has created an economic situation that is so difficult right now. All those things kept gripping my mind. . . . I had too many hurts. I was no longer as effective as I used to be. The empty seats bothered me more than the losses.[46]

Bill Giles, the guy who, above all, wanted "to make people smile," had told acquaintances, according to reports, that he used to end his workdays saying, "Well, I made a million people unhappy today and it's killing me."[47]

Giles went on to say, "Retirement isn't the right word. I've just decided it's time to stop working so hard. I wasn't forced out. It was a strong suggestion, but it was my decision. The business part of the game had gotten to me. I wasn't as effective as I had been. Some of the partners said, 'Don't you think it's time to let a younger man worry about all those things?'"[48]

Frank Fitzpatrick wrote about why Giles made the move, noting, "Whether it was the Phanatic or giveaways, Bill Giles always found a way to get people to the Vet when the Phillies were bad. This season, though, that magic failed him."[49] Sportswriter Jim Salisbury wrote, "Bill Giles evidently thinks this move will make the Phillies better, or he wouldn't have stepped aside. This is a man who dearly loved waking up in the morning and being the president of a major league baseball franchise."[50]

One player's reaction said it all. Darren (Dutch) Daulton, a player whom Bill Giles loved and who was a true clubhouse leader on the Phillies, said, "Bill is much more than an employer. He's been like an uncle to me for a long time. If he did this, he must feel it's the best thing for the club, because that's all he's ever cared about."[51]

One phase of Bill Giles' life with the Phillies had ended. The new phase was already in place and would eventually lead to one of Bill's greatest dreams—Citizens Bank Park.

10

Bill Giles and His Ballparks

Bill Giles is a baseball traditionalist and an unabashed baseball romantic. Having almost literally grown up in a ballpark at Crosley Field in Cincinnati, it is only fitting that such a big part of his career has been planning, developing, designing, opening, running, and even closing ballparks. As a young man traveling to out-of-town games with his dad, Giles experienced all of the old-time "jewel" ballparks in the National League. He developed a particular fondness for Wrigley Field, even before it became such an icon in baseball. He saw the "spite fence" in right field at Connie Mack Stadium in Philadelphia. As a "hometowner," he knew all about the terrace in the outfield at Crosley Field. He experienced the character of Ebbets Field, nestled in a neighborhood in Brooklyn, and the special relationship between the team and the fans created by the intimacy that characterized the bandbox ballparks of the day. Later, he helped open the Astrodome, close Connie Mack Stadium, and open and close Veterans Stadium. All of these experiences eventually led to one of his lifetime achievements, the building of Citizens Bank Park, a ballpark that changed the fortunes of the Phillies.

Baseball in Houston: Heat, Humidity, Mosquitoes

Walter O'Malley and Horace Stoneham left Brooklyn and Manhattan, respectively, and took their teams, the Dodgers and the Giants, to the West Coast after the 1957 season. Almost immediately, pressure grew to place a National League team back in New York City. Unable to find a team that wished to relocate to New York, Bill Shea, Mayor Wagner's emissary, decided that the next best strategy was to start an expansion franchise. Shea concocted the idea of a third major league, the Continental League, and recruited Branch Rickey, former president of the Dodgers, as new league president, as well as moneyed individuals in several cities as potential franchise owners. The Continental League never came to be, but the work by Shea and Rickey to create the league, along with political pressure from Congress, led baseball to expand by four teams.

The Senators had played in Washington since the beginning of the American League, but after the days of the great Walter Johnson, the team was known by the old ditty, "Washington: first in war, first in peace, last in the American League." During the 1950s, like most cities, Washington experienced a dramatic change in its demographic makeup, and the Senators struggled economically as well as competitively. Longtime owner Calvin Griffith was eager to move his team to greener pastures in Minneapolis, but that move would not have been approved without a "replacement" team, the new, expansion Washington Senators.

American League owners witnessed the incredible success that O'Malley's Dodgers experienced after they moved to Los Angeles. They decided that the American League needed to be on the West Coast as well and therefore awarded a franchise to Los Angeles, whose owner was "the singing cowboy," Gene Autry. The Angels began play in Wrigley Field in Los Angeles, which had been home to the Cubs' Triple-A franchise before Phil Wrigley traded his rights to Los Angeles to O'Malley for rights to Fort Worth. (Along with Brock for Broglio, this was one of the worst trades ever made by the Cubs!)

Awarding a franchise to the interests in New York brought that city back into the National League after a four-year hiatus. Houston was a growing metropolitan area, new home to the space program, and a city that had been targeted for one of the Continental League's franchises. The new Houston franchise was sought by a group headed by Judge Roy Hofheinz, an entrepreneur, former mayor of Houston, and a major political power broker, and Bob Smith, an oil man and real estate magnate of considerable wealth and influence. Along with some other local businessmen and newspapermen, they had formed the Houston Sports Association in pursuit of a major league baseball team for the city.

In the late 1950s, after he graduated from college and served in the Air Force, Giles worked as business manager for the Nashville Vols, a Double-A affiliate of the Reds in the old Southern League. He then returned to Cincinnati and continued his baseball apprenticeship, working in the front office of the Reds for General Manager Gabe Paul. Paul was a Warren Giles protégé who had been groomed by the elder Giles to succeed him as general manager when he became National League president in 1951. The judge and Bob Smith hired Paul as Houston's first general manager, and Gabe Paul brought the younger Giles and Tal Smith, another young Reds executive, along to the join the organization.

Warren Giles and the National League owners had concerns about the heat and humidity in Houston. Thus, approval of a franchise for Houston was contingent on the building of an indoor, air-conditioned facility. Such a facility was certainly novel in major league baseball. Judge Hofheinz was aware of Walter O'Malley's discussions years before with Buckminster Fuller, the noted architect, futurist, and creator of the geodesic dome. In the early 1950s, when O'Malley started his quest for a new stadium for the Dodgers, Fuller had given O'Malley a design for a domed stadium to replace aging Ebbets Field. Hofheinz learned about this concept and contacted Fuller, who told him that a domed stadium could be built to hold 50,000 people. Hofheinz was thus able to convince the National League president and owners of the feasibility of playing indoors, and the franchise was awarded as a result.

Once the franchise was awarded, the ownership of the new ball club had to determine where to play during the time it would take to build the domed stadium. The new Houston team was scheduled to start play in April 1962. The first idea was to upgrade and expand the ballpark that was being used by the Houston Buffs. The Buffs, a minor league team in the American Association, had been purchased by the Houston Sports Association for that very purpose. However, the judge, always a forward thinker, had a different idea.

Hofheinz had already acquired the site for the new stadium, which was to be financed with revenue bonds. Giles recalls that the judge was interested in marketing and promotion, so he decided to build a temporary facility on the site where the dome was to go up. The idea was that the fans who came to the games would see the progress on the new domed stadium that was going up before their eyes, and this would whet their appetites to buy tickets to see the new facility. Knowing that the facility was temporary, Hofheinz didn't want to spend a lot of money, but the facility had to have adequate capacity and had to be a good enough structure for major league baseball.

Building the new Colt Stadium on the site where the Astrodome was going up took less than a year and cost approximately $2 million. The stadium sat 32,000 on bench seats on one level of grandstands. Giles recalls, "Unfortunately, the site on which we built was marshland and the mosquitoes that had been nesting there didn't vacate the area. The conditions at Colt Stadium were awful—heat, humidity, and mosquitoes that descended in squadrons on the poor fans." The Colt .45s—as they were known at that time—wound up playing in Colt Stadium for three years, during which time the new dome was designed and built. Giles says, "The one thing that sustained us was the progress we witnessed on the new stadium."

The Eighth Wonder of the World

The Astrodome was originally to be called Harris County Domed Stadium. Since both Candlestick Park in San Francisco (1960) and Shea Stadium in New York (1964) were publicly funded, multipurpose facilities, the Astrodome was not first in that regard, but it certainly had a significant effect on all subsequent stadium designs. Giles notes that, with clubs now spending more than $1 billion for a new stadium, it is hard to believe that the initial cost of the Astrodome was only $35 million.

Giles recalls some of the design decisions:

> Six people from the organization worked on the details of the new facility, and I was involved in several specific areas of the design, as well as the subsequent stadium operation. The judge had lots of ideas, true to his grandiose dreams about what the stadium was to be. He knew, for example, that many people want to sit 'behind the dugouts' at the ballgame, so the crew designed by far the biggest dugouts in baseball, which were 120 feet long. At the very top of the stadium, the initial plan was to put $5 "cheap seats," but the judge had another idea. He was aware that the old Roman Coliseum had special boxes for dignitaries, so we created Skyboxes around the top rim of the stadium, in effect taking the worst seats in the house and selling them for the most money.

The fifty-three Skyboxes were each outfitted with a couch, bar, refrigerator, telephone, radio, closed circuit television, and Dow Jones ticker, plus a toilet. Each one had a distinct theme for its design and décor, with names such as "Roman Holiday" and "Las Vegas." According to Giles, "We made one mistake, and that was to make the seats separate from the box itself. While Dodger Stadium had a very popular stadium club, I believe that the Astrodome had the first party suites anywhere in U.S. professional sports." This is one way in which the Astrodome significantly affected subsequent stadium design.

Given his outsized personality, it wasn't surprising that the judge placed a private suite in the stadium that he made sure would be the envy of all other baseball owners. This space included, among other amenities, a bowling alley, a nondenominational wedding chapel, and a tilted bar with trick magnets to help sliding refreshments defy gravity. The office had deep gold carpeting, plush velvet scarlet and gold chairs, gold telephones, and a Louis XIV desk. Even the toilets in the private bathrooms were sprayed with gold.

The judge decided to name the building the "Astrodome," using a space theme that made sense because Houston had recently become home to NASA. Everything in the place reflected the astronaut theme. Giles recalls, "I helped come up with some ideas for the astronaut theme. The usherettes were called 'Spacettes,' and members of the ground crew were called 'Earthmen' and wore orange faux spacesuits and white helmets. Among the five eating places in the Dome, we had a large cafeteria called the 'Countdown Cafeteria.'" The judge called the Astrodome "the eighth wonder of the world," and it was truly that. It became a major tourist attraction and hosted guided tours and a huge program book full of advertising that was done in the same color scheme as the seats. Giles adds, "I designed that book, and I also wrote the text for the tour guides. I was surprised to find out that when I went back to the Astrodome twenty years later, they were still using my spiel."

One of the interesting features of the Dome was the AstroTurf. The dome was designed with Lucite panels, an inside panel and an outside panel with prisms in the middle. The role of Lucite panels was designed to keep out the hot, humid air while allowing in enough sunlight for the grass to grow. Giles says, "We needed the prisms to diffuse the light; otherwise, during the day the sun shining through the framework that held the panels would have made the field look like a waffle iron." Unfortunately, the glare that was created by the sunlight shining through the translucent panels made picking up a fly ball off the bat almost impossible for the outfielders, a sad fact that Hofheinz and his crew discovered when the Astrodome first opened in spring 1965 for a series of exhibition games, three against the Yankees and two versus the Orioles.

As Giles recalls:

> So, we had the inside of the roof in the southwest corner of the stadium painted, over home plate and the infield. This reduced the glare but blocked the sunlight. So the grass died. We wound up painting the infield grass green to get through the season. There were a few ideas for how to handle the situation. We tried orange baseballs, but they were too slippery, and I doubt if the league would have approved such a novel idea anyway. Our general manager, Paul Richards, suggested removing the infield grass and having a skin infield, like they do for some youth leagues and high schools. That might have been a disaster for pitchers and third basemen with no grass to slow down hot grounders.

Always the innovator, the judge searched for solutions and someone told him about the Monsanto Company and their new nylon artificial turf called ChemGrass, which was green and looked something like grass. He had the Monsanto reps come to see him to present their artificial turf, and he decided that it was the way to go. Giles recalls, "He then asked how much it would cost to replace the dying grass with artificial turf, and when the Monsanto rep told him the cost would be $1 million, he responded, 'That's interesting as it is the exact amount I planned to charge you for the promotional value. You can call it AstroTurf and sell it around the world.'" The turf was installed just before the 1966 season, and baseball was changed forever—or at least until 1992, when the opening of Camden Yards launched a return to classic design and grass fields.

Giles explains:

> One of my big responsibilities as promotions director was the scoreboard. Like everything else in the Astrodome, the scoreboard was Texas-sized. It cost $2 million, was 474 feet long, and included a huge electronic board for both still pictures and animation. We engaged the fans by sounding "Charge!" and we did a whole lot of other innovative messaging to make the fans feel part of the game. I helped design a "Home Run Spectacular," a demonstration that included six-gun-shooting cowboys, snorting bulls, and skyrockets. We ran this for a full forty-five seconds. It was loud and really got under the skin of the visiting teams, especially the pitchers who gave up the home runs. Nothing has ever been quite as noisy or dramatic.
>
> I also decided on the messages that went up on the boards, and sometimes I got in trouble when I kidded the commissioner—which I only did once—or the umpires, especially since my dad, as president of the National League, was also supervisor of the umpires. Leo Durocher, manager of the Cubs in the late 1960s, hated that scoreboard and, of course, I would take every opportunity to give him the old needle.

[*Note:* For some great stories about operating the scoreboard and getting in trouble with his dad as a result, check out Giles's memoir, *Pouring Six Beers at a Time.*]

The Astrodome represented a number of innovations that had a real impact on subsequent stadium design, both good and bad. These included artificial turf, which fell out of favor in the 1990s but was all the rage for the large number of multipurpose stadiums that were built later in the 1960s and 1970s; the oversized scoreboard with a video message board and the Home Run Spectacular; the five restaurants in the facility; the Skyboxes, and more than 5,000 seats that moved on railroad tracks so that different sports, including football, and other events could be accommodated. While the Astrodome is now basically abandoned, during its day, it was indeed the "eighth wonder of the world."

Giles recalls:

> When the Dome first opened, I thought it was fantastic. The Houston people were not that much into baseball—they were big football fans in Texas—and the Dome became an attraction in and of itself, and as I said before, a big tourist attraction. We had to do a lot of promotions and marketing to bring the people out to the games, and the Dome really helped. The turf made the game exciting because of the speed of the ball getting through the infield and getting through the outfield gaps, leading to a lot of triples, which I think is the most exciting play in baseball. It was the first stadium to really create a full entertainment experience. But as time went by, I became less enamored with indoor baseball and I began to feel that it was not real baseball.

Giles was offered the chance to return to "real baseball" when, in August 1969, he received a call from the Carpenter family in Philadelphia with an offer to join the front office of the Phillies. Unfortunately, at that time, while the Phillies played "real baseball" on the grass at Connie Mack Stadium, the former home of the departed Athletics that had been named "Shibe Park," the Phillies also played bad baseball.

Coming to Philly and Closing Connie Mack Stadium

In 1969 the manager of the Astros was a guy named Harry Walker. Jim Bouton immortalized "Harry the Hat" in his classic book *Ball Four.* Giles recalls:

> Harry was a great baseball man and a tremendous hitting coach. I had roomed with Harry and came to know him well. I owe a lot to Harry because he told the Carpenters, owners of the Phillies, that I was the best marketing and promotions guy in baseball. Bob Carpenter and his son Ruly decided to bring me to Philadelphia in 1970 because the Phillies were scheduled to move to a new stadium the following year and they wanted to do a lot better job of filling the seats after they moved.

When Giles went to Philadelphia for what was to be the last season the team played at venerable Connie Mack Stadium, he came to a team that had been doing almost nothing in the area of marketing. About the only real promotions were the periodic "bat days" and "ball days" and weekend special baseball excursions that ran from Harrisburg and Lancaster on the old Pennsylvania Railroad to North Philadelphia Station, which was only a few blocks from the ballpark, to allow fans from those "out-of-town areas" to see a Phillies game.

Connie Mack Stadium, one of the original "jewel" ballparks of the early 20th century, had been built by the Shibe Brothers, owners of the A's, some sixty years before. The ballpark, like most of the ballparks built during that era, was located in a city neighborhood, and its design and dimensions were determined by the shape of the plot of land on which it was constructed. At one time Shibe Park had been considered a palace, but by the late 1960s the ballpark, renamed Connie Mack Stadium in honor of the venerable A's manager, was in a declining area of North Philadelphia, at 21st Street and Lehigh Avenue, had virtually no parking, and was in an increasingly dilapidated condition. Of course, the Phillies had no real interest in maintaining the park once the team decided to move to a new facility. A new, 60,000-plus-capacity, artificially surfaced, concrete behemoth was going up in South Philadelphia. Construction of the facility was one year behind schedule, and the delay meant that Connie Mack Stadium was really in bad shape during its last couple of years.

Notes Giles:

> When I first got to Philadelphia, I was surprised to find that in my exalted new position, I had an office that was more of a closet, with exposed pipes and very little room. At least I had my own desk, which is more than I could say for the poor ticket salesmen, who had to share a desk. The marketing and promotion operation was very small, and there were fewer than a dozen people responsible for marketing, ticket sales, group sales, and advertising sales.

This type of operation was really the norm for most teams at the time. Some forward thinkers like Walter O'Malley put more resources into marketing, but most teams relied on a few promotions like "bat day" and a few radio and TV spots, very much unlike the large, sophisticated marketing organizations that the Phillies and other clubs employ today.

Connie Mack was a tough place to reach, and it was very difficult to find parking.

> If you parked on the residential streets in the area, it was almost inevitable that a kid would come up to you and say, "Watch your car for a dollar, Mister!" For a long time, it had been a "quarter," but inflation affects every transaction. This meant that if you didn't pay, you could expect that something bad would happen to your car before you returned to it after the game. Getting people to come to the games, especially at night, proved to be really tough.

To make matters worse, the start time for night games back then was 8:05 P.M., meaning that even with the shorter games of that era, fans were not leaving the ballpark until 10:30 P.M. or later.

Inside the ballpark, however, it was a great place to watch the game. The seats, especially in the upper deck, were literally almost on top of the field. The area in foul territory was small. The upper deck almost overhung the lower deck, and it actually did in left field; there were no seats in right field because the outfield fence butted up against the sidewalk on 20th Street. The park's capacity wasn't overly large, at about 33,000, but even so, the Phillies never filled it because the team was going through a really bad period in the late 1960s. Giles recalls, "We did, however, have a near-capacity crowd on October 1, 1970, the night we played our last game in Connie Mack. Of course, most of those in attendance seemed to be there just to get souvenirs, pretty much whatever they could pry loose. You could hear hammers pounding the whole game, and you could watch people with wrenches trying to unfasten seats from the concrete floor of the grandstands." The game ended with the Phillies scoring the winning run in the bottom of the 10th inning. Even before the runner crossed the plate, fans were on the field, grabbing whatever they could. "It was a melee, and the experience taught me a valuable lesson about last games at ballparks that I carried to Veteran's Stadium the following year."

It Seemed Like a Great Idea at the Time— Veterans Stadium

Philadelphia's new multipurpose stadium was located on a huge plot of land north of the Philadelphia Navy Yard and accessible from a main highway, route 276, the infamous "Schuylkill Expressway." The area became known in Philadelphia as "the sports complex," and it included the new stadium; the two-year old Spectrum, where the NHL Flyers and NBA 76ers played; and the old Municipal Stadium, which had been renamed "John F. Kennedy Stadium" and hosted the Army-Navy game each year. Veterans Stadium was named by Philadelphia City Council to honor veterans of the U.S. military—this was back before the days of naming rights. The stadium was designed as a multipurpose facility that would house both the Phillies and the NFL Eagles. "The Vet" was one of several "cookie cutter" facilities, as they came to be known derisively later, along with Pittsburgh (Three Rivers), Atlanta (Fulton County), Cincinnati (Riverfront), and St. Louis (Busch).

"By the time I joined the Phillies, the new stadium had been in the planning stages for some years, had already been designed, and was pretty far along in construction," notes Giles. Therefore, he adds, "I had relatively little to do with the design of the facility." Veterans Stadium had a unique design. It was called an "octorad," an architect's term, and was basically shaped like a rounded rectangle. The design was necessitated by the fact that the facility had to work for both baseball and football. This idea was popular in major pro sports cities throughout the United States in the 1960s and early 1970s, especially as the funding source shifted from private entities to municipalities that owned the facilities and leased them to their tenants, which were the NFL and MLB teams in those cities. The stadium's capacity was enormous, approximately 62,000 for baseball and 66,000 for football. In addition, the shape of the facility created very large expanses of foul territory because the seats were located far back from the field. The top deck, which included the 500, 600, and 700 levels, was very high, and the top rim, which housed the 700-level seats, was far above home plate and set far back from the field. The resulting sight lines were certainly not ideal for either sport, but they were much better for watching football than for watching baseball. "However, I always thought that perhaps 45,000 of the 62,000 seats available for baseball were pretty good seats," says Giles.

Recalling his early days in Philadelphia, Giles says:

> My dad had always thought that one of the worst things that you can see in a ballpark is a huge expanse of empty seats. It is really hard to draw 62,000 fans to a baseball game. You can do so if you have a really good team that is in a pennant race or playing in the postseason, or perhaps if you are running a really popular promotion. Certainly, no one could expect to fill 62,000 seats for baseball on any sort of regular basis. The idea, therefore, was to drape a large curtain across the seats in the upper reaches of the outfield, reducing capacity and limiting the number of empty seats.

Oakland has used this tactic recently, and you also see it in large arenas for some basketball tournaments. He continues:

> However, I really believed in myself and my creative ability to promote baseball games, or any event, for that matter, so I convinced everyone that we should not have a curtain. That turned out to be a good decision on opening days, evenings on which we had fireworks displays, and during the really good seasons of the late 1970s through 1983, and again in 1993. Not so good during other seasons. It was no fun having the Vet look like what we used to see in Florida at Marlins games. And it could look like that even if we drew 30,000, which during those years was considered a good major league crowd pretty much everywhere but in Dodger Stadium.

He adds:

> My other major design recommendation was to put what we called "super boxes" in at the 400 level. This is an idea I brought from Houston, since we had installed suites on the top level of the Dome. The super boxes at the Vet were of different sizes, ranging in capacity from eighteen to twenty-eight. We shared the suites with the Eagles. Ticket revenue for Eagles games went to the Eagles, and ticket revenue for Phillies games went to the Phillies. Initially, we let suite owners use their own caterers, but after a while, we changed the policy and the occupants had to use the caterer who had the contract for the Vet.

Suite owners received eight tickets to baseball games and could purchase additional tickets. He explains:

> We wanted to make the additional tickets affordable, so we priced them at the level of box seats. But to create more suite revenue, we charged additional rent for the suite based on the additional number of seats sold above the original allotment of eight. The additional rent was shared by the city and the ball club. We felt that the ball club's share was too low, but as tenants, we didn't have a lot of power to change things. When [Eagles owner] Leonard Tose demanded renegotiation of revenue distribution in the 1980s, we wound up getting a somewhat higher share of suite rentals.

One of the big issues that the Phillies had with Veterans Stadium was financial. According to Giles:

> The city planned, designed, funded, and built the Vet. They owned it, and they dictated the terms of the leases with the tenants. The

> parking lots were city-owned, and we received none of the parking fees. Our share of concessions was also very low, and there was no signage and advertising to speak of, as there is today in the new ballparks. Finally, there were no naming rights. As a result, our bottom line really suffered. Revenue levels were really depressed, and despite the fact that Philadelphia is one of the largest cities and one of the largest media markets in the country, we couldn't make enough money to do the things we really wanted to do, specifically in terms of the level of player payroll.

The Eagles were equally distressed by the financial situation at the Vet, and ultimately, in the 1980s, Tose demanded that the city renegotiate the terms of the lease and threatened to move the Eagles from Philadelphia. At one time, it seemed very likely that the Eagles would "fly the nest" and head to Phoenix. As a result of Tose's threat, the city did renegotiate, giving both the Eagles and the Phillies a share of the parking and a better percentage of concessions, but the other revenue streams were still lacking, and with attendance lagging, the club still didn't generate enough revenue.

In 1993, John Kruk, Lenny Dykstra, Dutch Daulton, Curt Schilling, and many others, led by manager Jim Fregosi, surged to the top of the National League East and stayed there pretty much all year. The excitement about the team increased to virtual hysteria, and the Phillies drew more than 3 million for the first time. Giles laments:

> We likely would also have drawn 3 million the next year [1994] because there was still a lot of enthusiasm for the team, but the strike that started in August of that year ended that dream with a thud. We drew 2 million in 1995 after baseball returned, but our attendance went down from there and we drew in the 1.5 to 1.8 million range for the rest of the decade. I was disheartened by both the on-field performance and the lack of attendance, and the fans were very frustrated as well. It was a tough time to be an owner.

Bill Giles was never afraid to learn from someone else. One of his most important learning experiences took place when he learned that the Baltimore Orioles were planning, with the help of Baltimore Mayor and later Maryland Governor William Donald Schaefer, a new ballpark near the Inner Harbor. Larry Lucchino, who led the project for the Orioles when he worked for Edward Bennett Williams, said:

> Bill Giles was a keen and attentive observer to what was going on in Baltimore in the late eighties and early nineties with respect to the construction of the ballpark. We had several conversations about it. I remember we had the owners in town and we gave them an early tour of the ballpark. It seemed like Bill was the first one there, the last one to leave and full of questions about it because he obviously thought that [for the Phillies] this is something that can and should be done. And it took someone with the wherewithal that Bill had to realize [the significance of the ballpark project] early on and to work towards the new version of what a baseball park should be.[1]

The Orioles opened Camden Yards in 1992. With sellout crowds every night, it was clear that the uniqueness and ambience of this beautiful retro ballpark packed in the fans. When it became apparent how significantly the park affected the team revenues, Giles decided that the key to the future success of the Phillies required a new, baseball-only ballpark in Philadelphia. He recalls, "Back in 1992, I saw the handwriting on the wall. As far as revenue, we had always been between sixth and 12th in baseball. Then we saw the new stadium in Baltimore come in, the Orioles' revenue jumped by $70 million, and I said, 'Uh oh.'" The Phillies soon saw revenue fall to 20th as more and more new ballparks came online. He says, "I never anticipated the disparity getting so bad."

The economic reality of baseball drove the stadium project. Giles saw a new ballpark as the only way that the Phillies could be competitive. He explains, "The economic pressures have become so difficult. When I first came to the Phillies in 1970, our entire payroll was $1 million. Now [the 1990s] we pay our backup infielders that much." Even before Bud Selig talked about its importance in the context of competitive balance in baseball, Giles said, "The whole life of a fan is hope—hope that your team at least has a chance of winning half their games, hope that they'll at least be entertaining. It has become frustrating to see that it will be difficult for the Phillies to ever be a consistent pennant contender unless we change our revenue structure."[2]

Just after he stepped down as CEO in June 1997, Giles spoke about the importance of the revenue-generating capability of a new ballpark for the ownership group:

> Without a new ballpark, it's going to be difficult for this group to continue. It's getting more and more difficult for a Mom-and-Pop operation to survive. The next two years are critical. If we don't see a new stadium on the horizon by December of 1999, it's going to

> be difficult for this group to continue. The only way we're going to be able to be consistently competitive and interesting is to have enough revenue to keep our young players. It's not just the stadium revenue and the related revenue to the stadium; it's television revenue, because theoretically, the more revenue you have to work with, the better players you can have, the higher the TV ratings. The higher the TV ratings, the more revenue you can take in.

He went on to say, "By the year 2002 there will be 18 new (baseball) stadiums. The amount of revenue generated by new stadiums amounts to an average of $50 million more than you can generate at the Vet."[3]

Eventually, his vision realized, Giles was thrilled and proud when Citizens Bank Park opened in April 2004, "but," he says, "I was still sad and shed some tears when we imploded the Vet because we needed the room for a parking lot. The Vet is gone, but the memories of my thirty-three years there will be around as long as I am."

Building a "Ballpark"

Any sports facilities project revolves around three major decisions. The first involves funding. Except in rare instances, it is unlikely that club owners can build new facilities without some type of public support. The expense is just too great. The cost of ballpark projects, even in the 1990s, approached $400 million and sometimes was even higher. The operative model for the past couple of decades has been a combination of public and private funding, and the Phillies ballpark project would follow that model.

The second major decision is location. A stadium or an arena has a large geographic footprint, especially when parking is included, so adequate space is a concern. Do existing buildings have to be removed? How are the owners of these structures compensated and relocated? There are many other considerations in facility development, including adequate access via both automobile and public transportation, the effect on neighborhoods, the economic impact on surrounding businesses, and the ambience of the location. Just like ballpark funding, location involves politics.

The third decision is design. Decisions must be made about seating capacity, building materials, the shape and size of the playing field, and all of the other elements that make up a ballpark. In this era, facilities have to generate revenues far beyond ticket sales. Bill Giles wanted a ballpark to be intimate, comfortable, and attractive, with revenue-generating potential.

Giles recalls, "Dave Montgomery, Richard Deats, who at the time was VP of ticket sales and served as a liaison with various companies working on the project, Jerry Clothier, our VP of Finance, and Bill Webb, our corporate counsel, did most of the 'heavy lifting' in terms of negotiations with various government and community entities, especially after I stepped down as president, but I spent a lot of time and effort working in all three of these areas."

Funding

The original concept of a new baseball-only ballpark, with capacity of 42,000 to 43,000, carried an initial construction cost estimate of $320 million. Clearly, Giles' ownership group would not be able to fund the project on its own. The Phillies needed significant contributions from the governor and the mayor. The funding of the ballpark, from day one, was to be a one-third, one-third, one-third proposition among the Commonwealth of Pennsylvania, the City of Philadelphia, and the Phillies. This split had been mandated early on by Pennsylvania Governor Tom Ridge. The public-private funding partnership model had been in use for most of the new ballparks that had been built since 1991. That was the year that the White Sox opened the new Comiskey Park, now U.S. Cellular Field, largely financed with public funds appropriated by the Illinois State Legislature. As a result, the funding proposition itself didn't create a major issue, but getting the Pennsylvania Legislature and Philadelphia City Council to identify a source of funding and appropriate the funds was far from a done deal.

State funding came first. The Phillies received the necessary help because both Pittsburgh teams were demanding new facilities and the Pirates had threatened to move to another city if they could not procure funding for a new ballpark. The politicos who represented the City of Pittsburgh and the Commonwealth of Pennsylvania did not want to lose the Steelers or the Pirates, and the leases at Three Rivers Stadium were about to expire for both clubs. Pittsburgh's stadium was very similar to the Vet—an aging, multipurpose concrete stadium with little charm and little revenue-generating potential. Governor Ridge pushed the legislature to come up with a funding package to provide state money, which would be combined with municipal and private funds, for the Steelers and the Pirates to build new facilities. He created a task force that recommended in September 1996 that Pennsylvania contribute up to 35 percent of the cost of the new stadiums. Of course, the legislature had to do for Philadelphia what it was doing for Pittsburgh, so the funding plan extended to the Phillies and Eagles as well.

Many members of the Pennsylvania Legislature opposed public funding for new sports facilities, as did their constituents. The argument was simple: how we can we justify spending public money on new sports facilities that will only help millionaires (players) and billionaires (owners) when we don't have money for schools and teachers, roads and bridges, and other needs? At the same time, elected officials who lost professional teams to other cities on their watches could expect to no longer be elected officials. Thus, there was pressure in the halls of the State Capitol in Harrisburg to get the deal done.

Giles did not sit idly by and wait and hope for the state legislature to come up with money for a ballpark. He attended political fundraisers. He participated in many civic, charitable, and social events with important politicians. He dined with important politicians and invited them to ballgames. While he never resorted to "stadium blackmail," that is, threatening to move the team if he couldn't get public money to build a new ballpark, Giles made certain that the politicians at both the state and city levels understood how important a new ballpark was to the team and as an entity that would generate tax dollars. He recalls, "We had a lot of pretty pictures. We just tried to sell the excitement of a new ballpark." One of the advantages that Bill Giles had over other sports owners who had to convince politicians to grant public money was that he is a genuine person. Tom Muldoon, head of Philadelphia's Convention and Visitors Bureau, captured the Giles persona, saying, "Bill isn't seen as a fat-cat team owner. He's really just a fan who happens to own a baseball team. If you talk to all the politicians who dealt with people on this issue, they will all tell you the most genuine guy was Bill."[4]

The big question was where to find the money. Pennsylvania sells liquor through state-controlled liquor stores; the operation is run by the Pennsylvania Liquor Control Board. Ridge advocated selling the state liquor stores and privatizing the operation. This plan (as well as all subsequent plans to join the 20th—not even the 21st—century and get the state out of the liquor business) fell on deaf ears in the legislature.

Maryland created a sports lottery as one of the funding sources for Camden Yards, and Philadelphia Mayor Ed Rendell supported a similar plan for Pennsylvania. His rationale was strong: only sports fans and others interested in helping the state fund the new facilities would participate. Rendell said, "The beauty of the scratch cards is that, basically, the sports fans would pay for the construction of the sports stadium. If Mary Smith, in the Northeast [section of Philadelphia] on a fixed income, doesn't want any of her tax dollars going for the stadiums, she doesn't buy the scratch cards." Governor Ridge and others at the state level did not favor a sports lottery because they were concerned that sports lottery purchases would cannibalize purchases in the regular state lottery, which benefitted senior citizens—a "most adamant lobbying group."[5]

A year later, as the 1998 legislative session drew to a close, the legislature still had not passed a stadium funding bill, and while most legislators approved the plan, several members of the state House and Senate were claiming a great deal of opposition to the plan from their constituents. One public interest organization was running radio ads in Pittsburgh that stated, "It's just not right for the legislature to put your children into debt for 30 years just to bail out millionaire team owners." A measure to raise the commonwealth debt limit was before the legislature on the last day before the body adjourned the legislative session, but leaders saw little hope for passage.[6] Ultimately, the state house speaker pulled the bill before it came to a vote.

When the legislature reconvened in January 1999, a new stadium funding proposal emerged, one that involved interest-free loans to four teams. Bill Giles responded succinctly, "That will not work. It does not work economically. We've already agreed to pay more than most other teams have paid. Now they are trying to make it worse for us. It may get to the point where it won't work from a team standpoint." The teams responded to the new proposal with the argument that now they were being forced to pay for two-thirds of the cost, instead of the previously agreed-on one-third, with the result that too little revenue would remain to compete adequately in their respective leagues.[7]

The *Philadelphia Inquirer* reported that a survey of fan voters underwritten by Major League Baseball showed that, while the majority of fans expressed opposition to the proposal when asked simply if public money should be used for a new ballpark for the Phillies, 70 percent of the respondents said that they approved public funding if it meant no tax increase and a like number said that they would support public spending if "spending from fans attending the games would pay for the city's and state's share." Bill Giles responded, "We keep hearing from some politicians that their constituents are opposed to this. Most of the time, it's the people who are opposed to the project who speak out. We think there is a silent majority out there who will support stadiums when they know the facts. That's what this poll shows."[8]

The logjam was finally broken by a new idea that was proposed by Pennsylvania House Majority Leader John Perzel from Philadelphia. Perzel proposed giving each of the four teams approximately $80 million to help cover the costs of four new stadiums. The teams would not be bound to repay the grants as long as the increase in state tax revenues generated by the new facilities exceeded the amount each team received from the state, which would make an accounting every ten years. If the tax increment was not meeting the minimum return to the state, then the teams would make up the difference. Perzel came up with a novel solution that both supported the teams and protected the taxpayers, and it worked. The next day, the bill passed. Giles, expressing his satisfaction with the outcome and his admiration for the idea, said, “It’s certainly something that municipalities elsewhere may look at and say, ‘Gee, that’s a pretty good idea.’ This might be the forerunner for public funding throughout sports.”[9]

The first major hurdle to a new ballpark, procuring state funding, had been overcome. At that point, the Phillies still had to obtain a funding package from the city and get approval on a location for the new ballpark. Giles said, “We have quite a bit of work still to be done. We’ve had a lot of meetings [with city leaders], but we’ve not come to an agreement yet on the economics. The good news is that the mayor [Ed Rendell] is very much trying to make it happen.[10]

Working with the City of Philadelphia

Mayor Rendell had been a strong proponent of a new ballpark in a downtown location. His successor, John Street, felt likewise. In 1994, Bill Giles originally said that a new ballpark would “turn that whole South Philadelphia area into a great sports complex, one worthy of this great sports city.”[11] Two years later, as the Comcast deal to acquire Spectacor and the 76ers developed, Giles confirmed that he had been holding meetings with Spectacor CEO Ed Snider and Philadelphia developer Ronald Rubin about building the ballpark in South Philadelphia, which made sense with Comcast in the mix. Giles said, “Plans are under way, and we’re working on it.” He also said, “Comcast could be involved in the form of a loan or by buying rights to the stadium name.”[12]

Giles understood the advantages of building his new ballpark in South Philadelphia, where all of the teams already played and where the Eagles wanted to locate their new stadium. He also understood the benefits to the city of a neighborhood ballpark, one located in the heart of the city, near restaurants, bars, and hotels, and in a location where these local businesses would benefit from the patronage of people on their way to and from games. He also saw in Baltimore, Cleveland, and other cities the ambience of being able to view a downtown skyline over the outfield fences. Thus, by early 1998, he was strongly advocating for a ballpark located in Center City. His plan called for a new ballpark located just a couple of blocks north of the city center, which was City Hall. His preferred site was a parcel of land bound by Broad Street, the major north-south street that separated the east and west sides of Philadelphia; 16th

Street, two blocks to the west; and Spring Garden and Callowhill Streets, two parallel streets that ran east and west. Angling the ballpark so that home plate was at the northwest corner would yield a spectacular view of the city skyline.

He recalls the thinking that went into his preferred downtown location:

> Of course, if the commonwealth and the city were to use taxpayer dollars to fund the majority of the new ballpark's cost, the Phillies had to show that they would generate more tax dollars for the city to justify the city's contribution. This led to the idea that we needed to put the ballpark in a downtown location. I felt strongly that a downtown ballpark was necessary. First, the experience of teams in Baltimore, Cleveland, and other cities with downtown ballparks had clearly demonstrated the benefits of such a location to the ball club and its fans, but also to local merchants and to the vibrancy of the city itself. Second, we did some analysis of attendance figures of various ball clubs and found that, for teams with facilities in downtown locations, the win-loss record had less effect on attendance than it did for clubs with facilities in other locations. I really thought that a ballpark at Broad and Spring Garden Streets, our most favored potential location, would have great ambience, in terms of looking at the skyline from the seats in foul territory, and would create real excitement and enthusiasm for baseball in the areas surrounding the park, and ultimately create higher revenues. We had a prospective deal to acquire the land from the *Philadelphia Inquirer* and other landowners at a reasonable price, and we had a tentative design that would have put home plate in the northwest corner of the site so that Center City opened up in center field. With the Broad Street Subway located adjacent to the site, with Septa regional rail trains coming into Suburban Station just a few blocks to the southwest, and with access to both route 95 and the Schuylkill Expressway via Vine Street, we felt it was a prime location.

Other sites were considered, but none turned out to be feasible, for a variety of reasons. Daniel Keating, president of Keating Building Company, submitted a proposal to the Phillies and city officials for a new ballpark on a parcel of land owned by the U.S. Postal Service near the west bank of the Schuylkill River, close to the 30th Street train station (the main intercity train station in Philadelphia). The ballpark would be part of a $500 million redevelopment project. Giles recollects:

> The air rights over the tracks could have been acquired. We also looked a couple of blocks directly to the south of that site, around the main Philadelphia Post Office. For both sites, it would have been feasible to fit the ballpark into the site. However, the lack of open space for parking, coupled with the congestion that would have been created in the area, which was already significant, with Drexel [University], Penn [The University of Pennsylvania], and the train station, plus access ramps to the expressway at 30th Street and at South Street, made the idea untenable.

In addition, the University of Pennsylvania had major expansion plans for its campus to the east, that is, to the river, and Penn's senior leadership was dead set against a ballpark around 30th Street Station or the post office.

A Center City location for the ballpark, unfortunately, came with several problems and issues. The biggest problem was reluctance on the part of neighborhood residents to have a ballpark nearby, with the attendant traffic congestion, noise, and people clogging the neighborhood. A large state office building on the site created an issue because those offices would have to be relocated. Vincent Fumo, a state senator who wielded enormous power in local politics, took a stand against the Broad and Spring Garden location. Of Fumo, Giles had said, "We don't know what he's up to. We know publicly that he's against it, but privately we're not sure where he stands. We'd like to have him on board because he's a powerful guy."[13]

Another disadvantage of the Center City location was the incremental cost to build there as opposed to the South Philadelphia site, which was estimated by the Phillies to be $40 million and by the city to be $80 million. The funds would be needed for demolition, road enhancements, and parking facilities. Giles thought that since the city would benefit from additional tax revenues and the positive economic effect on businesses in the area, the additional cost should be borne at least in part by the city. The Central Philadelphia Development Corporation, aided by Andersen Consulting, had performed an economic analysis that reported that the annual economic impact of the Phillies on the city amounted to $229 million. Putting a new stadium at the sports complex would raise that figure by 40 percent, to $341 million, while putting a stadium in Center City would increase the total to a projected $417 million, a figure 22 percent higher than that of a South Philadelphia location.[14]

As the drama over the ballpark location played out, Giles admitted, wearily, "It's been a lot more of a struggle than I anticipated. There were a lot more hurdles than I anticipated and a lot more people involved from the political side as well as other issues." But he also knew that, with the state having stepped up to the plate, a new ballpark was going to happen; he just wasn't sure where. "We'll definitely have a deal[;] the question is where. The end is in sight. But I don't know where that's going to be."[15]

Ultimately, however, the ability to move ahead with the ballpark project came down to City Council. Giles recounts the situation:

> Philadelphia has an unwritten tradition that any major construction project that comes to a vote before City Council has to be introduced by the councilperson of the district in which the project is to be located. Darrell Clarke was and still is the councilman from the 5th District, which included the proposed site of the ballpark. Unfortunately, local politicians did not favor the site because there was a real "not in my backyard" type of feeling expressed by residents and business owners in neighborhoods near our desired site. We held public meetings with the neighborhood groups and explained how the traffic and parking would work in an attempt to allay their concerns, but we could not overcome the neighborhood resistance. One of our major opponents was Vincent Fumo, a very powerful member of the Pennsylvania Legislature, who lived about six blocks from the site. He simply did not want the crowds and the congestion of some 45,000 people as many as eighty-one times a season coming into center city, especially to a location near his home. Fumo also used some legislative tricks to stall the project. The Broad and Spring Garden location was dead.

In fall 2000, John Street, former head of Philadelphia City Council, was elected mayor, and he was very much in support of a downtown ballpark, stating that "[a center city ballpark] is one dream that some Philadelphians aren't ready to let go of."[16] Mayor Street favored a location in Chinatown, around the area of 12th and Vine, just blocks from Giles' preferred location. Giles noted, "But there was significant opposition from community residents, business owners in the area, and various activists and interest groups. Plus, we felt that parking, ingress, and egress were all problematic. None of the Phillies people were really interested in that site, and ultimately Mayor Street could not sell it." Moreover, the cost projections for a ballpark project at 12th and Vine Streets were astronomical compared with the site in South Philadelphia. Just to get the site ready for excavation would have required the acquisition of 135 properties owned by 107 different people. The incremental cost for land acquisition, demolition, and solving traffic and parking problems was projected to be

$300 million. The plan required knocking down an old Reading Railroad track and trestle, creating 4,500 parking spaces, and building walkways across Vine Street—a sunken, divided highway that runs through Center City.[17]

A group of area residents proposed a site at the old Schmidt's Brewery at 2nd Street and Girard Avenue in the Northern Liberties section. While area residents and civic groups supported the economic development aspect of the project, it never received serious consideration. Another possible location was suggested by State Representative Marie Lederer, whose district included a site near the Delaware River northeast of Center City on land owned by Conrail in the Port Richmond section. Neither the Northern Liberties site nor the Port Richmond site presented a viable alternative, and they were never candidates. By spring 2000, Dave Montgomery and the rest of the planning team did not favor any of the locations except for the original Broad and Spring Garden site, preferring to be located in South Philadelphia in the Stadium Complex. Montgomery said, "We believe there is no viable Center City site available at this time. We believe our neighbors would be better served if the Phillies were located at the sports complex."[18]

Because Pittsburgh had a ready location for its two facilities right across the river from downtown Pittsburgh, the Heinz Field and PNC Park projects moved along at a nice pace, and by the 2001 seasons, both of those facilities were open. Unfortunately, that wasn't the case in Philadelphia, and the delays in getting the ballpark location finalized were affecting not only the Phillies but also the Eagles.

Giles recounts that his NFL neighbors were growing impatient. He recalls, "Frankly, Jeffrey Lurie and Joe Banner, the owner and the president of the Eagles, respectively, were not too happy with the Phillies during this period." They knew exactly where they wanted to locate their facility—in the sports complex in South Philadelphia, where the Vet, the Spectrum, and the CoreStates Center were located. "But because the funding packages of our two facilities were linked, the Eagles could not proceed until our deal was finalized, and that couldn't happen until the mayor and the Phillies had finally and firmly decided on a site for the ballpark."

So, after a couple of years of appearing before neighborhood groups and both explaining and getting citizen reaction to the proposal, of meeting and dealing with politicians and trying to cut the right deals, and of both private and public disagreements over where to locate the new ballpark, Mayor Street announced his decision in November 2000. The Phillies new 43,000-seat ballpark would be located in South Philadelphia, in the existing stadium complex, right next to Vet Stadium and directly north of the Eagles' new facility and a parking lot. Giles recalls,

"At the time, I was not too pleased with the result, but we were left with no other option, so we had to make the best of it."

The Financials

The city still had to determine where the money to fund the project would come from. Mayor Rendell had floated different proposals, including the sports lottery, a regional surcharge on the state sales tax, a tax on auto rentals, and a surcharge on the price of tickets to the new stadiums, in addition to saving money that the city was spending to maintain Veterans Stadium, which would become the responsibility of the respective teams in their new buildings. When Mayor Street announced the decision to locate the ballpark in South Philadelphia, his office also disclosed a funding plan for the $304 million required to pay back investors in municipal bonds that the city would issue to raise its contribution. Street estimated $199 million in taxes generated by the ballpark and the Eagles' new stadium from city wage taxes paid by construction workers, athletes and team administrators, parking, and an amusement tax on game tickets, plus $105 million from a 2 percent additional tax on rental cars.

The total cost of the ballpark project was put at $458 million, including $348 million for construction and $110 million for site work. Giles recounts that the state put in $95 million (as limited by the bill passed by the legislature), the city contributed $150 million plus the land on which the ballpark is constructed; the Delaware River Port Authority invested between $5 and $10 million; and the Phillies put in the rest, about $200 million. He notes, "The Phillies have a $1 per year lease on the land as long as we want it. We pay an amusement tax on each ticket sold and contribute $1 million per year to a children's fund. The club keeps all concessions revenue less the concessionaire's share." Aramark runs all concessions in the ballpark except for McFadden's Restaurant, which is a leased operation. Parking is split among the Eagles, the Phillies, and Comcast-Spectacor (Ed Snider) in a complex arrangement, with all parties sharing to some extent in all events held at the three sports facilities, the ballpark, Lincoln Financial Field, and the (now) Wells Fargo Center, with the Phillies keeping a higher percentage of the parking take for their ballgames.

Designing a Ballpark

The design of the ballpark, according to Giles, started with a couple of assumptions. First, he said, "capacity would be in the 42,000–43,000 range, which we believe is optimal for baseball in Philadelphia. Scarcity is important in selling tickets because if capacity is too large, fans will never feel a sense of urgency to buy tickets ahead of time. So, smaller capacity actually helps advance sales."

The second assumption was that, as Giles recalls, "the ballpark would be a really fun place to visit, and fans would have a great experience and want to come back, even if the Phillies lost the game! This was absolutely crucial to the vision we had for the ballpark, and ultimately, much of what you see in the park is driven by the notion of having a great time."

The Phillies unveiled architectural plans for the ballpark in late June 1997. Phillies CEO David Montgomery told the press that day, "Our goal is simple: to make our new ballpark a special place for our fans. We want them to have a wonderful experience from the time they arrive at the ballpark until they head home. We believe the design is fundamental to creating a unique and enduring ballpark experience."[19]

Giles recalls the effort that went into designing Citizens Bank Park. He says that the project involved the senior management of the Phillies meeting almost nightly after completing their regular work day. He describes the situation, saying:

> So, now we had a funding package, and a location, so we had to figure out what the park was going to look like. We also had to begin to line up companies who would purchase in-venue advertising, and a potential naming sponsor, as these revenues are now absolutely crucial to the financial success of a major league baseball team, and make other decisions about the eventual operation of the park.
>
> I have said already that the idea was to design a ballpark—and I have to tell you that it was considered a violation, and you were fined a dollar—if anyone in the Phillies organization referred to the new facility as a "stadium." Most assuredly, the idea was to build an intimate, fan-friendly, fun place to watch a game, a "ballpark." We wanted to make the field asymmetrical, have some quirkiness to the outfield fences, and have excellent sightlines for the fans, plus a lot of attractions that would add to the experience.
>
> We had the advantage of being late in the cycle of building, and therefore we had the opportunity to visit places like Camden Yards in Baltimore, PNC Park in Pittsburgh, Coors Field in Denver, Jacobs Field in Cleveland, AT&T Park in San Francisco, and every other new ballpark that had been built since the White Sox replaced the old Comiskey Park in 1991. We were able to see for ourselves what was done right and what could be done better, all of which was key learning for the design team. One of the best ideas

we found was at Coors Field, where the concourses are open to the field and, even when you go for a hot dog or a T-shirt, you still are in touch with the game, and so that became one of our key design parameters.

The field is actually twenty-three feet below grade level, which means two things. One, about half of the people go down to their seats when they enter the ballpark and about half go up. Of course, this is reversed when they leave. Two, the ballpark appears smaller and more intimate from outside at street level, and less of a stadium. Also, since the level of the field itself is actually below sea level and it is built on land between two rivers, we had to install what amounts to a humongous bathtub under the entire facility and constantly pump out water.

One of the points I made repeatedly with the design team and the architects was "right angles." The Vet, you see, had no angles. Everything was an arc. About the only things that were straight in the whole facility were the baselines and the contour of the dugouts. So, for the new park, we wanted angles and no arcs. Another key design element was brick. The Vet was all concrete. After seeing the beauty of the outside of Camden Yards and other new ballparks, we wanted the fans to see lots of brick. The ballpark is designed with virtually no exposed concrete, and we painted the steel beams to blend in with the brick, as this was all really important to the look of the new park.

Another of the key design elements we wanted was for the wall in center field to be low enough so that the center fielder could leap above the wall to catch near-home runs. We could not do that in right field because that is where we planned to put the out-of-town scoreboard.

We had the idea for two premium seating locations in the ballpark. The first is what we eventually named the "Diamond Club," the best seats in the house in the lower bowl behind the plate and between the dugouts. The Diamond Club has a private restaurant. We found out from our fans that some of them like table service and some like a buffet, so we designed the Diamond Club restaurant with both options. We also feature waiter service in the extra-wide, cushioned seats so that fans can eat while watching the game.

One of the interesting and innovative things we did with the Diamond Club was coming up with the idea of "loaded tickets," that is, tickets that included stored value that could be used to buy food and merchandise. In the opening year, 2004, we charged $90

> for Diamond Club tickets, with each ticket containing a $30 credit for purchases in the ballpark. We did this for the convenience of the Diamond Club members, mainly companies, so that they could entertain clients and guests at the ballpark, and even if the host was not present, the guest would not have to "pull money out of his or her pocket" to buy a beer and a hot dog. This is an idea that has caught on throughout professional sports and has been expanded by many clubs to the idea of "all-you-can-eat" tickets. Subsequently, we added some stored value tickets to some outfield sections, which we named the "Scoreboard Porch."

The second premium area is the Hall of Fame Club, with an air-conditioned interior concourse featuring food, beverage, and merchandise sales, a selection of premium foods, and its own bathrooms—with floor tile designed to look like grass. This area also features a Hall of Fame display in the area behind home plate. This display honors all ballplayers who have Philadelphia ties and are in the National Baseball Hall of Fame. Other displays honor Harry Kalas and other greats from the past. The first picture on the wall is of Harry Wright, who managed the Cincinnati Red Stockings, the very first openly professional baseball team in 1869 and later managed the Phillies. Giles explains, "There was an issue regarding how to locate the Hall of Fame Club relative to a level of suites, and we ultimately decided to give the suites the location just above the lower bowl and therefore better sight lines."

He continues, "We wanted to make the ballpark a destination, so we needed attractions and gathering places above and beyond just the seats and concourses in the facility." At Camden Yards, the Orioles integrated the massive old B&O Railroad building that sits beyond right field into the facility itself and set up what amounts to a pedestrian mall between the building and the right field seats. In this mall, there are places to buy food, such as Boog's Barbeque, another idea the Phillies borrowed, places to buy merchandise, and places just to hang out and have fun. Giles goes on to say:

> I liked this idea, and I particularly wanted an Atlantic City Boardwalk type of concept, so the idea of Ashburn Alley, our homage to the late, great Phillies player and announcer Richie Ashburn, was born. We designed the park to have Ashburn Alley sit above center field and above the bullpens, which are in the outfield, next to the "batter's eye" wall in dead center field. We filled Ashburn Alley with food emporia and merchandise stores, featuring local food vendors and Philadelphia specialties. We made Ashburn Alley

open to the field of play, so people could gather or hang out there and watch the game.

Behind the batter's eye, we placed a display of pictures and a narrative that covers the history of baseball in Philadelphia, from the very beginnings after the Civil War. We profile the Phillies and the A's, and we also include the two great Negro League teams, the Hilldale Daisies, who played in Darby Township (southwest of Philadelphia), and the Philadelphia Stars, who played at 44th and Parkside (in West Philadelphia). This is just one more way to involve the fans in the great tradition of baseball in Philadelphia.

We decided to build the bullpens in the outfield and placed bullpens one on top of the other next to the batter's eye and directly under Ashburn Alley. At first, we put the Phillies bullpen on top, but thought better of it—we wanted to avoid having fans yell at our players—and put the Phillies' pen on the bottom. Having the bullpens open to the public not only lets fans in the stands see who is warming up but also creates an opportunity for an "up close and personal" interaction between fans and players.

We brought in McFadden's Restaurant, which is open and accessible to the public pretty much all of the time, and set it up with both inside and outside seating. This is a real gathering place for twenty- and thirty-somethings who want to enjoy a great time out at a sports bar and still be part of the action at a major league baseball game. McFadden's, along with the other attractions, has really had the effect of changing the demographics of Phillies crowds, and we now have a much younger crowd than we had at the Vet. This is great not only for the present but also for the future of both the Phillies and Major League Baseball.

To honor our Hall of Fame announcer, Harry Kalas, we designed a restaurant above the left field stands called "Harry the K's," giving us two sit-down facilities in addition to all of the other food concessions." Former Phillies player Greg "Bull" Luzinski, who works for the club in community and fan relations, provides the name and the personality of "Bull's Barbeque." Located in the right field corner, this is clearly a concept that the Phillies appropriated from the Orioles.

We thought that, given Luzinski's popularity in Philadelphia, plus the fact that he is a big, fun-loving kind of guy, he would be perfect for this attraction, and he agreed to do it. On most game nights, Bull sits in a booth next to where the food is served and chats with fans, signs autographs, and poses for pictures. The fans love it.

> We wanted to have a place for kids, so we put in a kids' playground and we have games where the kids can play running games and throw and hit a baseball. Every aspect of these attractions was about creating a fun experience. Plus, as parents appreciate, the kids can burn some of that boundless energy they have when they come to the ballpark.

The outfield dimensions are very important in terms of having a balance of offense and defense. Giles explains, "We didn't want balls flying out with regularity, but we also wanted to have a park that hitters found reasonably friendly and pitchers found fair." The ballpark design team did extensive wind studies and found that the wind typically blows from the southwest. He continues, "We decided that the fences in right center field needed to be deeper than those in left center field because of the prevailing winds. As it turns out, we made a mistake by assuming that balls wouldn't travel as well to left field, and in the first year Citizens Bank Park was open, we were near the top in total home runs." After the inaugural season of 2004, the Phillies decided to lengthen the fences in left field. This helped put the ballpark more in the middle of the pack regarding home runs, but Citizens Bank Park is still considered a hitter-friendly ballpark. To move the wall back, the team had to remove a few hundred seats, but found other places in the park to add seats and make up the deficit.

Giles notes:

> I also wanted to pay homage to two ballparks that are of particular importance to the Phillies and to me. The first is Connie Mack Stadium. We decided to make some of the outfield dimensions in the new ballpark identical to those in Connie Mack. So, left field is 329 down the line and right field is 330. Even when we moved the left field fence back, we kept the distance at the foul pole at 329 feet.

The design team also wanted to honor a tradition that first started back when Connie Mack was managing at Shibe Park and the Philadelphia A's were dominating baseball. Back in the late 1920s and early 1930s, when the right field wall at Shibe Park was only twelve feet high, people used to pay a nickel to homeowners on 20th Street and watch games from the rooftops. Of course, this tradition is now a big part of the Wrigley Field experience on the north side of Chicago. Giles explains, "So, we designed a section of 'roof top' seats in right center field. Finally, in homage to Wrigley and its ivy-covered walls, one of my favorite ballparks ever since I was a kid traveling with my dad when he ran the Cincinnati

Reds, we put up a red brick batter's eye and planted ivy. So, just like Wrigley Field, Citizens Bank Park now has 'ivy-covered walls' in the outfield."

The goal in opening up a new ballpark was to create a better experience for the players and the fans, but obviously the Phillies needed much more revenue to compete in the National League. According to Giles, "My original thought when I saw the impact of Camden Yards on the revenue of the Baltimore Orioles, and as I saw other teams dramatically raising their revenues as they opened new ballparks, was that in order to be competitive, we had to have more revenue so we could spend more on players and player development." Since the Phillies opened Citizens Bank Park, team revenues have increased dramatically, and as revenues have risen, player payroll has risen. By 2011, the Phillies had the second highest payroll in the majors. The Phillies were able to sign players such as Jimmy Rollins, Chase Utley, Ryan Howard, and Cole Hamels to long-term deals. In addition, the team won back-to-back National League Pennants in 2008 and 2009 and celebrated the second World Series Championship in Phillies history in 2008.

Giles continues:

> So, has Citizens Bank Park lived up to my expectations, and those of my ownership partners? Well, the proof is strictly in the results. Attendance is off the charts. We drew 2.2 million in 2003, our last year at the Vet, and drew over 3 million in our first year at Citizens Bank Park. We dropped a bit in 2005, but starting in 2006, we have drawn over 3 million each season. We reached 3.6 million in 2009, playing to 102 percent of capacity, and actually increased that to 104 percent of capacity in 2010. We had a 257-game sellout streak, which amounts to over three seasons of baseball, that just ended [in August 2012]. In 2011 and again in 2012, the Phillies led baseball in total attendance, surpassing even the Yankees and Dodgers, teams that both play in bigger ballparks in bigger cities. Our baseball people, fans, sportswriters, and the general public love the ballpark. And our annual revenues have gone from around $100 million in 2002 to approximately $300 million today. By any measure, Citizens Bank Park is phenomenally successful. And I couldn't be more proud of this ballpark and the great group of people who made it happen.[20]

Back in February 1999, when the Pennsylvania Legislature approved a funding package for stadium construction, Bill Giles talked about his greatest thrills in baseball, saying, "If and when we have that first pitch in the new stadium, it will be one of the top two or three highlights of my career. Right now, my two highlights are the 1980 World Championship and beating the Braves for the 1993 National League championship with what was probably the most exciting team I have ever seen. But if this thing gets built the way I dream it's going to be built, well, then, that will make my top drawer."[21]

11

From the Depths of 2002 to the Heights of 2012

Nine Reasons Why Baseball Is Booming

The issues and events discussed in this book focus on the period between the fall of 1981 and the end of August 2002. Bill Giles and his investment group purchased the Phillies in the fall of 1981, elevating Giles to the status of "partner" with his fellow club owners in the business of baseball. Although Giles had resigned as president of the Phillies during the summer of 1997, he continued to attend owners' meetings and stayed active on the ballpark project, which culminated in the opening of Citizens Bank Park in April 2004. August 30, 2002, is a significant date because on that day, just hours before what would have been the ninth work stoppage in baseball since 1972, the owners and players agreed to a labor deal without interrupting the season. Ever since, baseball has progressed mightily on the economic front, despite the steroid scandal and a major economic recession that started in 2008.

In the late summer and fall of 2002, baseball was an industry in administrative and financial peril. Fortunately, the players accepted the terms of the 2002 CBA, which included expanded revenue sharing, a "competitive balance" (luxury) tax on excessive payrolls, and debt limits for the thirty clubs. The commissioner's office reported operating losses of more than $400 million that year, substantially in excess of the $232 million loss reported after the 2001 season, when Selig publicly lamented baseball's dire economic situation before Congress. In the wake of the 2002 labor deal, baseball's financial fortunes turned around quickly.

A decade-plus later, baseball is riding a crest of financial success, as measured by industry revenues, operating profits, and franchise values.

The venerable Dodgers franchise sold for more than $2 billion in 2012. What Walter O'Malley created the regional sports networks have elevated beyond his wildest dreams.

I end this book with a look at the factors that Bill Giles, Andrew Zimbalist, Bob DuPuy, and other industry insiders and baseball writers believe are the key forces and factors in baseball's economic turnaround. With all due respect to Ken Burns, who used the nine innings format in his 1994 PBS series *Baseball*, and to Mr. DuPuy, who uses this format when discussing baseball's economic strides, I will identify nine innings worth of key factors, and then one more, MLB's new Fan Cave, in "The Tenth Inning."

The First Inning: Bud Selig and MLB's Senior Executive Team

During his tenure ruling baseball, from his time as chair of the Executive Council from 1992 to 1998, and then in the role of permanent commissioner since then, Bud Selig has been roundly criticized and has been characterized more than once as the least effective commissioner of the four major U.S. professional sports. Yes, baseball suffered a debilitating, unforgivable strike and cancellation of the World Series in 1994. Yes, Bud Selig presided over baseball during an era of inflated bodies, inflated heads, and inflated home run totals as a result of performance-enhancing drugs. Yes, he infamously shrugged his shoulders as he ended the 2002 All-Star Game in an extra-inning tie because the teams had run out of pitchers. Yes, he has neither the appearance nor the speaking skills of a polished business executive or a politician. Some see Bud Selig, who worked for years in his family's automobile dealership, as a "used car salesman," certainly not a term of respect and endearment.

But who can argue with success? Bud Selig possesses several characteristics that have made him, in the minds of many, including Bill Giles, the most effective commissioner baseball has ever had. Bud Selig has an honest and enduring love for the game. He respects its traditions, but knows that change has to come. He understands clearly that the industry cannot operate today as it did in the age of Landis, when the commissioner's office was new and baseball's integrity was at risk; in the age of Frick, during the postwar years that many traditionalists call "the golden age of baseball," or even in the age of Ueberroth, when owners were still trying to grasp the fundamental economic changes that Marvin Miller had wrought. In the mid-1960s Selig played a leadership role in trying to keep the Braves in Milwaukee. In 1970 he was a key part of the effort to bring baseball back to Milwaukee by working out a deal to transfer the bankrupt Pilots from Seattle. As the owner of the Brewers, Selig was deeply involved in the issues that most affect the game. He has a nuanced understanding of the owners of thirty clubs: their differing personalities, positions, and motivations. He is patient and understands that "slow and steady wins the race." He has said that he wants to "keep moving the sport ahead: slowly, cautiously, but ahead."[1] Selig is the ultimate consensus builder, willing to spend hours each day on the phone conversing with MLB's executives and owners and gaining a thorough understanding of the issues and viewpoints. He has the unique ability to get thirty owners with different agendas to agree on key issues.

Unlike his predecessors in the commissioner's office, Selig understands and has embraced the notion that the commissioner cannot represent owners, players, and fans equally. He publicly agrees with the contention, often voiced by Marvin Miller, that the players have their representative, the head of the Players Association, and the owners have theirs, the commissioner. Selig was clearly a labor "hawk" in the 1980s and early 1990s, yet his experience during the labor difficulties of 1994 and 1995 convinced him that labor peace was the key to baseball's economic growth. He worked very hard behind the scenes to move his fellow owners toward a similar position. According to Andrew Zimbalist, despite stepping into a situation fraught with tension and conflict among the owners and between the owners and the players, Selig managed to bridge the sizable gaps that existed and get the owners on the same page as much as that could ever happen. Building some type of consensus among the owners was necessary for baseball to achieve labor peace, innovate successfully, and build the sport globally.

Many changes and accomplishments have marked Bud Selig's twenty-plus years at the helm. In his book, *Pouring Six Beers at a Time,* Giles graded all of the commissioners, from Landis through Selig. Professor Giles awarded Selig the grade of "A–," the highest grade he awarded to any of the commissioners—no grade inflation here. He said during a 2009 interview, "Bud has accomplished more than any other commissioner, particularly on the business side of the game. Three divisions, the wild card, interleague play, the unbalanced schedule, the effort to do away with steroids, turning the All-Star game into a mega-event, attracting younger fans, BAM and the fact that we share BAM revenue, and anything related to the Internet, equally. This was not an easy thing to accomplish."[2]

He went on, saying, "Bud is very clever. He studied history, and he studied politics. He's a very political guy. He has a way of getting votes by doing favors, for example, awarding the All-Star Game to a certain club. The owners' meetings today are very different than in the past. Instead of gathering and discussing issues at length, Selig manages to have all of his ducks lined up prior to the meeting. Nowadays, the owners sit and listen to reports from all of Selig's department heads on issues like scheduling and BAM. Selig has already lined up unanimous or near-unanimous support on every issue [that] is scheduled to come to a vote. Most of the votes now go 30–0."[3]

Giles went on to say, "His public persona has never been good. But he is very effective at building consensus on important issues. He's also continued to maintain the integrity of the game, the public trust in the game, except for the steroid issue, which he has worked hard to clean up."[4]

When Selig became chair of the executive council and *de facto* commissioner in September 1992, baseball had about $1.2 billion in total revenue. In 2007, Selig recalled, "I remember saying to myself, 'How will we ever get to $2 billion?' I'd spend sleepless nights worrying about it."[5] By 2004, revenue had reached more than $4 billion and by 2012 was more than $7 billion. More teams are making more money. Industry operating profits are at an all-time high. Franchise values, as we have seen, are going through the roof. For example, the investment group assembled by Bill Giles paid a little over $30 million for the Phillies in 1981. By the beginning of the 2013 season, *Forbes* had the Phillies valued at $893 million. Four teams—the Yankees, Dodgers, Red Sox, and Cubs—were valued at more than $1 billion.[6] The sale of the Dodgers during the 2012 season showed that the $1.4 billion estimate of the club's franchise value in April 2012 amounted to a significant undervaluation.

Selig has taken his share of criticism over the years, but appears to be having the last laugh. "People used to say baseball was 'past its time.' Make no mistake about it. Our sport is more popular than ever and it is still the national pastime. No question about it. And I have a lot of statistics to back that statement."[7]

The commissioner believes that January 19, 2000, was a landmark date in turning the corner toward labor peace and competitive balance. Owners had consolidated power in the commissioner's office, and on that day the owners granted the commissioner unlimited economic power to attempt to solve the growing disparity between large and small markets. During the same meeting, the owners also voted unanimously to create the sport's own Internet company, Major League Baseball Advanced Media (MLBAM). At the time, they never dreamed how that area would grow exponentially, producing revenues that continue to soar. Subsequently, on January 1, 2009, MLB launched the MLB Network in 50 million homes.

According to Selig, "That [January 2000] meeting was historic. I said at the time that history would show that was analogous and as powerful as the 1961 meeting when [NFL Commissioner] Pete Rozelle talked the clubs into revenue-sharing." Moreover, he recalled, "None of us ever dreamed what BAM would grow to be. It's one of the great success stories of the sport."[8] I discuss BAM and digital properties in more depth in "The Seventh Inning."

Selig has appointed extremely capable senior executives to head baseball's various operations and divisions. As Giles explains, "Bud has surrounded himself with good people, including Bob DuPuy, Rob Manfred, Tim Brosnan, Bob Bowman, people like that."[9] Because these are the four people specifically mentioned by Giles, I focus on them. Limiting the discussion to four individuals is not in any way intended to denigrate the accomplishments and importance of other senior people, such as Sandy Alderson (who spent time working for Selig and is now general manager of the Mets), John McHale, Jr., and others; however, in discussions with owners and observers of the business of baseball, the names of DuPuy, Manfred, Brosnan, and Bowman are clearly the most prominent.

Bob DuPuy

Bob DuPuy is an Ivy League–educated attorney (A.B. from Dartmouth and J.D. from Cornell) who came to baseball in 1989 as outside legal counsel after having worked as an attorney for Selig in Milwaukee. He was involved in most of MLB's legal issues during the 1990s. DuPuy negotiated the settlement of the collusion grievance in 1990 and served as the principal outside counsel to the commissioner and the executive council from 1992 until 1998, when Selig appointed him as MLB executive vice president of administration and chief legal officer. DuPuy oversaw the consolidation of the leagues, the consolidation of MLB's office in Washington, D.C., and the formation of MLBAM as its first CEO.

DuPuy was named president and COO of Major League Baseball on March 7, 2002. In that capacity, he was responsible for all phases of baseball's central offices, including licensing, sponsorship, international, broadcasting, publishing, marketing, public relations, government relations, baseball operations, legal affairs, finance, Internet operations, and the labor relations committee.

According to a profile in *Sports Business Journal*, DuPuy became MLB's ultimate insider, with virtually nothing of importance getting done without his direct involvement. "Whether working on local stadium deals, labor relations or national TV contracts, DuPuy has remained unflappable in the heat of battle and has retained a lower public profile than may otherwise be expected of someone seen as an indispensable ally of Selig and the owners."[10] DuPuy left baseball in 2010 and rejoined the law firm of Foley and Lardner, where he is a partner, but has clearly left his mark on the baseball industry.

Rob Manfred

Robert Manfred is a Harvard-educated attorney who served as partner in the Labor and Employment Law Section of Morgan, Lewis & Bockius, which had been baseball's outside legal counsel. At "MLB" (it is interesting to note that Morgan, Lewis and Bockius ultimately ceded to Major League Baseball its web domain, MLB.com), Manfred represented employers in numerous industries, including transportation, health care, professional sports, and airlines. From the law firm, Manfred came to baseball where, from 1998 to 2013, he served as executive vice president, reporting directly to the commissioner. While he has been involved in all the major economic and operational issues in baseball, his primary area of responsibility has been the collective bargaining relationship with the Players Association. He served as the chief negotiator for baseball during the 2002, 2006, and 2011 labor negotiations. Many baseball insiders attribute the successful conclusion of each of those negotiations to Manfred's approach and bargaining skill. Manfred fostered a positive relationship with Michael Weiner, who succeeded Don Fehr as executive director of the MLBPA. Manfred is also responsible for the collective bargaining relationship with the World Umpires Association and the human resources function in the commissioner's office in New York.

In addition to Manfred's role in collective bargaining, Giles pointed out in 2006 that he had done "a magnificent job of educating owners on the economics and pitfalls of continued escalating salaries, and that player compensation should amount to about 52% of revenue."[11] The discipline shown by owners immediately after the signing of the 2002 labor agreement, according to Giles, took an industry that lost more than $400 million in 2002 to one that made $180 million in 2005. Manfred, regarded as a leading candidate to succeed Selig as commissioner, was named MLB's COO in 2013.

Tim Brosnan

Tim Brosnan has a law degree from Fordham University. He joined Major League Baseball as vice president of international business affairs in 1991 and was promoted to COO of Major League Baseball International in 1994 and to senior vice president, domestic and international properties, in 1998. In February 2000, he was named executive vice president, business, and in this role he oversees all domestic and international business functions of Major League Baseball's office of the commissioner, including licensing, sponsorship, domestic and international broadcasting, special events, and MLB Productions. In 2002, he was given additional responsibility as president/CEO of Major League Baseball Enterprises, the company that holds the collective business of the 30 major league clubs, including all licensing rights.

Brosnan heads up negotiations for all national media rights at MLB. In 2004, he led baseball's effort to negotiate a $650 million contract, the largest nontelevision media deal in sports, with XM Satellite Radio. That same year, Brosnan was named by ownership to develop and launch the MLB Network, which launched in nearly 50 million households in January 2009, the most successful launch of any network in cable television history. Brosnan currently serves on its board of directors. The MLB Network has been one of the fastest growing cable outlets on television and has added nearly 20 million homes since its launch.

In 2005 and 2006, he negotiated long-term deals with ESPN and with FOX and Turner Sports, respectively, totaling more than $5.4 billion.[12] In 2011, Brosnan headed up the effort to launch MLB's Fan Cave, based on his desire to "enter the social media conversation." I discuss the Fan Cave in the "Tenth Inning" section.

Bob Bowman

Bob Bowman, who holds a master's degree in business administration from the Wharton School, has served as president and CEO of MLBAM since 2000. MLBAM, jointly and equally owned by the thirty MLB owners, manages baseball's interactive and Internet rights. Before joining BAM, Bowman was president and COO of ITT Corporation from 1995 to 2000, where he previously served as chief financial officer from 1991 to 1995. He also held the position of treasurer of the State of Michigan. MLB's success in marketing its digital rights and using revenue from BAM as an economic equalizer could not work without success on the operations front, much of which is directly attributable to Bowman. It is impossible to discuss BAM without discussing Bowman. I address the incredible success of MLBAM in "The Seventh Inning."

The Second Inning: Labor Relations Peace

Giles has seen labor turmoil and has experienced labor peace. Clearly, he strongly prefers the latter and attributes much of the economic turnaround in baseball to the peace between the owners and players since the players went back to work in April 1995. In the two decades following free agency, much of the effort expended by the owners in dealing with the union involved slowing salary growth, and several different solutions were tried. The owners could never get the players to accept any direct constraints on salaries, and attempts to fix the market for free agents proved disastrous, both economically and in terms of the acrimony created between the owners and the players. Giles pointed out in 2010 that about the only thing that could derail labor talks in 2011 would be an attempt by the owners to impose a salary cap, but after the troubles of the 1980s and 1990s, that term is no longer in the owners' lexicon.

The labor relations wars came about for two main reasons. First, the owners couldn't adjust their thinking to the new economic reality created by free agency and did not see early on that free agency actually increased interest in baseball. Second, when revenue disparity grew, one of the concepts pursued by owners was that the way to address the imbalance was to reduce the players' share of revenue and return the difference to the low-revenue teams. Eventually, as some of the old-line owners departed, a new way of thinking was embraced. After much tumult among the owners and between the owners and players, the CBA of 1996 introduced significant revenue sharing for the first time and ushered in the period of labor peace that baseball has enjoyed since then. This peace will last until at least 2016, a period of twenty years. Given the acrimony, bitterness, and vitriol of labor relations between 1970 and 1995, the late, great Richie Ashburn, commenting on the labor relations peace of the current era, would have said, "Hard to believe, Harry!"

Both sides learned from the 1994 and 2002 experiences that negotiating in the media is a "lose-lose" situation. Both sides also learned that fans are not interested in labor confrontations; they want baseball. Selig was well aware of these realities and worked hard behind the scenes to have the owners stop trying to defeat the union and instead coexist peacefully and grow the game.

A year after successfully leading the owners to the groundbreaking 2002 labor settlement, Selig commented on his role in the negotiations:

> What I knew going in, as opposed to the past labor negotiations, which were not only haphazard in a certain sense, but we never dealt with the problems—so they just get worse. They were exacerbated by each failure. I knew how the clubs felt, because I'd really grown up with them. I knew what was reasonable, what most clubs needed to survive and why. Each club has its own indigenous characteristics. And it's up to the commissioner to understand those. In the end, that's how you wind up getting votes and that's where progress comes from. Yes, it's painful. Yes, there are always people upset about something. But if you've been fair, and you've ex-

> plained things to them and you've been honest, they work their way out. And so, painful as it's been, tough as it's been, I think no one will quarrel it's been the most active decade in baseball history.[13]

Labor relations peace has given fans the freedom to love the game without concern that rich owners and rich players will be taking it away again. Fans have much more fun discussing pennant races, pitching matchups, great catches, and walk-off home runs than they do lockouts and strikes. Peace has allowed for a significant increase in TV ratings and rights fees as well as a major increase in licensing and merchandise revenue and sponsorship dollars.

The Third Inning: Addressing Economic and Competitive Imbalance

A true baseball man like Bill Giles understands the importance of "hope" to a fan. Giles and Selig have echoed the same mantra that the economic success of a baseball team requires that the team's fans have "hope" that their team can compete and has a reasonable chance of reaching the postseason. The report of Selig's Blue Ribbon Panel pointed this out as well and lamented the competitive state of the game as revenue disparity among franchises exploded during the 1990s. The big-revenue teams, such as the Braves and the Yankees, dominated, and the small-market or at least small-revenue teams that could not afford to keep their best players when they reached free agency gave their fans little hope. The report recommended expanded revenue sharing and a competitive balance tax. Fortunately for baseball, that is what the 2002 CBA provided.

Giles contends that "the main reason why baseball has become financially healthy is because the 2002 labor agreement provided for revenue-sharing, which has helped foster competitive balance, the luxury tax, which has discouraged teams from spending too much on payroll, and the debt limit."[14]

Debt Limits for Individual Clubs

I discuss the debt limit in the labor chapters. The players see the debt limit as a drag on salaries, and the owners see it as a limit on spending. The original debt limit was pegged at a 60–40 ratio, meaning that a club has to maintain a ratio of 60 percent assets to 40 percent liabilities. The 2002 CBA changed the debt rule to a ratio of debt to EBITDA: a club may not have more debt than ten times EBIDTA, that is, earnings before interest, depreciation, taxes, and amortization, based on a three-year average. There is an exception for teams that have recently constructed new facilities; a team that has moved into a newly constructed ballpark within the past ten years may not have more debt than fifteen times EBIDTA. This rule was retained "with modifications" during the next round of negotiations in 2006. For the latest CBA, in effect from 2011 to 2016, the EBITDA multiplier is lowered from ten to eight and from fifteen to twelve for teams with stadium debt.

According to Giles, "The debt limit is valuable because teams, including the Phillies, used to say to themselves, 'Yes, I'll sign this player and my revenue will go up by $10 million. I'll lose $10 million and I just borrowed to cover the loss but the value of my franchise went up by about 2½ times the revenue growth, so I am up $25 million.' The debt limit prevents this type of behavior."[15]

Revenue Sharing

In an interview published in fall 2003, one season into the 2002 CBA, Selig said, "When I took over we [the twenty-eight clubs] were sharing less than $20 million. [The American League had shared 20 percent of ticket receipts, the National League only 5 percent.] Look at how that has grown because all the clubs, big-market clubs and medium and small, all had confidence that I in the end was going to do the right thing." By 2003, baseball was sharing $230 million in revenue, and this number was scheduled to reach $300 million in 2004.[16]

As I discuss in the labor chapters, revenue sharing was a divisive issue and the concept was not embraced willingly by some owners. George Steinbrenner used to characterize the revenue sharing system as "socialism." The confidential financial statements that Deadspin.com released in 2008 showed that teams such as the Marlins and the Pirates, the biggest recipients of revenue sharing dollars, were among the most profitable teams in baseball. John Henry, owner of the Red Sox, decries the fact that the Red Sox have had to contribute so much of their revenue to teams like the Pirates that have used the money to pay down debt instead of investing in players and player development and, in fact, has suggested that the revenue sharing model be overhauled.[17] Nevertheless, revenue sharing has created a new fiscal environment for baseball.

Critics of the plan that emerged from the 2002 labor agreement point out that teams in low-revenue markets were rewarded financially for making their teams weaker and that the plan created a disincentive to fielding a better team and raising revenue as more money coming in from tickets meant less money coming in from the shared pool of MLB revenues.

Lower-revenue teams paid a marginal rate of 48 percent of local revenues into the shared pool, while high-revenue teams paid 40 percent.[18]

The 2006 CBA reduced the marginal tax rate from 34 percent to 31 percent and allowed lower-revenue teams to retain more of the revenues generated by fielding a stronger team. In addition, a portion of MLB's central fund, which included revenues from sources such as national broadcast contracts, licensing agreements, and sponsorships, was disproportionately allocated to teams based on their relative revenues, so lower-revenue teams received higher shares. The revisions to the revenue sharing plan contained in the 2006 CBA were designed to create an incentive for teams to invest in improving their clubs as opposed to either paying down debt or letting the proceeds drop to the bottom line.

Despite some of the inherent weaknesses in the structure of revenue sharing, in the years since the 2002 CBA was approved, competitive balance has improved. Life remains difficult for teams that compete with the Yankees and Red Sox and for small-revenue teams such as Pittsburgh and Kansas City. Recently, in an attempt to build from within, the Royals have begun to assemble a strong farm system. The Pirates improved dramatically in 2012, before fading late in the season, and in 2013 the team battled the Cardinals for supremacy in one of baseball's strongest divisions, the National League Central. Fans in those cities definitely have more hope now than in the past.

Since 2002, three teams have won more than one World Championship: Boston, with three, including 2013, and St. Louis and San Francisco, each with two. Boston is the seventh-largest television market; the Bay Area, including Oakland, is sixth; and St. Louis is 21st. Between 2003 and 2011, when baseball sent four teams in each league to the postseason, ten different American League teams and fourteen different National League teams made the postseason. Only Baltimore, Toronto, Kansas City, and Seattle failed to make the postseason in the American League, and only Pittsburgh and Washington, transplanted from Montreal, were left out in the National League. In 2012, Baltimore in the American League and the Nationals in the National League created a great deal of excitement for their fans, and both made it to the postseason, and Pittsburgh made the postseason in 2013.

From 2003 to 2013, six different teams in each league have won pennants. Baseball hasn't seen such an array of postseason participants since the 1980s, when free agency improved competitive balance from what it had been earlier. Selig commented, "Without revenue-sharing, baseball wouldn't look like it does today." Without revenue-sharing, he contends, teams from small markets like Detroit, Cincinnati, Milwaukee, Minnesota, and Oakland would be nowhere.[19]

The Fourth Inning: New Ballparks

Why did Bill Giles return from a visit to Baltimore twenty-two years ago with the notion that his team's future economic success depended on finding the wherewithal to construct a new, baseball-only ballpark in Philadelphia? In retrospect, the answer is obvious. Soon after it opened, Oriole Park at Camden Yards became a showcase for baseball and for the City of Baltimore. This first-of-a-kind retro-style ballpark with all of the modern amenities served as a financial engine for the Orioles, thus creating an incentive for other teams, typically supported by hundreds of millions of public dollars, to invest in new facilities. Most of these new ballparks, mainly following the lead of Camden Yards, were designed by HOK Sports, the Kansas City–based architecture firm. HOK designed nineteen of baseball's new or retrofitted stadiums.

These new ballparks had several elements in common. According to executives at HOK Sports, the new parks invariably led to "soaring sales of higher-priced tickets, concessions, and advertising at new theme-park style stadiums." Their designs routinely increased square footage by up to 50 percent over earlier ballparks to make room for amenities and revenue generators. As an HOK executive told Business 2.0: "The event [baseball] is in the background. The foreground is all these other activities. It's 'I need to buy a sweater' or 'There's a beer garden.'"[20] The new ballparks provide naming rights opportunities and often feature enhanced sponsorship opportunities for attractions such as the Acela and Delta Club Patios at Citi Field in New York, the Majestic Clubhouse Store at Citizens Bank Park, and similarly sponsored attractions at many of the new facilities.

New ballparks have created energy and excitement on the part of fans. Only Fenway Park and Wrigley Field now remain of the great old ballparks, and both have reached iconic status because of the traditions and old-time feel they embody. The new parks, starting with Camden Yards, have allowed fans to experience the ambience formerly found only in the old jewel ballparks, but with modern amenities that significantly enhance the fan experience. Beyond the comfortable seats, wide concourses, retail space, and theme park attractions, nearly all of the new facilities have fewer seats than the stadiums they replaced. The twenty new ballparks that have opened since 1992 have more than 200,000 fewer seats than the older facilities they replaced. Smaller seating areas create intimacy, provide better sightlines, and enhance the energy of the crowd in a ballpark that is filled versus one that is half-empty. This is precisely why Bill Giles wanted his new ballpark to have no more than 42–43 thousand seats.

The Fifth Inning: Television Dollars

After years of having a difficult relationship with baseball, television has become enamored with our national pastime. There are two reasons for this. First, baseball provides the largest television and digital inventory of any of the major sports because of the sheer number of games played. Second, in an era when live sports programs represent the ultimate content in a reality television world, baseball provides networks with a plethora of both games and highlights. Television executives and advertisers have discovered that live sports are the only content that is immune to the digital video recorder (DVR) culture. Any other program can be recorded and viewed later—either online or via DVR—without the commercials. But sports are still best viewed live, even if it means sitting through the commercials. As a result, MLB benefits from increasingly large rights fees from national, regional, and local networks.

Another reason why television loves baseball is that, in the age of DVRs and digital fragmentation, baseball presents a captive audience for a game that provides plenty of time to look around. The more than 70 million people who attend major league games have time to view ballpark signage, and the millions more watching on TV get a chance to look at lots of virtual advertising displayed behind home plate. This in-stadium signage also shows up on both television and Internet sports highlights. Teams have added advertising space and flexibility, with giant scoreboards that routinely feature high-definition video screens playing thirty-second spots, plus programmable LED boards that encircle the stadium and changing signage behind home plate that is sold by the half-inning.[21]

An analysis of the economics of baseball since free agency makes two things eminently clear. First, as Jerry Reinsdorf would frequently say, before the ink is dry on national and local television deals, the owners have spent the money. Second, every time it seems that baseball revenue is flattening, the game finds a new source of revenue. A few years ago, baseball reached the $6 billion mark in total revenue, the new stadium building boom had begun to run its course, and it seemed that no new revenue streams loomed on the horizon. I asked Giles where he envisioned that any significant new revenue might come from. He pointed to two key potential sources of new money: revenues generated by baseball outside the United States, primarily from television and licensed merchandise, and distribution of digital properties. He felt that both could contribute, but had limited potential. Even Bill Giles, a guy who had been an innovator with TV deals in his time, did not envision the heights to which television dollars might rise.

In the ten-plus years since George Steinbrenner and his allies created the YES Network, it has become clear that sports programming represents the last bastion, so to speak, of live television, resulting in expanding local and national revenues and booming franchise valuations. The clubs have used their new deals, or new deals on the horizon, to make huge offers to free agents.

In 2011, the Texas Rangers and the Los Angeles Angels underwrote massive free agent commitments to Yu Darvish, Albert Pujols, and C. J. Wilson, with twenty-year local TV deals reported to be worth $150 million per year for Texas and a bit more for the Angels. The Angels announced a deal with Fox Sports West shortly after the news of the ten-year agreement with Pujols became public, and the entire $317 million commitment to Pujols and Wilson is covered by roughly two years of the value of their TV deal.

In 2012, Frank McCourt sold the Dodgers, much to the relief of Dodgers fans and Bud Selig. The new ownership group paid $2.15 billion for the franchise, including Dodger Stadium, and then went on a spending spree to upgrade the club. The Dodgers traded for Hanley Ramirez, Adrian Gonzalez, Carl Crawford, and Josh Beckett during the 2012 season and signed free agent pitchers Zack Greinke and Hyun-Jin Ryu during the off-season. The club's payroll exceeded $220 million in 2013, and the new ownership group—Guggenheim Baseball Management—has taken on more than $600 million in salary obligations since purchasing the team. Why and how did this happen? Fox Sports and Time Warner Cable competed for the Dodgers' new local television deal and eventually the Dodgers agreed to a twenty-five-year contract with Time Warner for more than $7 billion, more than three times what the owners paid for the ball club and Dodger Stadium. The Dodgers can afford to be in Yankees territory with player payrolls and likely will exceed the Yankees in payroll by 2014, all fueled by television dollars.

The Phillies enjoy a regional TV audience second only to that of the New York Yankees, and the Phillies' new local TV deal is worth multiples of its current deal, which runs out after the 2015 season.

The Phillies, according to *Forbes*, netted $24 million from their TV rights contracts with Comcast and PHL17 during the 2010 season. The Phillies also profit from TV advertising sales, which they still handle in-house, to avoid sponsor conflicts in ballpark signage. The amount that the Phillies earn from those sales is unknown. In their new local TV deal, the Phillies will increase rights fees plus split the advertising sales with Comcast SportsNet. An additional element of the deal is that the Phillies pick up an equity interest in the network. The new deal will at least triple their existing local television revenues.[22]

For nine straight seasons, the Phillies' local ratings had risen. Over that period, the growth was 176 percent. In San Diego, where the Padres signed a deal with Fox that could average $75 million per year over the life of the contract, the local ratings decreased 41 percent from 2010 to 2011.[23] San Diego is the 26th largest market in baseball. Their 2011 local TV ratings were 3.15, slightly more than one-third of the Phillies' local ratings of 9.12. In Houston, the Astros will earn an average of $80 million a year beginning in 2013 through a joint venture operation with Comcast. The Astros had baseball's worst local ratings in 2011.[24]

Beyond the deals that individual clubs are negotiating with Regional Sports Networks (RSNs) in various markets, team-owned RSNs have helped redefine the television landscape and are dramatically changing the economics of the game. Unlike a traditional fixed rights fee arrangement, having an ownership stake in an RSN reconnects a club's broadcast revenues to its on-field performance. Beyond the impact on revenues, the RSN is an asset whose value fluctuates depending on the team's on-field performance. A regional sports network can be a significant source of capital for teams, such as the Yankees and Dodgers, to continue to invest in expensive free agents and carry a large payroll. For example, the News Corporation (Fox Sports), for the purposes of negotiating to buy a 49 percent share in the YES Network, valued YES at $3.4 billion as of November 2012.[25] RSNs also contribute significantly to a team's efforts to build its brand through team-related programming. Zimbalist noted, "Since the late 1980s RSNs have been a powerful force boosting team revenues, particularly those in the larger markets. When the team owners also own RSNs, it can be a source of extraordinary revenue advantage."[26]

MLB's national television contracts that ran through 2013 generated annual rights fees totaling $711.7 million from ESPN, Fox, and Turner. Taking advantage of the mega-deals available to purveyors of live sports events, Major League Baseball inked separate eight-year media rights extensions with Fox Sports and Turner Broadcasting System that begin with the 2014 season and will pay a total of $6.8 billion. Baseball had previously renewed its deal with ESPN for $5.6 billion, covering the same period. MLB is now guaranteed a total of $12.4 billion in revenue from these three broadcast partners through 2021, an amount that is more than double the $5.2 billion with its current contracts.[27]

Unlike the NFL, major league baseball for television purposes is a regional enterprise. For the most part, fans are interested in their own club; they want to watch their local teams. Fans move to different cities, both temporarily as they travel and permanently as they relocate, but true fans tend to maintain original loyalties. Fans who want to watch teams other than the hometown team can buy subscriptions to Baseball's Extra Innings out-of-town television package to watch games on TV or MLB At Bat to watch video streams of games on a computer or personal digital device. These products have provided fans the ability to watch their favorite team, regardless of where the team is playing, subject to local blackouts, and have been moneymakers for MLB. Baseball secured $700 million over seven years from DirecTV and top cable operators in April 2007 for the Extra Innings package. According to media experts, the deal also paved the way for MLB Network's 2009 debut to be the most successful launch in cable history.[28] As Bill Giles concluded in our discussion of baseball's TV deals, the biggest change he has witnessed in his life in baseball is the relationship between baseball and television, extended now to include digital media.

The Sixth Inning: Major League Baseball Advanced Media

MLBAM, or simply "BAM," is a company that was formed in June 2000. The owners, at the urging of Selig and Jerry Reinsdorf, voted 30–0 to consolidate their Internet rights and sites into one equally shared and centrally operated entity. Each team contributed less than $3 million to the startup, and BAM has exceeded all but the most optimistic expectations. CEO Bob Bowman indicated in May 2012 that BAM had surpassed the $620 million mark in annual revenues.[29]

BAM began under the leadership of Bob DuPuy, who served as chairman of the company until his departure from baseball in 2010. Before the formation of BAM, teams had individually developed, designed, and operated their websites. In voting to centralize all rights, owners sacrificed individuality for the good of the group, reminiscent of the way in which the NFL decided under Pete Rozelle to share revenues from national television equally. The common design and format of the league (MLB.com) and individual club websites created significant synergy and helped build the MLB brand.

BAM provides MLB with a way to connect with fans on multiple levels and for a multitude of products. Visitors to the MLB.com website can find news about major league baseball and its individual clubs, including schedules, standings, and statistics from around MLB. Fans can shop the website to buy merchandise. MLB.com provides a ticket marketplace for both the primary and secondary ticket markets. BAM sells subscriptions for both radio broadcasts and live game video, plus game highlights. MLB.com links to the MLB Network and shows snippets of its programming and also connects to the Fan Cave, which I describe in "The Tenth Inning." Real baseball fans love "Game Day," which allows them to follow games pitch by pitch, tracking each pitch type (fastball versus curve, for instance), velocity, trajectory, and location relative to the strike zone, plus the result of each batted ball, while maintaining all game and player statistics.

During the season, MLB.com receives about 8 million unique visitors per day, sells more than half a million season subscriptions of live game video at $80 to $120 a pop, and streams nearly 3 million videos a day. BAM's digital expertise has led many outside agencies and events to have BAM handle their web traffic; BAM manages content for numerous online affiliates, including the NCAA basketball tournament and the French Open.

The first big turning point for BAM occurred during the 2002 season, when BAM launched MLB.TV, its first out-of-market game package. For the first time, fans could watch live games online. To this day, live game streaming is the core around which much of the company is built. Both the traffic on MLB.com and the distribution of digital media products appeal to those 25–49 years old as well as baseball fans from other countries. DuPuy recalled, "We felt very strongly there was a significant place for the sport on the Internet. And now with this content, particularly the live games, it's unquestionably helped baseball become more international and more relevant to younger audiences, both of which were and still are major priorities."[30]

MLBAM purchased Tickets.com in 2005, enhancing its capacity for selling tickets and facilitating its entry into the secondary ticket market. In 2007, it introduced mobile tickets, by which a bar code and all of the pertinent information can be sent to the fan's cell phone. At least one-third of all tickets sold are sold online through baseball's website. MLB has entered into different partnerships designed to make ticket sales more convenient and more responsive to marketing conditions, and it recently established the capability to offer dynamic pricing.

Giles commented on how baseball's marketing has changed in the new century, indicating that the Internet and digital media have made a huge difference. He gave an example of how the Internet has changed ticket sales and distribution:

> When we had the [World Championship] parade [in 2008], we filled up both our ballpark and the Eagles' stadium by distributing free tickets. We were able to disseminate about 80,000 tickets in thirty minutes because of the computer. It is so convenient to get tickets now. When I was president and we were at the Vet, I used to measure interest in the Phillies by how many people were lined up at the ticket windows on Pattison Avenue. Now, maybe there

> are ten all day because almost everybody goes online or uses the phone. And it's so easy to communicate with people to tell them we have a giveaway on this date or that a game time has changed or tonight's game is rained out.[31]

To better control and serve the secondary ticket market, BAM in 2007 entered into a five-year partnership with eBay subsidiary StubHub, an agreement that allowed StubHub to handle all of the league's online ticket resales. The partnership included twenty-nine MLB teams, all except the Red Sox, although they eventually joined in. Many of the teams then negotiated sponsorship deals with StubHub, including signs to promote the ticket reseller in their ballparks. Some clubs, including the Chicago Cubs, listed StubHub under the ticket navigation bar on their websites.

In December 2012, BAM and StubHub announced a new five-year deal. The deal continues the website's role as the official secondary ticket market for the sport while eliminating the cheap ticket listings that had become problematic for some clubs by potentially cannibalizing sales in the primary market. The minimum price for baseball tickets on StubHub in 2013 was $6, a far more appealing number for the league after some seats were listed for pocket change during the first five-year deal that expired after the previous season.

BAM's ticketing operation serves and protects fans who purchase tickets on both the primary and secondary markets. Moreover, the convenience and timeliness of the sale and distribution system leads to fewer unused tickets and higher attendance, with more fans in the ballpark exposed to advertising and signage. Having more people in the ballpark also creates greater potential for sales of concessions and merchandise.

In 2008, Apple opened its App Store to third-party developers. BAM developers took advantage of this key opportunity and developed MLB.com At Bat, an application that delivers live games, news, and analysis from the "Hot Stove," as well as current and archived highlights. At Bat works on most Apple mobile devices and, according to mlb.com, is considered the "Number one sports app of all time."

In an in-depth 2011 article in *Sports Business Journal*, Eric Fisher pointed out:

> MLBAM is now widely considered the gold standard of online sports operations. With expertise in nearly every major element of digital sports, the company has built a potent blend of paid and free content, advertising, online commerce, ticketing, analytics, and a fast-growing technology component supporting live online

> streaming for third parties such as ESPN, Turner, and CBS Sports. BAM streams the BCS Championship game for ESPN and all of the NCAA tournament games for Turner and CBS Sports. As a result, MLBAM is now at the front of the line with nearly every major advance in the industry, and is seeking to accelerate not only its technological capabilities but also its revenue growth.[32]

In discussing his operation, Bob Bowman said, "We take what's already great content, called a baseball game, and we try to present it on every device as best as possible and in as high a quality as we can in an economically rational basis. If you look at what we're proudest of, it's our [site] traffic."[33] Bowman expressed his satisfaction with MLBAM's achievements, saying, "Rights fees are up, attendance is up, viewership is up. Somehow the strategy of putting [baseball games] on every device that has a plug or a battery has worked for the business partners. Even more important, it's worked for our fans."[34]

With more than $600 million in revenue split equally among the thirty clubs, BAM has also made a contribution to baseball's attempts to give small-revenue clubs a break. MLBAM is a true success story for baseball. Bud Selig has said that MLBAM is "not only one of the great stories in American sports business in the past twelve years, but one of the great stories in American business."[35]

The Seventh Inning: Expanding Baseball's Global Footprint: International Baseball and the World Baseball Classic

Don Fehr, during his more than two decades in charge of the players' union, had an often adversarial relationship with Bud Selig. Selig and Fehr disagreed on issues from revenue sharing to players' use of performance-enhancing drugs. But one issue brought the players and owners, and Fehr and Selig, together—building baseball's global footprint. Fehr, like Selig, understood that growing the game was good for everyone. They agreed on the merits of expanding baseball beyond U.S. shores much more aggressively. Together they pushed the idea of a global baseball tournament that would feature the most outstanding stars in the game, including many of the best major leaguers. In one shining example of player-owner cooperation, MLB created the World Baseball Classic, which was inaugurated in 2006. The effort received a major push when the Olympic Committee decided to discontinue baseball as an Olympic sport.

The first tournament in 2006 achieved notable success, although Americans exhibited less interest than baseball fans in Japan and Latin

America. The thirty-nine-game event garnered total attendance of 737,112, above expected TV ratings and net profits in the range of $10 million.[36] The World Baseball Classic ran for the second time in 2009, with total attendance rising to more than 801,000. According to Bizof-Baseball.com, domestic television ratings for the 2009 Round one games broadcast on ESPN averaged a 1.3 rating, up more than 40 percent from 2006. The four games averaged 1,745,000 viewers, up almost 90 percent compared with 2006 Round one games. The Japan versus South Korea final game had ratings higher than the deciding game of the previous World Series.

The third edition of the World Baseball Classic was played in spring 2013, with some changes to the format. Sixteen teams comprised the brackets, as had been the case in the previous editions, but only the twelve countries that won games in the 2009 World Baseball Classic were guaranteed a spot in the tournament. The other four countries had to qualify in 2012 via a series of double elimination tournaments. By having a qualifying round, the International Baseball Federation expanded the field to a total of twenty-eight countries, sixteen of which played in the March 2013 tournament. The team from the Dominican Republic ran the table, finishing with an 8–0 record and winning the 2013 edition of the World Baseball Classic.

According to MLB.com, "The 2013 World Baseball Classic set records in attendance, licensing, viewership and sponsorship sales and social media activity as the tournament continued its mission of growing the sport of baseball around the world. Overall, the tournament drew a total attendance of 885,212, which surpassed the 2009 World Baseball Classic top total of 801,410 by more than 10%."[37]

Beyond the World Baseball Classic, baseball has continued to expand its global footprint and the World Series has become much more a true "World" Series as developments in satellite technology have allowed MLB to export the game even more aggressively. The World Series was broadcast in twenty countries in 1987 and by 2003 was broadcast in 224 countries. The event has become a platform for companies that sponsor baseball outside the United States. Promotions tied to the World Series have dramatically increased the visibility of MLB globally, "putting baseball in front of consumers at banks, grocery stores and other retail outlets."[38]

While baseball laments the decline in the number of African American players, African Americans have been replaced by players from multiple countries, cultures, and ethnicities. According to MLB.com, players from fifteen different countries comprised major league opening day rosters in 2012. Of 856 players (both active and inactive), 243 were born outside the United States, or 28.4 percent, the highest figure in history. Latin America has been a hotbed of baseball for decades, as has Japan. Now there is interest throughout the Pacific Rim, including Korea, China, and Australia. Baseball has staked out a position in Europe, and in 2012, for the first time, a player who was born and developed in Italy made a major league roster.

As we have witnessed, exciting players such as Fernando Valenzuela, Ichiro Suzuki, and other foreign-born stars significantly enhance interest in major league baseball in their native countries, which drives television viewership, merchandise sales, and sponsorship dollars.

The Eighth Inning: Scheduling: Three Divisions, the Wild Card, Expanded Postseason, and Interleague Play

Another factor behind the attendance boom is an innovation championed by Selig that once drew considerable criticism—divisional play and the wild card system. Even when some teams run away with their divisions, the wild-card format keeps others in the playoff hunt, resulting in continued fan interest. Baseball's national television audiences tend to be much larger in the postseason, and more postseason games means more revenue.

For the 2012 season, baseball expanded the postseason by adding a "play-in" game between the two wild card teams in each league. Although some critics took baseball to task for the suddenness of the departure of the two losing teams—one and done after the rigors of a 162-game season—the addition of a second wild-card team helped maintain interest, and hope, in a number of cities that would have found their teams eliminated from the possibility of postseason play at an earlier date.

Interleague Play

Bud Selig and Bill Giles both pushed for interleague play. By virtually every measure, interleague play has been a success, especially in terms of attendance, which has been as much as 21 percent higher than for intraleague games during some seasons. As Bud Selig said, "Bill Veeck and Hank Greenberg, who were talking about how we should do this years ago, they were right. Look at it now. Up 21% this year [2003] for interleague play. New rivalries have been created. What it does is it intensifies interest in the game."[39]

Some argue that the advent of interleague play has cheapened the World Series and especially the All-Star Game, but no more than interconference play in the NFL cheapens the Super Bowl. Bud Selig believes that baseball must respect its traditions but cannot be mired in the past. Interleague play, particularly intracity rivalries such as the Yankees versus the Mets, the Cubs versus the White Sox, the Dodgers versus the Angels, even including the Giants versus the A's, has really heightened fan interest. Teams that have national appeal, such as the Yankees and the Red Sox, raise attendance everywhere they go in the National League. I recall the excitement in Pittsburgh when the Yankees visited the Pirates in 2008, the first time the Yankees had played in Pittsburgh since Bill Mazeroski's famous walk-off home run to end the 1960 World Series.

The interleague experiment, introduced in 1997 for one year, has become institutionalized. The 2013 season was the 17th season of interleague play and introduced a new wrinkle—interleague play all season instead of during designated "interleague periods"—as the Astros move to the American League and balance the leagues at fifteen teams each. Interestingly, the idea of two fifteen-team leagues has been around since the mid-1990s, when MLB assigned the last two expansion franchises to Phoenix, Arizona, and Tampa Bay–St. Petersburg, Florida. At that time, Giles had advocated two fifteen-team leagues as an option during the realignment discussions that took place among the owners.

The Ninth Inning: Exciting Young Players Vitalize the Game

Ultimately, baseball's success as sport, cultural institution, and economic entity depends on what happens on the field. Memorable players, plays, games, and pennant races capture fans and their emotions. The eleven seasons since the end of 2002 have introduced baseball fans to a host of exciting young players, some of whom are aging veterans now, including Mark Texeira and Miguel Cabrera from the class of 2002. Great players, such as Robinson Cano, Justin Verlander, Prince Fielder, Matt Cain, and Tim Lincecum, joined baseball in 2005 and 2006.

In 2008, Joey Votto and Evan Longoria joined the Reds and the Rays, respectively, and rising star Andrew McCutcheon, the National League Most Valuable Player in 2013, came on the scene in 2009. Buster Posey, who has helped the Giants to win two World Championships during his brief career, came to San Francisco in 2010, the same year that Jason Heyward came to Atlanta. In the last few seasons, we have seen the ascensions of Matt Kemp, Pablo Sandoval, Wade Miley, and especially Stephen Strasburg, Bryce Harper, and Mike Trout. Yasiel Puig made a huge splash with the Dodgers in 2013. Puig, Strasburg, Harper, and Trout promise to excite fans in their hometowns of Los Angeles and Washington, D.C., barring injury (and the Nationals took a lot of criticism for putting Strasburg on an innings count in 2012), for years to come.

These young players not only have excelled on the field but also have become key parts of baseball's social media efforts and fantasy baseball, two elements that really create interest on the part of the younger demographic, which is absolutely key to baseball's future.

The Tenth Inning: The MLB Fan Cave

Major League Baseball's website includes a welcome to MLBFanCave.com, where new videos, photos, and blogs featuring baseball's biggest stars, along with celebrities, musical acts, and other guests, are posted every day, allowing fans to interact with the game in an entirely new way. Baseball describes the MLB Fan Cave, located at 4th Street and Broadway, in the heart of New York City's Greenwich Village, as a "first-of-its-kind space, mixing baseball with music, popular culture, media, interactive technology and art."[40]

The MLB Fan Cave, created in 2012, hosts fan events, concerts, and MLB player and celebrity appearances, plus the "Cave Dwellers," whose task it is to watch every game of the season while chronicling their experiences online through videos, blogs, and social media. At the same time, they compete with one another in a series of challenges, with fans online helping decide who gets to stay in the MLB Fan Cave and who gets eliminated, with one eventual winner crowned before the end of the World Series. Fans can follow all of the activity on Facebook and Twitter and, like *American Idol* and other reality shows, vote for their favorite Cave Dweller.[41]

The goal of the MLB Fan Cave is to promote baseball via social media and engage the demographic that uses social media frequently, which obviously skews substantially younger than baseball's traditional audience. While the Super Bowl had a social media command center for the game itself, MLB, under the innovative leadership of Tim Brosnan, took over a former Tower Records Store at 4th and Broadway in Lower Manhattan. Players, celebrities, and musicians stop by the Fan Cave to create video content and more that is distributed via Twitter and Facebook. The Fan Cave is integrated with broadcast partners, including FOX, ESPN, TBS, and MLB Network, and they use content from the Fan Cave as a means of reaching fans via social media.

In an interview with Lostremote.com, Brosnan explained why MLB pushed the development of the Fan Cave and what the Fan Cave is doing for MLB. According to Brosnan, "The MLB Fan Cave grew out of our desire to address three specific areas in which we saw opportunity for growth: engaging with fans via social media, both at the league level and through players; reaching younger fans and converting casual baseball fans into more avid followers; and raising the profile of our players by showcasing their off-field personalities." Brosnan went on to say, "We all know how important the second screen has become to people while watching live sports on TV. The MLB Fan Cave allows us to tap into that digital water cooler, giving fans a platform to engage with baseball 24/7." Finally, the Fan Cave "is accomplishing all our goals and then some. We have successfully reached a younger audience, as the average fan of the Fan Cave is 30 years old compared with 45–48 for the typical avid baseball fan. We have reached a highly engaged audience via social media, as more than a third of our Facebook followers have liked or shared a piece of content, up to six times the usual rate for sports pages."[42]

The Last Word

Major League Baseball has reached monumental heights in popularity, attendance, and revenues. Commissioner Selig's vision and approach to getting things done, combined with the basic attractiveness of live sports to television, are two of the main reasons. In this, the final chapter, I have attempted to identify key factors that have moved baseball from a state of economic difficulty to one where franchises are worth in the billions of dollars. With the new national and local TV deals, both those that have been signed and those to come, the future looks even brighter. If only the Cubs can one day win a World Championship . . .

Notes

Chapter 1: A Rapid-Fire Exposition of the Business of Baseball from the Beginning to 1981

1. Robert F. Burk, *Much More Than a Game: Players, Owners, and American Baseball since 1921* (Chapel Hill, NC: University of North Carolina Press, 2001), 109–110.

2. Stanley Glenn, Presentation at Saint Joseph's University, Philadelphia, PA, March 15, 2007.

3. David Mandell, "Danny Gardella and the Reserve Clause," *The National Pastime*, No. 26 (2006), 41–44.

4. Available at http://supreme.justia.com/cases/federal/us/346/356/case.html.

5. Available at http://a.espncdn.com/mlb/columns/bp/1427632.html.

Chapter 2: Bill Giles and Major League Baseball's Network TV Deals, 1983–1995

1. Jeff Friedman, "The Impact of Major League Baseball's Local Television Contracts," *Sports Lawyers Journal*, Spring 2003.

2. Robert V. Bellamy Jr. and James R. Walker, "Baseball and Television Origins: The Case of the Cubs," *Nine*, September 22, 2001.

3. John Helyar, *Lords of the Realm: The Real History of Baseball* (New York: Ballantine Books, 1994), 391.

4. Ibid.

5. Bowie Kuhn, *Hardball: The Education of a Baseball Commissioner* (Lincoln, NE: University of Nebraska Press, 1997), 287.

6. Bill Giles and Doug Myers, *Pouring Six Beers at a Time: And Other Stories from a Lifetime in Baseball* (Chicago: Triumph Books, 2007), 286.

7. Kuhn, *Hardball*, 287.

8. Helyar, *Lords of the Realm*, 394.

9. Interview with Eddie Einhorn, July 2, 2012.

10. Giles and Myers, *Pouring Six Beers at a Time*, 287.

11. Helyar, *Lords of the Realm*, 396.

12. Ibid., 397.

13. Interview with Eddie Einhorn, July 2, 2012.

14. Interview with Bill Giles, July 21, 2010.

15. Ibid.

16. Available at http://www.forbes.com/sites/kurtbadenhausen/2012/11/09/why-espn-is-the-worlds-most-valuable-media-property-and-worth-40-billion.

17. Dave van Dyck, "Baseball Mulls Own TV Network," *Chicago Sun-Times*, April 26, 1987.

18. Interview with Eddie Einhorn, July 2, 2012.

19. Interview with Bill Giles, August 6, 2010.

20. Giles and Myers, *Pouring Six Beers at a Time*, 290.

21. Interview with Bill Giles, July 21, 2010.

22. Jack Craig, "Ueberroth Tackles the TV Issue," *Boston Globe*, February 21, 1987.

23. Jack Craig, "A Ueberroth Nomination May Blow Cable Deal," *Boston Globe*, August 14, 1988.

24. Interview with Bill Giles, June 22, 2010.

25. Interview with Eddie Einhorn, July 2, 2012.

26. Helyar, *Lords of the Realm*, 412.

27. Andrew Zimbalist, *Baseball and Billions: A Probing Look inside the Big Business of Our National Pastime* (New York: Basic Books, 1992), 158.

28. Jack Sands and Peter Gammons, *Coming Apart at the Seams: How Baseball Owners, Players, and Television Executives Have Led Our National Pastime to the Brink of Disaster* (New York: Macmillan, 1993), 90.

29. Joseph Durso, "A Billion-Dollar Bid by CBS Wins Rights to Baseball Games," *New York Times*, December 15, 1988.

30. Ibid.

31. Martin Tolchin, "The Media Business; Leagues Get Warning on Cable Deals," *New York Times*, November 15, 1989.

32. Mark Maske, "Notebook; CBS's Fiscal Headaches May Spread to Players," *Washington Post*, May 12, 1991.

33. Sands and Gammons, *Coming Apart at the Seams*, 169.

34. Mark Potts, "Bonilla Deal Continues a Trend; Baseball Executives See Widening Gap Between Rich, Poor Teams," *Washington Post*, December 4, 1991.

35. Richard Sandomir, "World Series: When Ailing Pastime Meets TV Recession, Baseball Gets the K," *New York Times*, October 21, 1992.

36. "Networks Not Willing to Pay Enormous Fees," *Chicago Sun-Times*, January 18, 1993.

37. Sandomir, "World Series."

38. Geoffrey Foisie, "Revenue Sharing: Baseball, Networks Consider Teamwork," *Broadcasting & Cable*, March 29, 1993.

39. Richard Sandomir, "Baseball Breaks with Its Television Past," *New York Times*, May 9, 1993.

40. Steve McClellan, "Fear of Falling Fees, Ratings Haunt MLB," *Broadcasting & Cable*, March 15, 1993.

41. Leonard Shapiro, "Ratings Sink as Low as Baseball's Spirit," *Washington Post*, May 28, 1993.

42. Dave van Dyck, "Buying into Selling Game," *Chicago Sun-Times,* May 10, 1993.

43. Jack Craig, "Baseball Strikes Six-Year Joint Deal with ABC, NBC," *Boston Globe,* May 9, 1993.

44. "Baseball, TV Strike Deal; More Playoffs," *Chicago Sun-Times,* May 9, 1993.

45. Jayson Stark, "Baseball on TV Won't Be the Baseball that You're Used to; The Picture Tube Will Still Be the Same Shape (Probably). Very Little Else Will Be Familiar, However," *Philadelphia Inquirer,* April 2, 1994.

46. Jack Craig, "Fans Take a Hit in Baseball Deal," *Boston Globe,* May 11, 1993.

47. Claire Smith, "Baseball; Baseball Flips Channel on TV Future," *New York Times,* May 29, 1993.

48. Craig, "Fans Take a Hit."

49. Thomas R. Umstead, "PPV Strikes out on Baseball TV Contract," *Multichannel News,* June 7, 1993.

50. Jack Craig, "Selig: PPV Not in Plans," *Boston Globe,* June 7, 1993.

51. "Baseball Held Hostage—Part II: TBN's Survival Watch," *Sports Business Daily,* February 23, 1995.

52. Jack Craig, "Talk May Be Cheap, But Parcells' Won't Be," *Boston Globe,* September 2, 1994.

53. Leonard Shapiro, "To Many Fans, TV Strikes out," *Washington Post,* October 6, 1995.

54. Ibid.

55. Richard Sandomir, "Baseball: Baseball Seeks a Loophole for TV Talks," *Washington Post,* June 28, 1995.

56. "Around the Majors," *Washington Post,* July 14, 1995.

57. Sam Donnellon, "Foxed in with TV, Deal Dead, Owners Look to Fox," *Philadelphia Daily News,* June 27, 1995.

58. Jayson Stark, "Giles Grimly Counts the Losses. The Phillies President Paints a Bleak Financial Picture. But the Fans are Lining up in Florida," *Philadelphia Inquirer,* April 11, 1995.

59. "Baseball Hires IMG's Frank to Negotiate New TV Deal," *Sports Business Daily,* July 14, 1995.

60. Richard Sandomir, "TV Sports; Baseball Learns That It's Still Loved," *New York Times,* October 9, 1995.

61. "MLB to Announce Deal Today: Pact Boosts Team Revenue to $10M," *Sports Business Daily,* November 6, 1995.

62. Ibid.

63. Robert Kurson, "Baseball Strikes New TV Contract," *Chicago Sun-Times,* November 7, 1995.

64. James McConville, "Fox, CBS Swinging for Baseball," *Broadcasting & Cable,* October 23, 1995.

65. "MLB Goes Deep in TV Deals; But Is It Enough for Stability?" *Sports Business Daily,* November 7, 1995.

66. Ibid.

67. Ibid.

68. Ibid.

69. Ibid.

70. Richard Sandomir, "TV Sports."

71. Jim McConville, "Baseball Boon for Fox, ESPN, Fox Liberty," *Broadcasting & Cable,* January 22, 1996.

72. Sam Donnellon, "Baseball Fans Are Winners in TV Deal," *Philadelphia Daily News*, November 7, 1995.

73. "MLB Goes Deep in TV Deals."

74. Richard Sandomir, "Hidden Cameras and Wired Bases," *New York Times*, May 26, 1996.

75. Ibid.

76. Ibid.

77. Alan Pergament, "With Ratings on the Rise, Fox Welcoming Baseball Aboard," *Buffalo News*, June 1, 1996.

78. E-mail from Bill Giles, May 19, 2013.

Chapter 3: Collusion

1. Available at http://www.baseball-almanac.com/charts/salary/major_league_salaries.shtml.

2. Michael Haupert, "The Economic History of Major League Baseball," December 3, 2007. Available at http://eh.net/encyclopedia/article/haupert.mlb.

3. Interview with Bill Giles, July 19, 2012.

4. James Tuite, "Baseball Owners Use Right of Option," *New York Times*, February 20, 1981.

5. Available at http://www.personal.psu.edu/~dxl31/research/presentations/strikes.pdf.

6. Available at http://www.baseball-almanac.com/charts/salary/major_league_salaries.shtml.

7. Steve Beitler, "The Empire Strikes out," *Baseball Research Journal*, 36, 2007.

8. Dan Shaughnessy, "Orioles' Owner Pleads Not Guilty on Collusion," *Boston Globe*, March 22, 1987.

9. Helyar, *Lords of the Realm*, 361.

10. Giles and Myers, *Pouring Six Beers at a Time*, 290.

11. Maury Brown, "MLB's Landscape Leading up to the CBA, Part One," June 19, 2006. Available at BaseballProspectus.com.

12. Jerome Holtzman, *The Commissioners: Baseball's Midlife Crisis* (New York: Total Sports, 1998), 221.

13. Brown, "MLB's Landscape Leading up to the CBA."

14. Dave van Dyk and Joe Goddard, "Moreland: Drug Tests OK if Secret," *Chicago Sun-Times*, January 19, 1986.

15. Marc Edelman, "Has Collusion Returned to Baseball? Analyzing Whether a Concerted Increase in Free Agent Player Supply Would Violate Baseball's 'Collusion Clause,'" *Loyola of Los Angeles Entertainment Law Journal*, 24 (Fall 2004), 59.

16. Helyar, *Lords of the Realm*, 366.

17. Brown, "MLB's Landscape Leading up to the CBA."

18. Glen Macnow, "Free Agency/The Big Money and the Big Offers Are Disappearing as Major-League Owners Fashion the 'Era of Good Sense,'" *Houston Chronicle*, December 25, 1985.

19. Interview with Donald Fehr, September 26, 2011.

20. Benjamin G. Rader, *Baseball: A History of America's Game*, 3rd ed. (Urbana: University of Illinois Press, 2008), 216.

21. Craig Brown, "Collusion and the No-Risk Free Agents of 1988," February 29, 2008. Available at http://www.hardballtimes.com/main/article/collusion-and-the-no-risk-free-agents-of-1988.

22. Interview with Bill Giles, July 19, 2012.

23. Murray Chass, "Baseball: Dollars and Sense, or Collusion?" *New York Times*, February 1, 1987.

24. Interview with Bill Giles, June 22, 2010.

25. Interview with Jerry Reinsdorf, October 7, 2011.

26. Interview with Bill Giles, July 19, 2012.

27. Ibid.

28. Paul Hagen, "Labor Daze Baseball; Giles Plan: Phils Could Break Ranks, End Strike Slick Willie Bill Giles Says If Strike Continues, He Might Ask 10 to 15 Phils to Cross Line Giles Reveals Inviting Idea Might Ask Phils to Cross Line," *Philadelphia Daily News*, March 15, 1995. Available at http://articles.philly.com/1995-03-15/sports/25701430_1_cross-line-bill-giles-phils.

29. Available at http://www.baseball-reference.com/players/p/parrila02.shtml.

30. Jayson Stark, "Phillies' Giles Goes His Own Way," *Philadelphia Inquirer*, April 1, 1990.

31. Marc Edelman, "Moving Past Collusion in Major League Baseball: Healing Old Wounds, and Preventing New Ones," *Wayne Law Review*, 54, no. 3 (2008).

32. Murray Chass, "Baseball Owners Lose Arbitration On Free Agents; Football Players' Union Strikes on a Parallel Issue; Ruling Backs Players on Collusion Charges Against Teams in '85," *New York Times*, September 22, 1987.

33. Interview with Bill Giles, July 19, 2012.

34. Ibid.

35. Marc Edelman, "Moving Past Collusion in Major League Baseball."

36. Jerome Holtzman and Murray Chass, "Arbitrator Finds Baseball Owners in Second Free-Agent Conspiracy," *New York Times*, September 1, 1988.

37. Edelman, "Moving Past Collusion in Major League Baseball."

38. Zimbalist, *Baseball and Billions*, 89.

39. Andrew Zimbalist, *May the Best Team Win: Baseball Economics and Public Policy* (Washington, DC: Brookings Institution Press, 2003).

40. Available at http://www.baseball-reference.com/bullpen/collusion.

41. Helyar, *Lords of the Realm*, 366.

Chapter 4: The Rise and Fall of Fay Vincent

1. Interview with Bill Giles, September 12, 2012.

2. Murray Chass, "Major League Council to Meet on Commissioner," *New York Times*, September 12, 1989.

3. Interview with Bill Giles, September 12, 2012.

4. Ibid.

5. Holtzman, *The Commissioners: Baseball's Midlife Crisis*, 262.

6. Burk, *Much More Than a Game*, 267.

7. Available at http://www.bizofbaseball.com/index.php?option=com_content&task=view&id=1173&Itemid=81.

8. Giles and Myers, *Pouring Six Beers at a Time*, 297.

9. Interview with Bill Giles, September 12, 2012.

10. Leonard Koppett, *Koppett's Concise History of Major League Baseball* (New York: Carroll & Graf, 2004), 410.

11. Claire Smith, "Vincent Says Steinbrenner Inquiry Must Proceed," *New York Times*, June 14, 1990.

12. Ibid.

13. Kevin McCoy and Richard T. Pienciak, "Baseball Strikes out Yanks' Steinbrenner," *New York Daily News*, July 31, 1990.

14. Robert Thomas Jr., "Reorganizing the Yankees; Other Owners Either Silent or Still Quietly Surprised," *New York Times*, August 1, 1990.

15. "Vincent's Action Shocks Yankees," *Chicago Sun-Times*, July 31, 1990.

16. "Consensus: Vincent Acted Fairly," *Albany Times Union*, July 31, 1990.

17. Ibid.

18. Steve Berkowitz, "Vincent Says Haggling Can't Halt NL Expansion," *Washington Post*, February 12, 1991.

19. Available at http://deadspin.com/5883511/fbi-docs-how-george-steinbrenner-helped-kill-off-baseballs-last-real-commissioner.

20. Murray Chass, "Nederlander Gets Owners' Approval," *New York Times*, September 13, 1990.

21. Claire Smith, "On Baseball; Too Much Money Is Never Enough," *New York Times*, May 22, 1991.

22. Zimbalist, *Baseball and Billions*, 45.

23. Larry Whiteside, "Vincent Rules NL-AL Fee Split on Expansion," *Boston Globe*, June 7, 1991.

24. Steve Fainaru, "Owners at Odds over Process of Bringing in Clubs," *Boston Globe*, June 14, 1991.

25. Jerome Holtzman, "Vincent Decision Angers AL Owners," *Chicago Tribune*, June 7, 1991.

26. Whiteside, "Vincent Rules NL-AL Fee Split on Expansion."

27. Available at http://www.historylink.org/index.cfm?DisplayPage=output.cfm&file_id=9562.

28. Ibid.

29. Ibid.

30. Mark Potts, "Baseball Owners Rethink Ban; Recent Vote Would Prohibit Japanese-Led Offer to Buy Mariners," *Washington Post*, February 5, 1992.

31. Mark Potts, "Japan and Mariners: Quandary for Game; Nationalism, Globalism Bang Heads," *Washington Post*, February 28, 1992.

32. Ibid.

33. Larry Whiteside, "Nintendo Pushes the Right Buttons; Concessions Clear the Way for Mariners Sale," *Boston Globe*, June 10, 1992.

34. Thomas Boswell, "Ring Up Sale for the Mariners' Good," *Washington Post*, February 5, 1992.

35. Interview with John Ellis, September 28, 2012.

36. Bill Brubaker, "The Head of the Game, Faced with Trouble; Commissioner Fay Vincent Buffeted by Baseball's Tough Times, Waves of Criticism," *Washington Post*, August 16, 1992.

37. Burk, *Much More Than a Game*, 279.

38. Sands and Gammons, *Coming Apart at the Seams*, 224.

39. Andrew Zimbalist, *In the Best Interests of Baseball?: The Revolutionary Reign of Bud Selig* (Hoboken, NJ: John Wiley & Sons, 2006), 106.

40. Ibid., 107.

41. Vincent Fay, *The Last Commissioner: A Baseball Valentine* (New York: Simon & Schuster, 2002), 281.

42. Zimbalist, *In the Best Interests of Baseball*, quoting Helyar, *Lords of the Realm*, 513.

43. Murray Chass, "Baseball; Vincent Repels Move to Cut His Powers on Labor," *New York Times,* June 10, 1992.

44. "Major League Owners Rebuked by Vincent; Chides 'Undistinguished Behavior,'" *Washington Post,* June 12, 1992.

45. Larry Whiteside, "Seattle Sale, Vincent Upheld; Japanese Group Buys Mariners; Commissioner Keeps Authority," *Boston Globe,* June 12, 1992.

46. Murray Chass, "Baseball; Owners Are Swayed by Vincent's Speech: 'He's in Total Charge,'" *New York Times,* June 12, 1992.

47. Sands and Gammons, *Coming Apart at the Seams,* 184.

48. Ibid.

49. Ibid., 186.

50. Ibid., 186.

51. Bill Madden and Jeff B. Ley, "Vincent Threatens Suspensions after Yankee Trio Testifies on Howe's Behalf," *Buffalo News,* July 2, 1992.

52. Rosalind Rossi, "Cubs Sue on Shift—Injunction Sought against Realignment of NL," *Chicago Sun-Times,* July 7, 1992.

53. "National League Realignment Decision Draws Immediate Criticism," *Buffalo News,* July 7, 1992.

54. Dave van Dyck, "Cubs Ask Vincent for Three-Division Format," *Chicago Sun-Times,* July 7, 1992.

55. Interview with Bill Giles, August 6, 2010.

56. Mark Maske, "Notebook: Reds and Braves Can Move the East from Worst to First," *Washington Post,* July 12, 1992.

57. Brubaker, "The Head of the Game."

58. Ibid.

59. Ibid.

60. Maske, "Notebook: Reds and Braves."

61. Murray Chass, "Baseball; As Vincent Dispute Heats Up, Disagreement Is Everywhere," *New York Times,* August 30, 1992.

62. "Baseball's Chiefs Meet to Discuss Fay's Status," *Albany Times-Union,* August 25, 1992.

63. Chass, "Baseball; As Vincent Dispute Heats Up."

64. Dave Sell, "Owners Increasing Pressure on Vincent," *Washington Post,* September 1, 1992.

65. Ibid.

66. Ibid.

67. Ibid.

68. Ibid.

69. "Baseball's Chiefs Meet to Discuss Fay's Status."

70. Dave Sell and Mark Potts, "Owners Set Meeting about Vincent; Commissioner Stands Firm," *Washington Post,* August 25, 1992.

71. Murray Chass, "On Baseball; It's Time to Meet: What's the Agenda?" *New York Times,* September 3, 1992.

72. Giles and Myers, *Pouring Six Beers at a Time,* 297.

73. Larry Whiteside, "Owners Tell Vincent, 'You're Out' He's Asked to Resign But Vows to Stay on Job," *Boston Globe,* September 4, 1992.

74. Ibid.

75. Dave Sell, "Baseball's Vincent Resigns; Commissioner Accedes to Owners' Wishes," *Washington Post,* September 8, 1992.

76. Nick Cafardo, "Reaction Is Regret but Relief," *Boston Globe*, September 8, 1992.

77. Dave Sell, "Owners: Relieved, Dismayed; Few Names Surface to Succeed Vincent," *Washington Post*, September 8, 1992.

78. Availableathttp://deadspin.com/5883511/fbi-docs-how-george-steinbrenner-helped-kill-off-baseballs-last-real-commissioner.

79. Chass, "Baseball; As Vincent Dispute Heats Up."

80. Interview with Bill Giles, September 12, 2012.

81. Ibid.

Chapter 5: Era of Unrest: The Strike of 1994 and the 1996 Collective Bargaining Agreement

1. Available at www.baseballyarn.com/9X53.htm.

2. Available at www.themick.com/mickeyquotes.htm.

3. Don Boston, "Richie Ashburn from Cornfield to Cooperstown," *Morning Call* (Allentown, PA), July 28, 1995.

4. "Record Profit for Baseball in '89," *Chicago Sun-Times*, November 28, 1990.

5. "Baseball Owners: Profits Declined 33 Percent in '90," *Post-Tribune* (Indianapolis, IN), November 19, 1991.

6. Lee Lowenfish, *The Imperfect Diamond: A History of Baseball's Labor Wars* (New York: Da Capo Press, 1980), 269.

7. "Salary Cap May Prevent War between Rich, Poor," *Chicago Sun-Times*, January 18, 1993.

8. George Vecsey, "Sports of the Times; Bowie Kuhn Lives," *New York Times*, June 17, 1982.

9. Helyar, *Lords of the Realm*, 592.

10. Nick Cafardo, "Basic Agreement Revived; Owners' Vote is 15–13; Ravitch Sees No Sentiment for Work Stoppage," *Boston Globe*, December 8, 1992.

11. Ronald Blum, "Ravitch Asks Owners to Open Their Books," *Albany Times Union*, December 17, 1992.

12. James E. Miller, *The Baseball Business: Pursuing Pennants and Profits in Baltimore* (Chapel Hill: University of North Carolina Press, 1990), quoted in Zimbalist, *Baseball and Billions*, 177.

13. "Salary Cap May Prevent War between Rich, Poor."

14. Mark Maske, "Notebook; 18 Owners Quietly Talk Dollars," *Washington Post*, March 28, 1993.

15. Richard Sandomir, "Small-Screen Feud, Majors' Big Picture," *New York Times*, August 3, 1993.

16. Dave van Dyck, "Owners to Study Plan of Legalized Collusion," *Chicago Sun-Times*, August 11, 1993.

17. Zimbalist, *May the Best Team Win*, 141.

18. Interview with Jerry Reinsdorf, October 7, 2011.

19. Interview with John Harrington, September 21, 2011.

20. Murray Chass, "Baseball; Owners Take Steps to Prevent a Strike," *New York Times*, August 13, 1993.

21. Peter Schmuck, "Owners Come Up Vote Shy of Sharing Plan," *Baltimore Sun*, January 7, 1994.

22. Amy Niedzielka, "Top Issues May Present Uphill Battle for Owners," Knight Ridder/Tribune News Service, January 17, 1994.

23. Phil Rogers, "Revenue Sharing Steps to the Plate; Selig Needs OK from Players to Alter Economics," *Chicago Tribune*, January 10, 2002.

24. Zimbalist, *May the Best Team Win*, 88.

25. Bob Hertzel, "Baseball Owners Face Some Pressing Issues," *The Record* (Bergen County, NJ), January 17, 1994.

26. Rader, *Baseball*, 286.

27. Mark Maske, "Baseball to Share Revenue; Conditional Plan Adopted by Owners," *Washington Post*, January 19, 1994.

28. Bill Conlin, "How Can Anybody Trust These Owners?" Knight Ridder/Tribune News Service, August 9, 1994.

29. Peter Schmuck, "Players, Owners Take First Step in Negotiations," *Baltimore Sun*, March 8, 1994.

30. Zimbalist, *May the Best Team Win*, 86.

31. Ibid.

32. Burk, *Much More Than a Game*, 287.

33. Steve Adamek, "There's Little Hope of Striking a Deal," *The Record* (Bergen County, NJ), August 7, 1994.

34. Dave van Dyck, "On the Blink; Owners Eye an Unlikely Labor Win," *Chicago Sun-Times*, August 10, 1994.

35. "Labor 'Talks' Resume, but Settlement Doubtful Owners Unlikely to Change Demands," *Buffalo News*, August 24, 1994.

36. Available at http://www.phrases.org.uk/meanings/255800.html.

37. Van Dyck, "On the Blink."

38. Mark Maske, "Owners Ponder Point at Which Season Is Lost," *Washington Post*, August 18, 1994.

39. Frank Dolson, "Here's Hoping Strike Doesn't Alter Our Emotional Ties to Baseball," Knight Ridder/Tribune News Service, September 7, 1994.

40. Dave van Dyck, "Strike Owner Unity: Stoppage on; Steinbrenner Breaks Rank," *Chicago Sun-Times*, August 12, 1994.

41. Helyar, *Lords of the Realm*, 601.

42. "Owners Studying New Plan: 'Deadline' Looms for World Series," *Buffalo News*, September 9, 1994.

43. Holtzman, *The Commissioners: Baseball's Midlife Crisis*, 276.

44. Burk, *Much More Than a Game*, 290.

45. Ibid, 289.

46. Ronald Blum, "Owners Will Join in Talks; Negotiators to Resume Bargaining Next Week," *Albany Times-Union*, August 19, 1994.

47. Ibid.

48. Ross Newhan, "Putting an End to Strike Simple as Following Steps," *Buffalo News*, August 20, 1994.

49. Mark Maske, "Baseball Checks Its Pockets; In Wake of Strike, Teams Massage Fans, Advertisers," *Washington Post*, October 29, 1994.

50. Mark Maske, "Baseball Owners Warned; Forced Salary Cap May Spell Legal Loss," *Washington Post*, December 17, 1994.

51. Burk, *Much More Than a Game*, 290.

52. Mark Maske, "Baseball Owners Put off Salary Cap until Next Week; Sides Have until Thursday to Settle," *Washington Post*, December 16, 1994.

53. Murray Chass, "Baseball Antitrust Exemption Subject of Congressional Bills," *New York Times,* January 4, 1995.

54. Mark Maske and Frank Swoboda, "Congress to Receive Antitrust Bill; Legislation Would Limit, Not Repeal, Baseball's 73-Year-Old Exemption," *Washington Post,* February 11, 1995.

55. Mark Maske, "Owners Begin Setting Replacement Procedures," *Washington Post,* January 5, 1995.

56. Paul Hagen, "A Bitter Bill Giles Takes Hard Swing at Union Leaders," January 18, 1995. Available at http://articles.philly.com/1995-01-18/sports/25713241_1_ticket-prices-bill-giles-union-leaders.

57. Jennifer Frey, "Baseball; The Ticket-Sales Dilemma Requires Creative Approach," *New York Times,* January 18, 1995.

58. Michael Bamberger, "Mediator Ready to Offer Proposal to Settle Baseball Strike if Sides Don't Agree Quickly," Knight Ridder/Tribune News Service, February 5, 1995.

59. Zimbalist, *May the Best Team Win,* 89.

60. Mark Maske, "Labor Woes Could Hinder Expansion," *Washington Post,* February 10, 1995.

61. Mark Maske, "Players' Proposal Brightens Baseball Negotiations; Union Accepts Revenue-Sharing Plan," *Washington Post,* March 4, 1995.

62. Jayson Stark, "NLRB Ruling Brings End to Strike Talks," Knight Ridder/Tribune News Service, March 14, 1995.

63. Ibid.

64. Hagen, "Labor Daze Baseball."

65. Jayson Stark, "Sapped by Baseball Strike, Phils Brass Feels Powerless. Bill Giles and Lee Thomas Are Sick of Playing the Waiting Game. The Players Will Be Sorry, They Warn." *Philadelphia Inquirer,* March 21, 1995.

66. Steve Adamek, "Opening Day Rescheduled for April 26," *The Record* (Bergen County, NJ), April 3, 1995.

67. Steve Adamek, "The Forecast for Opening Day Looks Sunny," *The Record* (Bergen County, NJ), January 14, 1996.

68. Dave van Dyck, "MacPhail Speaks out vs. Players. Cubs CEO: Service Time Won't Fly," *Chicago Sun-Times,* March 26, 1996.

69. Mark Maske, "Baseball Agreement Is Near; Settlement of 6-Year Labor Deal Is Expected Today," *Washington Post,* August 11, 1996.

70. Dave van Dyck, "Don't Celebrate Just Yet. Talks Still Haven't Created Deal and Could Fall Apart over Details," *Chicago Sun-Times,* August 12, 1996.

71. "Owners Continue to Stall Baseball Talks," *Seattle Post-Intelligencer,* August 17, 1996.

72. Murray Chass, "Owners' Negotiator Sees a Path to Progress," *New York Times,* September 12, 1996.

73. Bruce Miles, "Reinsdorf Dissension Can't Stop New Labor Deal," *Daily Herald* (Arlington Heights, IL), November 27, 1996.

74. Ibid.

75. Jim Souhan, "Owners Vote for Labor Deal; 5 Years of Peace Ensured," *Star Tribune* (Minneapolis, MN), November 27, 1996.

76. Bill Knight, "Finally, Baseball Strikes a Deal; Revenue Sharing, Interleague Play Part of Labor Pact," *Seattle Post-Intelligencer,* November 27, 1996.

77. Souhan, "Owners Vote for Labor Deal."

78. Miles, "Reinsdorf Dissension Can't Stop New Labor Deal."

79. Andrew Zimbalist, "Does Baseball's Antitrust Exemption Still Matter? More than You Think," *Sports Business Journal*, July 9, 2001.

80. Andrew Zimbalist, *The Bottom Line, Observations and Arguments on the Sports Business* (Philadelphia: Temple University Press, 2006), 195.

81. Larry Moffi, *The Conscience of the Game: Baseball's Commissioners from Landis to Selig* (Lincoln: University of Nebraska Press, 2006), 88.

82. Interview with Bill Giles, November 1, 2012.

Chapter 6: Expansion, Realignment, and Interleague Play: Bringing Baseball into the 1990s

1. Ronald W. Cox and Daniel Skidmore-Hess, *Free Agency and Competitive Balance in Baseball* (Jefferson, NC: McFarland & Company, 2006), 148.

2. Interview with Bill Giles, June 9, 2009.

3. Dan Shaughnessy, "Talent Appears Too Thin for Expansion," *Boston Globe*, April 24, 1988.

4. Interview with Bill Giles, August 6, 2010.

5. Thomas Boswell, "Is Baseball Expansive, or What?" *Washington Post*, May 27, 1987.

6. Len Shapiro, "Ueberroth: 32 Teams Makes Sense; Says Owners Showing an Increased Interest in Expansion," *Washington Post*, June 13, 1987.

7. Richard Justice, "Expansion's Slow, Small Signs; Baseball Merges Committees to Discuss Logistics of Adding Teams," *Washington Post*, December 10, 1987.

8. "Florida Senators in Push for Baseball Expansion," United Press International, November 5, 1987.

9. Ibid.

10. "Senators Take a Cut at Baseball," *Chicago Sun-Times*, April 15, 1988.

11. Murray Chass, "Baseball Destined to Grow, but Not Any Time Soon," June 26, 1988.

12. Richard Justice, "Baseball Expansion Still Lacks Timetable," *Washington Post*, December 8, 1987.

13. Joseph Durso, "Baseball Expansion Won't Come Soon," *New York Times*, December 10, 1987.

14. "League's Expansion Plans, Agreement on Pact Linked," *Los Angeles Times*, June 15, 1989.

15. Interview with Jerry Reinsdorf, October 7, 2011.

16. Evan Weiner, *The Business & Politics of Sports: A Collection of Columns* (New Canaan, CT: TBE Press, 2005).

17. Lee Byrd, "Senate Panel Turns up Heat for Expansion," August 3, 1989.

18. Richard Justice, "Vincent's View of Expansion Not Encouraging for D.C." *Washington Post*, September 14, 1989.

19. Cox and Skidmore-Hess, *Free Agency and Competitive Balance in Baseball*, 159.

20. Larry Whiteside, "He Sits Well; Commissioner Back Among Fans," *Boston Globe*, March 22, 1990.

21. Steve Berkowitz, "Commissioner: Lottery, Baseball Don't Mix; Vincent Talks to Senators on Expansion," *Washington Post*, May 9, 1990.

22. Cox and Skidmore-Hess, *Free Agency and Competitive Balance in Baseball*, 150.

23. "Giles to AL: Expansion Fees All NL's; Phillies' President Says Split Is out," *Washington Post*, January 23, 1991.

24. Steve Berkowitz, “NL Nears Timetable for Adding 2 Teams,” *Washington Post,* June 14, 1990.

25. Shapiro, “Ueberroth: 32 Teams Makes Sense.”

26. Steve Berkowitz, “NL Committee Believes Area Can Support Two Teams,” *Washington Post,* April 18, 1991.

27. Richard Justice, “D.C. Toughens Up Baseball Strategy; Soft Sell Struck Out,” *Washington Post,* December 4, 1988.

28. Interview with Bill Giles, August 6, 2010.

29. Ed Giuliotti, “Giles Joins Expansion Committee,” January 19, 1991.

30. Steve Berkowitz, “NL Expansion Is Their Business; Committee Covers All Bases,” *Washington Post,* March 24, 1991.

31. Steve Fainaru, “Saying ‘Wish You Were Here’ to Major League Baseball, Three Florida Cities Are Sweating out Expansion in . . . a State of Hot Pursuit,” *Boston Globe,* June 9, 1991.

32. Andrew Zimbalist, “The Capitalist; A Miami Fish Story,” *New York Times,* October 18, 1998.

33. “Giles to AL.”

34. Peter Gammons, “This NL Expansion Just Doesn’t Add up,” *Boston Globe,* June 14, 1991.

35. Fainaru, “Owners at Odds over Process of Bringing in Clubs.”

36. Murray Chass, “Notebook: Baseball; New Teams, Not Some Owners, May Be Getting the Raw Deal,” June 23, 1991.

37. Zimbalist, *In the Best Interests of Baseball,* 107.

38. Sands and Gammons, *Coming Apart at the Seams,* 192.

39. Murray Chass, “4 Teams to Change Divisions as Baseball’s Map Is Redrawn,” *New York Times,* July 7, 1992.

40. Ibid.

41. Zimbalist, *In the Best Interests of Baseball,* 107.

42. Murray Chass, “Baseball; Newly Empowered Owners Rescind Order to Realign,” *New York Times,* September 25, 1992.

43. Mark Maske, “Realignment Is a Subject of Divisions,” *Washington Post,* February 14, 1993.

44. Murray Chass, “Baseball; Changes on Horizon for Major Leagues,” February 17, 1993.

45. Bob Costas, *Fair Ball: A Fan’s Case for Baseball* (New York: Random House, 2000), 123–148.

46. Frank Dolson, “Baseball Goes with the Lesser of Two Evils,” Knight Ridder/Tribune News Service, September 11, 1993.

47. Ibid..

48. Michael Madden, “Move Purely Unacceptable,” *Boston Globe,* September 10, 1993.

49. Interview with Bill Giles, August 6, 2010.

50. Ibid.

51. Murray Chass, “Baseball; Major Leagues Near Three-Division Format,” *New York Times,* September 9, 1993.

52. Interview with John Harrington, September 21, 2013.

53. Mark Maske, “Baseball Okays Realignment, Expanded Playoffs; Major Leagues Remain Without a Commissioner, So Selig Agrees to Continue on an Interim Basis,” *Washington Post,* January 20, 1994.

54. Mark Maske and Steve Berkowitz, "Owners Thinking Again of Expansion; Realignment of Divisions Could Put Washington Back in Fray," *Washington Post*, June 12, 1993.

55. Mark Maske, "Baseball Might Expand; Washington Could Get Another Chance at Franchise," *Washington Post*, July 24, 1993.

56. Richard Justice, "Baseball Eyes Addition of Its 29th, 30th Teams," *Washington Post*, March 3, 1994.

57. Larry Whiteside, "Baseball Owners Are Looking Ahead," *Boston Globe*, March 3, 1994.

58. Cox and Skidmore-Hess, *Free Agency and Competitive Balance in Baseball*, 164.

59. "Next Major League Baseball Expansion," *Kiplinger Letter*, December 5, 1997.

60. Koppett, *Koppett's Concise History of Major League Baseball*, 487.

61. Interview with Jerry Reinsdorf, October 7, 2011.

62. Paul Hagen, "Ready to See AL East Teams at the Vet?" *Philadelphia Daily News*, January 17, 1996.

63. Ibid.

64. Jayson Stark, "Interleague Play Grows Closer to Reality as Owners Begin Meetings," Knight Ridder/Tribune News Service, January 16, 1996.

65. Mark Maske, "Baseball's Owners Prepare to Vote for Interleague Play; There is Momentum for Change," *Washington Post*, January 17, 1996.

66. Mark Maske, "Baseball Owners Want Interleague Play; Vote Is Unanimous for 1997 Start if Players Consent," *Washington Post*, January 19, 1996.

67. Nancy Gay, "Why Interleague Play Appeals to Owners," *Chronicle*, January 18, 1996.

68. Mark Maske, "Interleague Approval Is Likely; Players Union Might Ask for DH Change," *Washington Post*, January 27, 1996.

69. Interview with Donald Fehr, September 26, 2011.

70. Interview with Jerry Reinsdorf, October 7, 2011.

71. Ibid.

72. Stark, "Interleague Play Grows Closer to Reality."

73. Hagen, "Ready to See AL East Teams at Vet?"

74. Koppett, *Koppett's Concise History of Major League Baseball*, 487.

75. Interview with Jerry Reinsdorf, October 7, 2011.

76. "Unbalanced Leagues, Schedule Are Likely," *Seattle Post-Intelligencer*, September 4, 1997.

77. Mark Maske, "Baseball Seeks to Make Changes in Its Lineup; Teams May Switch on the Basis of Geography," *Washington Post*, August 13, 1992.

78. "Unbalanced Leagues."

79. Larry Whiteside, "Is a Shuffle in the Cards? Realignment Seen by Some as Game's Best Bet for Future," *Boston Globe*, August 13, 1997.

80. Dave van Dyck, "Shuffle Could Put DH in NL," *Chicago Sun-Times*, July 14, 1997.

81. Dave van Dyck, "Talks on Realignment Going Nowhere Fast," *Chicago Sun-Times*, September 16, 1997.

82. Dave van Dyck, "Selig Pushing Realignment—Plan's Opponents Are Getting Squeezed," *Chicago Sun-Times*, August 17, 1997.

83. Dave van Dyck, "Owners Talk Realignment—New '16-14 Plan' Gaining Support in Management," *Chicago Sun-Times*, July 30, 1997.

84. Tracy Ringolsby, "Realignment Changes Shape with 'Moderate' Proposal Teams in NY, Chicago Won't Switch Leagues If Owners Approve Plan," *Rocky Mountain News*, August 30, 1997.

85. Dave van Dyck, "Owners Will Look at Plans B and C," *Chicago Sun-Times*, September 3, 1997.

86. Jayson Stark, "In Realignment, Phils Unlikely to Be Designated Switcher: New Proposals Are on the Owners' Front Burner This Week. Rerouting the Phillies is Not," *Philadelphia Inquirer*, September 17, 1997.

87. "Baseball Team Owners Take Rain Check on Realignment," *Chicago Sun-Times*, September 18, 1997.

88. "Royals Discussing Option of Joining NL," *Cincinnati Post*, October 16, 1997.

89. Interview with Bill Giles, October 20, 2012.

Chapter 7: The Evolution of Baseball's Governance System

1. Major League Agreement, 1921. Available at http://www.bizofbaseball.com/index.php?option=com_content&view=article&id=58:1921-major-league-agreemen&catid=37:1900-1960&Itemid=47.

2. The Commissionership: A Historical Perspective. Available at http://mlb.mlb.com/mlb/history/mlb_history_people.jsp?story=com.

3. Jonathan M. Reinsdorf, "The Powers of the Commissioner in Baseball," *Marquette Sports Law Review*, 7, no. 1 (Fall 1996), 211–255.

4. Interview with Bill Giles, November 14, 2012.

5. Craig F. Arcella, "Note: Major League Baseball's Disempowered Commissioner: Judicial Ramifications of the 1994 Restructuring," *Columbia Law Review*, 97, no. 8 (December 1997), 2420–2432.

6. Moffi, *The Conscience of the Game*, 51.

7. "Restructuring, TV Revenue Top Owners' Meetings," *Herald Journal* (Spartanburg, SC), June 15, 1982.

8. Ibid.

9. Vecsey, "Sports of the Times."

10. Holtzman, *The Commissioners: Baseball's Midlife Crisis*, 205.

11. Kenneth M. Jennings, *Balls and Strikes: The Money Game in Professional Baseball* (New York: Praeger, 1990), 89.

12. Ibid., 209.

13. Zimbalist, *In the Best Interests of Baseball*, 92.

14. Holtzman, *The Commissioners: Baseball's Midlife Crisis*, 261.

15. Chass, "Major League Council to Meet on Commissioner."

16. Claire Smith, "On Baseball; Again, Maddox Gets Himself in Position," *New York Times*, June 23, 1992.

17. Dave van Dyck, "Even CEO Couldn't End Baseball Funny Business," *Chicago Sun-Times*, August 20, 1992.

18. Sell, "Baseball's Vincent Resigns."

19. Murray Chass, "Baseball's Vincent Steps Down; Commissioner Yields to Big-League Owners," *New York Times*, September 8, 1992.

20. Ross Newhan, "Selig Gets Commissioner's Power: Baseball: Brewers' Owner to Take Position Temporarily. It Could Take a Year to Find Permanent Successor," *Los Angeles Times*, September 10, 1992.

21. Murray Chass, "On Baseball; Owners Play a Game in Which the Rules Are Forever Changing," *New York Times*, September 16, 1992.

22. Claire Smith, "Coming Eventually: A New Commissioner," *New York Times*, December 19, 1992.

23. Murray Chass, "Baseball; Council Still Holding Report on Commissioner's Role," *New York Times*, April 23, 1993.

24. "Captain Selig Doing His Best to Right Ship," *Boston Globe*, July 29, 1993.

25. Craig F. Arcella, "Note: Major League Baseball's Disempowered Commissioner."

26. Jason M. Pollack, "Take My Arbitrator, Please: Commissioner 'Best Interests' Disciplinary Authority in Professional Sports," *Fordham Law Review*, Vol. 67, Issue 4, Article 9, 1999.

27. Jonathan M. Reinsdorf, "The Powers of the Commissioner in Baseball," 231.

28. Ibid.

29. Murray Chass, "Commissioner's Powers Are Diluted by Owners," *New York Times*, February 12, 1994.

30. Murray Chass, "A Decision: No New Commissioner," *New York Times*, January 20, 1994.

31. Maske, "Baseball Okays Realignment, Expanded Playoffs."

32. Chass, "Commissioner's Powers Are Diluted by Owners."

33. "Owners Limit Commissioner's Powers," *Chicago Sun-Times*, February 12, 1994.

34. Chass, "Commissioner's Powers Are Diluted by Owners."

35. Ross Newhan, "Baseball Changes Top Job-Owners—Power of Commissioner is Severely Limited. Former Commissioners Say the Move Weakens the Office," *Los Angeles Times*, February 12, 1994.

36. Reinsdorf, "The Powers of the Commissioner in Baseball," 235.

37. Tracy Ringolsby, "Selig Should Step aside for Baseball's Sake," *Rocky Mountain News*, July 24, 1997.

38. "Selig Now Receptive to Top Baseball Post—The Acting Commissioner is Ready to Make the Title Permanent," *Philadelphia Inquirer*, June 19, 1998.

39. Jayson Stark, "Selig Set for Permanent Role—Centralized Operations and Changes Designed to Improve Marketing and Promotions Are Expected from the Commissioner," *Philadelphia Inquirer*, July 9, 1998.

40. George Offman and Bob Edwards, "Baseball Elects Commissioner," *NPR Morning Edition*, July 10, 1998.

41. Mark Maske, "Owners Set to Elect Selig as Full-time Commissioner," *Washington Post*, July 9, 1998.

42. "Major Leagues from the Top down," *Sports Business Journal*, June 19, 2000.

43. Murray Chass, "Baseball; White Reportedly Is Ready to Leave as N.L. Chief," *New York Times*, January 21, 1994.

44. "Baseball Rids Itself of Schott," *Albany Times Union*, September 16, 1999.

45. Ronald Blum, "Schott's Reign Ends with Reds; Coleman Quits," *Charleston Daily Mail*, September 16, 1999.

46. Bill King, "MLB Makes Moves to a More Businesslike Model," *Sports Business Journal*, September 27, 1999.

47. Ibid.

48. Ibid.

49. Ibid.

50. Ibid.

51. Interview with Bob DuPuy, September 12, 2011.

52. Interview with John Harrington, September 21, 2011.

53. Ibid.

54. "Owners Limit Commissioner's Powers," *Chicago Sun-Times*, February 12, 1994.

55. Major League Constitution, Article 2, Section 4, Major League Baseball, January 14, 2000.

56. Zimbalist, *In the Best Interests of Baseball*, 159–160.

Chapter 8: Toward a New Era of Labor Peace: The 2002 Collective Bargaining Agreement

1. Zimbalist, *May the Best Team Win*, 46.

2. Ronald Blum, "Only a Handful of Teams Making Money in Major Leagues; World Champion Diamondbacks among Big Losers," *Charleston Daily Mail*, December 6, 2001.

3. Phil Rogers, "Selig Loses Focus on Central Issue; Key Is Revenue Disparities, Not Forbes Report," *Chicago Tribune*, April 6, 2002.

4. Cox and Skidmore-Hess, *Free Agency and Competitive Balance in Baseball*, 33.

5. Available at http://www.stevetheump.com/Payrolls.htm.

6. Joel G. Maxcy, "Progressive Revenue Sharing in MLB: The Effect on Player Transfers." Available at http://college.holycross.edu/RePEc/spe/Maxcy_Transfers2.pdf.

7. Murray Chass, "Trying to Strike a Competitive Balance," *New York Times*, November 11, 1998.

8. Zimbalist, *The Bottom Line*, 70.

9. Joe Posnanski, "Teams Have to Share the Wealth to Save Baseball," *Knight Ridder/Tribune News Service*, November 17, 2001.

10. Zimbalist, *The Bottom Line*, 70.

11. Peter Schmuck, "Revenue Stream Is Waterfall for Small-market Teams," *Baltimore Sun*, December 6, 1998.

12. Mark Rosentraub, "Bah, Humbug! MLB Delivers a Bitter Christmas," *Sports Business Journal*, December 28, 1998.

13. Tim Leonard, "Baseball's Economics: Fair or Foul?" *The Record* (Bergen County, NJ), September 13, 1998.

14. Murray Chass, "Baseball; Trying to Strike a Competitive Balance as the Disparity in Payrolls Grows," *New York Times*, November 22, 1998.

15. Ibid.

16. Hal Bodley, "Baseball Gambling on Futures Market," *Albany Times Union*, December 13, 2000.

17. William B. Gould IV, *Bargaining with Baseball: Labor Relations in an Age of Prosperous Turmoil* (Jefferson, NC: McFarland & Company, 2011), 123–124.

18. Available at www.mlb.com/mlb/downloads/blue_ribbon.pdf.

19. Ronald Blum, "Baseball Owners Discuss Competition," *AP Sports*, January 17, 2001.

20. Jim Salisbury, "Baseball Trying to Avert Strike, But Will It Work?" Knight Ridder/Tribune News Service, January 20, 2001.

21. Zimbalist, *The Bottom Line*, 81.

22. Ronald Blum, "Selig Calls for Big Changes in Economics of Baseball," *Post-Tribune* (Gary, IN), November 22, 2000.

23. "Bush to Baseball—Don't Bother Me with Your Problems," *Charleston Gazette*, January 20, 2001.

24. Will Mcdonough, "Harrington: Stoppage Theory off Base," *Boston Globe*, January 28, 2001.

25. Scot Gregor, "Fehr Tells Sox Players Labor Climate 'Not as Poisoned' as '94," *Daily Herald*, February 26, 2001.

26. "Baseball Labor Atmosphere Not Like 1994; Rumblings: Owners Could Lock out Players after This Season," *Telegraph-Herald*, February 26, 2001.

27. Tracy Ringolsby, "Labor Talks Might Be Less Bitter," *Rocky Mountain News*, March 4, 2001.

28. Available at www.mlb.com/mlb/downloads/blue_ribbon.pdf.

29. "Selig: Teams May Be Eliminated," *Cincinnati Post*, March 5, 2001.

30. Zimbalist, *In the Best Interests of Baseball*, 162.

31. Barry Rozner, "Is Lockout on Tap for Baseball?" *Daily Herald*, December 27, 2001.

32. Eric Fisher, "Baseball Owners Ponder a Purge," *Washington Times*, November 2, 2001.

33. Zimbalist, *In the Best Interests of Baseball*, 171.

34. Scott Dochterman, "Royals Not Concerned of Possible Contraction," *St. Joseph News-Press*, May 21, 2001.

35. Tracy Ringolsby, "Contraction Could Help Game Come up with Its Next Contract," *Chicago Sun-Times*, September 30, 2001.

36. Ronald Blum, "Owners Approve Elimination of Two Teams, Don't Identify Them," November 6, 2001.

37. Jim Salisbury, "Labor War Begins with Contraction Vote," Knight Ridder/Tribune News Service, November 6, 2001.

38. "Taking on Contraction Issue," *Albany Times Union*, November 15, 2001.

39. Available at http://www.baseball-almanac.com/quotes/quogiam.shtml.

40. Mark Asher and Dave Sheinin, "MLB, Union Set Meetings; Will Discuss Contraction," *Washington Post*, November 29, 2001.

41. Zimbalist, *May the Best Team Win*, 56–57.

42. Ibid., 61–62.

43. Available at http://www.nytimes.com/1998/10/18/magazine/the-capitalist-a-miami-fish-story.html?pagewanted=all&src=pm.

44. Blum, "Only a Handful of Teams Making Money."

45. Jim Salisbury, "Skeptical Reception for Selig's Bad-Times Numbers," *Philadelphia Inquirer*, December 6, 2001.

46. Ronald Blum, "MLB to Name Bob DuPuy New President," *AP Online*, March 6, 2002.

47. Zimbalist, *The Bottom Line*, 209.

48. Phil Rogers, "Owners Trying to Take More Revenues from Rich Teams," *Chicago Tribune*, March 13, 2002.

49. Zimbalist, *The Bottom Line*, 208.

50. Eric Fisher, "Despite Happier Face, Another Labor Storm Is Gathering," *Washington Times*, January 20, 2002.

51. Mark Asher, "MLB Players Support More Sharing of Local Revenue," *Washington Post*, February 14, 2002.

52. Zimbalist, *May the Best Team Win*, 96.

53. Ron Rapoport, "Fehr: No-Lockout Pledge From Selig Fooling Fans,'" *Chicago Sun-Times*, March 27, 2002.

54. "Union Calls Selig's Statement a Threat: Commissioner Says Players Won't Be Locked out," *Charleston Daily Mail*, March 27, 2002.

55. "Forbes Disputes Baseball Claims; Profitable: Magazine Reports Most Teams Made Money in '01," *Telegraph-Herald*, March 30, 2002.

56. Ronald Blum, "Labor Talks Recess until Next Week," *AP Sports*, April 17, 2002.

57. John Lindsay, "Attendance Continues to Nosedive," *Cincinnati Post*, May 10, 2002.

58. Doug Doughty, "Alderson: Imbalance 'Most Critical Issue' MLB Vice President Speaks at W&L," *Roanoke Times*, May 15, 2002.

59. Phil Rogers, "Strike Date Comes into Sight; Players' Union Could Use Threat to Spur Talks," *Chicago Tribune*, May 15, 2002.

60. Claire Smith, "Labor Strife a Staple of Major League Baseball," Knight Ridder/Tribune News Service, May 16, 2002.

61. Chris De Luca, "Threat of Walkout Lingering; Revenue Sharing, Luxury Tax, Steroid Testing Complicate Negotiations," *Chicago Sun-Times*, July 8, 2002.

62. Ibid.

63. Richard Justice, "One Team Could Fold; Second Team Might Not Be Financially Able to Finish Season, Commissioner Says," *Seattle Post-Intelligencer*, July 11, 2002.

64. Ronald Blum, "Baseball Players Agree to Random Tests for Steroids," *Columbian*, August 8, 2002.

65. Zimbalist, *May the Best Team Win*, 99.

66. Peter Schmuck, "Fehr Calls Tax Attack on Salary Structure Under Projection, 7 Teams Would be Affected in Plan Proposed by Team Owners," *Baltimore Sun*, August 21, 2002.

67. Ronald Blum, "Owners Make Moves toward Compromise: Baseball Labor Talks," *Charleston Gazette*, August 26, 2002.

68. "Negotiations Getting Serious; Sides Meet Three Times; Teams Shuffle Travel Plans," *Chicago Sun-Times*, August 28, 2002.

69. Zimbalist, *The Bottom Line*, 214.

70. "Baseball—Labor Agreement—Settlement Details," *Yakima Herald-Republic*, August 31, 2002.

Chapter 9: Bill Giles and His Baseball Team

1. Helyar, *Lords of the Realm*, 268.

2. "Champ Phillies Keep up Appearances in Winter of Content," *Philadelphia Inquirer*, February 2, 1981.

3. Available at http://upstart.bizjournals.com/views/columns/the-windup/2008/09/19/Phillies-Former-Owner-Still-Faithful.html?page=all.

4. Jayson Stark, "Giles Is Hoping to Assemble—A Group to Buy the Phillies May Have Edge With Ownership, *Philadelphia Inquirer*, March 8, 1981.

5. Harry Harris, "Joey Bishop Show Will Not Begin on Ch. 29 This Month," *Philadelphia Inquirer*, March 10, 1981.

6. Stark, "Giles is Hoping."

7. Ibid.

8. Jayson Stark, "Phil's Giles Exploring the Options," *Philadelphia Inquirer,* March 13, 1981.

9. Ibid.

10. Ibid.

11. Jayson Stark, "Phils Sale: Alexander Bows Out—Strike a Factor in Withdrawal," *Philadelphia Inquirer,* June 23, 1981.

12. Giles and Myers, *Pouring Six Beers at a Time,* 166.

13. Jayson Stark, "Phillies Sold for Record Price," *Philadelphia Inquirer,* October 30, 1981.

14. Ibid.

15. Ibid.

16. "Giles Doubles Interest in Phillies," *Reading Eagle,* December 9, 1986.

17. Jayson Stark, "Analysis—Phils Won't Stay with Status Quo in Giles' Regime," *Philadelphia Inquirer,* November 1, 1981.

18. Ibid.

19. Steve Goldstein, "Phillies, Lacking a TV Safety Net, Face Struggle to Stay out of the Red," *Philadelphia Inquirer,* July 12, 1982.

20. Ibid.

21. Ibid.

22. Jayson Stark, "Missing Persons—Suddenly, City's Teams Draw Smaller Crowds," *Philadelphia Inquirer,* January 15, 1984.

23. Ibid.

24. Ibid.

25. Glen Macnow, "TV Past Gives Steinbrenner New Weapon in Free-Agent War," *Philadelphia Inquirer,* December 12, 1988.

26. Ibid.

27. Glen Macnow, "Phils in Major Accords with Prism, Sportschannel," *Philadelphia Inquirer,* January 24, 1990.

28. John Brennan, "Phils Shelve Pay-for-View—For Now," *The Record* (Bergen County, NJ), February 16, 1991.

29. "Phillies Returning to Channel 17 in '93," *PR Newswire,* January 6, 1992.

30. Sam Donnellon, "Giles: Cable Me; Phillies See Hook-up with Comcast as Channel to New Stadium; Comcast Looms as Ballpark Figure; Giles Wired over Prospects of Hook-up," *Philadelphia Daily News,* March 21, 1996.

31. Interview with Bill Giles, November 14, 2012.

32. Donnellon, "Giles: Cable."

33. Michael Sokolove, Jayson Stark, and Michael L. Rozansky, "Comcast Buying 76ers and Flyers—Phils Also May Get Involved with Firm," *Philadelphia Inquirer,* March 20, 1996.

34. Donnellon, "Giles: Cable."

35. Ibid.

36. Michael L. Rozansky, "Comcast Deal Isn't the End of Prism; It Could Benefit Both Firms to Leave the TV Rights as They Are," *Philadelphia Inquirer,* March 24, 1996.

37. Edward Moran and Bill Fleischman, "Comcast Puts Prism on Ropes; Phils Agree to Join Flyers, Sixers in Fledgling All-sports Cable Channel," *Philadelphia Daily News,* April 26, 1996.

38. Deni Kasrel, *Philadelphia Business Journal,* April 14, 1996.

39. "New Super Regional All-sports Channel Announced by the Phillies and Comcast-Spectacor," PR Newswire, April 25, 1996.

40. Ibid.

41. "Phillies Welcome Comcast into Their Broadcasting Family," *Sports Business Daily*, January 23, 1998.

42. Jayson Stark, "Why the Electricity, and Fans, Are Gone from Phillies; The Causes Are Varied and Sometimes Disputed, But the Effect Is Undeniable, the Phillies Aren't Drawing Like They Used To," *Philadelphia Inquirer*, May 16, 1996.

43. Paul Hagen, "Field of Echos, Phils Attendance Seems to Be Stuck on 'E' Paul Hagen," *Philadelphia Inquirer*, September 5, 1996.

44. Jim Salisbury, "Giles out as CEO of Phillies; He Will Stay on as Chairman, but David Montgomery, Co-General Partner, Will Be in Charge of Daily Operations," *Philadelphia Inquirer*, June 21, 1997.

45. Salisbury, "Giles out as CEO of the Phillies."

46. Jim Salisbury, "New Park Is Crucial, Says Phils' Giles. 'We Can't Survive without It' He Said. The Club Offered to Finance up to 33 Percent of the Cost," *Philadelphia Inquirer*, June 25, 1997.

47. Jim Salisbury, "The Beginning of Big Changes?"

48. Jim Salisbury, "Giles to Severely Scale Back His Role With Phillies; He Won't Use the Word 'Retirement'; He Will Keep the Title of Team Chairman. But as of Nov. 1, He Will Have No Day-to-Day Duties," *Philadelphia Inquirer*, October 1, 1999.

49. Frank Fitzpatrick, "Slow Days for Business that Depends on Phils Crowds—The Phils, in up Years and down, Used to be Very Good for Business in Eateries near Veterans Stadium. Used to Be," *Philadelphia Inquirer*, June 22, 1997.

50. Jim Salisbury, "Changing of the Guard; Why Bill Giles Departed, and What's Coming Now," *Philadelphia Inquirer*, June 22, 1997.

51. Jim Salisbury, "Giles out as CEO of Phillies."

Chapter 10: Bill Giles and His Ballparks

Note: All of Bill Giles' quotes in this chapter, unless otherwise noted, come from interviews with him in 2010.

1. Interview with Larry Lucchino, September 21, 2011.

2. Christopher K. Hepp, "A Salesman's Ultimate Deal for Bill Giles, A New Phillies Stadium Caps a Lifetime of Work," *Philadelphia Inquirer*, February 8, 1999.

3. Sam Donnellon, "Ballpark or Bust; Stadium Key to Giles Group Retaining Team," *Daily News*, June 25, 1997.

4. Hepp, "A Salesman's Ultimate Deal."

5. Howard Goodman, "Tax Increase for Stadium Strikes out—But the Pittsburgh-area Vote Won't Change the Game Plan Here," *Philadelphia Inquirer*, November 9, 1997.

6. Ken Dilanian, "Chances Dim for Stadium Proposal—State Legislators Do Not Believe That the Votes Required to Pass the Funding Measure are There," *Philadelphia Inquirer*, November 24, 1998.

7. Christopher K. Hepp, Peter Nicholas, and Ken Dilanian, "Free Loans to Teams to Build Stadiums Gain Support—Taxpayers Would Get Their Money Back over 30 Years. Teams and Mayor Rendell Strongly Oppose the Plan," *Philadelphia Inquirer*, January 29, 1999.

8. Christopher K. Hepp, "Survey—Support for Stadiums Grows When Details Are Known—When Told There Would Be No Tax Hike, Voters Tend to Drop Opposition to Plans for New Facilities," *Philadelphia Inquirer*, January 30, 1999.

9. Bill King, "Stadium Backers Find a Way in Pennsylvania," *Sports Business Journal*, February 8, 1999.

10. Ibid.

11. Robin Palley, "Giles Dreams on at Luncheon," *Daily News*, May 03, 1994.

12. Timothy Dwyer, "Giles—New Stadium Is on Drawing Board," *Philadelphia Inquirer*, March 23, 1996.

13. Bob Ford, "Giles Says a New Stadium for Phils Can't Be Ready Until 2003, He Said Neighborhood Opposition Was a Big Obstacle in Securing the Spring Garden Street Site," *Philadelphia Inquirer*, September 09, 1999.

14. Garland L. Thompson, "Downtown Stadiums Can Work," *Philadelphia Tribune*, June 2, 2000.

15. Edward Moran, "It's Political Baseball; Giles Never Expected Ballpark to Be Such a Struggle," *Daily News*, October 5, 1999.

16. Dave Davies and Harriet Lessy, "Stadium Dreams Revived? Street Panel Mulls Center City Sites for Baseball Park," *Daily News*, February 24, 2000.

17. Jack Chevalier, "Street—Downtown Stadium a Grand Slam for the Economy," *Philadelphia Tribune*, April 28, 2000.

18. Michael J. Rochon and Raven Tyler, "Proposed Stadium Sites Stimulate Debate," *Philadelphia Tribune*, April 14, 2000.

19. "Phillies Unveil Plans for New Ballpark," Knight Ridder/Tribune News Service, June 28, 2001.

20. Interview with Bill Giles, November 14, 2012.

21. Christopher K. Hepp, "A Salesman's Ultimate Deal."

Chapter 11: From the Depths of 2002 to the Heights of 2012: Nine Reasons Why Baseball Is Booming

1. "Learning from History While Making It," *Sports Business Journal*, October 6, 2003.

2. Interview with Bill Giles, June 9, 2009.

3. Ibid.

4. Ibid.

5. Tom Haudricourt, "Bases Loaded—MLB Boon Continues as Revenues Top $6 Billion Mark," *Milwaukee Journal-Sentinel*, October 20, 2007.

6. Available at http://www.forbes.com/mlb-valuations/list.

7. Tom Haudricourt, "Bases Loaded."

8. Ibid.

9. Interview with Bill Giles, June 9, 2009.

10. Baseball, *Sports Business Journal*, April 27, 2008.

11. E-mail from Bill Giles, October 20, 2006.

12. Available at http://www.sloansportsconference.com/?p=4616.

13. "Learning From History While Making It."

14. Interview with Bill Giles, October 14, 2006.

15. Interview with Bill Giles, June 23, 2010.

16. "Learning From History While Making It."

17. Nick Cafardo, "Sox Owner Wants to Overhaul MLB's Revenue-Sharing System," *Boston Globe*, December 1, 2009.

18. Available at http://www.cbsnews.com/8301-505125_162-51210897/mlbs-revenue-sharing-formula/?tag=bnetdomain.

19. Tom Verducci, "10 Reasons Baseball Is Back," *Sports Illustrated*, Vol. 101, Issue 1, July 5, 2004.

20. David Jacobson, "The Revenue Model: Why Baseball Is Booming," July 11, 2008.

21. Ibid.

22. Matt Gelb, "Inside the Phillies: Phils Swinging for Fences with Next TV Deal, Huge TV Contracts Are Now Common in Baseball, Which Gives the Fightin's More Leverage with Comcast," *Philadelphia Inquirer*, February 14, 2012.

23. Available at http://www.utsandiego.com/news/2012/Feb/14/padres-tv-haul-2012-could-reach-40m.

24. Ibid.

25. Available at http://www.forbes.com/sites/nathanvardi/2012/11/20/new-york-yankees-and-goldman-sachs-hit-home-run-with-yes-potential-deal-would-value-network-at-3-4-billion.

26. Available at http://www.bizofbaseball.com/index.php?option=com_content&task=view&id=1079&Itemid=99999999.

27. Available at http://www.forbes.com/sites/christinasettimi/2012/10/02/baseball-scores-12-billion-in-television-deals.

28. Baseball, *Sports Business Journal*, April 27, 2008.

29. Chuck Salter, "MLB Advanced Media's Bob Bowman Is Playing Digital Hardball. And He's Winning," March 19, 2012. Available at http://www.fastcompany.com/1822802/mlb-advanced-medias-bob-bowman-playing-digital-hardball-and-hes-winning.

30. Eric Fisher, "Ten Years Later, MLBAM Still Evolving," *Sports Business Journal*, March 21, 2011.

31. Interview with Bill Giles, June 9, 2009.

32. Fisher, "Ten Years Later."

33. Jorge Ortiz, "MLB's Advanced Media Arm Pulls in Profits," *USA Today*, December 5, 2007.

34. Jay Yarow, "MLB's Real Competitive Advantage," *Bloomberg Businessweek*, August 29, 2008. Available at http://www.businessweek.com/stories/2008-08-29/mlbs-real-competitive-advantagebusinessweek-business-news-stock-market-and-financial-advice.

35. Chuck Salter, MLB Advanced Media's Bob Bowman."

36. Baseball, *Sports Business Journal*, April 27, 2008.

37. MLB Press Release, World Baseball Classic Grows Baseball Globally with Record-setting 2013 Tournament, March 21, 2013. Available at http://newyork.yankees.mlb.com/news/article.jsp?ymd=20130321&content_id=43072146&vkey=pr_mlb&c_id=mlb.

38. Bill King, "League Strengthens Efforts to Reach a Worldwide Audience," *Sports Business Journal*, October 13, 2003.

39. "Learning from History While Making It."

40. About MLB Fan Cave. Available at http://mlb.mlb.com/fancave/about.jsp#fbid=gZSxj9fNX3C.

41. Ibid.

42. Natan Edelsburg, "How the MLB Fan Cave Became the League's Social Strategy," *Lost Remote* (blog), May 21, 2012. Available at http://lostremote.com/how-the-mlb-fan-cave-became-the-leagues-social-strategy-interview_b29700.

Bibliography

Abrams, Roger I. *Legal Bases: Baseball and the Law* (Philadelphia: Temple University Press, 1998).

Burk, Robert F. *Much More Than a Game: Players, Owners, and American Baseball since 1921* (Chapel Hill: The University of North Carolina Press, 2001).

Costas, Bob. *Fair Ball: A Fan's Case for Baseball* (New York: Random House, 2000).

Cox, Ronald W., and Daniel Skidmore-Hess, *Free Agency and Competitive Balance in Baseball* (Jefferson, NC: McFarland & Company, 2006).

Giles, Bill, with Doug Myers, *Pouring Six Beers at a Time: And Other Stories from a Lifetime in Baseball* (Chicago: Triumph Books, 2007).

Gould, William B., IV, *Bargaining with Baseball: Labor Relations in an Age of Prosperous Turmoil* (Jefferson, NC: McFarland & Company, 2011).

Helyar, John. *Lords of the Realm: The Real History of Baseball* (New York: Ballantine Books, 1994).

Holtzman, Jerome. *The Commissioners: Baseball's Midlife Crisis* (New York: Total Sports, 1998).

Jennings, Kenneth M. *Balls and Strikes: The Money Game in Professional Baseball* (New York: Praeger, 1990).

———. *Swings and Misses: Moribund Labor Relations in Professional Baseball* (Westport, CT: Praeger, 1997).

Jozsa, Frank P., Jr., *Baseball, Inc.: The National Pastime as Big Business* (Jefferson, NC: McFarland & Company, Inc., 2006).

Koppett, Leonard, *Koppett's Concise History of Major League Baseball* (New York: Carroll & Graf, 2004).

Korr, Charles P. *The End of Baseball as We Knew It: The Players Union, 1960–81* (Urbana: University of Illinois Press, 2002).

Kuhn, Bowie. *Hardball: The Education of a Baseball Commissioner* (Lincoln: University of Nebraska Press, 1997).

Lowenfish, Lee. *The Imperfect Diamond: A History of Baseball's Labor Wars* (New York: Da Capo Press, 1980).

Miller, Marvin. *A Whole Different Ball Game: The Inside Story of the Baseball Revolution* (Chicago: Ivan R. Dee, 2004).

Moffi, Larry. *The Conscience of the Game: Baseball's Commissioners from Landis to Selig* (Lincoln: University of Nebraska Press, 2006).

Rader, Benjamin G. *Baseball: A History of America's Game*, 3rd ed. (Urbana: University of Illinois Press, 2008).

Sands, Jack, and Peter Gammons, *Coming Apart at the Seams: How Baseball Owners, Players, and Television Executives Have Led Our National Pastime to the Brink of Disaster* (New York: Macmillan, 1993).

Vecsey, George. *Baseball: A History of America's Favorite Game* (New York: Modern Library, 2006).

Vincent, Fay, *The Last Commissioner: A Baseball Valentine* (New York: Simon & Schuster, 2002).

Zimbalist, Andrew. *Baseball and Billions: A Probing Look inside the Big Business of Our National Pastime* (New York: Basic Books, 1992).

———. *In the Best Interests of Baseball?: The Revolutionary Reign of Bud Selig* (Hoboken, NJ: John Wiley & Sons, 2006).

———. *The Bottom Line: Observations and Arguments on the Sports Business* (Philadelphia: Temple University Press, 2006).

———. *May the Best Team Win: Baseball Economics and Public Policy* (Washington, DC: Brookings Institution Press, 2003).

Index